THE ROUGH GUIDE TO

Dubai

WITHDRAWN

written and researched by

Gavin Thomas

D0524447

Contents

Introduction to
Dubai

Dubai is like nowhere else on the planet. Often claimed to be the world's fastest-growing city, over the past four decades it has metamorphosed from a small Gulf trading centre to become one of the world's most glamorous, spectacular and futuristic urban destinations, fuelled by a heady cocktail of petrodollars, visionary commercial acumen and naked ambition. Dubai's ability to dream (and then achieve) the impossible has ripped up expectations and rewritten the record books, as evidenced by stunning developments such as the soaring Burj Khalifa, the beautiful Burj al Arab and the vast Palm Jumeirah island – testament to the ruling sheikhs' determination to make the city one of the world's essential destinations for the twenty-first century.

Modern Dubai is frequently seen as a panegyric to consumerist luxury: a self-indulgent haven of magical hotels, superlative restaurants and extravagantly themed shopping malls. Perhaps not surprisingly the city is often stereotyped as a vacuous consumerist fleshpot, appealing only to those with more cash than culture, although this one-eyed cliché does absolutely no justice to Dubai's beguiling contrasts and rich cultural make-up. The city's headline-grabbing mega-projects have also deflected attention from Dubai's role in providing the Islamic world with a model of political stability and religious tolerance, showing what can be achieved by a peaceful and progressive regime in one of the planet's most troubled regions.

For the visitor, there's far more to Dubai than designer boutiques and five-star hotels – although of course if all you're looking for is a luxurious dose of sun, sand and shopping, the city takes some beating. If you want to step beyond the tourist clichés, however, you'll find that Dubai has much more to offer than you might think, ranging from the fascinating old city centre, with its higgledy-piggledy labyrinth of bustling souks interspersed with fine old traditional Arabian houses, to the memorably quirky

ABOVE BURJ AL ARAB **RIGHT** TEXTILE SOUK, BUR DUBAI

postmodern architectural skylines of the southern parts of the city. Dubai's human geography is no less memorable, featuring a cosmopolitan assortment of Emiratis, Arabs, Iranians, Indians, Filipinos and Europeans – a fascinating patchwork of peoples and languages that gives the city its uniquely varied cultural appeal. The recent credit crunch may have pushed Dubai to the verge of bankruptcy but pronouncements of the city's demise are likely to prove premature, and this remains one of the twenty-first century's most fascinating and vibrant urban experiments in progress. Visit now to see history, literally, in the making.

What to see

At the heart of the metropolis on the south side of the breezy Creek, **Bur Dubai** is the oldest part of the city and offers a fascinating insight into Dubai's traditional roots. This is where you'll find many of the city's most interesting Arabian heritage houses, clustered in the beautiful old Iranian quarter of Bastakiya and the waterfront Shindagha district, as well as the excellent Dubai Museum and the atmospheric Textile Souk. On the opposite side of the Creek, the bustling district of **Deira** is the centre of Dubai's traditional commercial activity, much of it still conducted in the area's vibrant array of old-fashioned souks, including the famous Gold and Spice

souks. Fringing Deira and Bur Dubai lie Dubai's **inner suburbs**, with a varied array of attractions ranging from the absorbingly workaday suburbs of Karama and Satwa – home to dozens of no-frills Indian curry houses, low-rent souks and some of the city's most entertaining street life – through to impressive modern developments like the kitsch Wafi complex and adjacent Khan Murjan Souk, both exercises in faux-Arabian nostalgia.

A few kilometres south of the old city centre, modern Dubai begins in spectacular style with **Sheikh Zayed Road**, home to a neck-cricking array of skyscrapers including the glittering Emirates Towers. Even these, however, are outshone by the massive **Downtown Dubai** development at the southern end of the strip, centred on the stupendous new Burj Khalifa, the world's tallest building, flanked by further record-breaking attractions including the gargantuan Dubai Mall and spectacular Dubai Fountain. West of the Sheikh Zayed Road, the sprawling beachside suburb of **Jumeirah** is the traditional address-of-choice for Dubai's European expats, its endless swathes of walled villas dotted with half a dozen shopping malls and a smattering of low-key sights.

At the southern end of Jumeirah, there are more iconic sights in the sleepy suburb of Umm Suqeim, including the wave-shaped *Jumeirah Beach Hotel*, the extraordinary mock-Arabian Madinat Jumeirah complex and the unforgettable **Burj al Arab** hotel. South of the Burj stretches the spectacular **Dubai Marina**

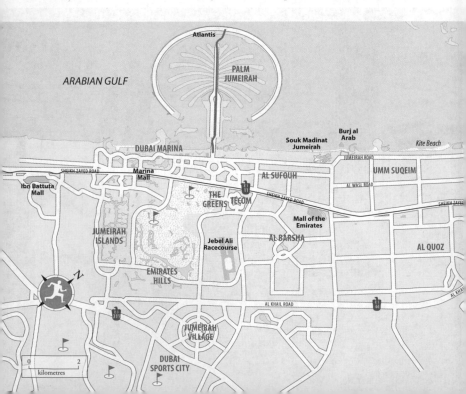

development, with its densely packed forest of glassy skyscrapers, while offshore lies the **Palm Jumeirah**, the world's largest man-made island, which ends in a flourish at the gigantic *Atlantis* resort.

A little over an hour's drive down the coast, the UAE's capital, **Abu Dhabi**, offers an intriguing contrast to its freewheeling neighbour – slightly smaller, and considerably more sedate, although here too a string of huge new developments are gradually transforming the city landscape. Leading attractions include the extravagant *Emirates Palace* hotel and the even more spectacular Sheikh Zayed Mosque, while the various attractions of Yas Island, home to the vast Ferrari World theme park, lie just down the road.

Elsewhere, there are a number of rewarding **day-trips** from Dubai, all offering an interesting alternative take on life in the twenty-first-century Gulf. Just 10km up the coast, the more conservative city of **Sharjah** hosts a rewarding selection of museums devoted to cultural and religious matters, including the excellent Museum of Islamic Civilization. Further afield, somnolent **Al Ain**, the UAE's only major inland city, offers a complete change of pace from life on the coast, with traditional mud-brick forts, old-fashioned souks and the country's finest oasis. Across country, it's only a two-hour drive from Dubai to the UAE's even more laidback **east coast**, with a string of beautiful and still largely deserted beaches to crash out on, backdropped by the dramatically craggy Hajar mountains.

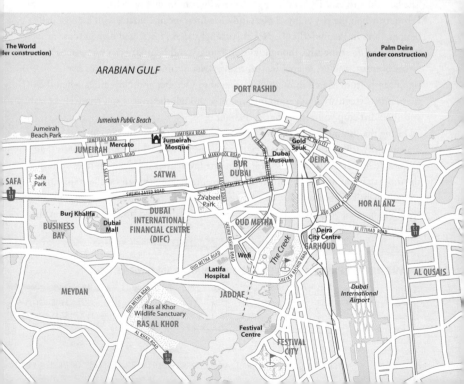

DUBAI: SECOND AMONG EQUALS

Given the city's soaring international profile, many people unfamiliar with the region think that Dubai is a country – which it isn't. Dubai is actually just one of the seven statelets which collectively form the United Arab Emirates, or **UAE**, a loose confederation founded in 1971 following the departure of the British from the Gulf. Technically the seven emirates are considered equal, and preserve a considerable measure of legislative autonomy, rather like the various states of the USA – which explains, for instance, why local laws in Dubai are so different from those in neighbouring Sharjah. In practice, however, a clear pecking order applies. **Abu Dhabi**, easily the largest and wealthiest of the emirates, serves as the capital (even if Abu Dhabi city is barely half the size of Dubai) and wields the greatest influence over national policy, as well as providing the UAE with its president. Dubai ranks second, followed by **Sharjah** and then the other emirates of **Umm al Quwain**, **Ras al Khaimah**, **Ajman** and **Fujairah**, which remain relatively undeveloped and even surprisingly impoverished in places.

The fact that the union has survived despite the sometimes considerable differences of opinion between Dubai and Abu Dhabi is a glowing tribute to local diplomacy, even it is has also created the anomaly whereby Dubai, with its headline international standing, isn't even the capital of its own low-key country. Abu Dhabi, meanwhile, continues to regard its upstart neighbour with a certain suspicion – although the true relative power of the rival emirates was vividly demonstrated during the credit crunch of 2009, when oil-rich Abu Dhabi was obliged to bail out its dazzling but virtually bankrupt neighbour to the tune of around US$20 billion.

When to go

The best time to visit Dubai is in the cooler winter months from December through to February, when the city enjoys a pleasantly Mediterranean climate, with average daily temperatures in the mid-20s ℃. Not surprisingly, room rates (and demand) are at their peak during these months, though skies in January and February can sometimes be rather overcast, and it can even be surprisingly wet at times. Temperatures rise significantly from March through to April and in October and November, when the thermometer regularly nudges up into the 30s, though the heat is still relatively bearable, and shouldn't stop you getting out and about.

During the summer months from May to September the city boils – July and August are especially suffocating – with average temperatures in the high 30s to low 40s (and frequently higher). Although the heat is intense (even after dark), room rates at most of the top hotels plummet by as much as 75 percent, making this an excellent time to enjoy some authentic Dubaian luxury at relatively affordable prices, so long as you don't mind spending most of your time hopping between air-conditioned hotels, shopping malls, restaurants and clubs.

AVERAGE TEMPERATURES AND RAINFALL IN DUBAI

	Jan	Feb	Mar	Apr	May	Jun	Jul	Aug	Sep	Oct	Nov	Dec
Max/min (℃)	24/14	25/15	28/17	32/20	37/24	39/26	41/29	40/29	39/26	35/23	31/18	26/15
Max/min (℉)	75/58	76/58	82/63	90/68	98/74	102/79	105/84	105/85	102/79	95/73	87/65	79/60
Rainfall (mm)	11	36	22	8	1	0	0	0	0	0	2	8

20

things not to miss

It's not possible to see everything that Dubai and the neighbouring emirates have to offer in a short trip – and we don't suggest you try. What follows, in no particular order, is a selective and subjective taste of the city's highlights, from traditional Arabian heritage houses and museums through to modernist landmarks, as well as the city's most spectacular malls, restaurants and bars. Each entry has a page reference to take you straight into the Guide, where you can find out more.

1 MADINAT JUMEIRAH
Astounding mock-Arabian city, home to a string of lavish hotels and leisure facilities – the quintessential Dubaian example of opulent kitsch on an epic scale.

2 DEIRA SOUKS
At the heart of old Dubai, the district of Deira comprises an atmospheric tangle of bazaars, ranging from the Gold Souk's glittering shop windows to the aromatic alleyways of the Spice Souk.

3 DUBAI MUSEUM
Unbeatable introduction to the city's history and traditional culture, housed in the quaint old Al Fahidi Fort.

4 DESERT SAFARIS
Go dune-bashing, try your hand at sand-skiing or quad-biking, then settle down over a shisha for a spot of traditional belly dancing.

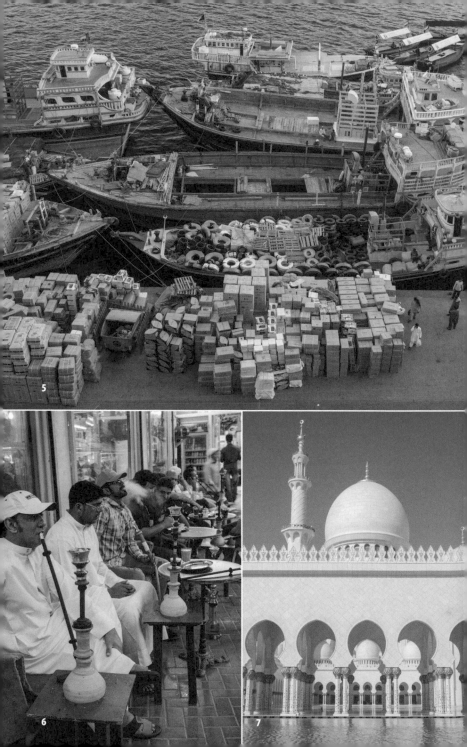

5 DHOW WHARFAGE
Home to hundreds of superb Arabian dhows moored up along the Deira creekside – one of central Dubai's most incongruous but magical sights.

6 ARABIAN FOOD AND SHISHA
Explore the Middle East's wonderful cuisine, from tempting mezze to succulent grills and kebabs, rounded off with an aromatic puff on a traditional shisha.

7 SHEIKH ZAYED MOSQUE, ABU DHABI
Abu Dhabi's most spectacular landmark, this monumental mosque is one of the world's largest, with huge courtyards, domes, and minarets enclosing a marvellously opulent prayer hall within.

8 BURJ KHALIFA
The world's tallest building, rising like an enormous space rocket above the streets of Downtown Dubai.

9 AL AIN OASIS
An idyllic retreat from the heat and dust of contemporary Al Ain, with peaceful little pedestrianized lanes running through shady plantations of luxuriant date palms.

8

9

13

14

15 BURJ AL ARAB
Page 77

One of the world's most instantly recognizable contemporary buildings, this superb, sail-shaped hotel towers gracefully above the coast of southern Dubai.

16 SKI DUBAI
Page 80

A surreal slope of Alpine mountainside attached to the vast Mall of the Emirates.

17 BASTAKIYA
Page 39

One of the city's best-preserved heritage areas, with a fascinating little labyrinth of old houses topped by innumerable wind towers.

18 KHAN MURJAN SOUK
Page 56

Check out the quirky Egyptian-themed Wafi and the atmospheric Khan Murjan Souk next door, a sumptuous re-creation of a traditional Arabian bazaar.

19 IBN BATTUTA MALL
Page 88

Kitsch and eye-poppingly extravagant, this mile-long mall takes its inspiration from the journeys of Moroccan traveller Ibn Battuta.

20 SHARJAH MUSEUM OF ISLAMIC CIVILIZATION
Page 146

State-of-the-art museum, showcasing the rich history of Islamic science, arts and culture.

15

16

METRO STATION, SHEIKH ZAYED ROAD

Basics

Getting there

Dubai is the Middle East's largest airline hub, boasting excellent connections worldwide with the city's own Emirates airline and other international carriers. These include numerous direct flights to various destinations in the UK, plus a number of places in the US and Australia.

Other options for getting to Dubai are contrastingly limited (for Western visitors, at least). It's possible to travel **overland** into the UAE from several points in neighbouring Oman, but not Saudi Arabia. There are no regular ferry services to Dubai, although the city is a popular stop on many **cruise** itineraries.

Flights from the UK and Ireland

Several airlines offer nonstop flights between the UK and Dubai; outbound flying time is around seven hours (slightly longer on the way back), with return fares starting at about £350. There are currently nonstop flights from Heathrow with Emirates, Virgin Atlantic, British Airways and Royal Brunei Airlines, plus indirect flights with many other European and Gulf airlines. Emirates also operates direct flights to Dubai from a number of regional UK airports including Birmingham, Manchester, Newcastle and Glasgow, as well as from Dublin (from around €420).

Flights from the US and Canada

There are currently nonstop flights to Dubai with Emirates from New York, Washington DC, Toronto, Houston, Dallas, Los Angeles, San Francisco and Seattle, plus innumerable other one- and two-stop options with a host of other carriers. Flights from the east coast take around 13–14 hours; from the west coast around 16 hours; and 14–16 hours from Houston and Dallas. Fares start at around US$900/Can$920 return from the east coast, and US$1100/Can$1120 from the west coast.

Flights from Australia, New Zealand and South Africa

There are nonstop flights to Dubai with Emirates from Perth (11hr), Sydney, Melbourne and Brisbane (14hr), plus one- and two-stop flights from Auckland (via Brisbane, Sydney or Melbourne; 19hr) and Christchurch (via Sydney and Bangkok; 22hr). Return fares start at around Aus$1500/NZ$2000. There are also numerous alternative routings via Asia, usually at slightly lower fares.

Travelling from South Africa, there are direct flights from Johannesburg, Cape Town and Durban (taking around 8–9hr), plus a few one-stop options including, most conveniently, Kenya Airways via Nairobi and Ethiopian Airlines via Addis Ababa. Return fares start at around ZAR6000.

By land

The UAE shares land borders with Oman and Saudi Arabia, though only the Oman border is open to visitors from outside the Gulf. There are currently four border crossings between the **UAE and Oman** open to non-Emirati and Omani citizens: at Tibat between Ras al Khaimah emirate and Oman's Musandam Peninsula; at Al Ain/Buraimi in Abu Dhabi emirate; just east of Hatta in Dubai emirate; and at Khatmat Malahah between Oman and Fujairah emirate on the east coast of the UAE.

It's about a five-hour drive from the Omani capital Muscat to Dubai, and there are also several daily buses operated by the Oman National Transport Company (there's a timetable at ⓦ www.omanet.om /english/useful/transport.asp, but don't assume it will be up to date) leaving from the bus station in Ruwi.

Airlines, agents and operators

AIRLINES

British Airways ⓦ ba.com.
Emirates ⓦ emirates.com.
Etihad Airways ⓦ etihadairways.com.
Royal Brunei ⓦ bruneiair.com.
Virgin Atlantic ⓦ virgin-atlantic.com.

A BETTER KIND OF TRAVEL

At Rough Guides we are passionately committed to travel. We believe it helps us understand the world we live in and the people we share it with – and of course tourism is vital to many developing economies. But the scale of modern tourism has also damaged some places irreparably, and climate change is accelerated by most forms of transport, especially flying. All Rough Guides' flights are carbon-offset, and every year we donate money to a variety of environmental charities.

AGENTS AND OPERATORS

North South Travel UK ☎ 01245 608291, ⊛ northsouthtravel .co.uk. Friendly, competitive travel agency, offering discounted fares worldwide. Profits are used to support projects in the developing world, especially the promotion of sustainable tourism.

STA Travel UK ☎ 0333 321 0099, US ☎ 1800 781 4040, Australia ☎ 134 782, New Zealand ☎ 0800 474 400, South Africa ☎ 0861 781 781; ⊛ statravel.co.uk. Worldwide specialists in independent travel; also student IDs, travel insurance, car rental, rail passes, and more. Good discounts for students and under-26s.

Trailfinders UK ☎ 020 7368 1200, Ireland ☎ 021 464 8800; ⊛ trailfinders.com. One of the best-informed and most efficient agents for independent travellers.

Travel CUTS Canada ☎ 1800 667 2887, US ☎ 1800 592 2887; ⊛ travelcuts.com. Canadian youth and student travel firm.

USIT Ireland ☎ 01 602 1906, Northern Ireland ☎ 028 9032 4073, Australia ☎ 1800 092 499; ⊛ usit.ie. Ireland's main student and youth travel specialists.

Arrival

Unless you're travelling overland from neighbouring Oman or sailing in on a cruise ship, you'll arrive at Dubai's sparkling modern international airport close to the old city centre – at least pending the opening of the new Al Maktoum International Airport (see box below). Once you've cleared customs and the crowds, getting into town is fairly straightforward. Information on arriving at Abu Dhabi or Sharjah airports is covered in the relevant guide chapters in the Guide (see p.175 & p.151).

The airport (⊛ dubaiairport.com; airport code DXB) is very centrally located in the district of Garhoud, around 7km from the city centre. There are three **passenger terminals**: Terminal 1 is where most international flights arrive; Terminal 3 is where all Emirates airlines flights land; and Terminal 2 is used by smaller regional carriers. All three terminals have plenty of ATMs and currency exchange booths, although if you want to rent a car, you'll have to head to Terminal 1 (see p.24).

There are several ways of getting into town from the airport and many hotels offer free airport transfers; check when you book. Both Terminal 1 and Terminal 3 have dedicated **metro stations**, offering quick and inexpensive transport into the city centre and beyond to southern Dubai: details of fares and train times are covered in "City transport" (see opposite). Alternatively, there are plentiful **taxis**, although note that they charge a 20dh flag fare (see p.22) when picking up from the airport rather than the usual 3dh, making them significantly pricier than usual. There are also various **buses** (see ⊛ dubai-bus .com) running from the airport into the city centre, although these are only really useful if you're staying in Deira or Bur Dubai and know where you're going; as for the metro, you'll also have to buy a Nol card or ticket (see box opposite) before boarding the bus. The two most useful services (every 30min, 24hr; 3dh) are airport bus #401, which travels via Baniyas Road to Al Sabkha Bus Station in central Deira, and airport bus #402, which runs via Al Mankhool Road and the Golden Sands area (see box, p.92) to Al Ghubaiba Bus Station in the middle of Bur Dubai.

City transport

Dubai is very spread out – it's around 25km from the city centre down to Dubai Marina – but getting around is relatively straightforward and inexpensive, thanks

---

AL MAKTOUM AIRPORT

Already one of the world's major air hubs, Dubai is now taking even more of a stranglehold on the aviation industry with the construction of the vast new **Al Maktoum International Airport** (AMIA; airport code DWC) in the far south of the city, slated to eventually become the world's largest airport, with five runways, three passenger terminals and capacity for up to 120 million passenger per year. The airport began receiving cargo flights in 2010 and, according to latest estimates, is due to open to passengers by late 2013.

The new airport is located around 15km inland from Jebel Ali port, roughly 22km by road from the marina, 30km from the Palm Jumeirah and around 50km from the old city centre. It's designed to supplement the existing Dubai International Airport rather than replace it, meaning that services to the older airport should continue more or less as before, although details of how it will all work are, at present, necessarily thin on the ground. From a practical point of view, however, unless you're staying in or near Dubai Marina, the old Dubai International Airport is likely to prove a far more convenient place to land than its new rival.

NOL CARDS

Almost all Dubai's public transport services – **metro**, **buses** and **waterbuses** (but not abras) – are covered by the **Nol** system (🅦 www.nol.ae), which provides integrated ticketing across the entire transport network. To use any of these forms of transport you'll need to buy a pre-paid Nol card or ticket ahead of travel. Cards can be **bought** and **topped up** at any metro station; at one of the machines located at 64 bus stops around the city; or at branches of Carrefour, Spinneys and Redha Al-Ansari Exchange; no tickets are sold on board metro trains, buses or waterbuses. You swipe the card or ticket as you pass through the metro ticket barriers or as you board a bus or waterbus, and the correct amount is automatically deducted from your pre-paid account.

TYPES OF CARDS AND TICKET

There are three types of Nol card; all three are valid for five years and can store up to 500dh worth of credit. The **Silver Card** costs 20dh (including 14dh credit). The **Gold Card** (same price) is almost identical, but also allows users to travel on Gold Class compartments on the metro (see below). The **Blue Card** is aimed squarely at residents, costs 70dh (including 20dh credit) and offers additional benefits including an automatic top-up facility and the chance to earn loyalty points; they aren't available over the counter, however (you'll have to submit a written or online application) so aren't much use to casual visitors.

An alternative to the three cards is the **Red Ticket** (a paper ticket, rather than a card). This has been specifically designed for tourists, costs just 2dh and is valid for 90 days, although it has to be pre-paid with the correct fare for each journey and can only be recharged up to a maximum of ten times. If you're going to be using public transport regularly while you're in the city it's well worth investing in a Silver or Gold card.

---

mainly to the city's excellent metro system. Taxis offer another convenient and relatively inexpensive form of transport, while there are also buses and boats, as well as cheap car rental.

Full information about the city's public transport is available on the Roads & Transport Authority (RTA) website at 🅦 rta.ae. The RTA also provide an excellent **online travel planner** at 🅦 wojhati.rta.ae.

By metro

Opened in September 2009, the **Dubai Metro** (🅦 rta.ae) has revolutionized transport within the city and offers a cheap, fast and convenient way of getting around, with state-of-the-art driverless trains running on a mixture of underground and overground lines, and eye-catching modern stations. Stand at the front or back of the train for the best views on overground sections – riding at the front of the driverless trains is the most (travel) fun you can have in the UAE outside a theme park.

The metro consists of two lines. The 52km-long **Red Line**, starts in Rashidiya, just south of the airport, and then runs via the airport and city centre south down Sheikh Zayed Road to Jebel Ali. The 22km-long **Green Line** arcs around the city centre, running from Al Qusais, north of the airport, via Deira and Bur Dubai and then down to Dubai Healthcare City (the two last stations on the line – Al Jadaf and Creek – had yet to open at the time of writing).

Trains run every 4–8 minutes, with services beginning at around 5.50am daily except on Fridays, when the metro doesn't start running until 1pm. Last trains leave at around 11am (or around midnight on Thursday & Friday). Despite the frequent departures, the popularity of the system means that it's often difficult to get a seat. **Fares** are calculated according to the distance travelled ranging from 1.80dh up to a maximum of 5.80dh for a single trip (or from 3.60dh to 11.60dh in Gold Class; see below), or 14dh for an entire day's travel (excepting Gold Class). Children under 5 or shorter than 0.9m travel free.

All trains have a dedicated carriage for **women and children** (look for the signs above the platform barriers) plus a **Gold Class** compartment at the front of/back of the train – costing double the standard fare charged to a Silver or Blue Nol card (and a little less than double on a Red Ticket), these have slightly plusher seating and decor, although the main benefit is that they're usually fairly empty, meaning that you're pretty much guaranteed a seat. Given how packed other carriages often are and how reasonably priced the system is, you might feel that paying a bit extra for Gold Class is well worth the modest sums involved.

By taxi

Away from areas served by the metro, the only way of getting around Dubai quickly and conveniently is by **taxi**. Cabs are usually plentiful at all times of day and night almost everywhere in the city with the important exception of Bur Dubai and Deira, where you might sometimes struggle to catch one, particularly during the morning and evening rush hours and after dark. Large malls and big hotels are always good places to pick up a cab; if not, just stand on the street and wave at anything that passes. Taxis are operated by various companies (see box below) and come in assorted colours, though all have yellow taxi signs on the roof, illuminated when the vehicle is available for rent.

Fares

Fares are pretty good value. There's a minimum charge of 10dh per ride, with a basic flag fare of 3dh (or 3.50dh from 10pm to 6am), plus 1.71dh per kilometre. The exception is for taxis picked up from the airport, where a 20dh flag fare is imposed; there's also a 20dh surcharge if you take a taxi into Sharjah. Booking by phone (see box below) adds an extra 3dh to the fare (or 3.50dh 10pm–6am). If you want a taxi to wait for you, it costs 0.50dh per minute. You'll also have to pay a 4dh surcharge if your taxi travels through a Salik tollgate (see p.24). For a full list of fares and charges, visit ⓦdtc.dubai .ae and click on the "Our Fares" tab. A small number of "ladies' cabs" (all with female drivers) are also available for the use of women and families only (flag fare 6dh, or 7dh from 10pm to 6am).

Drivers and complaints

The majority of taxi drivers (most are Indian or Pakistani, including many from Kerala) are well trained and will be familiar with all the main city landmarks, although if you're going anywhere more obscure you might have to help them find the way; if in doubt, try to have directions or a full address to hand. If you get completely stuck, get them to ring

up their control centre for help. Rumours of taxi drivers inflating fares by driving newly arrived tourists five times around the block occasionally surface, but appear to have no basis in reality; the whole industry is stringently regulated, and drivers are unlikely to risk their jobs for the sake of a few extra dirhams. Be aware, though, that Dubai's labyrinthine traffic systems often add considerably to the distances between A and B. If you get into a cab and the driver seems to head off in completely the wrong direction it's likely to be because he has to turn around or find the correct exit/entrance to a particular road. If you think you have a genuine grievance and you wish to lodge a **complaint**, phone the RTA call centre (☎800 90 90). Make sure you take the driver's ID number before you leave. **Tips** aren't strictly necessary, though many taxi drivers will automatically keep the small change from fares unless you specifically ask for it back.

Taxi drivers might occasionally **refuse to take you** if you're travelling only a short distance. This is most frequently the case outside hotels and malls where drivers are obliged to join a long queue to pick up a fare. Strictly speaking, they're obliged to take you however short the journey, though in practice if they've been waiting for an hour and you only want to go around the block you can see their point. If this happens, just walk back down the queue of taxis until you find a more willing driver. The only other occasion when a driver may refuse your fare is if it's likely to get them stuck in a massive traffic jam (such as when crossing the Creek during the morning or evening rush hours).

Finally, watch out for the **hotel limousines** which sometimes try to pass themselves off as conventional taxis (hotel doormen may sometimes try to get you into one of these, pretending they're ordinary taxis). These are metered, but usually cost around twice the price of a normal cab and have no perceptible benefits apart from leather upholstery and the overwhelming smell of cheap air freshener. Remember, if it doesn't have a yellow taxi sign on the roof, it's not a proper taxi.

By abra

Despite contemporary Dubai's obsession with modern technology, getting from one side of the Creek to the other in the city centre is still a charmingly old-fashioned experience, involving a trip in one of the hundreds of rickety little boats – or **abras** – which ferry passengers between Deira and Bur Dubai. It's a wonderful little journey, offering superb views of the fascinating muddle of creekside

---

TAXI NUMBERS

To book a cab, call any of the companies below:

Arabia Taxi ☎ 800 272 242
Cars Taxi ☎ 800 22 77 89
Dubai Taxi/Ladies Taxis ☎ 04 208 0808
Metro Taxi ☎ 600 566 000
National Taxi ☎ 600 54 33 22

buildings with their tangles of souks, wind towers, mosques and minarets. Note that small bumps and minor collisions between boats are common when docking and departing, so take care or you might find yourself not so much up the Creek as in it.

There are two main abra **routes**: one from the Deira Old Souk Abra Station (next to the Spice Souk) to the Bur Dubai Abra Station (at the north end of the Textile Souk), and another from Al Sabkha Abra Station (at the southern end of the Dhow Wharfage in Deira) to the Bur Dubai Old Souk Abra Station (in the middle of the Textile Souk). There's a third abra route from Al Seef Station at the southern end of Bur Dubai to Baniyas Station, near Baniyas Square in Deira. The **fare** is a measly 1dh per crossing. Boats leave as soon as full, meaning in practice every couple of minutes, and the crossing takes about five minutes. Abras run from 6am to midnight, and 24hr on the route from Bur Dubai Old Souk to Al Sabkha (though with a reduced service between midnight and 6am).

By waterbus

A more sedate but much less atmospheric way of getting across the Creek is aboard a **waterbus**. These were launched with the intention of providing a safer and more comfortable means of crossing the water than the traditional abra, although they have rather failed to catch on thanks to the higher fares, long waiting times between boats and general lack of atmosphere – boats are entirely glassed in behind tinted windows, effectively cutting you off from the views and sea breezes outside. They're worth considering if you might have problems hopping on and off an abra (if you have small children in tow, for instance) but otherwise don't have much to recommend them.

There are four different **routes**, mainly using the same "stations" as the city's abras, but following slightly different routings: Line **B1** runs from Bur Dubai to Al Sabkha; **B2** runs from Bur Dubai Old Souk to Baniyas Square; **B3** runs from Al Sabkha Station to Baniyas and Al Seef; and **B4** from Bur Dubai Old Souk to Al Seef and then on to Creek Park. Waterbuses run daily from around 7am to 10pm (line B1 10am–10pm only), with departures every 30 minutes. The **fare** is 2dh per trip, payable by Nol card or ticket (see box, p.21); tickets aren't sold on board.

By bus

Dubai has an extensive and efficient bus network, though it's mainly designed around the needs of low-paid expat workers so is of only limited use for tourists – most routes cover parts of the city that casual visitors are unlikely to want to reach. The majority of services originate at or terminate at either the **Gold Souk Bus Station** in Deira or **Al Ghubaiba Bus Station** in Bur Dubai (many services call at both). Bus stops are clearly signed, and many also boast air-conditioned shelters providing waiting passengers with refuge from the heat of the day; you'll also find a useful map of the bus network and other information inside each shelter.

For the casual visitor, the only really useful service is bus #8 (roughly every 20min from early morning till late evening), which runs from the Gold Souk station to Al Ghubaiba and then due south, down Jumeirah Road to the Burj al Arab and on to Dubai Marina, covering a big chunk of the city not served by the metro (although if heading to the southern city it's probably quicker to take the metro to the nearest jumping-off point, and then a cab for the last part of your journey). Buses are included in the **Nol ticket scheme**, meaning that you'll need to be in possession of a paid-up Nol card or ticket (see box, p.21) before you get on the bus; tickets aren't sold on board.

Buses to other emirates

Buses to neighbouring emirates all leave from Al Ghubaiba bus station in Bur Dubai (from the south side of station, opposite the *New Penninsula Hotel*), with regular services to **Sharjah** (every 20–25min; 45min–1hr 15min depending on traffic; services operate 24hr; 7dh), **Abu Dhabi** (every 30min, 5.30am–11.30pm; 2hr–2hr 30min; 15dh) and **Al Ain** (hourly 6.30am–11.30pm; 1hr 30min–2hr; 15dh). These buses aren't covered by the Nol scheme, and you'll need to buy a ticket at the relevant kiosk in the bus station before boarding.

By car

Renting a car is another option, but comes with a couple of major caveats. Driving in Dubai isn't for the faint-hearted: the city's roads are permanently busy and standards of driving somewhat wayward. **Navigational difficulties** are another big problem. Endless construction works, erratic signage, and road layouts and one-way systems of labyrinthine complexity can make getting anywhere a significant challenge. Outside the city you're less likely to get lost, although the main highways down to Abu Dhabi and up to Al Ain are notorious for the wildly aggressive driving styles of local Emiratis. Accidents are common, and considerable caution should be exercised.

Driving is on the right-hand side, and there's a 60 or 80km/h **speed limit** in built-up areas, and 100 or 120km/h on main highways (although locals regularly charge down the fast lane at 150km/h or more). **Parking** can be a major headache. Most hotels (apart from city-centre budget establishments) should have free spaces available but elsewhere you'll have to take your chances with finding an on-street space (most have metered parking at 1–2dh/hr). Finding on-street parking in the congested old city is particularly difficult, although there are plenty of small car parks dotted around Bur Dubai (fewer in Deira), most charging 10dh/hr. On the plus side, **petrol** is a bargain, at around 1.7dh per litre.

There are also four **road toll points**, run under the **Salik** (ⓦ salik.ae) scheme. These are located on Maktoum and Garhoud bridges and at two points along Sheikh Zayed Road (near Al Safa Park, and at Al Barsha, next to the Mall of the Emirates). You don't actually have to stop and pay the toll on the spot – it's automatically charged to your vehicle's account every time you drive through. If you're in a hire car, the rental company will subsequently deduct any toll fees (the basic 4dh toll, plus a 1dh service charge) from your credit card.

If you have an **accident**, local law prohibits you from moving your vehicle until the police have been called and the exact circumstances of the crash have been investigated. Note also that **drink-driving** is an absolute no-no. If you're caught behind the wheel with even the slightest trace of alcohol in your system you're facing either a hefty fine, or a spell in prison.

Car rental

All the major international car rental agencies have offices in Dubai, and there are also dozens of local firms, some of whom may slightly undercut rates offered by the international companies, although, equally, service and backup may not be quite as professional and comprehensive. Drivers will need to be aged 21 (25 for some larger vehicles) or over. Your driving licence from your home country should suffice, although you might want to check in advance. Rates are generally cheap – as little as 70dh (£16/US$19) per day for a basic vehicle including collision damage waiver (well worth taking). Some agencies will also deliver and collect vehicles from your address in Dubai, saving you the bother of picking up the car in person – check when you book.

For the locations and phone numbers of individual car rental offices, see the websites listed below. There are also car rental desks at all major hotels, while some of the tour operators (see p.25) also offer car

rental. The greatest concentration of offices is at the airport, in Terminal 1, although bizarrely these are located in an area which is technically accessible only to newly arrived passengers (just inside the main doors – you can see the offices clearly from outside). If you want to rent a car here and you haven't just got off a plane you'll have to try and duck in through the no-entry doors (usually easy enough, assuming there's no security guard hanging around, in which case you'll have to sweet-talk your way through) or call the relevant office and ask them to meet you outside. There are also lots of car rental offices scattered along Sheikh Zayed Road, a more convenient (and less stressful) starting point than the airport if you're heading south of the city.

CAR RENTAL AGENCIES

Avis ⓦ avisuae.ae
Budget ⓦ budget-uae.com
Europcar ⓦ europcar-middleeast.com
Hertz ⓦ hertzuae.com
Sixt ⓦ sixt-uae.com
Thrifty ⓦ thriftyuae.com

Tours, cruises and desert safaris

Dubai has dozens of identikit tour operators who pull in a regular supply of punters in search of the instant "Arabian" experience. The emphasis is firmly on stereotypical desert safaris and touristy dhow dinner cruises, although a few operators offer more unusual activities ranging from falconry displays to helicopter rides.

Top of most visitors' wish lists is the chance to get out into the **desert** – although it's worth bearing in mind the sandy hinterlands of Dubai are regarded more as a kind of enormous adventure playground rather than as a natural spectacle, and the emphasis is usually on petrol- and adrenaline-fuelled activities rather than on the quiet contemplation of the desert.

As well as the perennially popular **dhow dinner cruises** offered by pretty much every operator, there are numerous **city tours** available, as well as trips to neighbouring emirates. Some operators also offer various **watersports**, **snorkelling** and **diving** (although for diving it's better to contact a specialist dive operator; see p.139).

Prices can vary quite considerably from operator to operator, so it's worth shopping around. Most operators post the latest tariffs on their websites. It's usually easiest **to book** by phone, since few places have conveniently located offices, although many hotels have an in-house tour desk (bear in mind, however, that they'll most likely steer you in the direction of a particular operator).

Of the operators listed below, Hormuz Tourism are generally the cheapest, while Knight Tours probably have the most cultural kudos, having local (rather than the usual expat Asian) drivers. The one real standout operator, however, is **Arabian Adventures**, an offshoot of Emirates Airlines, which has tour desks in many of the city's top-end hotels including *Al Qasr*, *Mina A'Salaam*, *Atlantis*, *Hilton Jumeirah Beach*, the *Grand Hyatt* and *Hyatt Regency*, *Jumeirah Beach Hotel*, *Jumeirah Zabeel Saray*, and the *One&Only Royal Mirage*. This is easily the biggest tour operator in town, very professionally run and with a larger-than-average range of trips, including walking tours of old Dubai and Sharjah, visits to Ras al Khaimah and so on. They're more expensive than other operators, but it's usually money well spent.

GENERAL TOUR OPERATORS

Alpha Tours ☎ 04 294 9888, Ⓦ alphatoursdubai.com
Arabian Adventures ☎ 04 303 4888, Ⓦ arabian-adventures.com
Hormuz Tourism ☎ 04 228 0663, Ⓦ hormuztourism.com
Knight Tours ☎ 04 343 7725, Ⓦ knighttours.co.ae
Lama Tours ☎ 04 334 4330, Ⓦ lama.ae
Orient Tours ☎ 04 282 8238, Ⓦ orienttours.ae
Sunflower Tours ☎ 04 334 5554, Ⓦ sunflowerdubai.com
Travco ☎ 04 336 6643, Ⓦ travcotravel.ae

SPECIALIST OPERATORS

Absolute Adventure ☎ 04 345 9900, Ⓦ adventure.ae. Organize customized treks and other activities in the mountains of the UAE and Oman.
Nomad ☎ 04 450 2429, Ⓦ nomad4x4.com. 4WD desert-driving courses for beginners through to experienced off-roaders. Alternatively, Off-Road Zone (☎ 04 339 2449, Ⓦ offroad-zone.com) offers similar training.
Shaheen Xtreme ☎ 04 435 6550, Ⓦ shaheenxtreme.com. Falconry specialists offering a range of packages from simple two-hour flying displays through to complete training courses in the basic principles of falconry.
UAE Trekkers ☎ 055 886 2327, Ⓦ uaetrekkers.com. Local expat club arranging regular day-treks throughout the UAE and Oman, plus occasional overnight camping trips.

City tours

Generic city tours are offered by all our recommended general tour operators (see above), although the whistle-stop approach isn't likely to yield any particularly interesting insights, and you'll do better to follow your own itinerary unless severely pressed for time. Alternatively, more original views of the city are offered by the two operators listed under "City tour operators" (see below).

If you've got the cash you might consider an airborne tour of the city, offering peerless views of the Creek and coast. **Seaplane** tours are offered by Seawings (Ⓦ seawings.ae), while **helicopter** rides around the city can be arranged by several operators, including Arabian Adventures. Both start from around 1250dh per person.

CITY TOUR OPERATORS

Sheikh Mohammed Centre for Cultural Understanding (SMCCU) Bastakiya ☎ 04 353 6666, Ⓦ cultures.ae. Innovative tours of Jumeirah Mosque and Bastakiya, along with other cultural events (see box, p.40).
Wonder Bus Tours BurJuman centre ☎ 04 359 5656, Ⓦ wonderbustours.net. The bizarre-looking Wonder Bus – half bus and half boat – offers Dubai city tours with a difference. Departing from the BurJuman centre, you'll be driven down to Garhoud Bridge, where the bus-cum-boat dives into the water and motors all the way up the Creek to Shindagha. It then emerges back onto land, returning to BurJuman by road. Trips last about 1hr 30min (including 1hr on the Creek) and cost 140dh (95dh for children aged 3–11; family ticket 440dh). There are usually two trips daily in the morning and afternoon, depending on the tide; book at least one day ahead to make sure of a place and check latest timings.

Boat cruises

Getting out on the waters of the Creek is one of the highlights of a visit to the city, either via the short **abra** ride across the Creek (see p.22 & p.43) or via longer abra or **dhow** cruises.

Abra cruises

A more leisurely alternative to the standard Creek crossing by abra is to **charter** your own boat, which costs 120dh for an hour-long ride: starting from somewhere in the city centre, in an hour you can probably get down to the Dubai Creek Golf Club and back. To find an abra for rent, head to the nearest abra station and ask around. The rate is officially set (and posted in writing at all abra stations) and is the same regardless of how many people use the boat, so don't be talked into paying more.

Dinner cruises

A more comfortable alternative to chartering an abra is to go on one of the ever popular after-dark **Creek dinner cruises**, which can be booked through any tour operator (see p.25), as well as many of the city's hotels. Most of these use traditional old wooden dhows, offering the chance to wine and dine on the water as your boat sails sedately up and down the Creek. The experience has undeniable romance, although the food usually comprises a lame Arabian-style buffet at inflated prices, and you may feel that you can get a better (and much cheaper) sense of Dubai's maritime past simply by going for a ride on an abra. A number of operators also now offer similar dinner dhow cruises sailing between the skyscrapers of **Dubai Marina** in the southern city. Standard dinner cruises last two hours and cost anything from around 60dh up to 350dh, depending on which operator and boat you go with, inclusive of a buffet dinner and on-board entertainment; boats normally leave around 8–8.30pm.

DINNER CRUISE OPERATORS

Bateaux Dubai ☎ 04 814 5553, 🌐 bateauxdubai.com. The classiest of the city's myriad dinner-cruise operators, using a state-of-the-art modern boat (it looks a bit like a floating greenhouse) rather than a traditional dhow and with excellent food. Nightly cruises 350dh.

Cruises Dubai ☎ 05 871 7200, 🌐 cruisesdubai.net. Bargain-basement cruises from as little as 55dh, plus more expensive (150dh) Marina cruises.

Al Mansour Dhow ☎ 04 205 7033. One of the more reliable options, operated by the *Radisson Blu Dubai Deira Creek* hotel (see p.94). Nightly cruises 185dh.

Rikks Cruises ☎ 04 357 2200, 🌐 rikks.net. Long-running and popular cruises (nightly for around 150dh). Also runs dhow dinner cruises at the Marina.

Desert safaris

One thing that virtually every visitor to Dubai does at some point is go on a **desert safari**. The main attraction of these trips is the chance to see some of the desert scenery surrounding the city, and although virtually all tours put the emphasis firmly on cheap thrills and touristy gimmicks most people find the experience enjoyable, in a rather cheesy sort of way.

Sunset safaris

The vast majority of visitors opt for one of the endlessly popular **half-day safaris** (also known as "sunset safaris"). These are offered by every tour operator in town (see p.25) and cost from around 150dh up to 350dh. Whoever you decide to go with the basic ingredients remain the same, although staff employed by the cheaper operators are sometimes guilty of shockingly dangerous driving

en route to the dunes. More expensive tours will also generally offer superior service, better-quality food and a wider range of entertainments at their "Bedouin camps" (see below).

Tours are in large 4WDs holding around eight passengers. You'll be picked up from your hotel between 3 and 4pm and then, once you've driven around town collecting the other passengers in your vehicle, be driven out into the desert. The usual destination is an area 45 minutes' drive out of town on the road to Hatta, opposite the massive dune popularly known as Big Red (see box, p.164).

After a brief stop, during which your vehicle's tyres will be partially deflated as a preparation for going off-road, you'll be driven out into the dunes on the opposite side of the highway from Big Red for an hour or so to enjoy the traditional Emirati pastime of **dune-bashing**. This involves driving at high speed up and down increasingly precipitous dunes amid great sprays of sand while your vehicle slides, skids, bumps and occasionally takes off completely. Thrills apart, the dunes are magnificent, and very beautiful at sunset, and although it's difficult to see much while you're being bumped around inside the vehicle, your driver will probably stop near the highest point of the dunes so that you can get out, enjoy the scenery and take some photos. You might also be given the chance to try your hand at a brief bit of **sand-skiing**. Alternatively, some tour operators take you back to the main road, where you can go for a ride across the dunes on a quad bike – or "**dune buggy**" – generally for an additional fee.

As dusk falls, you'll be driven off to one of the dozens of optimistically named "**Bedouin camps**" in the desert, usually with various tents rigged up around a sandy enclosure and belly-dancing stage. Wherever you're taken you'll find pretty much the same touristy fare on offer, all included in the tour price. These typically include (very short) camel rides, henna painting, dressing up in Gulf national costume, and having your photo taken with an Emirati falcon perched on your arm. A passable international **buffet dinner** is then served, after which a **belly dancer** performs for another half-hour or so, dragging likely-looking members of the audience up on stage with her (choose your seat carefully). It's all good fun, although the belly dancer is more likely to be from Moscow than Muscat, and the floor tends to get rapidly swamped with jolly Indian businessmen. The whole thing winds up at around 9.30pm, after which you'll be driven back to Dubai.

Other desert safaris

For those who want to get more of a feel for the desert, some tour operators offer the chance to extend the sunset safari into an **overnight trip**, sleeping out in tents before returning to Dubai after breakfast the following morning. This offers you a much better chance of getting some sense of the emptiness and grandeur of the landscape than during the belly-dancing free-for-all.

Some companies also offer **full-day desert safaris**. These usually include a mixture of general sightseeing combined with activities like dune-bashing, camel riding, sand-skiing and dune-buggy riding before returning to Dubai at dusk. These tours are also the best way to experience the popular pastime of **wadi-bashing** – driving through the rocky, dried-up riverbeds that score the eastern side of the UAE around the Hajar Mountains. Some operators also offer tours focusing exclusively on particular activities like sand-skiing, camel trekking and dune-buggy riding.

The media

The media in Dubai and elsewhere in the UAE isn't renowned for its investigative journalism or controversial reportage. Although overt censorship is rarely applied, publications that question the status quo tend to find themselves losing large chunks of advertising revenue (most of which is likely to come from government-owned companies), while offending journalists (virtually all of whom are expats) are likely to have their visas cancelled. For more outspoken news sources, you'll have to look online (see p.35).

Newspapers and magazines

Easily the best English-language newspaper is **The National** (based in Abu Dhabi, but with extensive coverage of Dubai; Ⓦ thenational.ae). This has good international reporting and is generally well written and slightly less cringing in its coverage of UAE affairs than the country's other dailies. Of the two English-language broadsheets printed in Dubai, **Gulf News** (Ⓦ gulfnews.com) is usually a bit better than the **Khaleej Times** (Ⓦ khaleejtimes.com), though both are a bit turgid, with rather too many pictures of random ruling sheikhs attending official engagements and assorted "news" stories which quite clearly originated in a government press release. Look out, too, for the free and occasionally entertaining **7 Days** tabloid-style rag (Ⓦ 7days.ae).

Television and radio

There are a number of Emirati **television** channels, including the English-language Dubai One (Ⓦ dmi .ae/dubaione), which consists mainly of repackaged US shows and movies, along with a few local programmes. Local English-language **radio** stations include Virgin Radio Dubai (104.4 FM; Ⓦ virginradio dubai.com) and Dubai 92 (92FM; Ⓦ dubai92.com), though both largely subsist on an uninspiring diet of mainstream pop-rock and inane DJ chat.

Festivals

Despite Dubai's popular reputation as the land that culture forgot, the city hosts a number of world-class annual festivals showcasing film, music and the visual arts, while neighbouring Abu Dhabi also stages a number of leading cultural events. Annual sporting events are covered in the "Sports and outdoor activities" chapter (see p.137). For a complete listing of events in the city, see Ⓦ dubaicalendar.ae.

JANUARY/FEBRUARY

Al Dhafra Festival Fifteen days in Dec/Jan Ⓦ aldhafrafestival.ae. Held at the small town of Madinat Zayed in western Abu Dhabi emirate, this lively annual festival is devoted to traditional Bedouin desert culture and heritage. The centrepiece of the festival is a huge camel fair, with races, auctions and even beauty competitions for the best-looking dromedaries. Other events showcase the region's handicrafts, poetry, cooking and traditional date industry.

Dubai Shopping Festival One month in Jan/Feb Ⓦ dubaievents .ae/en. Only Dubai could dream up a festival devoted to shopping – and only in Dubai, one suspects, would it have proved so popular. The festival sees shops citywide offering all sorts of sales bargains, with discounts of up to 75 percent, while the big malls lay on lots of entertainment and children's events to keep punters' offspring amused during their parents' extended shopping binges. The festival also sees a spate of events at the Global Village in Dubailand (Ⓦ globalvillage.ae; open Oct–March), comprising a range of eye-catching international pavilions that showcase arts and crafts from countries around the world, as well as performances of world music and dance and other events.

Dubai International Jazz Festival One week in Feb Ⓦ dubaijazzfest.com. Top local and international jazz and pop acts perform at Festival City. Previous participants have included the Brand New Heavies, James Blunt, Macy Grey and Mica Paris.

RELIGIOUS FESTIVALS

The Islamic holy month of **Ramadan** is observed with great attention and ceremony in Dubai, and is the one time of the year when you really get the sense of being in an essentially Muslim city. For Muslims, Ramadan represents a period in which to purify mind and body and to reaffirm one's relationship with God. Muslims are required to fast from dawn to dusk, and as a tourist you will be expected to publicly observe these strictures, although you are free to eat and drink in the privacy of your own hotel room, or in any of the carefully screened-off dining areas set up in hotels throughout the city (alcohol is also served discreetly in some places after dark, but not during the day). Eating, drinking, smoking or chewing gum in public, however, is a definite no-no, and will cause considerable offence to local Muslims; singing, dancing and swearing in public are similarly frowned upon. In addition, live music is also completely forbidden during the holy month (though recorded music is allowed), while the city's nightclubs all close for the duration, and many shops scale back their opening hours.

Fasting ends at dusk, at which point the previously comatose city springs to life in a celebratory round of eating, drinking and socializing known as Iftar ("The Breaking of the Fast"). Many of the city's top hotels set up superb "Iftar tents", with lavish Arabian buffets, and things remain lively until the small hours, when everyone goes off to bed in preparation for another day of abstinence. The atmosphere is particularly exuberant, and the Iftar tents especially lavish, during **Eid ul Fitr**, the day marking the end of Ramadan, when the entire city erupts in an explosion of celebratory festivity.

Falling approximately 70 days after the end of Ramadan, on the tenth day of the Islamic lunar month of Dhul Hijja, **Eid al Adha** (the "Festival of the Sacrifice") celebrates the willingness of Ibrahim to sacrifice his son Ismail at the command of God (although having proved his obedience, he was permitted to sacrifice a ram instead). The festival also marks the end of the traditional pilgrimage season to Mecca. Eid al Adha is celebrated in Dubai with a four-day holiday, during which lambs are sacrificed and the meat divided among the poor. No alcohol is served on the day before the festival day itself.

DATES

Ramadan Scheduled to run from approximately June 28 to July 27, 2014; June 18 to July 16, 2015; June 6 to July 4, 2016; May 27 to June 24, 2017. Precise dates vary according to local astronomical sightings of the moon.

Eid ul Fitr Estimated dates: July 28, 2014; July 17, 2015; July 5, 2016; June 25, 2017.

Eid al Adha Estimated dates: Oct 4, 2014; Sept 23, 2015; Sept 11, 2016; Sept 1, 2017.

MARCH

Art Dubai Four days in mid-March ⓦ artdubai.ae. The biggest event in the Dubai visual arts calendar, this four-day art fair features exhibits from some 75 galleries from around the world at Madinat Jumeirah.

Abu Dhabi Festival Three weeks in March ⓦ www .abudhabifestival.ae/en. Long-running arts festival featuring a mix of classical music, ballet and theatre, with performances by top global stars.

Emirates Airline Festival of Literature Five days in March ⓦ eaifl.com. Established in 2009 and now the Middle East's largest literary festival, with five days of readings and discussions featuring over 100 leading local and international scribblers.

Dubai Fashion Week March and Oct ⓦ dfw.ae. Leading Middle Eastern fashion event, held twice yearly, with autumn/winter collections taken for a catwalk in late March, and spring/summer collections on show at the end of October.

Bastakiya Art Fair One week in mid-March ⓦ bastakiyaartfair .com. Held at the same time as Art Dubai, the lively week-long Bastakiya Art Fair offers a kind of fringe alternative to its more mainstream cousin, with shows of work by up-and-coming artists at venues throughout the historic Bastakiya quarter, backed up by film screenings, book readings and various talks.

Sharjah Biennial March to May ⓦ sharjahbiennial.org. The oldest (established 1993) and most famous art festival in the Gulf (see box, p.148), held over two months every other year (odd-numbered years) and showcasing major Arabian and international artists, along with other cultural events.

Taste of Dubai Three days in mid-March ⓦ tasteofdubaifestival .com. Three days of live cookery exhibitions in Dubai Media City by local and visiting international celebrity chefs, plus wine tastings and the chance to sample signature dishes from some of the city's leading restaurants at heavily discounted prices.

APRIL

Womad Abu Dhabi Three days in mid-April ⓦ womadabudhabi.ae. Abu Dhabi edition of the legendary world music festival, with three days of free concerts on the Abu Dhabi Corniche and at Al Jahili Fort in Al Ain.

JUNE/JULY

Dubai Summer Surprises Mid-June to mid-July ⓦ dubaievents .ae/en/dss. An attempt to lure visitors to Dubai during the blisteringly hot summer months, Dubai Summer Surprises (DSS) is a mainly mall-based event – really more of a marketing promotion than a genuine festival – with a decent selection of shopping bargains on offer and masses of live children's entertainment presided over by the irritating cartoon figure known as Modhesh, whose crinkly yellow features you'll probably quickly learn to loathe. Great if you've got kids in tow, however.

OCTOBER

Abu Dhabi Film Festival Ten days in mid-Oct Ⓦ abudhabifilm festival.ae. Established in 2007 to encourage the work of Arab filmmakers, and serving up a wide-ranging selection of films and documentaries from around the world, with guest appearances by assorted Hollywood, Bollywood and Middle Eastern celebrities.

Dubai Fashion Week (see opposite).

DECEMBER

Dubai International Film Festival One week in mid-Dec Ⓦ dubaifilmfest.com. This major film festival showcases international art house films, including a particular focus on home-grown work and usually a few well-known celebs in attendance.

National Day Dec 2. The UAE's independence day is celebrated with a raft of citywide events, including parades, dhow races and performances of traditional music and dance.

Culture and etiquette

Despite its glossy Western veneer and apparently liberal ways, it's important to remember that Dubai is an Islamic state, and that visitors are expected to comply with local cultural norms or risk the consequences. Recent Foreign Office figures have shown that Britons are more likely to get arrested in the UAE than in any other country in the world, mainly for the sort of actions – public drunkenness, "lewd" behaviour, or just eating, drinking or smoking in public during Ramadan – which would be considered unexceptional back home.

There are a few simple rules to remember if you want to stay out of trouble. Any public display of **drunkenness** outside a licensed venue contravenes local law, and could get you locked up. Driving while under any sort of influence is even more of a no-no. **Inappropriate public behaviour** with members of the opposite sex can result in, at best, embarrassment, or, at worst, a spell in prison. Holding hands or a peck on the cheek is probably just about OK, but any more passionate displays of public affection are severely frowned upon. The infamous case of Michelle Palmer and Vince Acors, who were jailed for three months after allegedly having sex on the beach and assaulting a policeman, received widespread coverage, although far less overt demonstrations of affection can potentially land you in big trouble; in 2010 two British citizens were sentenced to a month in jail for allegedly kissing one another on the lips in public at a restaurant. **Offensive gestures** are another source of possible danger. Giving someone the finger or even just sticking out your tongue might be considered rude at home but can get you jailed in Dubai. This is particularly worth remembering when driving, since even a frustrated flap of the hands could potentially land you in trouble.

In terms of general etiquette, except around the hotel pool, **modest dress** is expected of all visitors – although many expat women do pretty much the exact opposite. Dressing "indecently" is potentially punishable under law (even if actual arrests are extremely rare) although exactly what constitutes indecent attire isn't clearly defined – though obviously the shorter your skirt and the lower your top, the more likely you are to attract attention. Even men who wear shorts can raise eyebrows – to the locals it looks like you're walking around in your underwear. In addition, if you're fortunate enough to spend any time with Emiratis, remember that only the right hand should be used for eating and drinking (this rule also applies in Indian establishments), and don't offer to shake the hand of an Emirati woman unless she extends hers toward you.

Travel essentials

Costs

Dubai has never been a bargain destination, and although it's possible to get by without spending huge amounts of money, unless you're prepared to splash at least a certain amount of cash you'll miss out on much of what the city has to offer. The biggest basic cost is **accommodation**. At the very bottom end of the scale it's possible to find a double room for the night for around 250dh (£42/ US$70/€50). For more upmarket hotels you're looking at more like 600dh (£100/US$160/€120) per night, while you won't usually get a bed in one of the city's fancier five-stars for less than around 1200dh (£220/US$325/€260) per night at the absolute minimum; room rates at the very best places can run into thousands of dirhams.

Other costs are more fluid. **Eating** is very much a question of what you want to spend: you can eat well in the budget curry houses or shwarma cafés of

Bur Dubai and Karama for around 15dh (£2.50/US$4) per head, although a meal (with drinks) in a more upmarket establishment is likely to set you back around 300dh (£50/US$80) per head, and the sky is the limit in the top restaurants. **Tourist attractions** are also likely to put a big dent in your wallet, especially if you're travelling with children: the cost of a family day out at one of the city's water parks or kids' attractions is likely to set you back at least 600dh (£100/US$165). On the plus side, **transport** costs are relatively modest, given the city's inexpensive taxi services and metro system.

Taxes and tipping

Room rates at most of the city's more expensive hotels are subject to a ten percent **service charge** and an additional ten percent **government tax**; these taxes are sometimes included in quoted prices, and sometimes not. Check beforehand, or you may find your bill has suddenly inflated by twenty percent. The prices in most restaurants automatically include all relevant taxes and a ten percent service charge (though this isn't necessarily passed on to the waiters themselves); whether you wish to leave an additional **tip** is entirely your decision.

Crime, safety and the law

Dubai is an exceptionally safe city – although a surprising number of tourists and expats manage to get themselves arrested for various breaches of local law (see p.29). Violent crime is virtually unknown, and even instances of petty theft, pickpocketing and the like are relatively uncommon. The only time you're ever likely to be at risk is while **driving** (see p.23). If you need to **call the police** in an emergency, dial ☎999. You can also contact the police's Tourist Security Department toll-free on ☎800 4438 if you have an enquiry or complaint which you think the police could help you with. For the latest information about safety issues it's also worth having a look at the international government websites (see p.35).

Illegal substances and prescription drugs

You should not on any account attempt to enter (or even transit through) Dubai while in possession of any form of **illegal substance**. The death penalty is imposed for drug trafficking, and there's a mandatory four-year sentence for anyone caught in possession of drugs or other proscribed substances. It's vital to note that this doesn't just mean carrying drugs in a conventional sense, but also includes having an illegal substance in your **bloodstream or urine**, or

being found in possession of even **microscopic amounts** of a banned substance, even if invisible to the naked eye. Previous visitors have been convicted on the basis of minute traces of cannabis and other substances found in the fluff of a pocket or suitcase lining, or even in chewing gum stuck to the sole of a shoe. Note that **poppy seeds** (even in bakery products) are also banned, since the authorities believe they can be used to grow narcotics.

Even more contentiously, Dubai's hardline anti-drugs regime also extends to certain **prescription drugs**, including codeine and melatonin, which are also treated as illegal substances. If you're on any form of prescription medicine you're supposed to bring a doctor's letter and the original prescription from home, and to bring no more than three months' supply into the UAE. It's also a good idea to keep any medicines in their original packaging and to carry them in your hand luggage. A list of prohibited medicines (and other related information) is sometimes posted at ⓦbit.ly/dubai-arrival; if in doubt, ring your nearest embassy or consulate.

As a general rule, the more respectably dressed and boring you look, the less likely you are to get stopped at customs. Wait to make your fashion statement until you're safely inside the country.

Electricity

UK-style **sockets** with three square pins are the norm (although you might occasionally encounter Indian-style round-pin sockets in budget hotels in Bur Dubai and Deira). The city's **current** runs at 220–240 volts AC, meaning that UK appliances will work directly off the mains supply, although US appliances will probably require a transformer.

Entry requirements

Nationals of the UK, Ireland and most other Western European countries, the US, Canada, Australia and New Zealand are issued a **free thirty-day visa** on arrival (renewable for a further thirty days for 620dh). Always check visa requirements direct with your UAE embassy or consulate as this information is subject to change. You'll need a passport which will be valid for at least six months after the date of entry. Having an Israeli stamp in your passport shouldn't mean that you're denied entry to Dubai. For full details see ⓦbit.ly/dubai-immigration.

Customs regulations allow visitors to bring in up to 400 cigarettes (or 50 cigars or 500g of tobacco), four litres of alcohol (or two 24-can cases of beer), and cash and travellers' cheques up to a value of

40,000dh. Prohibited items include drugs (see opposite), pornographic material, material offensive to Islamic teachings, non-Islamic religious propaganda and evangelical literature and goods of Israeli origin or bearing Israeli trademarks or logos.

Foreign embassies are mainly located in the UAE's capital, Abu Dhabi, although many countries also maintain consulates in Dubai (see below).

EMBASSIES AND CONSULATES

Australia Consulate-General, Level 25, BurJuman Business Tower, Khalifa bin Zayed Rd, Bur Dubai ☎ 04 5087 100, ⓦ uae.embassy .gov.au.

Canada Consulate-General, 19th Floor, Emirates Towers, Sheikh Zayed Rd ☎ 04 404 8444, ⓦ canadainternational.gc.ca/uae-eau.

Ireland Embassy, 4th floor, Monarch Hotel Office Tower, 1 Sheikh Zayed Rd (opposite the World Trade Centre) ☎ 04 329 8382, ⓦ embassyofireland.ae.

New Zealand Consulate-General, Suite 1502, 15th Floor, API Tower, Sheikh Zayed Rd ☎ 04 331 7500, ⓦ immigration.govt.nz /branch/DubaiBranchHome.

Oman Embassy, Al Mushraf area (next to Immigration Department), Saeed bin Tahnon Square, Abu Dhabi ☎ 02 446 3333.

South Africa Consulate-General, 3rd Floor, New Sharaf Building, Khaleed bin al Waleed St, Bur Dubai ☎ 04 397 5222, ⓦ southafrica dubai.com.

UK Embassy, Al Seef Rd, Bur Dubai ☎ 04 309 4444, ⓦ ukinuae.fco .gov.uk/en.

US Consulate-General, Corner of Al Seef Rd and Sheikh Khalifa bin Zayed Rd, Bur Dubai ☎ 04 309 4000, ⓦ dubai.usconsulate.gov.

Gay Dubai

Dubai is one of the world's less-friendly gay and lesbian destinations. Homosexuality is illegal under UAE law, with punishments of up to ten years in prison – a useful summary of the present legal situation and recent prosecutions can be found at ⓦen.wikipedia.org/wiki/LGBT_rights_in_the_United _Arab_Emirates. Despite this, the city boasts a very clandestine gay scene, attracting both foreigners and Arabs from even less permissive cities around the Gulf, although you'll need to hunt hard to find it without local contacts. Relevant websites are routinely censored within the UAE, so you'll probably have to do your online research before you arrive. Useful resources include ⓦgaymiddleeast.com, ⓦfacebook .com/LGBTRightsUAE and ⓦgaysdubai.com.

Health

There are virtually no serious **health risks** in Dubai (unless you include the traffic). The city is well equipped with modern hospitals, while all four- and

five-star hotels have English-speaking **doctors** on call 24hr. **Tap water** is safe to drink, while even the city's cheapest curry houses and shwarma cafés maintain good standards of food hygiene. The only possible health concern is the **heat**. Summer temperatures regularly climb into the mid-forties, making sunburn, heatstroke and acute dehydration a real possibility, especially if combined with excessive alcohol consumption. Stay in the shade, and drink lots of water.

There are **pharmacies** all over the city, including a number run by the BinSina chain which are open 24hr. These include branches on Mankhool Road just north of the *Ramada* hotel; on the Creek side of Baniyas Square (in the building on the east side of the Deira Tower); in southern Jumeirah at the turn-off to the Majlis Ghorfat um al Sheif; and in Satwa on Al Diyafah Street between the *Al Mallah* and *Beirut* cafés.

There are three main government **hospitals** (more details at ⓦdha.gov.ae) and several private hospitals with emergency departments. You'll need to pay for treatment, though costs should be recoverable through your travel insurance.

GOVERNMENT HOSPITALS

Dubai Hospital Between the Corniche and Baraha St, Deira ☎ 04 219 5000.

Latifa Hospital (formerly Al Wasl Hospital) Oud Metha Rd (just south of Wafi), Oud Metha ☎ 04 219 3000.

Rashid Hospital Off Oud Metha Rd, near Maktoum Bridge, Oud Metha ☎ 04 219 2000.

PRIVATE HOSPITALS

American Hospital Off Oud Metha Rd (opposite the *Mövenpick* hotel), Oud Metha ☎ 04 336 7777, ⓦ ahdubai.com.

Emirates Hospital Opposite Jumeirah Beach Park, Jumeirah Beach Rd, Jumeirah ☎ 04 349 6666, ⓦ emirateshospital.ae.

Insurance

There aren't many safety or health risks involved in a visit to Dubai, although it's still strongly recommended that you take out some form of valid **travel insurance** before your trip. At its simplest, this offers some measure of protection against everyday mishaps like cancelled flights and mislaid

ROUGH GUIDES TRAVEL INSURANCE

Rough Guides has teamed up with WorldNomads.com to offer great travel insurance deals. Policies are available to residents of over 150 countries, with cover for a wide range of adventure sports, 24hr emergency assistance, high levels of medical and evacuation cover and a stream of travel safety information. Roughguides.com users can take advantage of their policies online 24/7, from anywhere in the world; you can also extend your policy and claim online. Roughguides.com users who buy travel insurance with WorldNomads.com can also leave a positive footprint and donate to a community development project. For more information, go to ⓦroughguides.com/travel-insurance.

baggage. More importantly, a valid insurance policy will cover your costs in the (admittedly unlikely) event that you fall ill in Dubai, since otherwise you'll have to pay for all medical treatment. Most insurance policies routinely exclude various "adventure" activities. In Dubai this could mean things like wall-climbing (see p.140) or tackling the black run at Ski Dubai (see p.80). If in doubt, check with your insurer before you leave home.

Internet

Dubai is a very wired city, although getting online can prove frustratingly difficult (or expensive) for casual visitors. All the better **hotels** provide internet access, either via computers in their business centres or via wi-fi or in-room cable connections. This is sometimes provided free, although more often is chargeable, often at extortionate rates (30dh/hr is common in more upmarket hotels).

There are frustratingly few **internet cafés** in the city. The best area to look is Bur Dubai, which boasts a scattering of small places, mostly catering to the area's Indian population. Aimei internet café (daily 8am–midnight; 3dh/hr) on 13c Sikka, the small road behind the *Time Palace* hotel, is one reliable option, as is Futurespeed (daily 8am–11pm; 10dh/hr) in the BurJuman centre (it's just inside the entrance by the *Dôme* café). Elsewhere, internet cafés are few and far between. In Deira, try the City Bird internet café between 11a and 13a streets (behind the *Dolphin Guest House* just off Corniche Road). In Oud Metha, try the Grano Coffee shop in Wafi (9am–11pm daily; 9dh/hr), although it doesn't have many machines so you may well have to wait.

Things are a lot easier if you have your own wi-fi-enabled laptop or other device. There are various free **wi-fi hotspots** around the city, including the whole of the Dubai Mall. You can also get online on the Dubai Metro for 10dh/hr. In addition, numerous wi-fi hotspots are operated by the city's two telecom companies, Etisalat (ⓦetisalat.ae) and Du (ⓦdu.ae). Both offer access at various places around the city, including most of the city's malls and numerous coffee shops, with several pay-as-you-go packages starting from 10dh for an hour's one-off surf time. See the websites for full details of charges and hotspot locations.

Internet access in Dubai is also subject to a certain modest amount of **censorship** – although this is now significantly less heavy-handed than in former years, during which mainstream sites such as Flickr, Myspace and Facebook were blocked (as was the website of the UK's Middlesex University thanks to its inadvertently suggestive name). There's a blanket ban on anything remotely pornographic, plus gambling and dating sites, and pages considered religiously or culturally offensive, although news pages (even those critical of the government) are generally left unblocked. The use of Skype and other types of **VOIP software** is technically forbidden by local telecom providers, although it's easy enough to find a way around the ban, which is seldom enforced in any case. Useful information about the latest internet censorship can be found at ⓦdubaifaqs.com/censorship-uae-internet.php.

Laundry

All larger hotels have a laundry service (usually expensive) while holiday apartments generally come with a washing machine as standard. There are no self-service launderettes in Dubai, though there are a few rather grubby places offering overnight laundry services dotted around the backstreets of Bur Dubai; you might prefer to wash your clothes yourself, however.

Mail

The two most convenient **post offices** for visitors are the Al Musalla Post Office (Sat–Thurs 7.30am–3pm) at Al Fahidi Roundabout, opposite the *Arabian Tea House Café* in Bur Dubai; and the Deira Post Office on Al Sabkha Road (Sat–Thurs 7.30am–9pm), near the intersection with Baniyas Road.

Airmail letters to Europe, the US and Australia cost 5dh (postcards 3.50dh); airmail parcels cost 50dh to Europe and 80dh to the US and Australia for parcels weighing 500g to 1kg.

Maps

The best general **city maps** are the pocket-sized *Dubai Mini Map* (around 50dh) and the larger *Dubai Map* (around 25dh) published by Explorer and widely available from bookshops around the city. Both combine a handy overview map of the city along with more detailed coverage of individual areas, with user-friendly cartography and all relevant tourist attractions and other local landmarks clearly marked. They're also updated on a regular basis, and make a laudable effort to keep pace with the city's constantly changing road layouts and other ongoing developments. The only A–Z-style **street atlas** currently available is the *Dubai Street Map* (also published by Explorer; around 90dh); this shows every road in the city, but is frustratingly lacking in other detail and not particularly useful.

Money

The UAE's currency is the **dirham** (abbreviated "dh" or "AED"), subdivided into 100 fils. The dirham is pegged against the US dollar at the rate of US$1=3.6725dh; other **exchange rates** at the time of writing were £1=5.93dh, €1=4.85dh. **Notes** come in 5dh, 10dh, 20dh, 50dh, 100dh, 200dh, 500dh and 1000dh denominations; there are also 2dh, 1dh, 50 fils and 25 fils coins. The 5dh, 50dh and 500dh notes are all a confusingly similar shade of brown; take care not to hand over the wrong sort (easily done if, say, you're getting out of a darkened cab at night) – a potentially very expensive mistake.

There are plenty of **ATMs** all over the city which accept foreign Visa and MasterCards. All the big shopping malls have at least a few ATMs, as do some large hotels. There are banks everywhere, almost all of which have ATMs. The most common are Mashreqbank, Commercial Bank of Dubai, National Bank of Dubai, National Bank of Abu Dhabi and Emirates Bank. All will also change **travellers' cheques** and **foreign cash**, and there are also plenty of **moneychangers**, including the reputable Al Ansari Exchange, which has branches all over the city (see Ⓦ alansariexchange.com/en /branches), as well as numerous places in Bur Dubai (try along and around Al Fahidi Street) and Deira (try Sikkat Al Khail Road, particularly the stretch closest to the Gold Souk).

Opening hours and public holidays

Dubai runs on an Islamic rather than a Western schedule, meaning that the city operates according to a basic **five-day working week** running Sunday to Thursday, with Friday as the Islamic holy day (equivalent to the Christian Sunday). Some offices also open on Saturday, while others close at noon on Thursday. When people talk about the **weekend** in Dubai they mean Friday and Saturday (and perhaps Thursday afternoon/evening as well). The most important fact to note is that many tourist sites and the Dubai Metro are **closed on Friday morning**, while **banks** usually open Saturday to Wednesday 8am–1pm and Thursday 8am–noon (some also reopen in the afternoon from 4.30 to 6.30pm).

Shops in **malls** generally open daily from 10am to 10pm, and until midnight on Friday and Saturday (and sometimes Thursday as well); shops in **souks** follow a similar pattern, though many places close for a siesta between around 1pm and 4pm depending on the whim of the owner. Most **restaurants** open daily for lunch and dinner (although some more upmarket hotel restaurants open for dinner only). **Pubs** tend to open daily from around noon until 2am; **bars** from around 6pm until 2/3am.

PUBLIC HOLIDAYS

There are seven public holidays in Dubai: two have fixed dates, while the other five shift annually according to the Islamic calendar (falling around 11 days earlier from year to year).

New Year's Day Jan 1.

Milad un Nabi (Birth of the Prophet Mohammed) Estimated dates: Jan 13, 2014; Jan 3, 2015; Dec 24, 2015; Dec 12, 2016.

Leilat al Meiraj (Ascent of the Prophet) Estimated dates: May 25, 2014; May 15, 2015; May 4, 2016; April 23, 2017.

Eid ul Fitr (the end of Ramadan; see box, p.28) Estimated dates: July 28, 2014; July 17, 2015; July 5, 2016; June 25, 2017.

Eid al Adha (the Festival of the Sacrifice; see box, p.28). Estimated dates: Oct 4, 2014; Sept 23, 2015; Sept 11, 2016; Sept 1, 2017.

Al Hijra (Islamic New Year) Estimated dates: Nov 5, 2013; Oct 25, 2014; Oct 14, 2015; Oct 2, 2016; Sept 21, 2017.

National Day (see p.29) Dec 2.

Phones

The **country code** for the UAE is ⓣ971. The **city code** for Dubai is ⓣ04; Abu Dhabi is ⓣ02; Sharjah is ⓣ06; Al Ain is ⓣ03. To **call abroad from the UAE**, dial ⓣ00, followed by your country code and the number itself (minus its initial zero). To call Dubai from abroad, dial your international access code, then ⓣ9714, followed by the local subscriber number (minus the ⓣ04 city code). Local mobile numbers begin with ⓣ050, ⓣ055 or ⓣ056 followed by a seven-digit number. If you've got a ⓣ04 number that's not working, try prefixing it instead with the various mobile phone prefixes – mobiles are so widely used now that many people don't specify whether a number is a landline or a mobile.

If you're going to be using the phone a lot while you're in Dubai, it might be worth acquiring a **local SIM card**, which will give you cheap local and international calls. The city's two telecoms operators are Etisalat (ⓦetisalat.ae) and Du (ⓦdu.ae). The cheapest options are currently the pay-as-you-go Du "Visitor Mobile Line" package (55dh, including 20dh credit) and Etisalat's Wasel package (40dh, including 5dh credit); see the websites for full details. Alternatively, you can pick up discounted SIM cards from phone shops around the city (particularly in Bur Dubai) from as little as 20dh. Either way, you'll need to present your passport when buying a SIM card.

Photography

Dubai is a very photogenic city, although the often harsh desert light can play havoc with colour and contrast – for the best results head out between around 7am and 9am in the morning, or after 4pm.

It's also worth noting that many upmarket hotels, restaurants and bars are extremely sniffy about people taking photographs of their establishments, particularly if other guests are likely to find their way into your shots – don't be surprised if you're asked to put your camera away. Outside of such establishments, things are more relaxed, although obviously it's polite to ask before you take photographs of people, and you risk causing considerable offence (or worse) if you shove your lens in the face of local Emiratis – ladies in particular – without permission.

USEFUL PHONE NUMBERS

Directory enquiries ⓣ181 (Etisalat), ⓣ199 (Du)
Police and ambulance ⓣ999
Airport enquiries ⓣ04 216 6666
Department of Tourism ⓣ04 223 0000 or ⓣ04 282 1111

Prostitution

Dubai maintains a bizarrely inconsistent attitude to sexual matters. A couple kissing on the lips in public can potentially face jail, and homosexuality is also illegal. Yet despite this high-handed moral stance, **prostitution** is endemic throughout the city – you won't get round many pubs or bars (particularly in the city centre) without seeing at least a few working girls perched at the bar in unusually short skirts and excessively bright lipstick. Prostitution is technically illegal, although arrests of male punters are virtually unheard of and the sex trade is tolerated by the city authorities, it is said, as part of the price to be paid in attracting expat professionals to the emirate, while it also reflects the city's overwhelmingly male demographic (see p.189). Dubai's sex workers come from all over the globe, with a sliding scale of charges to match: Arab girls are the most expensive, followed by Westerners, with Asians and Africans at the bottom of the pile – a snapshot in miniature of the city's traditional social and economic structure. The background of Dubai's working girls is equally varied: many are simply visitors or residents looking to make a bit of extra cash; others are the victims of human trafficking, with girls responding to adverts for "housemaids" and suchlike being sold into the sex trade on arrival. The Dubai government is making efforts to eliminate this illegal trade, although the problem persists.

Smoking

Smoking is banned in Dubai in the vast majority of indoor public places, including offices, malls, cafés and restaurants (although it's permitted at most – but not all – outdoor venues). At the time of writing you could still smoke in **bars and pubs**, although there has also been talk of including these in the ban at a future date. You can still smoke in the majority of **hotels**, though many places now provide non-smoking rooms or non-smoking floors – and a few places have banned it completely. During Ramadan, never smoke in public places in daylight hours.

Time

Dubai (and the rest of the UAE) runs on **Gulf Standard Time**. This is 4hr ahead of GMT, 3hr ahead of BST, 9hr ahead of North American Eastern

Standard Time, 12hr ahead of North American Western Standard Time, 6hr behind Australian Eastern Standard Time, and 8hr behind New Zealand Standard Time. There is no daylight saving time in Dubai.

Tourist information

Given the importance of tourism to the Dubai economy, there's a frustrating lack of on-the-ground visitor information – and not a single proper tourist office anywhere in the city. You could try ringing the head office of the **Department of Tourism and Commerce Marketing** (**DTCM**; ☎04 223 0000 or ☎04 282 1111, complaints toll-free on ☎800 7090; ⓦdubaitourism.ae and ⓦdefinitelydubai.com) or visiting one of their erratically manned information desks at Terminal 1 and Terminal 3 in the airport (both 24hr), and at Deira City Centre, BurJuman, Wafi and Ibn Battuta malls (all daily 10am–10pm), although none is especially useful. Otherwise, the only real sources of local info are the city's hotels and tour operators, although they can't be counted on to give impartial or particularly informed advice.

The best local **magazine** is the lively *Time Out Dubai* (7dh; ⓦtimeoutdubai.com), published weekly and available at bookshops all over the city, and carrying comprehensive listings about pretty much everything going on in Dubai. It's particularly good for information about the constantly changing nightlife scene, including club, restaurant and bar promotions and new openings. The glossy *What's On* (monthly; 10dh; ⓦfacebook.com /WhatsOnDubai) is also worth a look, though the listings aren't nearly as detailed.

DTCM TOURIST OFFICES OVERSEAS

Australia Suites 5 & 6, Level 14, 3 Spring St, Sydney NSW 2000 ☎02 9956 6620, ✉dtcm_aus@dubaitourism.ae.
South Africa Ground Floor, Block 4a, Bryanston Gate, Office, cnr Curzon and Main roads, Bryanston West, Johannesburg ☎011 702 9600, ✉dtcm_sa@dubaitourism.ae.
UK 4th floor, Nuffield House, 41–46 Piccadilly, London W1J 0DS ☎020 7321 6110, ✉dtcm_uk@dubaitourism.ae.
US 10th Floor, 215 Park Ave South, New York, NY 10003, US ☎212 725 0707, ✉dtcm_usa@dubaitourism.ae.

USEFUL WEBSITES

ⓦ**definitelydubai.com** Main consumer website of the DTCM, although it's not much more useful than a glorified press release.
ⓦ**abudhabitourism.ae** Official site of the Abu Dhabi Tourism Authority.
ⓦ**timeoutdubai.com** Latest listings and reviews of what's on in the city.

ⓦ**thenational.ae** Online home of the UAE's leading English-language newspaper.
ⓦ**gulfnews.com** Comprehensive news from the region.
ⓦ**dubaifaqs.com** Encyclopedic site with detailed information about pretty much everything you're ever likely to want to know about the city.
ⓦ**dubaiatrandom.blogspot.co.uk** Long-running site by an anonymous blogger on Dubai and the UAE.
ⓦ**beerandbloating.blogspot.co.uk** Entertaining blog by Chris Combe (who's also published a book of his Dubai experiences entitled *One Year in Wonderland: A True Tale of Expat Life in Dubai*).
ⓦ**dm-blog.blogspot.co.uk** Insightful blog by "B.D.", an American expat language teacher and UAE resident since 2000.
ⓦ**dubaisally.blogspot.co.uk** The "True life story of Filipino Maid in Dubai" – cult reading.
ⓦ**secretdubai.blogspot.com** Irreverent Dubai blog which attained cult status despite being repeatedly blocked by the government. No updates now since 2010, but still worth a look.
ⓦ**uaeprison.com** Alternative take on the modern UAE, including coverage of Dubai's sometimes murky human rights record.

GOVERNMENT WEBSITES

Australian Department of Foreign Affairs ⓦdfat.gov.au.
British Foreign & Commonwealth Office ⓦfco.gov.uk.
Canadian Department of Foreign Affairs ⓦinternational.gc.ca.
Irish Department of Foreign Affairs ⓦdfa.ie.
New Zealand Ministry of Foreign Affairs ⓦmfat.govt.nz.
South African Department of Foreign Affairs ⓦdfa.gov.za.
US State Department ⓦstate.gov.

Travellers with disabilities

Dubai has made considerable efforts to cater for visitors with disabilities, and ranks as probably the Middle East's most accessible destination. Most of the city's modern **hotels** now make at least some provision for guests with impaired mobility; many of the city's four- and five-stars have specially adapted rooms, although there's relatively little choice among three-star hotels and below. Quite a few of the city's **malls** also have special facilities, including disabled parking spaces and specially equipped toilets. Inevitably, most of the city's older heritage buildings are not accessible (although the Dubai Museum is).

Transportation is fairly well set up. The Dubai Metro incorporates facilities to assist visually and mobility-impaired visitors, including tactile guide paths, lifts and ramps, as well as wheelchair spaces in all compartments, while **Dubai Taxi** (☎04 208 0808) has specially designed vehicles equipped with ramps and lifts. The city's **waterbuses** can also be used by mobility-impaired visitors, and staff will assist you in boarding and disembarking. There are also dedicated facilities at the **airport**.

AL FAHIDI FORT

Bur Dubai

Strung out along the southern side of the Creek, the district of Bur Dubai is the oldest part of the city, and in many ways still the most interesting. This is where you'll find virtually all the bits of old Dubai that survived the rapid development of the 1960s and 1970s, and parts of the area's historic waterfront still retain their engagingly old-fashioned appearance, with a quaint tangle of sand-coloured buildings and a distinctively Arabian skyline, spiked with dozens of wind towers and the occasional minaret. Away from the Creek the district is more modern and mercantile, epitomized by lively Al Fahidi Street, lined with neon-lit stores stacked high with phones and watches. This is also where you'll get the strongest sense of Bur Dubai's status as the city's Little India, with dozens of no-frills curry houses, window displays full of glittery saris, and optimistic touts offering fake watches or a "nice pashmina".

Much of the charm of Bur Dubai lies in simply wandering along the waterfront and through the busy backstreets, although there are a number of specific attractions worth exploring. At the heart of the district, the absorbing **Dubai Museum** offers an excellent introduction to the city's history, culture and customs, while the old Iranian quarter of **Bastakiya** nearby is home to the city's most impressive collection of traditional buildings, topped with dozens of wind towers. Heading west along the Creek, the old-fashioned **Textile Souk** is the prettiest in the city, while still further along, the historic old quarter of **Shindagha** is home to another fine cluster of traditional buildings, many of them now converted into low-key museums, including the engaging **Sheikh Saeed al Maktoum House**.

Dubai Museum

Al Fahidi St • Sat–Thurs 8.30am–8.30pm, Fri 2.30–8.30pm • 3dh • ☎ 04 353 1862, Ⓦ bit.ly/DubaiMuseum • Al Fahidi metro

The excellent **Dubai Museum** makes a logical first stop on any tour of the city and the perfect place to get up to speed with the history and culture of the emirate. The museum occupies the old **Al Fahidi Fort**, a rough-and-ready little structure whose engagingly lopsided corner turrets – one square and one round – make it look a bit like a giant sandcastle, offering a welcome contrast to the city's other "old" buildings, most of which have been restored to a state of pristine perfection. Dating from around 1800, the fort is the oldest building in Dubai, having originally been built to defend the town's landward approaches against raids by rival Bedouin tribes; it also served as the residence and office of the ruling sheikh up until the early twentieth century before being converted into a museum in 1971.

Entering the museum you step into the fort's central **courtyard**, flanked by a few rooms containing exhibits of folklore and weaponry. Assorted wooden boats lie marooned around the courtyard, revealing the different types of vessel used in old Dubai, including a traditional abra, not so very different from those still in service on the Creek today. In one corner stands a traditional *barasti* (or *areesh*) hut, topped by a basic burlap wind tower – the sort of building most people in Dubai lived in right up until the 1960s. The hut's walls are made out of neatly cut palm branches,

---

THE CREEK

Cutting a broad, salty swathe through the middle of the city centre, the Creek (Al Khor in Arabic) lies physically and historically at the very heart of Dubai, all that now remains of a river that may once have flowed inland all the way to Al Ain. The Creek was the location of the earliest settlements in the area – first on the Bur Dubai side of the water, and subsequently in Deira – and also played a crucial role in the recent history of the city. One of the first acts of the visionary Sheikh Rashid – the so-called father of modern Dubai – on coming to power in 1958 was to have the Creek **dredged** and made navigable to larger shipping, thus diverting trade from the then far wealthier neighbouring emirate of Sharjah (whose own creek was allowed to silt up, with disastrous consequences). With its enhanced shipping facilities, Dubai quickly established itself as one of the Gulf's most important **commercial centres**. Indeed in hindsight it's possible to see Sheikh Rashid's opening up of the Creek, just as much as the later discovery of oil, as the key factor in the city's subsequent prosperity.

Although the Creek's economic importance has dwindled in recent decades following the opening of the enormous new docks at Port Rashid and the free-trade zone at Jebel Ali, it continues to see plenty of small-scale commerce. Almost all of this is transported on the innumerable old-fashioned wooden **dhows** which run between Dubai and neighbouring countries, and which moor up along the Deira side of the water at the Dhow Wharfage (see p.52). Commerce aside, the Creek remains the centrepiece of Dubai and its finest natural feature: a broad, serene stretch of water which is as essential a part of the fabric and texture of the city as the Thames is to London or the Seine to Paris.

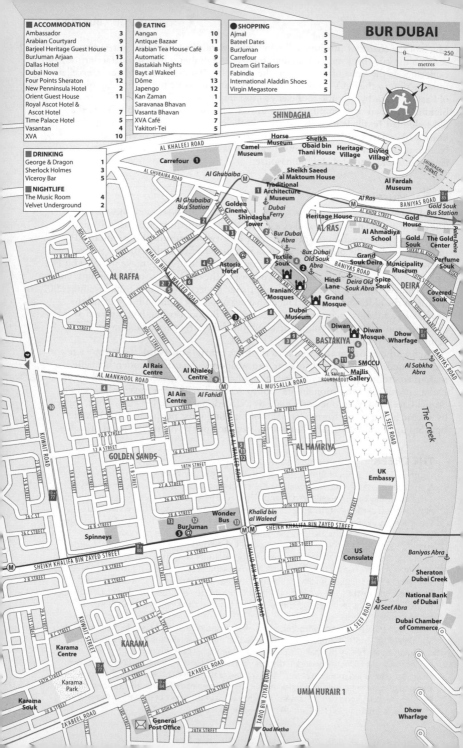

BUR DUBAI

● ACCOMMODATION	
Ambassador	3
Arabian Courtyard	9
Barjeel Heritage Guest House	1
BurJuman Arjaan	13
Dallas Hotel	6
Dubai Nova	8
Four Points Sheraton	12
New Penninsula Hotel	2
Orient Guest House	11
Royal Ascot Hotel &	
Ascot Hotel	7
Time Palace Hotel	5
Vasantan	4
XVA	10

● EATING	
Aangan	10
Antique Bazaar	11
Arabian Tea House Café	8
Automatic	9
Bastakiah Nights	6
Bayt al Wakeel	4
Dôme	13
Japengo	12
Kan Zaman	1
Saravanaa Bhavan	2
Vasanta Bhavan	3
XVA Café	7
Yakitori-Tei	5

● SHOPPING	
Ajmal	5
Bateel Dates	5
BurJuman	5
Carrefour	1
Dream Girl Tailors	3
Fabindia	4
International Aladdin Shoes	2
Virgin Megastore	5

■ DRINKING	
George & Dragon	1
Sherlock Holmes	3
Viceroy Bar	5

■ NIGHTLIFE	
The Music Room	4
Velvet Underground	2

spaced so that breezes are able to blow right through and meaning it stays surprisingly cool even in the heat of the day. It's also worth having a look at the rough walls of the courtyard itself, constructed from horizontal layers of coral held together with powdered gypsum – the standard building technique in old Dubai, but which is usually hidden underneath layers of plaster.

The museum's real attraction, however, is its sprawling **underground section**, a buried wonderland which offers as comprehensive an overview of the traditional life, crafts and culture of Dubai as you'll find anywhere. A sequence of rooms – full of the sound effects and life-size mannequins without which no Dubai museum would be complete – cover every significant aspect of traditional Dubaian life, including Islam, local architecture (and wind towers), traditional dress and games, camels and falconry. Interesting short films on various subjects are shown in many of the rooms, including fascinating historic footage of pearl divers at work. There's also a line of shops featuring various traditional trades and crafts – carpenters, blacksmiths, potters, tailors, spice merchants and so on. It's kitsch but undeniably engaging, populated with colourful mannequins in traditional dress, although the old black-and-white video clips of artisans at work add a slightly spooky touch.

Bastakiya

Al Fahidi metro

Stretching between the Creek and Al Fahidi Street just east of the Dubai Museum is the beautiful old quarter of **Bastakiya** (or Bastakia, with the stress on the *i*), a photogenic huddle of traditional Gulf houses, capped with dozens of wind towers and arranged around a rabbit warren of tiny alleyways, built deliberately narrow in order to provide pedestrians with welcome shade.

The houses here were originally put up in the early 1900s by merchants from Bandar Lengeh and other ports just over the Gulf in southern Iran, who had been lured to Dubai by the promise of low taxes and free land, and who in turn helped transform the commercial fortunes of their host city; they named their new suburb Bastakiya after their ancestral home, the Iranian town of Bastak. At a time when virtually the entire population of Dubai was living in palm-thatch huts, the houses of Bastakiya were notably solid and sophisticated, with the added luxury of primitive air-conditioning provided by the wind towers which rise from virtually every rooftop in the district.

WIND TOWERS

Often described as the world's oldest form of air-conditioning, the distinctive **wind towers** (*barjeel*) that top many old Dubai buildings (as well as numerous modern ones constructed in faux-Arabian style) provided an ingeniously simple way of countering the Gulf's searing temperatures in a pre-electrical age. Rising around 6m above the rooftops on which they're built, wind towers are open on all four sides and channel any available breezes down into the building via triangular flues; the largest and most highly decorated wind tower was traditionally placed over the bedroom, with smaller ones over other rooms. Of course, wind towers don't produce the arctic blasts generated by modern air-conditioning, but stand next to one and you'll notice a slight but significant drop in temperature – particularly welcome in summer, and doubtless a life-saver back in the city's pre-air-con days.

Although the wind tower has become one of the iconic architectural symbols of Dubai and the UAE, it was actually introduced to the city by Iranian merchants who settled in the city in the early twentieth century. Many built houses in Bastakiya, whose collection of wind towers is the largest and finest in the city, with subtle variations in design from tower to tower, meaning that no two are ever exactly alike.

1

OPEN DOORS, OPEN MINDS

Based in an office on the eastern edge of Bastakiya, the pioneering **Sheikh Mohammed Centre for Cultural Understanding**, or **SMCCU** (Sun–Thurs 8am–6pm, Sat 9am–1pm; ☎04 353 6666, ⊛cultures.ae) was set up in the laudable attempt to break down the entrenched barriers that generally separate Dubai's legions of Western expats from local Emiratis. The former can spend years in the city without having any meaningful contact with their hosts, while native Dubaians, in turn, tend largely to keep within their own circles. Running under the slogan "Open doors, open minds", the SMCCU runs popular **tours** of Jumeirah Mosque (see p.72) and a number of activities in Bastakiya itself, including walking tours, Gulf Arabic classes and "cultural" breakfasts and lunches, during which you get the chance to sample some traditional food while chatting to the centre's Emirati staff.

By the 1980s, Bastakiya had become increasingly run-down as the wealthy Iranian families who had previously lived here began to move out to more spacious houses in the new suburbs. Many of the old houses were turned into warehouses and the entire area was threatened by demolition, although in the end around two-thirds of the original quarter was rescued from the developers and meticulously restored to its former splendour. It now looks every bit as grand – and certainly a lot cleaner – than it ever did in the past. Unfortunately, despite the work that's been put into the place, the whole quarter still feels rather moribund and under-used, only really coming to life during the vibrant **Bastakiya Art Fair** (see p.28), during which a rabble of artists and assorted performers descend, transforming the normally somnolent streets into a riot of activity.

Bastakiya museums
Various locations on the north side of Bastakiya, near the entrance to the Diwan Mosque (see p.43) • Free

A number of old Bastakiya houses have now been opened to the public as small-scale museums. Most boast only a few sparse and uninteresting exhibits, although they do give you the chance to nose around inside and have a look at the various houses' often unexpectedly ornate courtyards.

The only place with any half-decent exhibits is the **Coins Museum** (Sat–Thurs 8am–8pm; ☎04 353 9090), containing a well-presented collection of over four hundred Ummayad, Sassanian, Abbasid and later Islamic coins through to the Ottoman era, backed up by explanatory touchscreens. Other places open to the public include the **Architectural Heritage Society** (Sat–Wed 8am–1pm & 5–8pm), next to the Coins Museum; the **Philately House** (Sat–Wed 9am–1pm & 4–8pm, Thurs 9am–1pm), with a pretty little courtyard and some token exhibits on postal history in the UAE and abroad; and the **Architectural Heritage Department** (Sun–Thurs 8am–2pm), boasting a particularly large and chintzy courtyard, and fine views over Bastakiya and the Creek from its roof.

The Textile Souk and around
Al Ghubaiba metro

At the heart of Bur Dubai, the **Textile Souk** (also sometimes referred to as the "Old Souk") is easily the prettiest in the city, occupying an immaculately restored traditional bazaar, its long line of sand-coloured buildings shaded by a fine arched wooden roof, blissfully cool even in the heat of the day and illuminated by traditional Moorish hanging lights after dark. This was once the most important bazaar in the city although its commercial importance has long since faded – almost all the shops have now been taken over by Indian traders flogging reams of sari cloth and fluorescent blankets alongside assorted tourist tat (if you're hankering for an I ♥ DUBAI T-shirt, Burj Khalifa paperweight or spangly camel, now's your chance).

CLOCKWISE FROM TOP LEFT INTERNATIONAL ALADDIN SHOES, TEXTILE SOUK (P.132); IRANIAN MOSQUE (P.42); GRAND MOSQUE (P.43) >

1

It's also worth exploring the lanes off the souk's main drag, dotted with further examples of traditional (albeit heavily restored) local architecture, including long wooden balconies, latticed windows and the occasional wind tower.

Bayt al Wakeel

At the western end of the souk, near the main entrance, the **Bayt al Wakeel** ("Agent's House"), originally known as the Mackenzie House, was the first office in Dubai when it opened in 1935 as the headquarters of local shipping agents, Gray Mackenzie and Company. The building now houses the low-key *Bayt al Wakeel* restaurant (see p.106), worth a peek inside for a glimpse of the attractively restored ground floor, which once housed the company's office (the manager lived upstairs).

Iranian mosques

Ali bin Abi Taleb St (11c St) • No entry to non-Muslims • Al Ghubaiba metro

Hidden away amid Bur Dubai's endless curry houses and sari shops, evidence of one of the city's other long-established immigrant communities can be found in the fine pair of **Iranian Shia mosques** which sit on the southern edge of the Textile Souk. The more easterly of the two mosques (set just back from the road) is particularly eye-catching, with a superb facade and dome covered in a lustrous mosaic of predominantly blue tiling decorated with geometrical floral motifs. The second mosque, about 50m west along the road close to the *Time Palace Hotel*, is a contrastingly plain, sand-coloured building, its rooftop enlivened by four tightly packed little egg-shaped domes and its minaret illuminated a distinctive phosphorescent green after dark, like a slightly spooky-looking lighthouse stranded in the middle of Bur Dubai.

Hindi Lane

Al Ghubaiba metro

Hidden away at the eastern end of the Textile Souk, the colourful little alleyway popularly known as **Hindi Lane** is one of Dubai's most curious and appealing little ethnic enclaves. From the far (eastern) end of the Textile Souk, turn right by T. Singh Trading and then left by Mohammadi Textiles and you'll find yourself in a tiny alleyway lined with picturesque little Indian shops selling an array of bangles, bindis, coconuts, flowers, bells, almanacs and other religious paraphernalia.

Sikh Gurudaba and Shri Nathje Jayate Temple

Both open at various times for puja daily from around 6am to midnight

On the north side of Hindi Lane is the tiny hybridized Hindu-cum-Sikh temple sometimes referred to as the **Sikh Gurudaba** (no photography). Go up the stairs (leaving your shoes in the lockers at the bottom) to reach the improvised temple; its diminutive size and obscure location give it an engagingly secretive, almost clandestine air. The first floor is home to various Hindu shrines, decorated with images of Shiva, Hanuman and Ganesh, along with the revered South Indian guru Sai Baba and a few swastikas. From here, further stairs (cover your head with a piece of cloth from the box at the top) lead up to a miniature Sikh temple, adorned with pictures of the ten Sikh gurus, with the Sikh mantra "Satnam Waheguru" ("Oh God your name is true") painted on the walls.

Continue along Hindi Lane and you'll shortly come out at the back of the Grand Mosque (see opposite). Turn right at the end of the lane and then right again, past Perumal Stores, to reach the tree-shaded entrance to a second Hindu temple, the **Shri Nathje Jayate Temple**. It's not signed, but just look for the piles of shoes and follow the crowds upstairs, where you'll find yourself in a marbled hall decorated with assorted Hindu icons and regalia. These include emblems of Shiva (tridents and peacocks) and black-skinned images of Krishna in the form of Shri Nathji, showing him lifting Mount Goverdhan above his head to protect the people of Vrindavan from a devastating deluge unleashed by the jealous Indra, king of the gods.

1

BUR DUBAI AND BEYOND BY BOAT

The Textile Souk (see p.40) is where you'll find Bur Dubai's two main abra stations: **Bur Dubai Abra Station**, just outside the main entrance to the souk, and **Bur Dubai Old Souk Abra Station**, inside the souk itself. From these stations, old-fashioned little wooden abras shuttle back and forth across the Creek at all hours of the day and night (see p.22), operated by boatmen from India, Bangladesh, Pakistan and Iran. The boats' basic design has changed little for at least a century, apart from the addition of a diesel engine (abras were formerly rowed) and an awning to provide passengers with shade. Up until the opening of Al Maktoum Bridge in 1963, abras provided the only means of getting from one side of the Creek to the other, and despite the fact that they are now effectively floating antiques, they still play a crucial role in the city's transport infrastructure, carrying a staggering twenty million passengers per year for a modest 1dh per trip.

The two Textile Souk stations are also served by regular **waterbuses** (see p.23). For longer trips, you can either charter your own abra (see p.25) or take a tour aboard the sleek new **Dubai Ferry**. Leaving from its berth in Al Ghubaiba opposite Shindagha Tower, the 100-seater ferry offers 1hr cruises (at 9am, 11am, 5pm and 7pm; 50dh, or 75dh in Gold Class) heading down the coast as far as the Burj al Arab – an exhilarating and memorable trip, although as ferries require a minimum of ten passengers (and may not venture out of the Creek in rough weather) it can be pot luck as to whether you find a boat that's actually running. Similar trips are also offered from Marina Mall in Dubai Marina, with similar caveats. Occasional ferries also run one way from Al Ghubaiba to Marina Mall, or vice versa, offering a wonderful overview of the city from the waves in a single trip.

The Grand Mosque

Ali bin Abi Taleb St (11c St), behind Dubai Museum · No entry to non-Muslims · Al Fahidi metro

The **Grand Mosque** – historically Dubai's leading place of Islamic worship – has had something of a chequered past. The original Grand Mosque was built around 1900 but demolished in the 1960s, although its replacement lasted only three decades being razed in its turn to make way for the current edifice, completed in the 1990s. This is the biggest mosque in Dubai: an impressively large if rather plain structure, the general austerity relieved only by an elaborate swirl of Koranic script and some intricately carved windows over the main doors. Above rise eighteen tiny domes and the city's tallest minaret, soaring proudly above the rooftops of Bur Dubai and the Creek beyond.

The Diwan

Beside the Creek, between the Grand Mosque and Bastakiya · Al Fahidi metro

Hugging the creekside east of the Grand Mosque sits the **Diwan**, or Ruler's Court, although current ruler Sheikh Mohammed and his Executive Council now conduct most of the city's major business from their offices near the summit of the Emirates Towers on Sheikh Zayed Road – leaving the Diwan in possession of various less exalted government officials. The building itself, guarded by a long line of ostentatiously high black railings, is a large but uninspiring modern edifice topped by a few oversized wind towers. Rather more eye-catching is the attached **Diwan Mosque** (with its main entrance in Bastakiya), topped by an unusually flattened onion dome and a slender white minaret which rivals that of the nearby Grand Mosque in height.

Al Fahidi Street

Al Fahidi and Khalid bin al Waleed metros

South of the Textile Souk lies **Al Fahidi Street**, Bur Dubai's de facto high street, bisecting the area from east to west and lined with a mix of shops selling Indian clothing, shoes and jewellery along with other places stacked high with mobile

1

phones and fancy watches (not necessarily genuine). This is Dubai at its most intensely Indian, and great fun, particularly after dark, when the crowds come out, the neon comes on and the whole strip gets overrun with shoppers, sightseers and off-duty labourers just shooting the breeze – like a slightly sanitized version of the Subcontinent, minus the cows.

The area around the eastern end of Al Fahidi Street and neighbouring Al Hisn Street is often loosely referred to as **Meena Bazaar**. The centre of the district's textile and tailoring industry, it's home to a dense razzle-dazzle of shopfronts stuffed with colourful dresses and sumptuous saris.

Khalid bin al Waleed Road

A couple of blocks south of Al Fahidi Street lies the broad **Khalid bin al Waleed Road** (also known as "Computer Street", and occasionally by its old colonial name of Bank Street). There's a distinct change of pace here from the narrow streets and souks of the old city centre to the more modern districts beyond, epitomized by the huge **BurJuman** mall (see p.134), which nestles on a corner near the road's eastern end. The strip is best known for its plethora of computer and electronics shops, concentrated around the junction with Al Mankhool Road – a good place to pick up cheap digital stuff or simply to enjoy the after-dark atmosphere, when it's lit up in a long blaze of neon, and locals emerge to haggle over the laptops, phones and mysterious bits of cable.

Shindagha

Although now effectively swallowed up by Bur Dubai, the historic creekside district of **Shindagha** was, until fifty years ago, a quite separate and self-contained area occupying its own spit of land, and frequently cut off from Bur Dubai proper during high tides. This was once the most exclusive address in town, home to the ruling family and other local elites, who occupied a series of imposing coral-walled and wind-towered houses lined up along the waterfront. Many of these old houses, now sprucely restored, have survived, making this part of town – along with Bastakiya – the only place in the city where you can still get a real idea of what old Dubai looked like. A growing number have also been converted into low-key museums, including the absorbing **Sheikh Saeed al Maktoum House** and **Traditional Architecture Museum**, along with a number of other places which are hardly worth bothering with, despite being free.

The edge of the district is guarded by the distinctive waterfront **Shindagha Tower**, one of only two of the city's original defensive watchtowers to survive (the other is the Burj Nahar; see p.54) and instantly recognizable thanks to the slit windows and protruding buttresses on each side, arranged to resemble a human face.

A WALK ALONG THE CREEK

The walk along the Bur Dubai waterfront is far and away the nicest in the city, pedestrianized throughout, and with cooling breezes and wonderful views of the city down the Creek – particularly beautiful towards sunset. For the best views, begin in Shindagha and head south; it takes about 20–25 minutes to reach Bastakiya.

Starting outside the Diving Village, a spacious promenade stretches all the way down the Shindagha waterfront as far as Shindagha Tower, from where a narrow walkway extends to the Bur Dubai Abra Station and Textile Souk. Walk through the souk, exiting it via Hindi Lane (see p.42) to emerge by the Grand Mosque. Head left from here to regain the waterfront by the high black railings of the Diwan, from where the creekside promenade continues to the edge of Bastakiya and beyond, past the old Bur Dubai cemetery flanking Al Seef Road.

1

Sheikh Saeed al Maktoum House

Shindagha waterfront • Sat–Thurs 8am–8.30pm, Fri 3–9.30pm • 2dh • ☎ 04 393 7139, Ⓦ bit.ly/SheikhSaeedHouse • Al Ghubaiba metro

Easily the most interesting of the various Shindagha museums is the **Sheikh Saeed al Maktoum House**, the principal residence of Dubai's ruling family from 1896 to 1958. Work on the house was begun in 1896 – making it one of the oldest buildings in Dubai – by Sheikh Maktoum bin Hasher al Maktoum, and three further wings were added by subsequent members of the Maktoum family, including Sheikh Saeed bin Maktoum al Maktoum, former ruler of Dubai, who lived here until his death in 1958. Dubai's current ruler, Sheikh Mohammed (grandson of Sheikh Saeed), himself spent the early years of his life in the house, sharing living space with a hundred-odd people and assorted animals, including guards, family slaves, goats, dogs and the occasional camel – basic living conditions for someone who would go on to become one of the world's richest men.

The house is now home to one of the city's most interesting museums, featuring assorted exhibits relating to the history of Dubai. Pride of place goes to the superb collection of old **photographs**, with images of the city from the 1940s through to the late 1960s, showing the first steps in its amazing transformation from a remote Gulf town to global megalopolis. There are also fine shots of fishermen at work and old dhows under their distinctive triangular lateen sails, plus a couple of photos showing the rather biblical-looking swarm of locusts that descended on the town in 1953. (Locusts have played a surprisingly important role in Dubai's history. One theory holds that the town's name derives from a type of local locust, the *daba*, while during the starvation years of World War II, locusts – netted and fried – provided a valuable source of food for impoverished locals.) Another room is devoted to photos of the various craggy-featured Al Maktoum sheikhs – the startling family resemblance makes it surprisingly difficult to tell them apart – including the prescient image of Sheikh Rashid and the young Sheikh Mohammed poring over a petroleum brochure which can also be seen in the Al Ahmadiya School (see p.50).

Elsewhere you'll find some interesting wooden models of traditional dhows, colourful colonial-era stamps and an extensive exhibit of local **coins**, featuring a large selection of the East India Company and Indian colonial coins which were used as common currency in Dubai from the late eighteenth century right through until 1966, when Dubai and Qatar introduced a joint currency to replace them. Upstairs a couple of further rooms are filled with lovely old **maps** of Dubai and the Arabian peninsula, plus some **documents** detailing assorted administrative and commercial dealings between the British and Dubaians during the later colonial period, including the agreement allowing Imperial Airways seaplanes to land on the Creek from 1938, the first commercial service to touch down in Dubai.

Camel Museum

Shindagha waterfront, behind Sheikh Saeed al Maktoum House • Sun–Thurs 8am–2pm • Free • ☎ 04 392 0368 • Al Ghubaiba metro

Occupying a former horse and camel stable once belonging to the legendary Sheikh Rashid, the **Camel Museum** offers a modest attempt to trace the history and cultural significance of this iconic beast in Dubai and the Emirates. Like many of the city's recently opened museums the overall effect is half-hearted and patchy, with plenty of rather didactic displays but precious few actual exhibits, barring an absolutely surreal pair of animatronic dromedaries in the room devoted to camel racing, which the resident caretaker may be persuaded to fire into life, assuming they're working.

Horse Museum

Shindagha waterfront, next door to the Camel Museum behind Sheikh Saeed al Maktoum House • Sun–Thurs 8am–2pm • Free • ☎ 04 392 0368 • Al Ghubaiba metro

In a traditional house formerly belonging to Sheikha Moza, a daughter of Sheikh Saeed (see p.183), Dubai's puny **Horse Museum** provides a lacklustre overview of the history of the horse in Arabia from 3000 BC through to current Dubai ruler Sheikh

1

Mohammed's own horse-breeding exploits, covered in displays of spectacular incoherence: make what you will of "The cavalry Sheikh Mohammad has come to fore in this revered sport for he was known of courage, cavalry, and a tooth for horses", for example.

Sheikh Obaid bin Thani House

Shindagha waterfront, a few steps beyond Sheikh Saeed al Maktoum House • Sat–Thurs 8am–10pm, Fri 4–10pm • Free • ☎ 04 393 3240, ⓦ bit.ly/ObaidThani • Al Ghubaiba metro

The grandiose **Sheikh Obaid bin Thani House** of 1916 is one of the largest and most striking in Shindagha, with a flamboyantly decorated exterior and an impressively large courtyard within. The upper floor is now home to a small and not very edifying exhibition on the rich heritage of Arabic calligraphy, charting its development from antique Kufic through flowing Diwani and Persian Ta'liq scripts to modern Naksh.

Traditional Architecture Museum

Shindagha waterfront, halfway between Shindagha Tower and Sheikh Saeed al Maktoum House • Sat–Thurs 7am–6pm, Fri 8am–6pm • Free • ☎ 04 392 0093 • Al Ghubaiba metro

One of the most interesting of the hotchpotch of Shindagha museums, the **Traditional Architecture Museum** occupies the former home of Sheikh Juma al Maktoum, brother of Sheikh Saeed (see p.183), a rather grand affair with the usual sandy courtyard, wind towers and elaborate latticed wall-panels decorated with geometrical and floral patterns moulded from the traditional mix of gypsum, coral, limestone and sand. Inside, informative displays cover the story of architecture in the Emirates generally and Dubai in particular, including insightful explanations of the region's various different types of building, local materials and construction techniques, accompanied by a good spread of exhibits and the usual life-size mannequins pounding and plastering silently away.

Heritage and Diving Villages

Shindagha waterfront • Sun–Thurs 8.30am–10.30pm, Fri & Sat 4.30–10.30pm • Free • ☎ 04 393 7139, ⓦ bit.ly/HeritageDiving • Al Ghubaiba metro

At the far end of the Shindagha waterfront, the so-called **Heritage Village** comprises a string of traditional buildings surrounding a large sandy courtyard, at the back of which are a few souvenir shops. The atmosphere is fairly moribund most of the time, but livens up somewhat after dark during national holidays and festivals, particularly Ramadan and the Dubai Shopping Festival, when locals put on cookery and craft displays, occasionally accompanied by performances of Emirati music and dancing.

The adjacent **Diving Village** offers more of the same, with further traditional buildings around another courtyard dotted with a couple of wooden boats and a few *barasti* huts, plus two boat-shaped phone booths – a rather lame tribute to the pearl-diving trade which underpinned the city's economy up until the 1930s.

A further 100m past the Diving Village, five mannequins unloading a small dhow on the waterfront mark the site of the diminutive **Al Fardah Museum**, devoted to the history of Dubai customs (as in customs and excise, rather than cultural customs), although it had yet to open at the time of writing.

Deira

North of the Creek lies Deira, the second of the old city's two principal districts, founded in 1841, when settlers from Bur Dubai crossed the Creek to establish a new village here. Deira rapidly overtook its older neighbour in commercial importance and remains notably more built-up and cosmopolitan than Bur Dubai, with a heady ethnic mix of Emiratis, Gulf Arabs, Iranians, Indians, Pakistanis and Somalis thronging its packed streets, along with a healthy contingent of African gold traders and camera-toting Western tourists. Specific attractions are thin on the ground, but this remains the city's best place for aimless wandering and even a short exploration will uncover a kaleidoscopic jumble of cultures. Indian curry houses jostle for space with Iranian grocers, Somali shisha-cafés and backstreet mosques – not to mention an endless array of shops selling everything from formal black *abbeya* to belly-dancing costumes.

For the visitor, Deira's main attraction is its myriad souks – most obviously the famous **Gold Souk** and the small but atmospheric **Spice Souk** – although in many ways the entire quarter is one enormous bazaar through which it's possible to wander for mile after mile without ever surfacing. The district is also home to the interesting traditional **Heritage House** and **Al Ahmadiya School** museums, while along the banks of the Creek itself you'll find the atmospheric **Dhow Wharfage**, an authentic taste of Dubai past, plus a clutch of striking modernist buildings centred on the landmark **National Bank of Dubai**, an icon of Dubai's dazzling present.

2

Gold Souk

Between Sikkat al Khail Rd and Old Baladiya Rd • Most shops open from around 10am to 10pm • Al Ras metro

Deira's famous **Gold Souk** is usually the first stop for visitors to the district and attracts a cosmopolitan range of customers, from Western tourists to African traders buying up pieces for resale at home. There are over three hundred shops here, most of them lined up along the souk's wooden-roofed main arcade, their windows packed with a staggering quantity of jewellery. It's been estimated that there are usually around ten tons of gold in the souk at any one time, and walking from one end of the place to the other it's easy to believe.

The souk's main attraction is its prices: the gold available here is among the cheapest in the world, and massive competition keeps prices keen. The jewellery on offer ranges from ornate Arabian creations to elegantly restrained pieces aimed at European visitors. Particularly appealing are the traditional Emirati bracelets, fashioned from solid gold (and often exquisitely embellished with white-gold decoration) and hung in long lines in shop windows; these were traditionally used for dowries, as were the heavier and more ornate necklaces also on display. There are also plenty of places selling **precious stones**, including diamonds and a range of other gems.

SHOPPING IN THE GOLD SOUK

The gold industry in Dubai is carefully regulated, so there's no danger of being ripped off with substandard or fake goods, but there are still a few useful basic things to know. First, gold jewellery is **sold by weight** (the quality and detail of the decoration and workmanship, however elaborate, isn't usually factored into the price). Second, the **price** of gold is fixed in all shops citywide (the daily price is displayed on video screens at either end of the souk; the exact figure fluctuates daily depending on the international price of gold). Therefore, if you ask how much a piece of jewellery is, it will first be weighed, and the cost then calculated according to the day's gold price.

Once you've established this basic price, it's time to start **bargaining**. A request for "best price" or "small discount" should yield an immediate discount of around 20–25 percent over the basic price; you may be able to lower the price still further depending on how canny you are and how desperate the shop staff are for a sale. As ever, it pays to shop around and compare prices; tell the shop you're in that you've found a better deal elsewhere, if necessary. If you're buying multiple items, press for further discounts.

If you can't find what you want in the Gold Souk, try one of the sizeable **malls** – Gold Land, The Gold Center and Gold House – stuffed full of gold and jewellery shops lined up along Al Khaleej Road opposite the Gold Souk bus station, a short distance to the north.

Shopping for **precious stones** is more complicated, and it pays to do some research before leaving home. Diamonds are a particularly good buy in Dubai, often selling at up to half the price they would retail for in the West. If you're buying diamonds, it's also well worth visiting the excellent Gold and Diamond Park in southern Jumeirah (see p.134). The area around the Gold Souk is also one of the major centres of Dubai's flourishing trade in **designer fakes** (see box, p.135).

Heritage House

Old Baladiya Rd (exit the rear end of the Gold Souk, then turn right along Old Baladiya Rd, following it for a few minutes as it veers around to the left) • Sat–Thurs 8am–7.30pm, Fri 2.30–7.30pm • Free • ☎ 04 226 0286 • Al Ras metro

One of the city's oldest museums, and still one of its best, the engaging **Heritage House** offers the most complete picture of everyday life in old Dubai you'll find anywhere in town. The house was originally built in 1890 and subsequently enlarged at various times over the next fifty years, most notably in 1910 by the pearl merchant Sheikh Mohammed bin Ahmed bin Dalmouk, who was also responsible for establishing Al Ahmadiya School next door (see p.50).

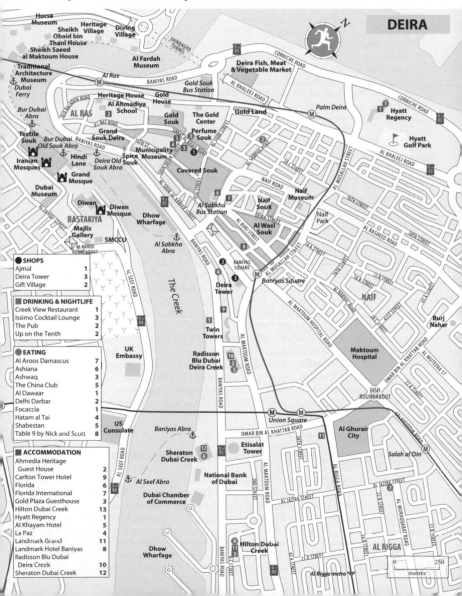

DEIRA

● SHOPS
Ajmal	1
Deira Tower	3
Gift Village	2

■ DRINKING & NIGHTLIFE
Creek View Restaurant	1
Issimo Cocktail Lounge	3
The Pub	2
Up on the Tenth	2

● EATING
Al Aroos Damascus	7
Ashiana	6
Ashwaq	3
The China Club	5
Al Dawaar	1
Delhi Darbar	2
Focaccia	1
Hatam al Tai	4
Shabestan	5
Table 9 by Nick and Scott	8

■ ACCOMMODATION
Ahmedia Heritage Guest House	2
Carlton Tower Hotel	9
Florida	6
Florida International	7
Gold Plaza Guesthouse	3
Hilton Dubai Creek	13
Hyatt Regency	1
Al Khayam Hotel	5
La Paz	4
Landmark Grand	11
Landmark Hotel Baniyas	8
Radisson Blu Dubai Deira Creek	10
Sheraton Dubai Creek	12

2

TRADITIONAL EMIRATI HOUSES

The heritage houses in Dubai (and other places around the Emirates) follow a standard pattern – although it's worth remembering that these elaborate stone mansions were far from typical of the living arrangements enjoyed by the population at large, most of whom lived in simple and impermanent palm-thatch huts. Virtually all traditional houses are built around a central **courtyard** (*housh*) and veranda (*liwan*). These provided families with their main living area, and a place where they could cook, play and graze a few animals in complete privacy; some also had a well and a couple of trees. Exterior walls are usually plain and largely windowless in order to protect privacy. Rooms are arranged around the courtyard, the most important being the **majlis** (meeting room), in which the family would receive guests and exchange news (larger houses would have separate *majlis* for men and women). More elaborate houses would also boast one or more **wind towers** (see box, p.39).

Traditional houses make ingenious use of locally available natural materials. Most coastal houses were constructed using big chunks of coral stone, or *fesht* (look closely and you can make out the delicate outlines of submarine sponges, coral and suchlike on many of the stones). The stones were cemented together using layers of pounded gypsum, while walls were strengthened by the insertion of mangrove poles bound with rope. Mangrove wood was also used as a roofing material along with (in more elaborate houses) planks of Indian teak. Away from the coast, coral was replaced by bricks made from a mixture of mud and straw, or adobe (a word deriving from the Arabic *al tob*, meaning "mud").

Local architecture is remarkably well adapted to provide shelter from the Gulf's scorching summer: walls were built thick and windows small to keep out the heat, while both coral and adobe have excellent natural insulating properties. Houses were also built close to one another, partly for security, and also to provide shade in the narrow alleyways between. And although most houses look austere, the overall effect of plainness is relieved by richly carved wooden doors and veranda screens, and by floral and geometrical designs around windows, doorways and arches, fashioned from gypsum and coloured with charcoal powder.

The building is a classic example of a traditional Gulf mansion, with imposing but largely windowless exterior walls (except at the front) and rooms arranged around a large sandy courtyard with a couple of trees in the middle – a miniature desert at the heart of an urban mansion. Each of the rooms is enlivened with exhibits evoking aspects of traditional Emirati life. Mannequins loll around on cushions drinking coffee in the main *majlis*, where male guests were traditionally received, business was conducted and news exchanged, while in the ladies' *majlis* a child has her hands painted with henna while others spin thread, work on their embroidery or grind spices. Finely carved teak doors with stylized palm and floral motifs lead into the main room (*al makhzan*), where further mannequins in rich traditional dress and jewellery pose amid incongruous Western imports, including an old gramophone, a wireless and a Seth Thomas clock – the unintentionally comic signs admonishing visitors to "Please keep away from the exhibits" may be taken with the appropriate pinch of salt.

Al Ahmadiya School

Old Baladiya Rd • Sat–Thurs 8am–7.30pm, Fri 2.30–7.30pm • Free • ☎ 04 226 0286, ⓦ bit.ly/AlAhmadiya • Al Ras metro

Tucked away directly behind the Heritage House, the **Al Ahmadiya School** is one of the city's finest surviving examples of traditional Emirati architecture, and now houses an interesting museum devoted to the educational history of the emirate. Founded in 1912 by pearl merchant Sheikh Mohammed bin Ahmed bin Dalmouk, Al Ahmadiya was the first public school in UAE, and many of the city's leaders studied here, including Sheikh Rashid (see p.183). The school was also notably egalitarian – only the sons of wealthy families were expected to pay, and education for poorer pupils was free. The curriculum initially focused exclusively on the traditional Islamic disciplines of Koranic study, Arabic calligraphy and mathematics, though the syllabus was later expanded to cover practical subjects such as diving and the pearl trade, as well as more modern disciplines including English, geography and science. After the overcrowded school was relocated in 1962, the original building was allowed to fall into ruin, but in 1995 was meticulously restored by the city authorities – part of a belated attempt to rescue surviving examples of traditional architecture and culture amid the swiftly modernizing city.

The building itself is a simple but attractive two-storey affair arranged around a sandy courtyard and topped by a solitary wind tower; the lower floor is particularly fine, with unusual, richly carved cusped arches surrounding the courtyard, while the rear wall is decorated with a sequence of Koranic inscriptions set into recessed panels. The upper storey is plainer, although one of the rooms still preserves some of the old-fashioned wooden desks used by former pupils. Touchscreens and displays cover the history of the school, along with an interesting ten-minute film containing interviews with former students, plus some intriguing old footage of the school in its heyday showing neatly robed pupils lined up for inspection in the courtyard. The modest exhibits include old photos and the inevitable mannequins, including three tiny pupils being instructed by a rather irritable-looking teacher brandishing a wooden cane. A photograph in the same room shows Dubai's present ruler, Sheikh Mohammed, as a young boy in 1954, sitting with his father, Sheikh Rashid, the pair of them hunched over a book about petroleum – a touching snapshot of the two men most responsible for Dubai's spectacular transformation over the past five decades.

Grand Souk Deira

Between Al Ras and Baniyas roads • Most shops open from around 10am to 10pm, although some may close between around 1pm and 4/5pm, and also on Fri mornings • Al Ras metro

Southwest of the Gold Souk stretches the extensive covered souk formerly known as Al Souk al Kabeer ("The Big Souk"), once the largest and most important market in Deira. Now rechristened **Grand Souk Deira**, the whole area has recently been given a major makeover, with the former mishmash of shopfronts and signs now replaced with uniform facades in traditional-looking stone, similar to those in Bur Dubai's Textile Souk, across the Creek. Renovation has come at a price, however, largely destroying the area's former ramshackle charm and quiet, while many of the touts who used to roam the Gold Souk now hang out along the main drag here instead, attempting to lasso passing tourists with the usual offers of copy bags, nice pashminas and genuine fake watches. Most of the shops, meanwhile, remain as unexciting as before, selling a humdrum assortment of household goods and cheap toys.

Spice Souk

Grand Souk Deira, roughly opposite Deira Old Souk Abra Station and the Municipality Museum • Most shops open from around 10am to 10pm, although some may close between around 1pm and 4/5pm, and also on Fri mornings • Al Ras metro

Tucked into the southeast corner of the Grand Souk, the diminutive **Spice Souk** (now signed "Herbs Market") is perhaps the most atmospheric – and certainly the most fragrant – of the city's many bazaars. Run almost exclusively by Iranian traders, the shops here stock a wide variety of culinary, medicinal and cosmetic products, with tubs of merchandise set out in front of each tiny shopfront. All the usual spices can be found – cinnamon, cardamom, cumin, coriander – along with more unusual offerings such as dried cucumbers and lemons (a common ingredient in Middle Eastern cuisine), incense and heaps of hibiscus and rose petals, used to make a delicately scented tea. The souk is also famous for its frankincense, sold in various different forms and grades – the most common type looks like a kind of reddish, crumbling crystalline rock; frankincense burners can be bought in the souk for a few dirhams. Most stalls also sell natural cosmetic products such as pumice and alum, a clear rock crystal used to soothe the skin after shaving. Male visitors in search of a pick-me-up will also find plentiful supplies of so-called "natural viagra".

2

Museum of the Poet Al Oqaili

Off Arsa Court, Grand Souk Deira · Sun–Thurs 8am–2pm · Free · ☎ 04 234 2385, ⓦ bit.ly/AlOqaili · Al Ras metro

The Spice Souk apart, the nicest part of the Grand Souk is the diminutive **Al Arsa Court**, usually full of boxes, trolleys and lounging porters. From here, signs point into the back alleys towards the **Museum of the Poet Al Oqaili**, in the former house of noted poet Mubarak bin Hamad al Manea al Oqaili (1875–1954), who was born in Al Ahsa in present-day Saudi Arabia but eventually settled in Dubai after an itinerant life in Oman, Abu Dhabi and Bahrain. The house itself (built in 1923, and comprehensively restored before reopening as a museum in 2012) is well worth a look, with two storeys set around a shady central courtyard, embellished with delicately carved stone windows and wooden balustrades – although the exhibits on Al Oqaili plumb impressive depths of dullness.

Municipality Museum

Al Souk al Kabeer St, opposite the Spice Souk (facing Deira Old Souk Abra Station) · Sun–Thurs 9am–2.30pm · Free · ☎ 04 345 3636, ⓦ bit.ly/DubaiMunMus · Al Ras metro

The run-of-the-mill **Municipality Museum** occupies the quaint old balconied building which originally housed the city's first municipal offices from 1958 to 1964 – the 1950s municipality had just six employees compared to over 20,000 today. Exhibits include assorted charts, municipal stamps and other documents including the 1966 decree ordering traffic to drive on the right (vehicles had previously driven, British-style, on the left) and the groundbreaking city plan of 1960 showing the proposed development of Deira and Bur Dubai – extremely small beer compared to more recent developments, but impressively ambitious for its time.

Dhow Wharfage

Al Ras metro

Stretching along the Deira creekside east of the Grand Souk between Deira Old Souk and Al Sabkha abra stations, the **Dhow Wharfage** offers a fascinating glimpse into the maritime traditions of old Dubai that have survived miraculously intact at the heart of the twenty-first-century city. At any one time, the wharfage is home to dozens of beautiful

SANCTIONS-BUSTING IN OLD DUBAI

Dubai is one of the Middle East's major entrepôts. Huge quantities of goods are imported and then re-exported through the city, with extensive shipping routes stretching up and down the Gulf and beyond to India and East Africa. The city's convenient geographical location and laissez-faire trading environment has also made it one of the region's major **smuggling centres**. Dubai's famous gold trade was built on the back of long-established smuggling routes into India, while in recent decades the city has served as an important trans-shipment point for diamonds, hashish, opium and weapons.

A particular bone of international contention – especially with the US – is Dubai's thriving trade with **Iran**, a large part of which is channelled through the dhow wharfage in Deira. Many of the boats here head straight across the Gulf to Iranian ports like Bandar Abbas, just 100km distant, and although most cargoes consist of harmless domestic items, a small but significant proportion do not. Smuggled goods range from simple contraband like American scotch and cigarettes through to more sophisticated items which are exported in contravention of UN sanctions and the long-standing US trade embargo. These include computers, mobile phones and various electronic components, as well as more sophisticated hardware ranging from aeroplane parts to weapons and explosives, including items that, it's thought, could potentially be used in Iran's nuclear programme. Continued attempts to crack down on illegal trade with Iran in the past few years have been made, although given the number of boats in service and the virtually nonexistent security infrastructure at the wharfage, such efforts are inevitably flawed. "Dubai," as one observer put it, "is an absolute sieve."

wooden dhows (see box, p.59), some as much as a hundred years old, which berth here to load and unload cargo; hence the great tarpaulin-covered mounds of merchandise – anything from cartons of cigarettes to massive air-conditioning units – that lie stacked up along the waterfront. The dhows themselves range in size from the fairly modest vessels employed for short hops up and down the coast to the large ocean-going craft used to transport goods around the Gulf and over to Iran, and even as far afield as Somalia, Pakistan and India. Virtually all of them fly the UAE flag, although they're generally manned by foreign crews who live on board, their lines of washing strung out across the decks and piles of cooking pots giving the boats a quaintly domestic air in the middle of Deira's roaring traffic. Hang around long enough and you might be invited to hop on board for a chat (assuming you can find a shared language) and a cup of tea.

Perfume Souk

Sikkat al Khail Rd • Most shops open roughly 10am–10pm, although some may close between around 1pm and 4/5pm, and also on Fri mornings • Al Ras metro

Immediately east of the Gold Souk lies the so-called **Perfume Souk** – although there's no actual souk building, just a collection of streetside shops, mainly along Sikkat al Khail Road but also spilling over into Al Soor and Souk Deira streets. Most places sell a mix of international brands (not necessarily genuine) along with the much heavier and more flowery oil-based *attar* perfumes favoured by local ladies. Keep an eye out for fragrances made with the highly prized *oud*, derived from agarwood (or aloes wood, as it's called in the West). At many shops you can also create your own scents, mixing and matching from the contents of the big bottles lined up behind the counter before taking them away in chintzy little cut-glass containers, many of which are collectibles in their own right.

Deira Fish, Meat and Vegetable Market

Between Al Khaleej and Corniche roads (take the footbridge over Al Khaleej Rd opposite Gold Land shopping centre) • No set hours, but usually busy from early in the morning until dark, or later • Palm Deira metro

Occupying a large warehouse on the north side of Al Khaleej Road, away from the hustle and bustle of central Deira, is the extensive **Deira Fish, Meat and Vegetable Market**. The fruit and vegetable section features a photogenic array of stalls piled high with all the usual fruit alongside more exotic offerings such as rambutans, mangosteens, coconuts, vast watermelons, yams and big bundles of fresh herbs, as well as a bewildering array of dates in huge, sticky piles. The less colourful – and far more malodorous – fish section is stocked with long lines of sharks, tuna and all sorts of other fish right down to sardines; if you're lucky someone will offer you a prawn. There's also a small but rather gory meat section tucked away at the back.

Covered Souk

South of Sikkat al Khail Rd between Souk Deira St and Al Sabkha Rd • Most shops open roughly 10am–10pm, although some may close between around 1pm and 4/5pm, and also on Fri mornings • Al Ras metro

Deira's sprawling **Covered Souk** (a misnomer, since it isn't) comprises a rather indeterminate area of small shops arranged around the maze of narrow, pedestrianized alleyways which run south from Sikkat al Khail Road down towards the Creek. Most of the shops here are Indian-run, selling colourful, low-grade cloth for women's clothes, along with large quantities of mass-produced plastic toys and cheap household goods. It's all rather down-at-heel, but makes for an interesting stroll, especially in the area at the back of the Al Sabkha bus station, the densest and busiest part of the bazaar, particularly after dark – expect to get lost at least once. The souk then continues, more or less unabated, on the far side of Al Sabkha Road, where it's known variously as the **Naif Souk** and **Al Wasl Souk**, before reaching Al Musallah Street.

Naif Museum

Naif Police Station, Naif Fort, Sikkat al Khail Rd · Sun–Thurs 8am–2pm · Free · ☎ 04 226 0286, ⓦ bit.ly/NaifMuseum · Baniyas Square metro

Celebrating Dubai's formidable reputation for law and order, the modest **Naif Museum** lies tucked away in a corner of the imposing Naif Fort (originally built in 1939, but restored to death in 1997). The museum was created at the behest of Sheikh Mohammed, who himself served as Chief of the Dubai Police for three years from 1968 – his first job, aged just 19 – before graduating to minister of defence in 1971. It's actually a lot less tedious than you might fear, with mildly diverting exhibits on the history of law enforcement in Dubai from the foundation of the police force in 1956 (with just six officers under a British captain) up to the present day. Exhibits include assorted old weapons and uniforms, a trio of short films including some interesting historical footage, and various old photos, among them a shot of a youthful-looking, clean-shaven Sheikh Mohammed as Chief of Police.

Burj Nahar

Omar bin al Khattab Rd · ⓦ bit.ly/BurjNahar · Salah al Din metro

Next to busy Omar bin al Khattab Road on the eastern outskirts of Deira is the little-visited **Burj Nahar**, set in a pretty little garden studded with palm trees. Built in 1870 to guard the city's landward approaches, it's one of only two of Dubai's original watchtowers to survive (the other is Shindagha Tower; see p.44). The virtually impenetrable round structure is completely devoid of doors and windows in its lower half, with only the narrowest of slits above.

The National Bank of Dubai and around

Creekside, off Baniyas Rd immediately south of the *Sheraton Dubai Creek* · Union metro

Next to the Creek in the southern part of Deira you'll find several of Dubai's original modernist landmarks, whose quirky design provided a blueprint for the ever growing crop of magnificent, maverick and sometimes downright loony high-rises which can now be found across the city. Pride of place goes to the **National Bank of Dubai** building (1998), designed by Uruguayan architect Carlos Ott, who was also responsible for the nearby *Hilton Dubai Creek* and the Bastille Opera House in Paris. The bank's Creek-facing side is covered by an enormous, curved sheet of highly polished glass, modelled on the sail of a traditional dhow, which acts as a kind of huge mirror to the water below and seems positively to catch fire with reflected light towards sunset – although for the best views of the bank you'll need to head over to the opposite side of the Creek.

Next to the bank sits the shorter and squatter **Dubai Chamber of Commerce** (1995), an austerely minimalist glass-clad structure which seems to have been designed using nothing but triangles – a pattern subliminally echoed in the adjacent **Sheraton Dubai Creek**, whose wedge-shaped facade pokes out above the creekside like the prow of some enormous concrete ship. Opposite the *Sheraton* on Omar bin al Khattab Road stands the **Etisalat Tower** (1986), designed by Canadian architect Arthur Erikson and instantly recognizable thanks to the enormous golf ball on its roof. The design proved so catchy it's since been repeated at further Etisalat buildings across the UAE, including the Etisalat building at the north end of Sheikh Zayed Road and on its two buildings in Abu Dhabi.

There's another large **Dhow Wharfage** here, just east of the Chamber of Commerce. It's much less visited than central Deira's but just as eye-catching, with the old-fashioned boats surreally framed against the sparkling glass facades of the surrounding modernist high-rises.

WAFI

The inner suburbs

Fringing the southern and eastern edges of the city centre – and separating it from the more modern areas beyond – are a necklace of low-key suburbs: Garhoud, Oud Metha, Karama and Satwa. South of Deira, workaday Garhoud is home to the Dubai Creek Golf Club, with its famously futuristic clubhouse, and the adjacent yacht club, where you'll find a string of attractive waterside restaurants alongside the lovely *Park Hyatt* hotel. Directly over the Creek, Oud Metha is home to the quirky Wafi complex and the lavish Khan Murjan Souk, while north of here the enjoyably downmarket suburbs of Karama and Satwa are both interesting places to get off the tourist trail and see something of local life among the city's Indian and Filipino expats, with plenty of cheap curry houses and shops selling designer fakes.

A handful of additional attractions can be found slightly further afield. Just beyond Oud Metha the suburb of Jaddaf is home to the city's last surviving traditional **dhow-building yard**, while over the Creek rises the shiny new **Festival City** development. A few kilometres further along the Creek, the **Ras al Khor Wildlife Sanctuary** protects a rare surviving patch of undeveloped wetland, home to colourful flocks of flamingo, while a short drive southwest from here brings you to the spectacular **Meydan Racecourse**, home to the Dubai Cup, the world's richest horse race.

Garhoud

Deira City Centre metro

Covering the area between the airport and the Creek, the suburb of **Garhoud** is an interesting mishmash of up- and downmarket attractions. The **Deira City Centre** mall (see p.134) is the suburb's main draw, eternally popular with an eclectic crowd running the gamut from Gulf Arabs and Russian tourists to the many expat Indians and Filipinos who live in the down-at-heel suburbs on the far side of the airport.

Dubai Creek Golf and Yacht Clubs

On the far side of Baniyas Road from Deira City Centre lies the **Dubai Creek Golf Club** (see p.140), an impressive swathe of lush fairways and greens centred on the quirky **clubhouse**, built in 1993 and still one of the city's most instantly recognizable modern landmarks, with its uniquely spiky white roofline echoing the shape of a dhow's sails and masts – like a Dubai remake of the Sydney Opera House.

Enclosed within the grounds of the golf club next to the Creek lies another local landmark, the **Dubai Creek Yacht Club**, occupying a full-size replica of a ship's bridge, with dozens of beautiful yachts moored alongside. There are several good restaurants (see p.107) in the golf and yacht club buildings, as well as in the **Park Hyatt** hotel (see p.94) between, whose serene white Moroccan-style buildings, topped with vivid blue-tiled domes, add a further touch of style to the creekside hereabouts.

Oud Metha

Across the Creek from Garhoud lies the slightly more upmarket district of **Oud Metha**, a rather formless area dotted with assorted malls, hotels and lowbrow leisure attractions. The district is centred on the area around the *Mövenpick* hotel, the old-fashioned Lamcy Plaza and the even more old-fashioned Al Nasr Leisureland amusement park, though there are also some surprisingly good restaurants here (see p.108), as well as one of Dubai's biggest clubs, *Domeland by Chi* (see p.124).

Wafi and Raffles

Oud Metha/Sheikh Rashid roads · Daily 10am–10pm (Thurs & Fri until midnight) · ☎ 04 324 4555, ⓦ wafi.com · Dubai Healthcare City metro

The leading attraction hereabouts is the wacky Egyptian-themed **Wafi** complex, a little slice of Vegas in Dubai, dotted with obelisks, pharaonic statues, random hieroglyphs and assorted miniature pyramids. The mall is home to myriad boutiques and restaurants (see p.135 & p.108). The Egyptian theme is continued in the opulent **Raffles** hotel next door, built in the form of a vast pyramid, its summit capped with glass – particularly spectacular when lit up after dark.

Khan Murjan Souk

Oud Metha/Sheikh Rashid roads · Daily 10am–10pm (Thurs & Fri until midnight) · ☎ 04 324 4555, ⓦ bit.ly/KhanMurjan · Dubai Healthcare City metro

Hidden away between Wafi and *Raffles*, **Khan Murjan Souk** is one of Dubai's finest "traditional" developments, allegedly modelled after the fabled fourteenth-century Khan Murjan Souk in Baghdad. The souk is divided into four sections – Egyptian,

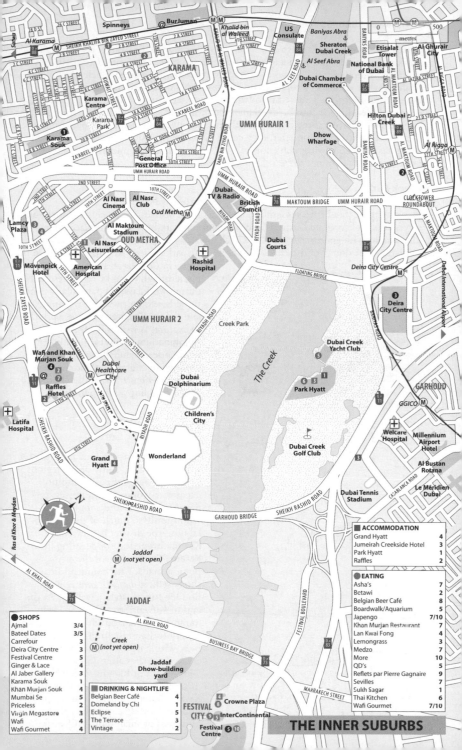

THE INNER SUBURBS

Syrian, Moroccan and Turkish (not that you can really tell the difference) – spread over two underground levels with a lovely outdoor restaurant at its centre (see p.108) and some 125 shops selling all manner of traditional wares. It's a great (albeit pricey) place to shop, while the faux-Arabian decor is impressively done, with lavish detailing ranging from intricately carved wooden balconies to enormous Moroccan lanterns and colourful tilework. Of course, it's all about as authentic as a Mulberry bag from Karama (see below) – indeed, if the city authorities are serious about clamping down on the local trade in fakes and forgeries, they could do worse than start here. Still, the whole thing has been done with such enormous panache and at, presumably, such enormous expense that it's hard not to be at least a little bit impressed.

Creek Park

Riyadh Rd • Daily 8am–10pm (Thurs–Sat until 11pm) • 5dh • Dubai Healthcare City or Oud Metha metros

Flanking the Creek between Garhoud and Maktoum bridges, the expansive **Creek Park** serves as one of congested central Dubai's major lungs and is a pleasant place for an idle ramble, with good views over the Creek towards the golf and yacht clubs and the miniature blue domes of the *Park Hyatt* hotel. The park is nicest towards dusk, when the temperature falls and the place fills up a bit, although it can be eerily deserted during weekdays. It's particularly good for kids, with plenty of playgrounds and the fun **Children's City** (see p.142) to explore, as well as the **Dubai Dolphinarium** (see p.142). Children (and, indeed, adults) may also be tempted by the park's **cable car**, which offers half-hour trips (25dh; children 15dh) dangling 30m up in the air.

Karama

Karama metro

Karama is the classic Dubai inner-city suburb, home to some of the legions of Indian, Pakistani and Filipino expatriate workers – waitresses, taxi drivers, builders and shopkeepers – who supply so much of the city's labour. The district is centred on **Kuwait Street** and the bustling little **Karama Centre**, one of the city's pokiest malls, with colourful little shops selling *shalwar kameez* and flouncy Indian-style jewellery. At the end of Kuwait Street lies the lively **Karama Park**, surrounded by cheap and cheery Indian restaurants and usually busy with a dozen simultaneous cricket matches after dark.

Just south of Karama Park is the district's main tourist attraction, the **Karama Souk** (see p.135), an unprepossessing concrete mall of hundreds of small shops stuffed full of fake designer clothes, watches, glasses, DVDs and other items (or "copy watches" and "copy bags" as the souk's enthusiastic touts euphemistically describe them).

Satwa

The unpretentious district of **Satwa** is the southernmost of Dubai's predominantly low-rise, low-income inner suburbs before you reach the giant skyscrapers of Sheikh Zayed Road and the beginnings of the supersized modern city beyond. It's also one of the few places in Dubai where the city's different ethnic groups really rub shoulders, with its mix of Arab, Indian, Filipino and even a few European residents reflected in an unusually eclectic selection of places to eat, from cheap-and-cheerful curry houses to Lebanese shwarma cafés and Western fast-food joints. A massive plan, announced in 2008, to raze the entire suburb and redevelop it with a glamorous new district of parks, artificial islands and hi-tech high-rises – provisionally named **Jumeirah Garden City** – has gone the way of several similar mega-projects in the wake of the credit crunch, although pictures of some of the planned buildings – fanciful even by Dubai standards – can still be seen online.

At the centre of the district lies **Satwa Roundabout**, overlooked by the *Chelsea Plaza* hotel. The streets south of here are mainly occupied by Indian and Pakistani shops and cafés, including the well-known *Ravi's* (see p.110). West from the roundabout stretches

3

THE ARABIAN DHOW

The inhabitants of the Arabian Peninsula were among the greatest seafarers of medieval times, using innovative shipbuilding techniques and navigational instruments to establish extensive maritime trading connections. Early Arab traders established outposts as far afield as India, Sri Lanka and East Africa, and the legacy of these early adventurers can be still be seen in the religious and cultural heritage of places like Lamu in Kenya and Zanzibar in Tanzania, where the distinctive form of the lateen-sailed Arabian **dhow** survives to this day.

The word "dhow" itself is simply a generic name used to apply to all boats of Arabian design. Classic designs include the **sambuq**, a sizeable ocean-going vessel incorporating Indian and European features, including a square stern which is thought to have been influenced by old Portuguese galleons (traditional Arabian dhows are tapered at both ends), and the **boom**, another large seafaring dhow. Other smaller dhows still in use around the Gulf include the **shu'ai** and the **jalibut**, both formerly used for trading, pearling and fishing, as well as the **abra**, hundreds of which still ply the Creek today (see p.22).

CONSTRUCTION

Perhaps the most distinctive feature of the traditional dhow was its so-called **stitched construction** – planks, usually of teak, were literally "sewn" together using coconut rope. Nails were increasingly used after European ships began to visit the region, although stitched boats were made right up until World War II. Traditional dhows are also unusual in being built "outside-in", with exterior planking being nailed together before the internal framework is added (the exact opposite of European boat-building techniques).

The traditional dhow's most visually notable feature was its distinctive triangular **lateen** sails, which allows boats to sail closer to the wind when travelling against the monsoon breezes. These have now disappeared on commercial vessels around the Gulf following the introduction of engines, though they can still be seen on local racing dhows (see p.138).

Traditional wooden dhows still play an important part in the local economy, and continue to prove an efficient and cost-effective way of shipping goods up and down the Gulf and, particularly, over to Iran – as well as finding a new lease of life in the local tourist industry. There are still a number of traditional **dhow-building yards** around the UAE: in Dubai at Jaddaf (see p.60), in Abu Dhabi, and also in the neighbouring emirates of Ajman, Umm al Quwain and Ras al Khaimah, although the incredibly labour-intensive production costs and a gradual erosion of the traditional skills required in dhow-construction (local boat-builders are famed for their ability to work entirely without plans, building entirely by eye and experience) may yet lead to an eventual end to dhow-building.

Satwa's principal thoroughfare, the tree-lined **2nd December Street** (still widely referred to by its old name, Al Diyafah Street), one of the nicest in Dubai – and one of the few outside the city centre with any real street life – with wide pavements, dozens of cafés and restaurants and an interestingly cosmopolitan atmosphere. It all feels rather Mediterranean, especially after dark, when the cafés get going, the crowds come out, and young men in expensive cars start driving round and round the block in a vain effort to impress.

Jaddaf

Taxi to Creek metro station (not yet operational, although the station building itself is finished), then walk left (north) along the Creek

On the southern edge of Oud Metha, the district of **Jaddaf** is home to the very last of Dubai's traditional **dhow-building yards**, where you may be lucky enough to see craftsmen at work constructing these magnificent ocean-going vessels using carpentry skills which appear not to have changed for generations. The yards aren't really set up for visitors and are essentially places of work, rather than tourist attractions, while there's also a certain degree of pot luck involved depending on how many vessels are under construction at any given time – although the mainly Indian workforce are usually happy to chat to visitors and the yard owners don't generally mind visitors having a look around.

As an alternative to approaching via Creek metro station, you can get a long-distance view of the dhow-building yards from the other side of the Creek, along the waterfront at Festival City.

Festival City

Festival Boulevard · ⓦ dubaifestivalcity.com

Facing Jaddaf on the opposite side of the Creek, **Festival City** is one of Dubai's newest and largest purpose-built neighbourhoods – a self-contained city within a city, complete with villas and apartments, offices, golf course, marina, shopping mall and a pair of swanky five-star hotels. The centrepiece of the development is the bright, modern **Festival Centre** shopping mall; there's nothing here that you won't find (and generally done better) at other

---

GODOLPHIN AND THE RACING MAKTOUMS

Ruler and architect of contemporary Dubai, **Sheikh Mohammed bin Rashid al Maktoum** is also celebrated in racing circles as one of today's leading owners and breeders of thoroughbreds in his role as the founder of **Godolphin**, established in 1994 and now one of the world's largest and most successful racing stables. Sheikh Mohammed's love of horses runs deep: he is said to have shared his breakfast with his horse en route to school as a boy, to have competed in his first horse race aged 12, and to have been able to tame wild horses considered unrideable by others. His love of the turf dates back to his time as a student at Cambridge in England in the 1960s, and within a decade he and his brothers Hamdan and Ahmed all had horses in training at nearby Newmarket. The first of many Maktoum family triumphs came in 1982, when Hamdan's Touching Wood won that year's St Leger classic at Doncaster, followed up by Derby wins in 1989 and 1994.

Godolphin now have over 1500 horses in training across the globe and have won more than 2000 races in fourteen different countries, becoming one of the biggest buyers and breeders of racehorses on the planet, with a total investment in bloodstock, stud farms and various related properties now totalling a cool US$2.4 billion. In 2013, they also had the less enviable distinction of finding themselves at the centre of one of the biggest **scandals** to hit racing in years when 22 horses at their Newmarket stables in the UK were found to have been dosed with anabolic steroids by their trainer, Mahmood al Zarooni. Al Zarooni was swiftly banned from horse racing for eight years while Sheikh Mohammed professed himself "absolutely appalled" by the actions of one of his own trainers. Nevertheless, the affair's potential long-term damage to Godolphin's reputation – and perhaps even to that of Sheikh Mohammed himself – may take years to repair.

malls around the city, although the canalside cafés at the Creek end of the centre are pleasant enough, and there are also "sofa boats" for rent (50dh/15min) if you fancy a sedate turn around the waterways. The development's best physical feature is its creekside location, with sweeping views from the waterfront promenade by the Festival Centre mall and hotels across the water to the dhow-building yards at Jaddaf and the long line of skyscrapers beyond. The panorama is particularly fine towards dusk, when the sun sets behind the Burj Khalifa and towers along Sheikh Zayed Road, turning them a smoky grey, like the outline of some kind of surreal bar chart.

Ras al Khor

Some 5km southwest of Festival City, the Dubai Creek comes to an impressive end at **Ras al Khor ("Head of the Creek")**, forming an extensive inland lagoon dotted with mangroves and surrounded by intertidal salt and mud flats – a unique area of unspoilt nature close to the city centre. This being Dubai, much of Ras al Khor's rare natural habitat is under threat, earmarked for the vast new **The Lagoons** development, featuring seven interconnected artificial islands along with the usual malls, five-star hotels and the city's first opera house. The project has been plagued with problems (not least the arrest on corruption charges of four of the developer's senior executives), and although construction work continues to limp along, exactly what will ever get built (and when) remains unclear.

Ras al Khor Wildlife Sanctuary

Ras al Khor/Oud Metha roads • Sat–Thurs 9am–4pm • Free, but permits required; apply by phone at least 2 days in advance • ☎ 04 606 6822 or ☎ 04 606 6826, ⓦ wildlife.ae

The southern end of the lagoon provides, for now at least, a home for the low-key **Ras al Khor Wildlife Sanctuary**, best known for its aquatic birdlife. The sanctuary is an important stopover on winter migratory routes from East Africa to West Asia and almost seventy different species have been spotted here. It's best known for the colourful flocks of bright pink flamingoes which nest here – one of Dubai's most surreal sights when seen perched against the smoggy outlines of the city skyscrapers beyond. You can't actually go into the sanctuary, but you can birdwatch from one of three **hides** on its edge. Signage for the hides is minimal and you'll need a car to reach them, but don't expect taxi drivers to know where they are. Free binoculars are provided, although the roar of the nearby motorways isn't particularly conducive to the relaxed contemplation of nature. The quietest but most difficult to reach is on Al Buhaira ("Lagoon") hide, on the north side of the sanctuary in Jaddaf; the other two are Fantir ("Flamingo") hide on the west side of the sanctuary, beside the E66 Highway just north of the junction with the Hatta road; and Gum ("Mangrove") hide on the south side of the sanctuary, on the north side of the Hatta road – although to reach it from central Dubai you'll need to do an annoying 8km loop to get back on the correct side of the highway.

Meydan

Meydan Rd (take exit 7 off the E66 Al Ain Rd, or exit 20 of Al Khail Rd (E44)) • ⓦ meydan.ae

Around 4km south of Ras al Khor, the vast **Meydan** complex provides conclusive proof of the ruling Maktoum family's passion – bordering on obsession – for all things equine (see box opposite). Centrepiece of the complex is the superb **racecourse**, opened in 2010 to replace the old track at nearby Nad al Sheba and provide a new and more fitting venue for the **Dubai World Cup** (see p.138), the world's richest horse race with a massive US$10 million in prize money. The complex also contains the usual fancy five-star hotel along with a few other buildings in a mixed residential and business development which is eventually intended to form a self-contained "city" along the lines of Festival City down the road.

3

Sheikh Zayed Road and Downtown Dubai

Around 5km south of the Creek, the upwardly mobile suburbs of modern Dubai begin in spectacular style with the massed skyscrapers of Sheikh Zayed Road and the huge Downtown Dubai development: an extraordinary sequence of neck-cricking high-rises which march south from the landmark Emirates Towers to the cloud-capped Burj Khalifa, the world's tallest building. This is the modern city at its most futuristic and flamboyant, and perhaps the defining example of Dubai's insatiable desire to offer more luxury, more glitz and more retail opportunities than the competition, with a string of record-breaking attractions which now include not just the world's highest building but also its largest mall, tallest hotel and biggest fountain.

Emirates Towers

Sheikh Zayed Rd · Emirates Towers metro

Opened in 2000, the soaring **Emirates Towers** remain one of modern Dubai's most iconic symbols, despite increasing competition from newer and even more massive landmarks. The larger office tower (355m) was the tallest building in the Middle East and tenth highest in the world when it was completed, though such has been the pace of development that it now barely scrapes into the top ten tallest buildings in the city. Size (or lack of) notwithstanding, the twin towers remain among the most beautiful in the city, their highly reflective surfaces mirroring the constantly changing play of desert light and shadow, and their unusual triangular groundplan and spiky cutaway summits giving them a kind of thrusting sci-fi glamour – like a pair of alien rockets about to blast off into space.

The taller tower houses the offices of Emirates airlines, plus the offices of Dubai ruler Sheikh Mohammed and his inner circle of senior advisers; the smaller is occupied by the exclusive *Jumeirah Emirates Towers* hotel (see p.95). One curiosity of the buildings is that the office tower, despite its considerable extra height (355m versus 305m), has only two more floors than the hotel tower (53 versus 51). The taller tower isn't open to the public, apart from the ground floor where you'll find the posh (if now rather moribund) Emirates Towers Boulevard, but there are plenty of opportunities to look around the hotel tower, most spectacularly from the 50th- and 51st-floor *Vu's* bar and restaurant (see p.120 & p.112). It's also worth popping in to have a look at the dramatic atrium, with its little pod-shaped glass elevators shuttling up and down the huge orange wall overhead.

4

Dubai International Financial Centre

Between Sheikh Zayed Rd and 312 Rd · ⓦ difc.ae · Emirates Tower or Financial Centre metros

Virtually in the shadow of the Emirates Towers, the **Dubai International Financial Centre (DIFC)** is the city's financial hub and home to myriad banks, investment companies and other enterprises, along with the flagship NASDAQ Dubai exchange. Opened in 2005, NASDAQ Dubai is a key element in the government's attempts to exploit the city's location midway between European and Asian financial markets and become the region's leading financial trading centre – and, ultimately, a major player in global markets to rival the City of London, Wall Street and Tokyo, although progress so far has been slower than hoped for. The exchange is also a leader in the rapidly growing international market for *sukuk*, so-called "Islamic Bonds", devised to be acceptable under Shariah law, which (in accordance with the Koran's strictures against usury) forbids the charging of interest, stipulating that investors profit only from transactions based on the sale or purchase of actual assets.

The DIFC's northern end is marked by **The Gate**, a striking building looking like a kind of postmodern Arc de Triomphe-cum-office block. The Gate is surrounded on three sides by further buildings linked by "The Balcony", an attractive raised terrace

---

SHEIKH ZAYED ROAD

Technically, Sheikh Zayed Road – christened after the much-loved first president of the UAE (see box, p.172) – is the name of the highway that runs all the way from Dubai to Abu Dhabi. In practice, however, when locals refer to "Sheikh Zayed Road" they are usually talking about the section of highway in central Dubai **between Interchange no. 1 and the Trade Centre Roundabout** (also known as Za'abeel Roundabout) – in other words, from the *Dusit Thani* hotel to just north of the Emirates Towers, which is where you'll find most of the road's hotels, restaurants and shops. This is the sense in which the name is used in the Guide. Attractions further south along Sheikh Zayed Road past Interchange no. 1 – such as the Mall of the Emirates, Dubai Marina and Ibn Battuta Mall – are covered in later chapters.

lined with assorted cafés and shops. The entire pedestrianized complex is pleasantly sedate, almost collegiate, with sober expat financial types shuttling between meetings and a high-financial solemnity which feels more like London or Frankfurt than anywhere in the Gulf. Off on the east side of the complex lies a further cluster of buildings known as the **Gate Village**, now one of the focal points of Dubai's burgeoning visual arts scene, with virtually every building occupied by assorted galleries (see p.127), with a couple of top-end restaurants (see p.111 & p.112) thrown in for good measure.

Dubai World Trade Centre

Sheikh Zayed Rd, by Trade Centre Roundabout • Ⓦ dwtc.com • World Trade Centre metro

North of the Emirates Towers stretches the sprawling **Dubai International Convention and Exhibition Centre**, on whose far side rises the venerable old **Dubai World Trade Centre** tower, Dubai's first skyscraper and formerly the tallest building in the Middle East. Commissioned in 1979 by the visionary Sheikh Rashid (see p.183), this 39-storey edifice was widely regarded as a massive white elephant when it was first built, standing as it did in the middle of what was then empty desert far from the old city centre. In fact, history has entirely vindicated Rashid's daring gamble. The centre proved an enormous success with foreign companies and US diplomats, who established a consulate in the tower and used it as a major base for monitoring affairs in nearby Iran – their covert intelligence-gathering vastly aided by the large number of Dubai-based Iranians who arrived at the

consulate to apply for US visas. The centre also served as an important anchor for future development along the strip, and it's a measure of Sheikh Rashid's far-sighted ambition that his alleged *folie de grandeur* has long since been overtaken by a string of far more impressive constructions further down the road.

South along Sheikh Zayed Road

South of the Emirates Towers, Sheikh Zayed Road continues in a more or less unbroken line of high-rises, looking like contestants in a bizarre postmodern architectural beauty parade. Heading down the strip brings you immediately to **The Tower**, a slender edifice rising to a neat pyramidal summit, with three tiers of stylized leaf-shaped metal protuberances sprouting from its sides. Right next door sits the thoroughly daft **Al Yaqoub Tower** (not quite finished at the time of writing): effectively a postmodern replica of London's Big Ben, although at 330m it's well over three times the height of the 96m-tall UK landmark. Two buildings down, the quirky **Maze Tower** (wmazetower.com), its facade covered in labyrinthine doodles, looks almost understated in comparison.

Further south the eye-catching **Al Attar Tower** (not to be confused with the nearby Al Attar Business Tower) appears to have been constructed entirely out of plate glass and enormous gold coins, while close by rises the graceful **Rose Rayhaan** – a beautifully slender and delicate structure, topped by a small globe which is

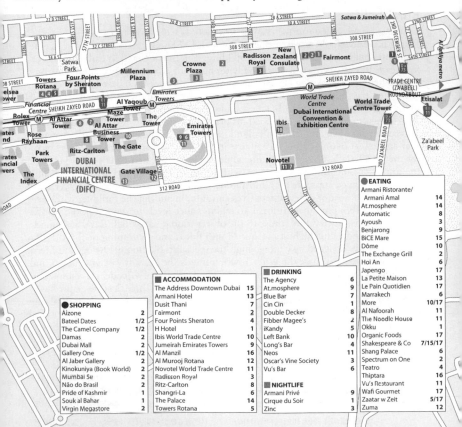

illuminated prettily after dark. At 333m this was formerly the world's tallest hotel until the recent opening of the new *JW Marriott Marquis Dubai* just down the road in Business Bay (see p.70). Slightly further down stands the **Rolex Tower**, a rather severe rectangular mass of black glass with (apparently) a kind of card slot cut out of its uppermost floors, while across the road is the soaring **Chelsea Tower**, topped by what looks like an enormous toothpick. A short walk further south the strip reaches a suitably dramatic end with the iconic **Dusit Thani** hotel, a towering glass-and-metal edifice inspired by the traditional Thai *wai*, a prayer-like gesture of welcome, though it looks more like a huge upended tuning fork thrust into the ground.

An increasing number of wacky high-rises are also mushrooming in the area behind the *Dusit Thani* off Sheikh Zayed Road, including the pod-shaped **Park Towers**, the ovoid **Emirates Financial Towers**, the **Islamic Bank Towers** (aka Central Park Towers), with their unusual wedge-shaped summits, and the gargantuan **The Index** tower. The last is a rare (for Dubai) example of environmentally intelligent design, with the building's main facades aligned exactly north–south, reducing the effects of the penetrating, low-angle morning and evening sun, while sunshades are used to keep the north and south fronts cool – all of which substantially reduces the need for air-conditioning, so that even in the hottest summer months the building's internal temperature never exceeds 28°C, even without a/c – a far cry from most of the city's glass-encased, energy-guzzling skyscrapers (see p.192).

Burj Khalifa

4

Sheikh Mohammed bin Rashid Blvd (Emaar Blvd) • ☎ 04 888 8888, ⊕ burjkhalifa.ae • Burj Khalifa/Dubai Mall metro

Rising imperiously skywards at the southern end of Sheikh Zayed Road, the needle-thin **Burj Khalifa** is the world's tallest building. The Burj opened in early 2010 after five years' intensive construction, finally topping out at a staggering 828m and comprehensively smashing all existing records for the world's tallest man-made structures, past and present. Among the superlatives it took were those of Taipei 101 in Taiwan (formerly the world's tallest building at 509m), the KVLY-TV mast in North Dakota (the world's tallest extant man-made structure at 629m), and the Warsaw Radio Mast, at Gąbin in Poland (previously the tallest man-made structure ever erected, at 646m, before its collapse in 1991). The Burj also returned the record for the world's tallest structure to the Middle East for the first time since 1311, when the towers of Lincoln Cathedral surpassed the Great Pyramid of Giza, which had previously reigned supreme for almost 4000 years. Not surprisingly, the tower also accumulated a host of other superlatives en route, including the building with the most floors (163, plus an additional 46 maintenance levels in the spire), the world's highest and fastest elevators (those to the observation deck, which travel at around 10m per second), plus highest mosque (158th floor) and swimming pool (76th floor).

The tower was designed by Chicago high-rise specialists Skidmore, Owings and Merrill, whose other credits include the Willis Tower, formerly the Sears Tower, in Chicago, and New York's One World Trade Center. The building consists of a slender central square core, surrounded by three tiers arranged in a Y-shaped plan. These tiers are gradually stepped back as the building rises, forming a series of 27 terraces, before the central core emerges to form the culminating spire – a plan which makes the optimum use of available natural light, as well as providing the best outward views. The shape of the tower has often been compared to that for Frank Lloyd Wright's visionary (but unrealized) plans for The Illinois, a mile-high skyscraper designed for Chicago, while chief architect Adrian Smith has said that the tower's Y-shaped footprint was inspired by the flower *Hymenocallis*.

The astonishing scale of the Burj is difficult to fully comprehend – the building is best appreciated at a distance, from where you can properly appreciate the tower's jaw-dropping height and the degree to which it reduces even the elevated high-rises

BURJ DUBAI OR BURJ KHALIFA?

The biggest surprise at the Burj's spectacular opening party in January 2010 was the announcement that the tower, previously known as the Burj Dubai, was to be renamed the Burj Khalifa, in honour of **Khalifa bin Zayed al Nahyan**, ruler of Abu Dhabi and president of the UAE. Announcing the name change, Dubai ruler Sheikh Mohammed stated: "This great project deserves to carry the name of a great man" – although the naming rights to the world's tallest building may owe less to Sheikh Khalifa's personal qualities and more to the US$15-billion-plus bailout that Abu Dhabi provided to cash-strapped Dubai following recent financial difficulties. Oddly enough, Sheikh Khalifa himself didn't bother showing up to the unveiling of the building that will now make his name familiar to millions.

which surround it to the status of undernourished pygmies. Distance also emphasizes the Burj's slender, elegantly tapering outline, which has been variously compared to a shard of glass, a latter-day Tower of Babel and, according to Germaine Greer, "a needle stuck in the buttock of the Almighty".

Most of the tower is occupied by some 900 residential apartments (these allegedly sold out within eight hours of launch, and subsequently changed hands, at the height of the Dubai property market, for a cool US$43,000 per square metre); lower floors are occupied by the world's first **Armani hotel** (see p.98).

At the Top observation deck

At the Top tours depart from the ticket desk in the lower-ground floor of the Dubai Mall • Sun–Wed 9am–midnight, Thurs 8.30am–midnight, Fri & Sat 4.30pm–midnight • Pre-booked tickets 100dh, immediate entry tickets 400dh • Reserved tickets can be purchased in advance on the website or from the ticket desk; immediate entry tickets must be purchased in person from the ticket office • ☏ 04 888 8888, ⓦ burjkhalifa.ae

Access to the Burj Khalifa is strictly controlled. Most visitors take the expensive tour up to the misleadingly named **"At the Top"** observation deck (on floor 124, although there are actually 163 floors in total) for sensational views over the city. The tour also includes some interesting displays on the creation of the tower, although you should expect large crowds and long queues whenever you visit.

A plausible alternative is to take a drink or meal in **At.mosphere** (see p.112 & p.120), on level 122, just below the observation deck. If you just go up for a drink in the lounge (daily noon–2am) there's a minimum spend of 200dh per couple, exactly what you'd fork out on the At the Top tour, which lets you avoid the crowds and queues and enjoy the view in a much more relaxed environment – and with a drink thrown in for good measure.

Dubai Mall

Financial Centre Rd • Daily 10am–10pm, Thurs–Sat until midnight • ⓦ thedubaimall.com • Burj Khalifa/Dubai Mall metro; Dubai Mall is linked directly to the metro station by an 820m-long elevated walkway with airport-style travelators – around a 10min walk

Right next to the Burj Khalifa, the supersized **Dubai Mall** is the absolute mother of all malls, with over 1200 shops spread across four floors and covering a total area of over a million square metres – making it easily the largest mall in the world measured by total area (although other malls contain more shopping space). Just about every retail chain in the city has an outlet here, with flagship names including Galeries Lafayette, Bloomingdale's, an offshoot of London's famous Hamleys toy store and a superb branch of the Japanese bookseller Kinokuniya. There are also lashings of upmarket designer stores, mainly concentrated along the section of the mall called **Fashion Avenue** – a positive encyclopedia of labels, complete with its own catwalk and Armani café – as well as a self-contained **Souk**, with attractive contemporary Arabian design and a further 220 shops. Look out too for the eye-catching **The Waterfall**, complete with life-size statues of fibreglass divers, which cascades from the top of the mall down to the bottom, four storeys below.

DUBAI MALL SHOPPERS' SURVIVAL GUIDE

Not surprisingly given its size, even a casual shopping visit to the Dubai Mall can be an exhausting experience – expect to walk several miles at minimum, even if you're just looking for the nearest toilet. Maps of the mall are available from various information desks – useful to plan your visit and save endless backtracking.

Despite its size, the mall also suffers from massive crowds, especially at weekends and on holidays, when it's best avoided. If you want a break from the masses, the coffee shops on the top (2nd) floor such as *Caribou Coffee* are often significantly quieter than those downstairs, and there's also a pleasant little café in Kinokuniya (see p.130) offering bird's-eye views of the Dubai Fountain below and often surprisingly peaceful when other places are rammed.

Other amenities include some 120 **cafés and restaurants**, divided between various interior food courts and the bustling waterside terrace at the back of the mall overlooking the Dubai Fountain. There are also a couple of five-star hotels (see p.97), a 22-screen multiplex, the state-of-the-art SEGA Republic theme park (see p.142), the KidZania "edu-tainment" centre (see p.142), an Olympic-size ice rink (see p.140) and the Dubai Aquarium and Underwater Zoo (see below).

Dubai Aquarium

Dubai Mall • Sun–Wed 10am–10pm, Thurs–Sat 10am–midnight • 80dh including underwater tunnel, 110dh including glass-bottom boat ride; dive packages from 590dh • ☎ 04 448 5200, ⊛ thedubaiaquarium.com

Assuming you come in the mall's main entrance off Financial Centre Road, one of the first things you'll see is the spectacular viewing panel of the **Dubai Aquarium and Underwater Zoo**: a huge, transparent floor-to-ceiling aquarium filled to the brim with fish large and small, including sand-tiger sharks, stingrays, colourful shoals of tropical fish and some large and spectacularly ugly grouper. The viewing window holds the record for the world's largest acrylic panel: at around 8m high and over 30m wide, with 33,000 fish, 70 species and 10 million litres of water, it's effectively the largest fish tank on the planet, although the similarly huge aquarium at The Lost Chambers (see p.85) runs it close.

The **Underwater Zoo** upstairs is relatively unexciting compared to the enormous tank, and more likely to appeal to children than to adults. Displays are arranged according to different marine habitats like freshwater, "rocky shore" and rainforest, with representative fauna from each, ranging from tiny cichlids, poison-dart frogs and soapfish through to otters, penguins and seals. The entrance ticket also allows you to walk through the underwater tunnel which runs through the middle of the tank, while for an extra 30dh you can take a glass-bottom boat ride across the top. Qualified divers can even go diving in it (by prior arrangement only) – although you won't see anything you can't already see from the mall, and for free.

Dubai Fountain

Burj Khalifa Lake, Downtown Dubai; access from the Dubai Mall via the lower-ground (LG) floor of the Star Atrium • Displays daily at 1pm & 1.30pm and then every 30min 6–11pm (Thurs–Sat until 11.30pm) • ☎ 04 362 7500, ⊛ bit.ly/TheDubaiFountain • Burj Khalifa/Dubai Mall metro

Winding through the heart of Downtown Dubai between the Dubai Mall, Burj Khalifa and Old Town Island is the large **Burj Khalifa Lake**. The section of the lake closest to the Dubai Mall doubles as the spectacular 275m-long **Dubai Fountain**, the world's biggest, capable of shooting jets of water up to 150m high, and illuminated with over 6000 lights and 25 colour projectors. The fountain really comes to life after dark, spouting carefully choreographed watery flourishes which "dance" elegantly in time to a range of Arabic, Hindi and classical songs, viewable from anywhere around the lake for free.

Old Town

Access by crossing the small bridge at the exit from the Dubai Mall's Star Atrium · Souk al Bahar Sat–Thurs 10am–10pm, Fri 2–10pm · Burj Khalifa/Dubai Mall metro

On the far side of the Dubai Fountain, directly in the shadow of the Burj Khalifa, is the chintzy **Old Town** development: a low-rise sprawl of sand-coloured buildings with traditional Moorish styling. The overall concept, with a soaring futuristic tower placed next to a cod-Arabian village with waterways, is effectively a blatant copy of the Madinat Jumeirah/Burj al Arab concept (see p.79), except not quite as impressively done. The centrepiece of the development is the **Souk al Bahar** ("Souk of the Sailor"; see p.136), a small, Arabian-themed mall specializing in traditional handicrafts and independent fashion, though it feels rather underpowered after the excesses of the neighbouring Dubai Mall. A string of restaurants line the waterfront terrace outside, offering peerless views of Burj Khalifa – although they tend to get absolutely rammed after dark, and none is of any particular culinary distinction. On the far side of the Souk al Bahar stands the Old Town's opulent showpiece hotel, **The Palace** (see p.98), its rich Moorish facade offering a surreal but quintessentially Dubaian contrast with the needle-thin outline of the Burj Khalifa rising imperiously behind.

Business Bay

Business Bay metro

Dubai's last big hurrah before the credit crunch hit town in 2008, the vast new **Business Bay** project was originally intended to comprise a swanky new high-rise district mixing offices and residential towers around a man-made extension of the Creek, although the entire scheme has got stuck in what is beginning to feel like a perpetual limbo. The Creek extension and a fair number of buildings were completed as planned before the crunch bit, but many others are struggling to get finished (or, if finished, tenanted) and the whole area is still very much a work in progress.

For the time being, it remains one of the largest building sites in Dubai, and a reminder of the Wild West days of the mid-noughties, when large swathes of the city looked a lot like this. In the meantime, a few completed (or almost completed) buildings are worth a look. Exiting the metro, and heading right at the first main intersection brings you to the **JW Marriott Marquis Dubai** hotel, opened in late 2012 and currently the tallest hotel in the world at a cool 355m (having taken that particular record off the nearby *Rose Rayhaan* hotel on Sheikh Zayed Road, which in turn took it off the Burj al Arab). The hotel occupies one of a soaring pair of identical blue-glass-clad towers whose strangely contoured outlines appear to be modelled on the trunk of a palm tree, each topped with a spiky little crown.

Opposite the Marriott, you can't fail to notice the unfinished **Iris Bay**, an extraordinary crescent-shaped building (like an eye turned sideways – hence the name), while back down the road, next to the intersection opposite the metro, stands **One Business Bay** tower, like an enormous popcorn carton made out of shiny black glass. From here down the road ahead in the distance your eye is drawn to the funky O-14 tower, popularly known as the **Swiss Cheese Tower** thanks to the undulating layer of white cladding which envelops the entire structure, dotted with around 1300 circular holes. It's said to have been inspired by the Arabian *mashrabiya* (traditional, elaborately carved wooden screens) but actually looks like nothing so much as an enormous piece of postmodern Emmenthal.

Jumeirah

Around 2km south of the Creek, the beachside suburb of Jumeirah marks the beginning of southern Dubai's endless suburban sprawl. The area's swathes of chintzy low-rise villas are home to many of the city's European expats and their wives – immortalized in Dubai legend as the so-called "Jumeirah Janes" who (so the stereotype runs) spend their days in an endless round of luncheons and beach parties, while their hard-working spouses slave away to keep them in the style to which they have very rapidly become accustomed. The suburb is strung out along the Jumeirah Road, which arrows straight down the coast, lined with a long string of low-key shopping malls and cafés. Attractions include the Jumeirah Mosque (the only one in Dubai currently accessible to non-Muslims), the old-fashioned Majlis Ghorfat um al Sheif, the former summer retreat of Dubai's erstwhile ruler Sheikh Rashid, and the enigmatic Jumeirah Archeological Site.

5

Jumeirah Mosque

Jumeirah Rd · 1hr tours Tues, Thurs, Sat & Sun at 10am; 10dh (under-5s not allowed; no pre-booking required) · ☎ 04 353 6666, ⓦ cultures.ae · Bus #8, C10 or X28

Rising proudly above the northern end of the Jumeirah Road, the stately **Jumeirah Mosque** is one of the largest and most attractive in the city. Built in quasi-Fatimid (Egyptian) style, it's reminiscent in appearance, if not quite in size, of the great mosques of Cairo, with a pair of soaring minarets, a roofline embellished with delicately carved miniature domes and richly decorated windows set in elaborate rectangular recesses. As with many of Dubai's more venerable-looking buildings though, medieval appearances are deceptive – the mosque was actually built in 1979.

It also has the added attraction of being the only mosque in Dubai that non-Muslims can visit, owing to the four weekly **tours** run by the Sheikh Mohammed Centre for Cultural Understanding (SMCCU). These offer a good opportunity to get a look at the mosque's rather chintzy interior, with its distinctive green-and-orange colour scheme and delicately painted arches. The real draw, however, are the entertaining and informative guides, who explain some of the basic precepts and practices of Islam before throwing the floor open for questions – a rare chance to settle some of those perplexing local conundrums, whether it be a description of the workings of the Islamic calendar or an explanation of exactly what Emirati men wear under their robes.

Iranian Hospital and Mosque

Al Wasl Rd · Bus #7, #12 or #88

Standing on either side of Al Wasl Road, the striking **Iranian Hospital** and nearby **Imam Hossein Mosque** (generally known simply as the "Iranian Mosque") add a welcome splash of colour to the pasty concrete hues which rule in this part of the city. The hospital is a large, functional, modern building improbably covered in vast quantities of superb blue-green tiling in the elaborate abstract floral patterns beloved of Persian artists. The mosque is even finer, its sumptuously tiled dome and two minarets particularly magical, especially in low light early or late in the day. Unfortunately the mosque is walled off and you can only see it from a certain distance – the best view is from the small residential side street which runs around the back of it, rather than from Al Wasl Road itself.

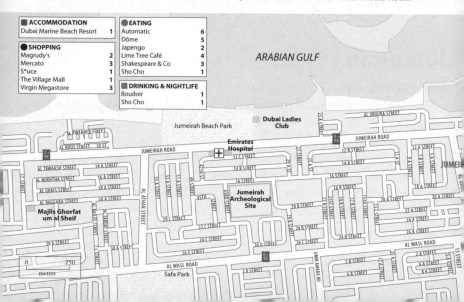

■ ACCOMMODATION		■ EATING	
Dubai Marine Beach Resort	1	Automatic	6
		Dôme	5
● SHOPPING		Japengo	2
Magrudy's	2	Lime Tree Café	4
Mercato	3	Shakespeare & Co	3
S*uce	1	Sho Cho	1
The Village Mall	1		
Virgin Megastore	3	■ DRINKING & NIGHTLIFE	
		Boudoir	1
		Sho Cho	1

ARABIAN GULF

JUMEIRAH: A NOTE ON NAMES

Area names in Dubai are often used with a certain vagueness – Bur Dubai and Deira, for example, are both employed in varying ways, while no one seems entirely certain yet whether Dubai Marina should be called Dubai Marina, or New Dubai, or perhaps something else entirely. None, however, has proved as enduringly slippery as Jumeirah. Strictly speaking, **Jumeirah proper** covers the area from roughly around the *Dubai Marine Beach Resort* in the north down to around the Majlis Ghorfat um al Sheif in the south. In practice, however, the name is often used loosely to describe the whole of coastal Dubai south of the Creek down to the Burj al Arab, and sometimes even beyond.

Further confusion is added by the fact that Jumeirah has been adopted as the name of the city's leading luxury hotel chain. The **Jumeirah Beach Hotel** and **Madinat Jumeirah**, for instance, aren't strictly speaking in Jumeirah, but in the adjacent suburb of Umm Suqeim (although both are owned by the Jumeirah chain – as is the *Jumeirah Emirates Tower* hotel, which is actually on Sheikh Zayed Road, and the *Jumeirah Creekside Hotel*, in Garhoud). Further south the J-word crops up again at the *Sheraton Jumeirah Beach* hotel and *Hilton Dubai Jumeirah Resort*, both in what is now the Marina, while the name has also wandered off and attached itself to the **Palm Jumeirah** artificial island, **Jumeirah Lakes Towers** and the stalled **Jumeirah Garden City** – none of them in, or (except for the latter) even particularly near, Jumeirah proper. And that's not the end of it: thanks to the Jumeirah group the name can now be found attached to properties as far afield as London, New York and Shanghai – an impressive feat of global colonization for the name of what was, until fifty years ago, little more than a humble fishing village.

Dubai Zoo

Jumeirah Rd • Daily except Tues 10am–5.30pm • 2dh • ☎ 04 349 6444 or ☎ 04 344 0462 • Bus #8, #88 or C10

The first zoo on the Arabian peninsula when it was founded in 1967, **Dubai Zoo**, about 1.5km south of Jumeirah Mosque, serves as the overcrowded and rather unappealing home to a wide range of animals, almost all of whom arrived at the zoo having been taken from smugglers apprehended by UAE customs officials. The resultant mishmash of haphazardly acquired animals includes giraffes, tigers, lions, chimps, brown bears, Arabian wolves and oryx, plus assorted birds, though it's difficult to see very much thanks to the ugly cages, covered in thick wire-mesh (installed, ironically, to protect the

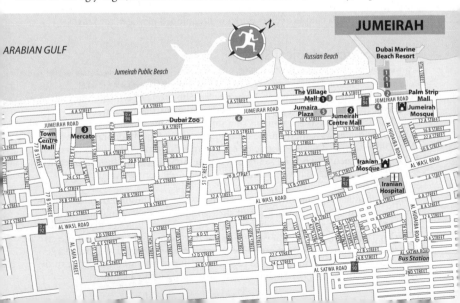

5

animals from visitors; when the zoo first opened, locals would turn up armed with sticks to prod depressed animals into action, and sadly the behaviour of many of today's visitors is little better). Plans for a replacement zoo have been in the pipeline for over a decade now, and in 2012 it was announced that a spacious new wildlife park named **Dubai Safari** will be created on the city outskirts, off the Hatta road, with a provisional opening date of the end of 2014 – although whether this ever actually sees the light of day is anyone's guess.

Mercato

Jumeirah Rd · Daily 10am–10pm (Thurs–Sat until midnight) · ⓦ mercatoshoppingmall.com · Bus #8, #88, C10 or X28

About halfway down Jumeirah Road, the eye-popping **Mercato** mall is well worth a visit even if you've no intention of actually buying anything. Looking like a kind of miniature medieval Italian city rebuilt by the Disney Corporation, the mall comprises a series of brightly coloured quasi-Venetian-cum-Tuscan palazzi arranged around a huge central atrium overlooked by panoramic balconies, while side passages lead to miniature piazzas on either side – a memorable example of the sort of brazen kitsch that Dubai does so well. Not surprisingly, it's all proved immensely popular, and the fake-Florentine thoroughfares are thronged most hours of the day and night by a very eclectic crowd, with Jumeirah Janes ducking in and out of the mall's designer boutiques and crowds of white-robed Emirati men lounging over coffee in the ground-floor *Starbucks* while their veiled wives and Filipino maids take the kids upstairs for burgers and fries at *McDonald's* – a picture-perfect example of the multicultural madness of modern Dubai.

Jumeirah Beach Park

Jumeirah Rd · Daily 8am–10.30pm (Thurs–Sat until 11pm); Mon ladies and boys aged up to 4 only · 5dh · Bus #8, #88, C10 or X28

Squeezed in between the sea and Jumeirah Road near the suburb's southern end, **Jumeirah Beach Park** is easily the nicest park and public beach in Dubai – wildly popular both with city residents and with sand-starved tourists staying in city-centre hotels. The beach itself is large enough to soak up the crowds, with a fine wide swathe of white sand manned with lifeguards and equipped with loungers and parasols, while the pleasantly wooded strip of park behind has lots of shaded grass for picnics, barbecue facilities, a couple of cafés and a well-equipped play area for kids.

Jumeirah Archeological Site

16 St (reachable via 27 St or 49 St from Jumeirah Rd) · Officially the site isn't open to the public although the caretaker might let you in if you hang around the gate (a small tip is nice to give) · ☏ 04 3496874, ⓦ bit.ly/JumeirahAS · Bus #8, #88, C10 or X28

The slight but intriguing **Jumeirah Archeological Site** is one of Dubai's best-kept secrets, scattered over several acres of prime real estate in the heart of Jumeirah. First excavated in 1969, the site protects the remains of a small settlement which grew up here thanks to the area's strategic location on the caravan route between Mesopotamia and Oman. Originally established in pre-Islamic or early Ummayad times (fifth to sixth centuries AD), the settlement reached its zenith during the Abbasid period (ninth to tenth centuries) and appears to have remained inhabited until perhaps as late as the eighteenth century.

The fragmentary remains of seven structures lie scattered around the site, all now largely vanished apart from the bases of their coral-stone walls. Buildings include several residential dwellings, a small mosque, souk (signed "Market Place") and a "ruler's palace", still dotted with the stumps of its original pillars. Most impressive are the remains of a sizeable **caravanserai**, with small rooms arranged around a large central courtyard, its antique outline providing a memorably weird contrast to the hypermodern skyscrapers of Sheikh Zayed Road rising loftily behind.

Safa Park

Between Al Wasl and Sheikh Zayed roads, by Al Hadiqa St • Daily 8am–10.30pm, Thurs–Sat until 11pm • 3dh • Bus #12 or #93

Flanking Al Wasl Road a couple of blocks inland from the coast, **Safa Park** offers a refreshing expanse of grassy parkland impressively backdropped by the skyscrapers of Sheikh Zayed Road. The park is well supplied with children's attractions, including numerous play areas, a boating lake and a miniature fairground area featuring a merry-go-round, a (small) big wheel, dodgems, a games arcade, trampolines and a giant slide, although some attractions only operate in the evenings, if at all.

Majlis Ghorfat um al Sheif

17 St (signed off Jumeirah Rd by the BinSina pharmacy; turn down 17 St for about 50m and the *majlis* is on your left) • Sat–Thurs 8.30am–8.30pm, Fri 2.30–8.30pm • 1dh • ☎ 04 852 1374 • Bus #8, #88 or X28

Tucked away off the southern end of Jumeirah Road, the **Majlis Ghorfat um al Sheif** offers a touching memento of old Dubai, now incongruously marooned amid a sea of chintzy modern villas. Built in 1955 when Jumeirah was no more than a small fishing village, this modest traditional house was used by Sheikh Rashid, the inspiration behind modern Dubai's spectacular development, as a summer retreat and hosted many of the discussions about the city's future, which in turn led to its dramatic economic explosion during the 1960s and 1970s. The two-storey building serves as a fetching reminder of earlier and simpler times: a sturdy coral-and-gypsum structure embellished with fine doors and window shutters made of solid teak, the whole of it enclosed in an old-fashioned Arabian garden complete with date palms and *falaj* (irrigation) channels. The *majlis* itself is on the upper floor, with cushions laid out around its edges and the walls and floor adorned with a modest selection of household objects, including an old-fashioned European radio and clock, rifles, oil lamps and coffee pots which in 1950s Dubai were considered all the luxury necessary, even in a residence of the ruling sheikh – a far cry from the seven-star amenities enjoyed by today's Emiratis.

BURJ AL ARAB AND JUMEIRAH BEACH HOTEL

The Burj al Arab and around

Some 18km south of the Creek, the suburb of Umm Suqeim marks the beginning of Dubai's spectacular modern beachside developments, announced with a flourish by three of Dubai's most famous landmarks: the Madinat Jumeirah complex, the roller-coaster-like *Jumeirah Beach Hotel*, and the iconic sail-shaped Burj al Arab hotel. There are further attractions at the thrills-and-spills Wild Wadi water park and at Ski Dubai, the Middle East's first ski slope, while more sedentary pleasures can be found at the vast Mall of the Emirates, next to Ski Dubai, of whose snowy pistes it offers superbly surreal views. Close to the Mall of the Emirates on the far side of Sheikh Zayed Road, the industrial area of Al Quoz provides an unlikely home to a number of Dubai's leading art galleries (see p.127).

The Burj al Arab

Off Jumeirah Rd, Umm Suqeim • Access for non-guests only possible with a reservation (see box below) • ⓦ burj-al-arab.com

Rising majestically from its own man-made island just off the coast of Umm Suqeim is the peerless **Burj al Arab** ("Tower of the Arabs"), one of the world's most luxurious hotels and de facto symbol of the city. Commissioned by Dubai's ruler, Sheikh Mohammed, the aim of the Burj al Arab was simple: to serve as a global icon which would put Dubai on the international map. Money was no object. The total cost of the hotel was perhaps as much as US$2 billion, and it's been estimated that even if every room in it remains full for the next hundred years, the Burj still won't pay back its original investment.

As a modern icon, however, the Burj is unmatched. Although not much more than a decade old, the building's instantly recognizable outline has already established itself as a global symbol of Dubai to rival the Eiffel Tower, Big Ben and the Sydney Opera House. Even the top-floor helipad has acquired celebrity status: André Agassi and Roger Federer once famously played tennis on it, while Tiger Woods used it as a makeshift driving range, punting shots into the sea (before ringing room service for more balls), and more recently it was turned into an impromptu green for Rory McIlroy to practise his bunker shots on.

The Burj is home to the world's first so-called **seven-star hotel**, an expression coined by a visiting journalist to emphasize the unique levels of style and luxury offered within (officially, of course, such a category doesn't exist). Staying here is a very expensive pleasure (see p.98), and even just visiting presents certain financial and practical challenges (see box below). Fortunately the building's magnificent exterior can be enjoyed for free from numerous vantage points nearby.

The building

Designed to echo the shape of a dhow's sail, the Burj al Arab forms a kind of maritime counterpart to the adjacent *Jumeirah Beach Hotel*'s "breaking wave" (see p.79). Its sail-like shape offers a contemporary tribute to Dubai's historic seafaring traditions, enhanced (as is its very exclusive aura) by its location on a specially reclaimed island some 300m offshore. The building was constructed between 1993 and 1999 by UK engineering and architectural firm W.S. Atkins under lead designer Tom Wright. The statistics alone are impressive. At 321m, the Burj is the third tallest dedicated hotel in the world. The spire-like superstructure alone, incredibly, is taller than the entire *Jumeirah Beach Hotel*, while the atrium (180m) is capacious enough to swallow up the entire Statue of Liberty – or, for that matter, the 38-storey Dubai World Trade Centre (see p.64).

The sheer scale of the Burj is overwhelming, and only really appreciated in the flesh, since photographs of the building, perhaps inevitably, always seem to diminish it to the size of an expensive toy. The Burj's scale is tempered by its extraordinary grace and the

---

VISITING THE BURJ AL ARAB

Non-guests are only allowed into the Burj with a prior **reservation** at one of the hotel's bars, cafés or restaurants (call ☎04 301 7600 or email ✉BAArestaurants@jumeirah.com). The cheapest option is to come for a cocktail at the 27th-floor **Skyview Bar** (see p.121; minimum spend 250dh/person), perhaps the best way of getting a good look at the hotel without going bankrupt. Alternatively, a visit for one of the Burj's sumptuous afternoon teas (285–450dh) in either the *Skyview Bar* or at the *Sahn Eddar* **atrium lounge** is another possibility. Moving up the scale, the Burj boasts two of the city's most spectacular (and pricey) **restaurants**: *Al Muntaha* and *Al Mahara* (see p.114 & p.113), and there are also two cheaper but significantly less appealing buffet restaurants: the Arabian-style *Al Iwan* or the slighty nicer pan-Asian *Junsui* (lunch/dinner buffets 360/410dh at both) – although you'd be better off taking afternoon tea or a drink. If you want to go the whole hog, try the novel "**Culinary Flight**" (lunch/dinner 800/1000dh) comprising drinks at the *Skyview Bar* followed by a four-course meal, with each course served in a different restaurant, rounded off with dessert at *Sahn Eddar*.

sinuous simplicity of its basic design, broken only by the celebrated cantilevered helipad and (on the building's sea-facing side) the projecting strut housing *Al Muntaha* ("The Highest") restaurant and the *Skyview Bar*. The hotel's shore-facing side mainly comprises a huge sheet of white Teflon-coated fibreglass cloth – a symbolic sail which is spectacularly illuminated from within by night, turning the entire building into a magically glowing beacon. Less universally admired is the building's rear elevation, in the shape of a huge cross, a feature that caused considerable controversy among Muslims at the time of construction, though it's only visible from the sea, and is almost never photographed.

Most of the **interior** is actually hollow, comprising an enormous atrium vibrantly coloured in great swathes of red, blue, green and gold. The original design comprised a far more restrained composition of whites and soft blues, but was significantly altered at the insistence of Sheikh Mohammed, who called in interior designer Khuan Chew (responsible for the colourful lobby at the adjacent *Jumeirah Beach Hotel*) to jazz things up. The contrast with the classically simple exterior could hardly be greater, and the atrium and public areas look like something between a Vegas casino and a James Bond

6

movie set, the casual extravagance of it all encapsulated by enormous fish tanks flanking the entrance staircase which are so deep that cleaners have to put on diving suits to scrub them out (a performance you can witness daily 2–4pm). For many visitors, the whole thing is simply a classic example of Middle Eastern bling gone mad (that's not gold paint on the walls, incidentally, but genuine 22ct gold leaf). Still, there's something undeniably impressive about both the sheer size of the thing and Chew's slightly psychedelic decor, with huge expanses of vibrant primary colour and endless balconied floors rising far overhead, supported by massive bulbous golden piers – like a "modern-day pirate galleon full of treasure", as Wright himself neatly described it.

6

Jumeirah Beach Hotel

Jumeirah Rd, Umm Suqeim · ⓦ bit.ly/JBHhotel · Bus #8, #88 or X28

On the beach right next to the Burj sits the second of the area's landmark buildings, the huge **Jumeirah Beach Hotel**, or "JBH" as it's often abbreviated. Designed to resemble an enormous breaking wave (although it looks more like an enormous roller coaster), and rising to a height of over 100m, the hotel was considered the most spectacular and luxurious in the city when it opened in 1997, although it has since been overtaken on both counts. It remains a fine sight, however, especially when seen from a distance in combination with the Burj al Arab, against whose slender sail it appears (with a little imagination) to be about to crash.

Wild Wadi

Off Jumeirah Rd, Umm Suqeim · Daily: March–May, Sept & Oct 10am–7pm; June–Aug 10am–8pm; Nov–Feb 10am–6pm · 220dh, children under 1.1m 175dh; locker and towel rental 50dh extra · ⓣ 04 348 4444, ⓦ wildwadi.com · Bus #8, #88 or X28

Directly behind the JBH, the massively popular **Wild Wadi** water park offers a variety of attractions to suit everyone from small kids to physically fit adrenaline junkies. The park is modelled on a Sinbad-inspired fantasy tropical lagoon, with cascading waterfalls, whitewater rapids, hanging bridges and big piles of rocks. Get oriented with a circuit of the Whitewater Wadi (MasterBlaster) ride, which runs around the edge of the park, during which you're squirted on powerful jets of water up and down eleven long, twisting slides before being catapulted down the darkened Tunnel of Doom. Dedicated thrill-seekers should try the Wipeout and Riptide Flowriders, simulating powerful surfing waves, and the park's stellar attraction, the **Jumeirah Sceirah**, the tallest and fastest speed slide outside North America, during which you're likely to hit around 80kph and experience temporary weightlessness. There are also less demanding attractions such as gentle tube-rides down Lazy River, family-oriented water games in Juha's Dhow and Lagoon and the chance to bob up and down in the big simulated waves of Breaker's Bay. Many people make a day of it, and you can buy food and drinks inside the park using money stored on an ingenious waterproof wristband.

Madinat Jumeirah

Al Sufouh Rd, Al Sufouh · ⓦ madinatjumeirah.com · Bus #8, #88 or X28

Just south of the Burj al Arab lies the huge **Madinat Jumeirah**, a vast mass of faux-Moorish-style buildings rising high above the coastal highway. Opened in 2005, the Madinat is one of Dubai's most spectacular modern developments: a self-contained miniature "Arabian" city comprising a vast sprawl of sand-coloured buildings topped by an extraordinary quantity of wind towers (best viewed from the entrance to the *Al Qasr* hotel), the whole thing arranged around a sequence of meandering waterways along which visitors are chauffeured in replica abras. The complex is home to a trio of ultra-luxurious five-star hotels (see p.99), the labyrinthine **Souk Madinat Jumeirah** bazaar (see p.136), a vast spread of restaurants and bars (see p.114 & p.121), and one of the city's best spas (see p.97).

6

There's an undeniable whiff of Disneyland about the Madinat, admittedly. The vision, according to the developers, was "to re-create life as it used to be for residents along Dubai Creek, complete with waterways, abras, wind towers and a bustling souk", although in truth Madinat Jumeirah bears about as much relation to old Dubai as Big Ben does to your average grandfather clock. Even so, the sheer scale of the place, with its relentlessly picturesque array of wind towers, wood-framed souks and palm-fringed waterways, is strangely compelling, and a perfect example of the kind of thing – mixing unbridled extravagance with a significant dose of sugar-coated kitsch – which Dubai seems to do so well. The Madinat also offers some of the most eye-boggling views in Dubai, with the futuristic outlines of the Burj al Arab surreally framed between medieval-looking wind towers and Moorish arcading. The fact that the fake olde-worlde city is actually newer than the ultramodern Burj is, by Dubai's standards, exactly what one would expect.

The obvious place from which to explore the complex is the Souk Madinat Jumeirah, though it's well worth investigating some of the superb restaurants and bars in the *Al Qasr* and *Mina A'Salam* hotels, several of which offer superlative views over the Madinat itself, the Burj al Arab and coastline. Thirty-minute **abra cruises** around the Madinat's waterways depart from the kiosk outside *Left Bank* bar-restaurant on the waterfront (75dh per person, kids 40dh).

Mall of the Emirates

Interchange 4, Sheikh Zayed Rd · Daily 10am–10pm (Thurs–Sat until midnight) · ⓦ malloftheemirates.com · Mall of the Emirates metro

The second largest mall in Dubai (outdone only by the Dubai Mall), the swanky **Mall of the Emirates** is one of the most popular in the city, packed with some five hundred shops and crowds of locals and tourists alike. Centred around a huge, glass-roofed central atrium, the mall is spread over three levels, crisscrossed by escalators and little wrought-iron bridges, and topped by the pink, five-star *Kempinski Hotel*. For dedicated shopaholics it's arguably the best place in Dubai to splash some cash (see p.134) – and there's also the added bonus of surreal views of the snow-covered slopes of Ski Dubai through huge glass walls at the western end of the mall, or from one of the various restaurants and bars overlooking the slopes, such as *Après* (see p.113).

Ski Dubai

Mall of the Emirates, Interchange 4, Sheikh Zayed Rd · Daily: Sun–Wed 10am–11pm, Thurs 10am–midnight, Fri 9am–midnight, Sat 9am–11pm · 2hr ski slope session adult 180dh, children 150dh; ski slope day-pass 300/275dh; snow park 130/120dh; lessons from 220/190dh for 90min; prices include clothing, boots and equipment for both slope and snowpark, but not hats and gloves · ☎ 800-FUN, ⓦ skidxb.com · Mall of the Emirates metro

Attached to the Mall of the Emirates, the huge indoor ski resort of **Ski Dubai** is unquestionably one of the city's weirder ideas. The idea of a huge indoor snow-covered ski slope (the first in the Middle East) complete with regular snowfall is strange enough amid the sultry heat of the Gulf – but the sight of robed Emiratis skiing, snowboarding or just chucking snowballs at one another adds a decidedly surreal touch to the already unlikely proceedings. If a peek is all you're after, you can take in the whole spectacle for free from the viewing areas at the attached Mall of the Emirates.

The complex contains the world's largest indoor snow park, comprising a huge 3000 square metres of snow-covered faux-Alpine mountainside, complete with chairlift. Accredited skiers and snowboarders (you'll need to undergo a brief personal assessment to prove you possess the necessary basic skills to use the main slope) can use the five runs of varying height, steepness and difficulty, ranging from a beginners' track through to the world's first indoor black run, as well as a "freestyle zone" for show-off winter sports aficionados. There's also a Snow School ski academy for beginners and improvers, as well as a twin-track bobsled ride, a snowball-throwing gallery, snow cavern and adventure trail, plus tobogganing and snowman-building opportunities.

ATLANTIS

The Palm Jumeirah and Dubai Marina

Nowhere is the scale of Dubai's explosive growth as staggeringly obvious as in the far south of the city, home to the vast Palm Jumeirah artificial island and Dubai Marina development – evidence of the emirate's magical ability to turn sand into skyscrapers and raise entire new city suburbs up out of the waves. Ten years ago the district was the largest building site on the planet – at one point it was estimated that Dubai was home to a quarter of the world's total number of construction cranes. Now the building crews have gone, leaving a brand-new city and the world's largest man-made island in their wake, with a forest of densely packed skyscrapers lined up around the glitzy marina itself and the fronds of the Palm spreading out into the waters beyond.

The Palm Jumeirah

Access either via monorail (see p.84) or by taxi from Nakheel metro (if available)

Lying off the coast around 5km south of the Burj al Arab, **The Palm Jumeirah** is far and away the largest example of modern Dubai's desire not just to master its unpromising natural environment but to transform it entirely. Billed as the "Eighth Wonder of the World" and stretching 4km out into the waters of the Arabian Gulf, the Palm is currently the world's largest man-made island, and has doubled the length of the Dubai coastline at a total cost of over US$12 billion – although even this grandiose feat is only the first in a series of four artificial islands currently under development (see box, p.84).

As its name suggests, the Palm Jumeirah is designed in the shape of a palm tree, with a central "trunk" and a series of sixteen radiating "fronds", the whole enclosed in an 11km-long breakwater, or "crescent", lined with a string of huge resorts. The design has the merit of providing an elegantly stylized homage to the city's desert environment while also maximizing the amount of oceanfront space in relation to the amount of land reclaimed (as Jim Krane puts it in *Dubai: The Story of the World's Fastest City*: "It was Dubai at its most cunning. Since seafront properties are the most valuable, why not build a development that has nothing but seafront?").

Construction work began in 2001, with the first apartments opening in 2006, and the island's landmark **Atlantis** resort (see p.84) opening to enormous fanfare in 2008, although as of early 2013 several of the landmark hotels ringing the Crescent were still either under construction or yet to open, including the vast Yemeni-style *Kingdom of Sheba* resort, modelled after the mud-brick skyscrapers of Sana'a, and the Mughal-style *Taj Exotica*.

Despite the size and ambition of the development, however, the Palm feels disappointingly botched (the "Eighth Blunder of the World", as local wags put it). The palm-shaped layout remains largely invisible at ground level – although it looks terrific from a plane – and the architecture is deeply undistinguished, with a string of featureless high-rises lining the main trunk road and endless rows of densely packed Legoland villas strung out along the waterside "fronds". The developer, Nakheel, was allegedly forced to almost double the number of villas on the island to cover spiralling construction costs, resulting in the overcrowded suburban crush you see today – much to the chagrin of those who had bought properties off-plan at launch, only to move in and discover that they were virtually living in their neighbours' kitchens. Only towards the far end of the island does the Palm acquire a modest quotient of drama, as the main trunk road dips through a tunnel before emerging in front of the vast *Atlantis* resort – although by then, one feels, it's probably too late.

NEW DUBAI: FAILURE TO LAUNCH

Dubai Marina and the Palm Jumeirah were at the epicentre of the accelerating megalomania which engulfed Dubai developers before the credit crunch brought the emirate back to its financial senses – resulting in the cancellation or indefinite postponement of a string of widely publicized world-breaking initiatives, most of which now seem unlikely ever to be realized. Headline schemes included a project to build the world's first luxury **underwater hotel** (the "ten-star" Hydropolis), which never managed to get off the seabed, while plans to redevelop the retired **QE2** cruise liner as a floating hotel off Palm Jumeirah have also been scuppered (the legendary cruiser currently languishes in Port Rashid, its future still undecided). **The Universe** archipelago (see box, p.84) has been another casualty of Dubai's reduced circumstances, as has the futuristic **Trump Tower**, a grandiose high-rise hotel planned but now abandoned by the US entrepreneur, which was meant to provide the Palm Jumeirah with one of its two key landmarks. Even more extravagant were plans for the **Nakheel Tower**, a kilometre-high colossus which would have smashed the current record for the world's tallest building but which was finally cancelled in 2009, although its name, if nothing else, lives on at Nakheel Tower and Harbour metro station – a sad memento of vanished ambitions.

THE PALM JUMEIRAH AND DUBAI MARINA

■ DRINKING
101 Dining Lounge and Bar	3
Bar 44	7
Barasti Bar	4
C Club	2
Rooftop Bar	5
Siddharta Lounge	7
Voda Bar	2
West Beach Bistro & Sports Lounge	6

■ NIGHTLIFE
Arabian Courtyard	5
Dubai Media City Amphitheatre	8
Al Hakawati	9
Kasbar	5
The Music Hall	2
Nasimi Beach	1
N'dulge	1

■ ACCOMMODATION
Amwaj Rotana	10
Arjaan by Rotana Dubai Media City	16
Atlantis	1
Grosvenor House	15
Hilton Dubai Jumeirah Resort	7
Jumeirah Zabeel Saray	4
Kempinski	3
Le Méridien Mina Seyahi	12
Le Royal Méridien Beach Resort and Spa	11
Oasis Beach Tower	14
One&Only Royal Mirage	5
One&Only The Palm	8
Ritz-Carlton	2
Rixos	9
Sheraton Jumeirah Beach	6
The Westin Dubai	13

■ EATING
Amala	2
Automatic	8
BiCE	3
Buddha Bar	10
Dôme	14
Eauzone	9
Frankie's	7
Indego by Vineet	10
Japengo	14
Nina	9
Le Pain Quotidien	6
Al Qaherah 1940	11
Rhodes Mezzanine	10
Rhodes Twenty10	4
Ronda Locatelli	1
Shakespeare & Co	12
Tagine	9
Vôi	2
Zaatar w Zeit	5/13/14

● SHOPS
Borders	1/2
The Camel Company	2
Carrefour	1
Ginger & Lace	2
Ibn Battuta Mall	2
Al Jaber Gallery	1
Marina Mall	1
Mumbai Se	1

Atlantis

Kingdom of Sheba

Palm Atlantis Monorail Station

Aquaventure, Dolphin Bay

Kempinski

PALM JUMEIRAH

Taj Exotica

Jumeirah Zabeel Saray

ARABIAN GULF

One&Only The Palm

Skydive Dubai

Sheraton Jumeirah Beach

Hilton Dubai Jumeirah Resort

THE WALK

Ritz-Carlton

Le Royal Méridien Beach Resort

Dubai International Marine Club

Le Méridien Mina Seyahi

The Westin Dubai

One&Only Royal Mirage

Gateway Monorail Station

KNOWLEDGE VILLAGE

Jebel Ali & Abu Dhabi

JUMEIRAH BEACH RESIDENCE

AL SUFOUH ROAD

Grosvenor House

Princess Tower

Infinity Tower

Elite Residence

DUBAI MEDIA CITY

AL SUFOUH ROAD

Arjaan by Rotana Dubai Media City

DUBAI INTERNET CITY

Marina Mall

MARINA WALK

DUBAI MARINA

Dubai Media City Amphitheatre

Hard Rock Café

Jumeirah Lake Towers

SHEIKH ZAYED ROAD

Dubai Marina

SHEIKH ZAYED ROAD

INTERCHANGE NO. 5

Nakheel

SHEIKH ZAYED ROAD

Al Kazim Towers

Nakheel Harbour & Tower

Almas Tower

JUMEIRAH LAKES TOWERS

Emirates Golf Club

THE GREENS

Dubai Internet City (metro)

EMIRATES HILLS

0   500
metres

Montgomerie Golf Club

The Palm Jumeirah Monorail

2–3 trains per hour from around 10am to 10pm • 15dh one way, 25dh return

The best way to see the Palm is from the **Palm Jumeirah Monorail**, whose driverless trains shuttle along an elevated track between *Atlantis* and Gateway station on the mainland, taking around ten minutes to complete the trip – a fine ride offering sweeping views over the Palm and the long chain of high-rises behind. Unfortunately, the monorail is a bit of a white elephant since it doesn't connect with the Dubai metro or anywhere else useful, and Gateway station itself is in a hopeless location hemmed in by busy roads, and usually without a taxi in sight. In addition, the two intermediate stations between *Atlantis* and Gateway – Trump Tower and Palm Mall – are not yet open and show no signs of opening any time soon, which further reduces the trains' usefulness.

Atlantis

Crescent Rd • ☏ 04 426 0000, ⊛ atlantisthepalm.com

At the furthest end of the Palm, sitting in solitary splendour on the oceanfront Crescent, the vast **Atlantis** resort is the island's major landmark and a focal point for the entire development. It's a near carbon copy of its sister establishment, the *Atlantis Paradise Island* resort in the Bahamas: a blowsy pink colossus, undeniably huge, vaguely outlandish, and just a little bit camp ("like the tomb of Liberace," as the UK's *Sun* newspaper aptly put it). In fact it's probably the only one of Dubai's recent

7

DUBAI'S ARTIFICIAL ISLANDS

For a city-state with aspirations of taking over the world's tourism industry, Dubai has a serious lack of one thing: **coast**. In its natural state, the emirate boasts a mere 70km of shoreline, totally insufficient to service the needs of its rocketing number of beach-hungry tourists and residents.

Dubai's solution to its pressing lack of waterfront was characteristically bold: it decided to build some more. The Palm Jumeirah has already added 68km to the emirate's coastline, although this was just the first (and smallest) of four proposed offshore developments which were intended to create anything up to 500km of new waterfront. Two further palm-shaped islands – the **Palm Jebel Ali**, 20km further down the coast, and the gargantuan **Palm Deira**, right next to the old city centre – were also planned. Reclamation work on the former has apparently been complete since around 2008, although development of the island's infrastructure (slated to eventually house a quarter of a million people) has been on hold for several years, and shows little side of resuming. Work on Palm Deira is at a much earlier stage, and although significant amounts of land have already been reclaimed, it seems unlikely that much progress will be made in the foreseeable future.

The current status of the even more fanciful **The World** development is similarly uncertain. Lying around 5km off the coast (accessible by boat only, unlike the three palm developments, all of which are connected directly to the mainland), this complex of artificial islands has been constructed in the shape of an approximate map of the world (weirdly impressive when seen from the air). It was originally hoped that developers would buy up individual islands and create themed tourist developments, perhaps based on the "nationality" of the island they occupy, but although physical reclamation of the islands has been complete since around 2006, little development has yet occurred and most of the islands remain uninhabited dots of sand in the ocean – while 2011 saw persistent (though unsubstantiated) rumours that the entire archipelago had begun to sink back into the sea. The only way of currently seeing the islands is by visiting the **Royal Island Beach Club** (☏ 04 368 0900, ⊛ royalislandbeachclub.ae), opened in 2012 on the island of Lebanon and offering the first public access to any part of the archipelago. Visitors have the use of the club's restaurant, beach and swimming pool, while the island has also staged several Friday DJ club nights, aptly entitled "Stranded". At present, however, unless the club nights resume or you can get a group together, the cost of renting a boat to the island for a casual visit is likely to prove prohibitively expensive.

Finally, plans for a fifth and even more extravagant artificial archipelago, christened **The Universe** (with a design based on the solar system) were announced in 2008, but were put on hold soon afterwards and now seem highly unlikely ever to leave the drawing board.

mega-developments to really live up to the city's widespread reputation for tasteless extravagance and shameless bling – slightly ironic, given that it actually had nothing to do with the Dubai government, being the brainchild of Jewish South African billionaire Sol Kerzner. Like many of Dubai's newer landmarks it's best from a distance, especially after dark and from the mainland, when its vast illuminated outline looks like some kind of weird triumphal archway twinkling far out to sea.

Inside, the **hotel** itself is as satisfyingly over-the-top as one would hope, featuring all manner of gold columns, crystal chandeliers and random twinkly bits, not to mention Dale Chihuly's extraordinary sculptural installation in the lobby – a 10m-high blown-glass creation resembling a waterfall of deep-frozen spaghetti – and the spectacular viewing window into the vast Ambassador Lagoon (see below).

Aquaventure

Atlantis • 225dh, or 180dh for children under 1.2m (free to in-house guests), or 275/215dh adults/children including The Lost Chambers; locker rental an extra 50dh • ☎ 04 426 0000, ⓦ atlantisthepalm.com

Atlantis boasts a heap of in-house activities – but they come with a steep price tag. Best is the spectacular **Aquaventure** water park, which features an adrenaline-charged array of master-blasters, water-coasters, speedslides, inner-tube rides and power-jets. It's all centred on the dramatic "Ziggurat", where'll you'll find the park's headline Leap of Faith waterslide, 27.5m tall and 61m long, which catapults you at stomach-churning speed down into a transparent tunnel that runs through a lagoon full of sharks. There are also various gentler rivers and rapids, plus a children's play area, and you can also use the impressive stretch of adjacent private beach.

Dolphin Bay

Atlantis • Prices vary according to season: shallow-water "interactions" cost around 800dh, deep-water interactions (over-8s only) around 900dh; observer passes 300dh (only available to visitors accompanying those taking part in shallow- or deep-water interactions); tickets also include same-day admission to Aquaventure and the Atlantis private beach • ☎ 04 426 1030, ⓦ atlantisthepalm.com

There are further watery attractions at **Dolphin Bay**, next door to Aquaventure, which offers the chance to swim with the hotel's troupe of resident bottlenose dolphins. Choose between a child-friendly shallow-water interaction (30min), open to all ages, including non-swimmers, and allowing you to "connect to your dolphin through kisses, hugs and dancing"; and a deep-water interaction (30min; confident swimmers aged 8 and above only) in 3m-deep water, which includes a ride on your designated underwater chum's belly along with further opportunities to hug, kiss and dance. Exactly what the dolphins think of all this is not recorded.

The Lost Chambers

Atlantis • Daily 10am–11pm • 100dh; children aged 3–11 70dh; under-2s free • ☎ 04 426 0000, ⓦ atlantisthepalm.com

For a slice of pure historical hocus-pocus, head to **The Lost Chambers**, a sequence of halls and tunnels running through the hotel's vast underground aquarium, dotted with assorted "ruins". Hotel publicity and wide-eyed guides will attempt to convince you that these are the remains of the legendary city of Atlantis, which vanished (according to Plato) in the western Mediterranean around 10,000 BC, but which has now fortuitously turned up in the waters underneath Dubai's largest hotel. It's all nonsense, of course, and the real reason for visiting is to get a better look at the spectacular aquarium and its extraordinary array of 65,000-odd tropical fish and other marine creatures. Unfortunately, the po-faced cynicism with which this theme-park bunkum is presented is more or less guaranteed to insult the intelligence of anyone aged over five, while the racked-up admission price is a further turn-off.

If you're not staying at the hotel you can alternatively buy a ticket (30dh) to see the so-called **Ambassador Lagoon**, which is actually just that part of the aquarium visible from the hotel public areas, similar to – but a lot more expensive than – the one at the Dubai Mall (see p.69).

Dubai Marina

Dubai Marina or Jumeirah Lake Towers metros

A kilometre further south along the coastal road beyond the Palm Jumeirah turn-off, a vast phalanx of tightly packed high-rises signals the appearance of **Dubai Marina**, Dubai's brand-new city-within-a-city, built at lightning speed since 2005 and now very nearly finished. There's no real precedent anywhere in the world for urban development on this scale or at this speed, and the area's huge new residential developments and commercial and tourist facilities have already shifted the focus of the entire emirate decisively southwards, and may in time perhaps even eclipse the old city centre itself.

Like much of modern Dubai, the marina is a mishmash of the good, the bad and the downright ugly. Many of the high-rises are of minimal architectural distinction, and all are packed so closely together that the overall effect is of hyperactive urban development gone completely mad – the result of unregulated construction during the massive real-estate boom in Dubai, which coincided with the marina's creation. The whole area feels oddly piecemeal and under-planned, while the lack of pedestrian facilities (excepting the pleasant oceanfront promenade and **Marina Walk**) means that you're unlikely to see much more of it than can be glimpsed while speeding down Sheikh Zayed Road by car or metro. It's weirdly impressive, even so, especially by night, when darkness hides the worst examples of gimcrack design and the whole area lights up into a fabulous display of airy neon (or, if you prefer, a display of a high-rise ecological catastrophe waiting to happen).

7

Jumeirah Beach Residence and The Walk

Dubai Marina metro

Most of Dubai Marina's tourist development is focused on the string of luxurious **beachside hotels** which established themselves here when the coast was largely undeveloped, but now find themselves rather tragically hemmed in by densely packed high-rises on all sides. Much of the area is now dominated by the unlovely **Jumeirah Beach Residence** (JBR), the world's largest single-phase residential complex, comprising a 1.7km-long sprawl of forty high-rises with living space for ten thousand people. The development was widely touted as the latest thing in luxury beachside living when it was launched, although the massive apartment complexes actually look a bit like some kind of low-grade housing project out of Soviet Russia, their towers packed so closely together that you fancy flat-dwellers could open their windows and shake hands with people in neighbouring blocks.

The JBR's one redeeming feature is **The Walk**, an attractive promenade lined with a long straggle of boutiques, pizzerias, coffee shops, burger joints and fast-food outlets, which stretches along the seafront between the *Sheraton* and *Le Royal Méridien* hotels – always busy, and often rammed at weekends. It's one of the very few places south of the old city centre which actually encourages people to get out of their cars, and boasts a modicum of street life including, during the winter months, the pleasant **Covent Garden Market** (Wed & Thurs 5pm–midnight, Fri & Sat 10am–9pm; ⓦcoventgardenmarket.ae), with around fifty stalls selling clothes, jewellery and other

---

DUBAI: THE WORLD'S TALLEST CITY

Dubai is now officially the tallest city on the planet. At the time of writing the city was home to 23 of the world's 100 highest buildings. By comparison, traditional high-rise hotspots Hong Kong and Chicago muster just seven top-100 buildings apiece, while New York and Shanghai manage just four – the same as Abu Dhabi. The landmark example of Dubai's sky-high ambition is provided by the staggering Burj Khalifa (see p.66), the world's tallest building, while other high-rise icons include the Burj al Arab (see p.77) and the glittering Emirates Towers (see p.63), as well as less well-known buildings such as the twin towers of the recently opened *JW Marriott Marquis Dubai* (see p.70), the world's tallest hotel, and the Princess Tower (see opposite), soaring high above the Dubai Marina.

MARINA BEACHES

All Dubai's **beach hotels** allow non-guests to use their beaches, swimming pools and other facilities for a (usually hefty) fee – the best deal is usually at the *Sheraton* (weekdays at the Hilton are also cheap, although the beach and grounds are small compared to other places). Some places close to outsiders when occupancy levels rise above a certain percentage – it's always best to ring in advance to check the latest situation wherever you're planning to go, since individual hotel policies and charges change frequently. Given the wallet-emptying amounts of money involved, many people prefer to head to the stretch of **free beach** between the *Sheraton* and *Hilton* hotels, which has plenty of white sand to loll about on (see box, p.143). There are **watersports centres** at all the marina beach hotels, offering a wide range of activities including windsurfing, sailing, kayaking, waterskiing, wakeboarding and parasailing (but not jet-skiing, which the authorities have banned).

Hilton Dubai Jumeirah Resort ☎ 04 399 1111. Sun–Wed 85dh, Thurs–Sat 250dh; under-12s free.
Jumeirah Beach Hotel ☎ 04 301 0000. Daily 350dh; children 250dh.
Le Méridien Mina Seyahi ☎ 04 399 3333. Sun–Thurs 200dh, Fri & Sat 300dh (children 125dh/175dh).
Le Royal Meridien ☎ 04 399 5555; 350dh, children under 12 100dh; prices may rise at weekends.

One&Only Royal Mirage ☎ 04 399 9999; advance reservations required. Daily 250dh.
Ritz-Carlton ☎ 04 399 4000; call in advance to check availablility. A painfully expensive 500dh, children 300dh.
Sheraton Jumeirah Beach ☎ 04 399 5533. Sun–Thurs 100dh, children 60dh; Fri & Sat 180dh/100dh.
Westin ☎ 04 399 4141. Sun–Thurs 200dh, Fri & Sat 300dh (children 125dh/175dh).

7

collectibles by local and expat craftsmen, designers and artists. The **beach** itself comprises a fine wide swathe of white sand.

Marina Walk
Marina or Jumeirah Lake Towers metros

The **marina** itself (apparently inspired by the Concord Pacific Place development along False Creek in Vancouver) is actually a man-made sea inlet, lined with luxury yachts and fancy speedboats, which snakes inland behind the JBR, running parallel with the coast for around 1.5km. Encircling the water is the attractive pedestrianized promenade known as **Marina Walk**. The section between the Marina Mall and Infinity Tower (see below) is now one of the city's most enjoyable after-dark destinations, lined with a long straggle of waterfront cafés and restaurants including a large number of Middle Eastern joints, with classic Egyptian and Lebanese tunes warbling out into the night, accompanied by vast clouds of shisha smoke – offering an incongruous flavour of downtown Cairo or Beirut amid the thrusting marina high-rises. Various kiosks around Marina Walk offer a mix of expensive boat charters alongside much cheaper dhow cruises for those who want to take to the water.

Presiding over the northern sea inlet into the marina is the quirky **Infinity Tower** (330m), designed by high-rise specialists Skidmore, Owings & Merrill, who were also responsible for the Burj Khalifa. The latest in Dubai's increasingly long list of iconic skyscrapers, the tower is instantly recognizable thanks to its distinctively twisted outline, which rotates through 90 degrees from base to summit – a bit like the famous Turning Tower in Malmö, Sweden.

Close by rise the city's most dramatic pod of super-tall skyscrapers, clustered tightly together. None is of any particular architectural distinction, although the impression of sheer height is impressive, and a guaranteed neck-stretcher. Tallest of the lot is the **Princess Tower** (414m), the second highest building in Dubai (almost precisely half the height of the 830m-tall Burj Khalifa) and the fourteenth highest in the world – and also the world's highest residential building. A couple of buildings along is the **Elite Residence** (380m), fifth tallest building in the city, with its distinctive, vaguely tent-shaped, summit.

Jumeirah Lakes Towers

Dubai Marina or Jumeirah Lake Towers metros

On the far side of the marina, inland from the metro and Sheikh Zayed Road, stretches the new suburb of **Jumeirah Lakes Towers** (commonly referred to as **JLT**), with a pleasant artificial lake. The lake is surrounded by a further cluster of rather humdrum high-rises, dominated by the vast **Almas Tower** (363m), the fifth tallest building in Dubai, and thirtieth tallest in the world.

Dubai Internet and Media cities

Nakheel metro

At the north end of Dubai Marina lie the twin business areas known as **Dubai Internet City** and **Dubai Media City**. These two districts were the first and most successful in a string of initiatives undertaken by the government to encourage foreign firms to set up offices in designated areas of the city under preferential commercial terms (including no income or corporate tax), obviating the bundles of red tape and restrictive local legislation which have traditionally stood in the way of foreign investment in the Gulf. The schemes were so successful that they have now been repeatedly copied in Dubai (Studio City, Sports City, Maritime City and Healthcare City among others) and in neighbouring countries. There's not much really to see here, though travelling down the coastal road you'll notice a number of large signs advertising the offices of international corporate heavyweights such as Microsoft, CNN and Reuters. Along Sheikh Zayed Road or the metro line, you also won't miss the soaring **Al Kazim Towers** (on the north side of Internet City just south of Dubai Internet City station) – a pair of quirky skyscrapers styled after New York's iconic Chrysler Building.

Ibn Battuta Mall

Between interchanges 5 and 6 (exits 25 and 27), Sheikh Zayed Rd • Daily 10am–10pm (Thurs–Sat until midnight) • Ⓦ ibnbattutamall .com • Ibn Battuta metro

Situated way down along Sheikh Zayed Road south of the marina, the outlandish, mile-long **Ibn Battuta Mall** is worth the trip out to the furthest reaches of the city suburbs to sample what is undoubtedly Dubai's wackiest shopping experience (which is

---

DUBAILAND

Occupying a huge swathe of land some 10km inland from the marina, the vast new **Dubailand** development (Ⓦ dubailand.ae) has become the major symbol of Dubai's overreaching ambition – and ongoing financial difficulties. Dubailand was originally slated (according to plans announced at launch in 2003) to become the planet's largest and most spectacular tourist development, with an extraordinary mix of theme parks and sporting and leisure facilities covering a staggering 280 square kilometres – twice the size of the Walt Disney World Resort in Florida. Major attractions were to have included a massive water park and snowdome; the Great Dubai Wheel, the Gulf's answer to the London Eye (although, naturally, quite a lot bigger); the Restless Planet dinosaur theme park featuring over a hundred animatronic dinosaurs; and the Falcon City of Wonders, comprising full-scale replicas of the Seven Wonders of the World. Other mega-projects within Dubailand were to have included the Mall of Arabia (the world's largest) and the Bawadi development, with over thirty hotels including – it goes almost without saying – the world's largest hotel, *Asia-Asia* (6500 rooms), plus reams of other leisure and residential facilities.

Despite all the hubris, parts of the complex did actually manage to get built before the credit crunch hit town, including the Dubai Outlet Mall, Global Village (see p.27), Dubai Autodrome and Dubai Sports City (see p.139), complete with international cricket stadium and The Els Club golf course. Unfortunately, despite all the publicity, the remainder of the development now appears to be stalled – most likely for good – so that it now seems unlikely that any of Dubailand's more ambitious attractions will ever succeed in seeing the light of day.

saying something). The mall is themed in six different sections after some of the countries – Egypt, Andalusia, Tunisia, Persia, India and China – visited by the famous Arab traveller Ibn Battuta, with all the architectural kitsch and caprice you'd expect. Highlights include a life-size elephant complete with mechanical mahout (rider), a twilit Tunisian village and a full-size Chinese junk, while the lavishness of some of the decoration would seem more appropriate on a Rajput palace or a Persian grand mosque than a motorway mall. As so often in Dubai, the underlying concept may be naff, but it's carried through with such extravagance, and on such a scale, that it's difficult not to be at least slightly impressed – or appalled. In addition, the 1.6km walk from one end of the elongated mall to the other is the most pleasant stroll you can have in Dubai's pedestrian-hating suburbs, especially in the heat of summer.

7

JUMEIRAH ZABEEL SARAY HOTEL

Accommodation

Dubai has a vast range of accommodation, much of it aimed squarely at big spenders, though there's also a decent selection of mid-range places; travellers on a tight budget will struggle to find suitable accommodation. At the top end of the market, the city has some of the most stunning hotels on the planet, from the futuristic Burj al Arab to traditional Arabian-themed palaces such as *Al Qasr* and the *One&Only Royal Mirage*. When it comes to creature comforts, all Dubai's top hotels do outrageous luxury as standard, with sumptuous suites, indulgent spa treatments, spectacular bars and gorgeous private beaches. The size and style of the very best places makes them virtually tourist attractions in their own right – self-contained islands of indulgence in which it's possible to spend day after day without ever feeling the need to leave.

Many of the top hotels are spread out along the beach in **Umm Suqeim** and **Dubai Marina** and around **the Palm**, although the overall shortage of oceanfront accommodation means these places tend to get booked solid way in advance, especially during the winter months (even in the stifling summer months, occupancy levels remain high). There are also several superb top-end places dotted around the city centre, along **Sheikh Zayed Road** and around **Downtown Dubai**.

There are a vast number of **mid-range** options scattered across the city, although virtually all establishments in this price range tend towards the functional and characterless, providing comfortable lodgings but not much else. There's no real **budget accommodation** in Dubai, and you won't find a double room anywhere for much less than about 250dh (US$70), or a single for much under 200dh (US$55). The good news is that stringent government regulations and inspections mean standards are reliable even at the cheapest hotels – all are scrupulously clean and fairly well maintained, and come with en-suite bathroom, plenty of hot water, satellite TV and fridge. **Internet** access (either wi-fi or via cable, or both) is general available in all except the cheapest hotels, although may be charged for separately, sometimes at extortionate rates.

All hotels are graded by the government according to a **star-rating** system comparable to that used in other countries worldwide, starting at one star and rising to five-star-deluxe, while the city is also home to the world's first "seven-star" hotel, as the Burj al Arab is often described – although not, it must be said, by the hotel itself.

BUR DUBAI

Central Bur Dubai is, along with Deira, where you'll find pretty much all the city's **budget** accommodation (although places in Bur Dubai are generally very slightly more expensive than over the water). When booking into a place it's worth looking out for in-house nightclubs, which can make some of the district's cheaper hotels unbearably noisy. More upmarket places are strung out along Khalid bin al Waleed Road, though the majority are fairly uninspiring, with a couple of honourable exceptions.

Ambassador Al Falah St ☎04 393 9444, ⓦastamb .com; Al Ghubaiba metro; map p.38. Claiming to be the oldest hotel in the city (opened 1968), this old-fashioned three-star is still a reasonable place to stay, despites its age. Rooms are functional but well maintained, while facilities include pricey wi-fi (10dh/hr), a swimming pool, a couple

8

ROOM RATES

Hotels in all price ranges chop and change their **room rates** constantly according to the time of year and demand, so a place may be brilliant value one week, and a rip-off the next. The rates given in our reviews are only a very rough guide to average prices; actual costs may sometimes be significantly lower or higher, with fluctuations of up to 100 percent at the same property quite common. Prices usually (but not always) depend on the **season**. In general, they're highest during the cool winter months from November to February (especially during the Dubai Shopping Festival) and cheapest in high summer (June to August), when rates at some places can tumble by thirty percent or more. **Taxes** (a ten percent service charge and a ten percent municipality tax) are sometimes included in the quoted price, but not always, so check when booking or you might find yourself suddenly having to cough up an extra twenty percent.

The best room rates at the big hotel chains (particularly more business-oriented places) tend to be available on the relevant hotels' own **websites**, although it's always worth having a look to see if there are cheaper deals available at places like Expedia, Agoda.com, Asiarooms.com and Hotels.com. For cheaper deals at the big beach resorts your best bet may be to book a traditional **package** (including flights) from a high-street or online travel agent.

All the prices given in the reviews below are for the **cheapest double room in high season** (excluding Christmas and New Year), inclusive of all taxes. Note that relatively few hotels have **single rooms**, and (except in some budget places in Deira and Bur Dubai) solo travellers are usually charged the full two-person rate when staying in a double room (minus any charges for breakfast or other included meals).

of in-house restaurants (Indian and international) and the cut-price English-style *George & Dragon* pub (see p.118). B&B **450dh**

★ **Arabian Courtyard** Al Fahidi St ☎ 04 351 9111, ⓦ arabiancourtyard.com; Al Fahidi metro; map p.38. In a brilliantly central location opposite the Dubai Museum, this attractive four-star is a distinct cut above the other mid-range places in Bur Dubai – and usually excellent value too. Decor features a nice mix of modern and Arabian styles, including attractive wood-furnished rooms, while facilities include a jacuzzi, a small gym, health club and spa – though the pool is disappointingly tiny. There's also a couple of passable in-house restaurants (Indian and Asian) plus the convivial *Sherlock Holmes* pub (see p.118). **650dh**

Barjeel Heritage Guest House Shindagha ☎ 04 393 8700, ⓦ barjeelguesthouse.com; Al Ghubaiba metro; map p.38. Located between Al Ghubaiba metro station and Sheikh Saeed al Maktoum House, this newly opened heritage guesthouse occupies a rather grand old historic building in Shindagha. Rooms are arranged around a beautiful internal courtyard and attractively furnished in traditional Arabian style. **850dh**

BurJuman Arjaan Sheikh Khalifa bin Zayed St ⓦ rotana.com/arjaanhotelapartments; map p.38. Slick, modern apartment-hotel in a smart high-rise directly behind the BurJuman centre, offering a range of spacious suites with kitchen, balcony and living area – usually at very competitive rates. **775dh**

Dallas Hotel Al Nahda St ☎ 04 351 1223, ⓦ dallashotel -dubai.com; Al Ghubaiba or Al Fahidi metro; map p.38. Reliable two-star cheapie, with neat little rooms and a modest in-house café, but no bars or nightclubs, so it's all reasonably peaceful. **250dh**

Dubai Nova Al Fahidi St ☎ 04 355 9000, ⓦ dubai novahotel.com; Al Fahidi metro; map p.38. Well-run modern hotel in a very central location, with comfortable rooms and extremely attentive service. **250dh**

Four Points Sheraton Khalid bin al Waleed Rd ☎ 04 397 7444, ⓦ fourpoints.com/burdubai; Al Fahidi metro; map p.38. One of the classiest hotels in Bur Dubai, this understated but very comfortable four-star has nicely furnished rooms in simple international style and good facilities including a gym, (smallish) swimming pool, the excellent *Antique Bazaar* restaurant (see p.105) and the cosy *Viceroy Bar* (see p.118). Rates are usually surprisingly good value given the quality. **600dh**

New Penninsula Hotel Al Raffa St ☎ 04 393 9111; Al Ghubaiba metro; map p.38. This slightly dog-eared old hotel is usually one of the cheapest places in town. Rooms, set around a cool white atrium, are old-fashioned but cosy and reasonably well maintained, although noise from in-house Indian clubs may be a problem on lower floors. **300dh**

Orient Guest House Bastakiya ☎ 04 353 4448, ⓦ orientguesthouse.com; Al Fahidi metro; map p.38. Attractive heritage hotel (albeit not quite as atmospheric as the nearby *XVA*), occupying an old Bastakiya house arranged around a pair of pretty little courtyards. There are eleven rooms, attractively decorated with old wooden furniture and four-poster beds – choose between the smallish Heritage Rooms or the slightly pricier but considerably more spacious Mumtaz Rooms. Guests have free use of the pool and gym at the *Arabian Courtyard* hotel just over the road. Free wi-fi. B&B **700dh**

Royal Ascot Hotel & Ascot Hotel Khalid bin al Waleed Rd ☎ 04 355 8500, ⓦ royalascothotel-dubai.com; Al Fahidi metro; map p.38. The swanky faux-Georgian-style *Royal Ascot* is one of the classiest places in Bur Dubai, with plush and decidedly chintzy rooms. Alternatively there are a few plainer and slightly cheaper rooms in the older *Ascot* hotel next door. Facilities comprise a couple of decent in-house restaurants, including the *Yakitori-Tei* restaurant (see p.106), plus pool, spa, gym and the attached *Velvet Underground* club (see p.125). *Ascot* **600dh**, *Royal Ascot* **750dh**

★ **Time Palace Hotel** Just off Al Fahidi St ☎ 04 353 2111, ⓦ time-palace.com; Al Ghubaiba metro; map p.38. The most consistently reliable and best-value

---

HOTEL APARTMENTS

A good alternative in Dubai to a conventional hotel is to book into one of the city's myriad **hotel apartments**. These can often provide significantly better value than hotels, assuming you don't mind doing without some of the usual hotel facilities (although some apartments do have a few amenities, which might include a pool and/or a basic café/restaurant).

Most of the city's **budget** hotel apartments are in Bur Dubai – in fact the entire city block south of the BurJuman centre is pretty much entirely taken up with them. The main operator is Golden Sands (ⓦ goldensandsdubai.com; studios from around 350dh), which has about ten huge apartment blocks scattered across the area. Other operators offering similar places include Al Faris (ⓦ alfarisdubai.com), Savoy (ⓦ savoydubai.com), Winchester (ⓦ winchest.com), Xclusive (ⓦ xclusivehotels.ae) and Flora (ⓦ florahospitality.com). More **upmarket** options include the *BurJuman Arjaan* (see above), *Arjaan by Rotana Dubai Media City* (see p.100), and *Oasis Beach Tower* (see p.101).

TOP 5 HOTELS FOR ARABIAN AMBIENCE

Ahmedia Heritage Guest House
See below
One&Only Royal Mirage See p.101
The Palace See p.98
Al Qasr See p.99
XVA See below

Vasantan Al Nahda St (around the back of the Astoria Hotel) ☎04 393 8006, ⓦthevasantabhavan.com /Vasantam.html; Al Ghubaiba metro; map p.38. This simple hotel is one of the cheapest options in Bur Dubai – old-fashioned and a bit ramshackle compared to other nearby places, but perfectly comfy and peaceful, and often has vacancies when other places are full. Also home to the excellent *Vasanta Bhavan* restaurant (see p.106). **250dh**

★ **XVA** Bastakiya ☎04 353 5383, ⓦxvahotel.com; Al Fahidi metro; map p.38. Dubai's most memorable heritage hotel, this atmospheric place has nine guest rooms tucked away around the back of a fine old Bastakiya house, as well as a lovely café (see p.106). Rooms are on the small side but brimming with character, featuring Arabian furnishings, slatted windows and four-poster beds, plus captivating views over the surrounding wind towers. B&B **650dh**

budget hotel in Bur Dubai, with spacious and very well-maintained rooms in an unbeatable location just up from the main entrance to the Textile Souk, though it's surprisingly quiet given how central it is – only the local mosque disturbs the peace. Tends to get booked up, so reserve well in advance. **250dh**

DEIRA

Deira has easily the city's biggest selection of **budget** hotels, with literally dozens of places around the Gold Souk and elsewhere, particularly along Sikkat al Khail Road, as well as plenty of mid-range options and a few top-end establishments located along the side of the Creek. And with the opening of the Metro Green Line it's now also a lot better connected with other parts of the city.

Ahmedia Heritage Guest House Old Baladiya Rd ☎04 225 0085, ⓦahmediaguesthouse.com; Al Ras metro; map p.49. Formerly the *Al Hijaz Motel*, this is a new addition to Dubai's modest collection of heritage hotels, owned by the same group as the *Orient Guest House* (see opposite). It has a very central but peaceful location right next to Al Ahmadiya School, with fifteen rooms attractively done up with traditional wooden furniture and four-poster beds; an extra 100dh gets you one of the bigger and more lavishly furnished Mumtaz rooms. Free wi-fi. B&B **600dh**

Carlton Tower Hotel Baniyas Rd ☎04 222 7111, ⓦcarltontower.net; Baniyas Square metro; map p.49. Pleasantly old-fashioned four-star, enjoying an excellent location right in the thick of the city. Rooms are comfortable, if dated; some boast fine Creek views though road noise can be slightly intrusive on lower floors. Facilities include a second-floor pool and health club, plus Russian and international restaurants. There's also a free shuttle to the public beach at either Jumeirah Beach Park or Al Mamzar Park. **600dh**

Florida Al Sabkha Rd ☎04 226 8888, ⓦflorahospitality .com; Baniyas Square metro; map p.49. Sister hotel to the *Florida International* just down the road, though slightly cheaper. Rooms (all with wi-fi; 30dh/day) are neatly refurbished and modern, and some have bird's-eye street views – although they're well soundproofed, so remain pleasantly quiet. **350dh**

Florida International Opposite Al Sabkha Bus Station, Al Sabkha Rd ☎04 224 7777, ⓦflorahospitality .com; Baniyas Square metro; map p.49. One of Deira's more upmarket budget hotels, right in the heart of the

downtown action. Rooms (all with wi-fi; 30dh/day) are nicely furnished for the price, while decent soundproofing means they're reasonably quiet despite the location on a busy main road (although there are also rooms around the back if you prefer). **450dh**

Gold Plaza Guesthouse Souk Deira St ☎04 225 0240, ⓔgoldplaza@asteco.com; Al Ras metro; map p.49. Long-standing cheapie next door to the Gold Souk entrance, popular with visiting African traders and other mercantile types – you may find the corridors occasionally stacked up with piles of merchandise waiting to be shipped abroad. Rooms (of varying sizes and prices) are basic but among the cheapest in town, and there are also a few ultra-cheap singles (160dh), though you'll probably need to book in advance. **230dh**

Hilton Dubai Creek Baniyas Rd ☎04 227 1111, ⓦhilton.com/dubai; Al Rigga metro; map p.49. Deira's smartest hotel, the Carlos Ott-designed *Hilton* is as cool as it gets in this part of town, from the chrome-clad public areas through to the soothing wood-panelled corridors with blue floor lights. Rooms are well equipped and stylishly decorated in minimalist whites and creams; most also have grand Creek views, framed by floor-to-ceiling windows. There's also a health club, a small rooftop pool and the excellent *Table 9* restaurant (see p.107). **1100dh**

Hyatt Regency Corniche Rd ☎04 209 1234, ⓦdubai .regency.hyatt.com; Palm Deira metro; map p.49. Standing in monolithic splendour on the northern side of Deira, this gargantuan five-star could easily pass for a medium-sized nuclear power station from a distance, but is a lot more appealing close up. The spacious rooms are

8

attractively decorated in pine-and-cream minimalist style and boast fine city and/or water views (those from the higher floors are spectacular). Facilities include an attractive spa and a good selection of in-house restaurants, and you're conveniently close to the Gold Souk and city centre. **1100dh**

Al Khayam Hotel Souk Deira St ✆04 226 4211, ✉khayamh@emirates.net.ae; Al Ras metro; map p.49. Friendly two-star with a mix of cosy and slightly chintzy "modern" doubles and a few "old" (slightly shabby) singles (180–200dh) and twins – all accessible via the world's smallest lift. There's also an attractive little first-floor café overlooking the street. **230dh**

La Paz Souk Deira St ✆04 226 8800, ✉lapazhtl @emirates.net.ae; Al Ras metro; map p.49. This "family hotel" (so no alcohol or disreputable ladies) is perhaps the quietest of the guesthouses clustered around the entrance to the Gold Souk. Rooms are a bit old-fashioned, but perfectly clean and comfortable, and rates are often among the cheapest in the city (including bargain singles at 180dh). **280dh**

Landmark Grand Al Rigga Rd ✆04 250 1111, ⊛landmarkhotels.net; Union metro; map p.49. This well-run four-star opposite Al Ghurair Mall is one of the best of the numerous mid-range hotels on this side of Deira – nothing terribly exciting, but offering comfortable modern rooms close to the city centre and metro at a reasonable price, plus a healthclub and rooftop pool. **550dh**

Landmark Hotel Baniyas Baniyas Square ✆04 228 6666, ⊛landmarkhotels.net; Baniyas Square metro; map p.49. Perhaps the best of several almost identikit options along the north side of Baniyas Square – and

usually full of Russian visitors, who flock to this part of town. It's a good option if you want a reasonably inexpensive hotel in the thick of Deira but don't fancy the real cheapies nearer the Gold Souk, with comfy modern rooms and facilities including a small rooftop pool, health club and a couple of restaurants. The *Landmark Plaza* hotel a few doors down is owned by the same group and very similar. **550dh**

Radisson Blu Dubai Deira Creek Baniyas Rd ✆04 222 7171, ⊛radissonblu.com/hotel-dubaideiracreek; Union metro; map p.49. The oldest five-star in the city, this *grande dame* of the Dubai hotel world still has plenty going for it: an extremely central location, a good spread of restaurants and a scenic position right on the Creek, of which all rooms have a view. The style is engagingly old-fashioned and European, with rather chintzy public areas and plush rooms (but small bathrooms) and a certain understated swankiness. There's also a pool and a good range of health and fitness facilities. Generally excellent value, and one of the cheapest of the Deira five-stars. **850dh**

Sheraton Dubai Creek Baniyas Rd ✆04 228 1111, ⊛sheraton.com/dubai; Union metro; map p.49. This old-fashioned five-star enjoys a scenic creekside setting, opulent public areas with lots of shiny white marble and an unusual wedge-shaped atrium dotted with palm trees. Roughly half the rooms have Creek views (the higher the better), though the decor is rather dated and dull, and bathrooms are small. Leisure facilities include a sauna, well-equipped gym and a small pool, plus good in-house restaurants (including *Ashiana*; see p.106), while rates are usually the cheapest of all the city-centre five-stars. **850dh**

THE INNER SUBURBS

There aren't many standout places to stay in the inner suburbs, although the area does boast Dubai's two finest city hotels – the opulent *Raffles* and the idyllic *Park Hyatt*.

Grand Hyatt Sheikh Rashid Rd, Oud Metha ✆04 317 1234, ⊛dubai.grand.hyatt.com; Dubai Healthcare City metro; map p.57. This colossus of a hotel (the second biggest in Dubai, with 674 rooms spread over sixteen floors) is grand in every sense – the vast atrium alone could easily swallow two or three smaller establishments and comes complete with fake tropical rainforest and the wooden hulls of four large boats poking out of the ceiling. Rooms are larger than average and have grand views through big picture windows, though the decor itself is uninspiring. The range of facilities is vast: four pools (including a nice indoor one with underwater music), spa, kids' club, gym and fourteen restaurants and bars. The only real drawback of the whole place is its middle-of-nowhere location, although it's conveniently close to the metro and major roads north and south. **1200dh**

Jumeirah Creekside Hotel Sheikh Rashid Rd,

Garhoud ✆04 230 8555, ⊛jumeirah.com; GGICO metro; map p.57. Sleek new five-star by the city's leading hotel chain – although it's not actually by the side of the Creek, whatever the name says. Rooms are nicely done up in funky reds and whites (with fine views from higher floors), and there are a pair of pools and a spa, plus access to various sports facilities at the attached Aviation Club, while rates include free entrance to Wild Wadi water park and the private Madinat Jumeirah beach, with free shuttle bus provided. **1000dh**

★ **Park Hyatt** Dubai Creek Golf and Yacht Club, Garhoud ✆04 602 1234, ⊛dubai.park.hyatt.com; Deira City Centre metro; map p.57. One of Dubai's accommodation gems, this alluring five-star occupies a beautiful complex of white-walled, blue-domed buildings in quasi-Moroccan style, surrounded by extensive grounds with plenty of palm trees – a beguiling mixture of golf and

TOP 5 HOTELS WITH CONTEMPORARY CHIC

The Address Downtown Dubai
See p.97
Fairmont See below
Grosvenor House See p.100
Raffles See below
Shangri-La See p.97

Gulf. Rooms (some with beautiful Creek views) are unusually large, with cool white and cream decor and spacious bathrooms. Facilities include a large pool and the superb Amara spa (see box, p.96), plus the innovative *Thai Kitchen* restaurant (see p.108) and attractive *The Terrace* (see p.119) marina-side bar. **1700dh**

★ **Raffles** Sheikh Rashid Rd, Oud Metha ☎ 04 324 8888, ⓦ raffles.com/dubai; Dubai Healthcare City metro; map p.57. Vying with the *Park Hyatt* for the title of Dubai's finest city-centre hotel, the spectacular new *Raffles* takes its cue from the Egyptian theme of the Wafi complex next door and pushes it to new levels of opulence. The hotel is designed in the form of an enormous postmodern pyramid, with a beautifully executed blend of Egyptian and Asian styling (the lobby, with huge columns covered in hieroglyphs and enormous hanging lanterns, is particularly dramatic). Rooms feature silky-smooth contemporary decor and fine city views, while facilities include a good selection of eating and drinking establishments plus the appealing Amrita spa. Outside there's a big pool and surprisingly extensive grounds complete with their own botanical garden, stuffed with some 130,000 plants. **1700dh**

SHEIKH ZAYED ROAD AND DOWNTOWN DUBAI

Sheikh Zayed Road is lined with a long sequence of mainly upmarket hotels aimed mainly at visiting businessmen, with superb views and classy facilities – although, of course, no beach. There are several places to stay dotted around the **Downtown Dubai** district, including a trio of new establishments tucked away in the chintzy "Old Town" development, and the flagship *Armani* hotel in the Burj Khalifa itself.

SHEIKH ZAYED ROAD

Dusit Thani Sheikh Zayed Rd ☎ 04 343 3333, ⓦ dusit .com; Financial Centre metro; map pp.64–65. This *wai*-shaped Sheikh Zayed Rd landmark (see p.66) is one of the nicest five-stars hereabouts. Thai-owned and styled, the whole place has a distinctive ambience which combines serene interior design and ultra-attentive service. Rooms are stylishly decorated in soothing creams and browns (and cleverly designed so that you can even watch TV from the bath), and there are all the usual upmarket facilities, including the excellent *Benjarong* restaurant (see p.110). Prices fluctuate, but it's generally good value compared to other places hereabouts. **1000dh**

Fairmont Sheikh Zayed Rd ☎ 04 332 5555, ⓦ fairmont .com; World Trade Centre metro; map pp.64–65. Designed to resemble an enormous wind tower, this Sheikh Zayed Rd landmark is instantly recognizable after dark thanks to its four luridly spotlit turrets. Inside, the hotel is one of the most stylish on the road, huddled around a soaring glass-and-steel atrium illuminated with multi-coloured splashes of changing light. Rooms are beautifully furnished, with soothing cream decor, huge TVs and all the usual mod cons, plus larger-than-average bathrooms. The whole of the ninth floor is given over to leisure facilities, including a sumptuous spa (see box, p.97) and sunset and sunrise pools on opposite corners of the building. **1500dh**

Four Points Sheraton Sheikh Zayed Rd ☎ 04 323 0333, ⓦ fourpoints.com/sheikhzayedroad; Financial Centre metro; map pp.64–65. This efficient modern business hotel lacks the facilities and panache of other places along the strip – although if you just want a place to

sleep it generally offers some of the cheaper rates along the road. Facilities include Moroccan and Italian in-house restaurants, a smallish rooftop pool with spectacular views, plus a gym and sauna. **1000dh**

H Hotel Sheikh Zayed Rd ☎ 04 501 8888, ⓦ h-hotel .com; World Trade Centre metro; map pp.64–65. Formerly the *Monarch Hotel*, this stylish modern five-star is a cut above most other places along Sheikh Zayed Rd, although slightly marooned at the far northern end of the strip. Suave contemporary designs are spiced up with discreet Arabian styling, the rooms are well equipped and there are some good places to eat and drink, including the super-cool *Okku* (see p.111). Competitively priced, and sometimes a real bargain during periods of low demand. **1250dh**

Ibis World Trade Centre Sheikh Zayed Rd ☎ 04 332 4444, ⓦ ibishotel.com; World Trade Centre metro; map pp.64–65. One of the modern city's best bargains during quiet periods. Rooms are small but comfortable, and the higher ones have nice views. In-house facilities are limited to the Italian *Cubo* restaurant and a pleasant bar, but guests can use the fitness centre and two pools at the adjacent *Novotel* for a small fee. Rates can fluctuate widely depending on whether there's a big event on in the attached World Trade Centre and can fall dramatically at weekends. **500dh**

Jumeirah Emirates Towers Sheikh Zayed Rd ☎ 04 330 0000, ⓦ jumeirahemiratestowers.com; Emirates Towers metro; map pp.64–65. Occupying the smaller of the two iconic Emirates Towers, this exclusive establishment is generally rated the top business hotel in the city, catering mainly to senior execs on very generous expense accounts. Rooms appear designed to calm the nerves of stressed-out CEOs, with muted colours and soothingly understated furnishings, and there's also a dedicated ladies' floor, plus a good-sized pool and health club, while the shops, restaurants and bars of the Emirates Boulevard mall are right on your doorstep. 1500dh

Al Murooj Rotana Financial Centre Rd ☎ 04 321 1111, ⓦ rotana.com; Financial Centre metro; map pp.64–65. In a handy location between Sheikh Zayed Rd and the Dubai Mall, this sprawling establishment feels more like a traditional resort than a business hotel. Outside, the extensive, attractively landscaped gardens are dotted with lively restaurants and bars, including the ever-popular *Double Decker* pub (see p.120). Inside there's plenty of contemporary style, with spacious and attractively furnished rooms (some with excellent Burj Khalifa views), plus a well-equipped health club and fitness centre. 1250dh

Novotel World Trade Centre Sheikh Zayed Rd ☎ 04 332 0000, ⓦ novotel.com; World Trade Centre metro; map pp.64–65. Tucked away at the back of the Dubai International Convention and Exhibition Centre, this business-oriented five-star is one of Novotel's more stylish offerings, from the chic minimalist foyer to the attractively designed rooms with cool cream and pine decor. Its direct connections to the World Trade Centre guarantee a steady flow of business visitors, but there's also a decent-sized pool, plus gym and spa and the enjoyable *Blue Bar* (see p.119). Rates vary hugely, sometimes falling as low as around 400dh. 700dh

Radisson Royal Sheikh Zayed Rd ☎ 04 308 0000, ⓦ radissonblu.com/royalhotel-dubai; World Trade Centre metro; map pp.64–65. Funky new hotel in the gleaming pair of skyscrapers (looking like a pair of enormous chisels) midway down the strip. It attracts a mainly business crowd, although comes with an above-average spread of leisure facilities, including a nice rooftop pool and bar, good dining options, a spa and the über-snooty *Mo*vida* nightclub – although you probably won't get into that unless you happen to be a crown prince, A-list movie star or mates with Paris Hilton. Rates vary wildly, but can sometimes be a real bargain. 900dh

Ritz-Carlton Dubai International Financial Centre ☎ 04 372 2222, ⓦ ritzcarlton.com; Emirates Towers

SPAS

Dubai has a gorgeous array of excellent spas, most of then in the city's various five-star **hotels**. A huge choice of treatments is on offer, from conventional facials, massages and beauty treatments through to everything from traditional Ayurvedic remedies to colour therapy rituals. All the following hotel spas are open to non-guests, though it's always best to reserve in advance. **Prices** are predictably steep: count on a minimum of around 250dh or more for a half-hour treatment, or 500dh for an hour.

Amara Park Hyatt Hotel (see p.94) ☎ 04 602 1660; Deira City Centre metro. One of the most idyllic spas in the city, with eight private treatment rooms in the hotel grounds, all with private walled garden and rain shower. Treatments are based around the "ancient healing philosophies of diamond, emerald, ruby and sapphire", featuring Thai, Swedish and Indian head massages, phyto-aromatic facials, marine-inspired scrubs and baths, aromatherapy, reflexology, ear candling and volcanic hot stone treatments. Taking an hour's treatment allows you all-day access to hotel's gorgeous pool. Daily 9am–10pm.

B/Attitude Tower 2, Grosvenor House Hotel (see p.100); Dubai Marina metro. This gorgeous new spa looks a bit like some kind of rather opulent Buddhist temple, with stunning Tibetan decor and a lovely hamman with five baths at a range of carefully controlled temperatures. Treatments take a holistic approach, aiming to nurture your chakras as much as your complexion and using a range of Tibetan, Thai, Ayurvedic and Arabian techniques. Daily 8am–10pm.

Caracalla Spa Le Royal Méridien Beach Resort and Spa (see p.101) ☎ 04 316 5322; Dubai Marina metro. Swanky Roman-themed spa specializing in Elemis-brand body treatments and Pevonia Botanica facials, including massages, reflexology and body wraps. Daily 9.30am–9pm.

Cleopatra's Wafi (see p.56) ☎ 04 324 0000, ⓦ cleopatrasspaandwellness.com; Dubai Healthcare City metro. This long-running favourite is relatively workaday compared to the opulent hotel spas, but considerably more affordable. Treatments include Elemis facials, a range of Thai, Balinese, Chinese and other massages, and fancy Royal Rituals including the signature "Cleopatra's Arabian Experience". Daily 9am–9pm.

Lime Spa Desert Palm (see p.102) ☎ 04 323 8888. Sumptuous Per Aquum spa in the chilled-out *Desert Palm* resort on the edge of the city. Treatments feature a range of Anne Semonin and Eve Lom products and personalized, holistic treatments like the Lime "Intuitive Massage", using a mix of Swedish, Thai, shiatsu, aromatherapy and Balinese massage techniques. Daily 9am–9pm.

metro; map pp.64–65. Swanky new five-star aimed at visitors to the adjacent DIFC – good for business, and not bad for pleasure either, if you don't mind the hefty price tag. The whole place is constructed on a palatial scale (especially compared to the space-poor skyscraper-hotels on Sheikh Zayed Rd), with unusually spacious rooms – beautifully kitted out with gorgeous pale yellow furnishings and all mod cons (including a mini-TV in your bathroom mirror) – and extensive facilities including indoor and outdoor pools, spa, gym and a good spread of restaurants. 1800dh

★ **Shangri-La** Sheikh Zayed Rd ☎04 343 8888, ⓦshangri-la.com; Financial Centre metro; map pp.64–65. The most stylish hotel on Sheikh Zayed Rd, the *Shangri-La* is pure contemporary class – a beguiling mix of Zen chic and Scandinavian cool. Rooms come with smooth pine finishes, beautiful artwork on the wall and mirrors everywhere, while leisure facilities include a spa, an unusually large and well-equipped gym, and one of the biggest pools in this part of town. There are also several excellent restaurants (see p.110 & p.111), plus the very chilled-out *iKandy* poolside bar (see p.120). 1500dh

Towers Rotana Sheikh Zayed Rd ☎04 343 8000, ⓦrotana.com; Financial Centre metro; map pp.64–65. This shiny four-star is usually one of the cheaper Shekih Zayed Rd options. It's a bit run-of-the-mill compared to other places in the area, but offers comfortable and nicely furnished rooms along with a decent range of leisure amenities including a pool, well-equipped gym, a couple of decent in-house restaurants and the ever-popular *Long's Bar* (see p.120). 900dh

DOWNTOWN DUBAI

The Address Downtown Dubai Sheikh Mohammed bin Rashid Boulevard (Emaar Boulevard) ☎04 436 8888, ⓦtheaddress.com; Burj Khalifa/Dubai Mall metro; map pp.64–65. Not to be confused with the nearby but considerably less impressive *The Address Dubai Mall* hotel, this OTT five-star occupies a huge high-rise directly opposite the Burj Khalifa. The interior is one of the city's most extravagant pieces of interior design, featuring lots of dark wood, moody lighting and huge quantities of dangling braided screens – it all looks a bit like some kind of weird, futuristic bordello. Facilities include a big range of

One&Only Spa and Oriental Hammam One&Only Royal Mirage (see p.101) ☎04 399 9999; Nakheel metro. Classy spa offering a range of wraps, scrubs, massages and facials (including special men's treatments). Alternatively, check out the picture-perfect Oriental Hammam, a marvellous little traditional steam bath with Arabian massages by experts from Morocco, Tunisia and Turkey, performed while you lie supine on a heated marble slab. Daily 9.30am–9pm.

Retreat Spa Tower 1, Grosvenor House Hotel (see p.100) ☎04 317 6761; Dubai Marina metro. Suave modern spa specializing in marine-based Phytomer products and treatments, including body wraps, sea holistic massages, and the Rasul skin ceremony using natural muds. Daily 8am–10pm.

Ritz-Carlton Spa Ritz-Carlton Hotel, Dubai Marina (see p.101) ☎04 318 6184; Dubai Marina metro. Upmarket hotel spa specializing in Balinese massages, Carita Paris facials, and fruity signature treatments ranging from wild berry body buff to raspberry-ripple hydrotherapy baths and Peruvian chocolate body scrubs. Daily 9am–8pm.

The Spa 9th floor, Fairmont Hotel (see p.95) ☎04 311 8800; World Trade Centre metro. Fancy, upmarket spa with Roman-style decor, separate male and female spas, hammam style steam rooms and a pair of pools outside on the fourth floor. Daily 9am–10pm.

The Spa at The Palace The Palace Hotel (see p.98) ☎04 428 7805; Burj Khalifa/Dubai Mall metro. Male and female spas, with opulent Moorish styling and a menu featuring unusual Arabian-inspired treatments, including the Oriental hammam scrub, the desert sand scrub (using desert sand and sea salt) and the award-winning Moroccan-inspired "One Desert Journey" sand scrub and massage. Daily 9am–10pm.

Talise Madinat Jumeirah (see p.79) ☎04 366 6818, ⓦtalise.jumeirah.com. Set in the beautiful grounds of the Madinat Jumeirah, Talise is more of a miniature health resort than a simple spa, with 26 villas-cum-treatment-rooms scattered around verdant gardens. The menu includes signature Sodashi spa treatments along with other wellness treatments and therapies ranging from yoga to cavitation, at above-average prices. Daily 10.15am–8pm.

Talise Ottoman Spa Jumeirah Zabeel Saray (see p.100) ☎04 453 0455. Claiming to be the largest spa in the Middle East, this is more like a self-contained health resort than a conventional spa, with gorgeous Ottoman styling throughout and 42 treatment rooms spread over two floors including garden pavilions for Thai massages, an indoor saltwater swimming pool and hot-stone seats – or try the combined snowbath and sauna to really work those pores. Daily 9am–9pm.

8

in-house eating and drinking options, including the signature *Hukama* Chinese restaurant and the spectacular *Neos* bar (see p.120) on the 63rd floor, and there's also a lavish spa, kids' club and a lovely infinity pool with superb views of the Burj Khalifa. **1800dh**

Armani Hotel Floors 5–8 & 38–39, Burj Khalifa ☎04 888 3888, ⓦarmanihotels.com; Burj Khalifa/Dubai Mall metro; map pp.64–65. Located in the iconic Burj Khalifa, this was the world's first Armani hotel when it opened in 2010 and is meant to be the ultimate in Dubaian cool (and has proved a big hit with label-conscious locals). The whole place is very much a shrine to Giorgio, kitted out in furnishings from his Casa Armani homeware range so that it all looks a bit like the world's biggest showhome (and with more branding than an Australian cattle ranch). If you like Armani's super-subdued minimalism you'll enjoy the hotel's soothing Zen decor, all muted whites, greys, browns and blacks, quietly but luxuriously finished with silk-covered walls and discreetly perfumed corridors – if you prefer more bling for your buck, this isn't the place to come. In addition, rooms are relatively low down the tower, so don't command the views you might hope for, while one drawback to staying in the Burj is that you can't actually see it. Facilities include a string of fine eating and drinking venues (see p.112 & p.124), a cool spa and pool. The entire hotel is non-smoking, apart from the dedicated cigar room. **2650dh**

Al Manzil Sheikh Mohammed bin Rashid Boulevard (Emaar Boulevard), Old Town ☎04 428 5888, ⓦalmanzilhotel.ae; Burj Khalifa/Dubai Mall metro; map pp.64–65. Stylish little modern hotel in the Downtown Dubai Old Town development, with an engaging mix of traditional Arabian styling and quirky contemporary touches – including walls made out of what looks like petrified vanilla and chocolate ice cream. Rooms are on the small side, although there's a decent spread of amenities including a reasonable-sized pool and gym, an attractive outdoor restaurant-cum-shisha café and the pleasant *Nezesaussi* sports-themed pub-restaurant. The nearby *Qamardeen* hotel (☎04 428 6888, ⓦqamardeenhotel.ae), run by the same company, is very similar. **1250dh**

The Palace Sheikh Mohammed bin Rashid Boulevard (Emaar Boulevard), Old Town ☎04 428 7888, ⓦtheaddress.com/en/hotel/the-palace-downtown-dubai; Burj Khalifa/Dubai Mall metro; map pp.64–65. One of the flagship properties of the vast Downtown Dubai development, this opulent, Arabian-themed "city-resort" offers a surreal contrast to the nearby Burj Khalifa. It's all beautifully done, with lavish, quasi-Moroccan styling and a perfect lakeside view of the Dubai Fountain and Burj (best enjoyed from the fine in-house *Thiptara* restaurant; see p.113), and there's also a superb spa (see p.97) and large lakeside pool. Right in the thick of the downtown action, although for real Arabian romance it comes a distant second best to beachside places like the *One&Only Royal Mirage* or *Al Qasr*. **1750dh**

JUMEIRAH

Dubai Marine Beach Resort Jumeirah Rd, near Jumeirah Mosque ☎04 346 1111, ⓦdxbmarine.com; map pp.72–73. This pocket-sized resort is more Sheikh Zayed Rd urban chic than bucket-and-spade beach resort. It's also the only five-star in Dubai where you can be on the beach but also within easy striking distance of the old city – although equally the central location means that facilities don't compare with places further south, with only a modest scrap of white-sand beach and the cranes of Port Rashid dominating the view. Accommodation is in a string of simple modern white villas dotted around lush gardens, while facilities include a couple of medium-sized pools and a spa. The resort's main selling point, however, is its lively collection of bars, restaurants and clubs including *Sho Cho* and *Boudoir* (see p.113, p.121 & p.124), which attract a steady stream of locals after dark when the whole place turns into a bit of a party palace. **1300dh**

THE BURJ AL ARAB AND AROUND

The suburb of **Umm Suqeim** is home to some of Dubai's most memorable beachfront hotels, including the world-famous Burj al Arab – though not surprisingly, none of them come cheap.

Burj al Arab ☎04 301 7777, ⓦburj-al-arab.com; map p.78. A stay in this staggering hotel (see p.77) is the ultimate Dubaian luxury. The "seven-star" facilities include fabulous split-level deluxe suites (the lowest category of accommodation – there are no ordinary rooms here), arrival in a chauffeur-driven Rolls and your own butler, while a paltry 80,000dh per night gets you the royal suite, complete with private elevator and cinema, rotating four-poster bed and your own Arabian *majlis*. Whatever form of suite you stay in there's pretty much every business and leisure facility you could imagine, including the superlative Assawan Spa, a handful of spectacular restaurants and bars (see pp.113–114 & p.121) and a fabulous stretch of beach. For unbridled luxury it all takes some beating, and offers the perfect playground for image-conscious wannabes, although the overwhelming atmosphere of super-heated opulence isn't necessarily conducive to a particularly peaceful or romantic stay compared to the less attention-grabbing (and considerably cheaper) beachside hotels further down the coast. **9700dh**

8

Dar al Masyaf Madinat Jumeirah ☎ 04 366 8888, ⓦ madinatjumeirah.com; map p.78. A more intimate and upmarket alternative to the Madinat Jumeirah's big two hotels, *Dar al Masyaf* consists of a chain of modest, low-rise private villas scattered around the edges of the Madinat complex within extensive, palm-studded gardens. Each villa contains a small number of rooms, sharing an exclusive pool and decorated in the deluxe Arabian manner of *Al Qasr* and *Mina A'Salam*, whose myriad facilities they share. **2800dh**

Ibis 2a St, near the Mall of the Emirates ☎ 04 382 3000, ⓦ ibishotel.com; Mall of the Emirates metro; map p.78. This cheery little no-frills hotel is usually the best bargain in southern Dubai, with superb-value rooms and a decent location on the south side of the Mall of the Emirates. There's another Ibis nearby, *Al Barsha* (☎ 04 399 6699), about 1.5km further south next to Sheikh Zayed Rd, which is often even cheaper, though the location is unappealing. **400dh**

★ **Jumeirah Beach Hotel** Jumeirah Rd ☎ 04 348 0000, ⓦ jumeirahbeachhotel.com; map p.78. The most luxurious and stylish place in town when it opened a fifteen years ago, this iconic hotel (see p.79) has come down in the world slightly since then, and now caters to a more lowbrow crowd of (mainly UK) families and couples. Facilities remain among the best in the city, including over twenty restaurants, several top nightspots (see p.121), seven pools, six tennis courts, a golf driving range and the Pavilion PADI diving centre (see p.139). It's particularly good for children, with the Sinbad kids' club, spacious grounds and a large and lovely stretch of beach with plenty of watersports available and jaw-dropping Burj views; guests also get unlimited access to the Wild Wadi water park next door. The hotel is

also home to the more upmarket and expensive *Beit al Bahar* (ⓦ beitalbahar.com): nineteen freestanding villas, set in lush gardens with beautiful Arabian decor and their own private plunge pools. **2400dh**

Mina A'Salam Madinat Jumeirah ☎ 04 366 8888, ⓦ madinatjumeirah.com; map p.78. Part of the stunning Madinat Jumeirah complex, *Mina A'Salam* ("Harbour of Peace") shares the Madinat's Arabian theming, with wind tower-topped buildings and quasi-Moroccan decorative touches, although the sheer size of the place lends it a faint package-resort atmosphere which sits incongruously with its refined styling. Rooms are beautifully furnished with traditional Arabian wooden furniture and fabrics, and the public areas are full of character. That said, the whole place can seem like a slightly watered-down version of the even more extravagant *Al Qasr* hotel on the opposite side of the Madinat, where rooms are often available at similar rates. Facilities include a nice-looking stretch of private beach, three pools, plus the forty-odd restaurants and bars (and myriad shops) of the Madinat complex outside. **3000dh**

Al Qasr Madinat Jumeirah ☎ 04 366 8888, ⓦ madinatjumeirah.com; map p.78. This extravagantly opulent Arabian-themed hotel looks like something out of a film set, from the statues of rearing horses and jaw-dropping views over the Madinat which greet you on arrival to the many-pillared foyer with cascading fountains and vast chandeliers inside. Rooms are similarly dramatic, with show-stopping views over the surrounding attractions, sumptuous Oriental decor and pretty much every luxury and mod con you can imagine. There's also a huge pool and all the facilities of the Madinat complex on your doorstep. **3200dh**

THE PALM JUMEIRAH AND DUBAI MARINA

Dubai Marina is where you'll find the majority of the city's big beachside resorts, lined up in a long row along the seafront. There's also a growing number of more business-oriented hotels slightly inland, like the suave *Grosvenor House*, wedged in amid the skyscrapers of the Marina proper. Even seven years after its official opening, the **Palm Jumeirah** remains very much a work in progress, with several large-scale resorts – including the *Royal Amwaj*, Rajasthani-style *Taj Exotica* and bizarre, faux-Yemeni *Kingdom of Sheba* still not yet open, although all three should come into service sometime in 2013–2014.

THE PALM JUMEIRAH

Atlantis ☎ 04 426 0000, ⓦ atlantisthepalm.com; map p.83. This vast mega-resort (see p.84) is the exact opposite of tasteful, but can't be beaten when it comes to in-house attractions, including a water park, dolphinarium, celebrity-chef restaurants, kicking bars and clubs, luxurious spa and vast swathes of sand. There are also excellent kids' facilities, making it a good place for a (pricey) family holiday, with everything you need under one very large roof, while staying here also gets you free or discounted admission to the otherwise expensive ream of on-site activities. It's not the most peaceful place in town, however, more suited to an up-tempo family holiday than a romantic break – the fact

that 3000-odd people work here, including more than 500 chefs serving over 15,000 meals a day should give you an idea of the scale of the place, while the public areas often feel like a major railway terminus in rush hour. **2000dh**

> **TOP 5 HOTELS BY THE BEACH**
>
> **Atlantis** See above
> **Jumeirah Beach Hotel** See above
> **Le Méridien Mina Seyahi** See p.100
> **Le Royal Méridien Beach Resort and Spa** See p.101
> **Sheraton Jumeirah Beach** See p.101

8

★ **Jumeirah Zabeel Saray** West Crescent ☎ 04 453 0000, ⊛ jumeirah.com; map p.83. Easily the most extravagant of the many hotels to have opened in Dubai in recent years, the *Zabeel Saray* looks relatively understated from outside compared to other places around the Palm but is a riot of quirky opulence within, looking like the brainchild of some slightly mad but very wealthy Bollywood film producer. Public areas and rooms are designed in lavish quasi-Ottoman style (you might recognize the lobby from *Mission: Impossible IV*), while the hotel's spectacular array of bars and restaurants (see p.114, p.121 & p.126) range through a whole encyclopedia of styles – fake Rajasthani palace, faux French chateau, burlesque music hall and sci-fi spaceship – all beautifully done, and good fun besides. Facilities include the vast Talisse Ottoman Spa (see box, p.97) and in-house cinema, while outside there are beautiful grounds, a gorgeous infinity pool and extensive beach (with kids' club). Rates vary wildly, but are often good value, and can sometimes fall to as little as 1200dh – an absolute snip. **2000dh**

Kempinski West Crescent ☎ 04 444 2000, ⊛ kempinski.com/en/dubai/palm-jumeirah/welcome; map p.83. Big new Palm resort-hotel, looking like a vast pink wedding cake with rather too much icing. The whole place in a monumental exercise in naff opulence, from the marbled public areas to the chintzy rooms, although the huge private beach, immense pool, watersports centre and kids' club are good for families in search of sun and sand – if not style. **2300dh**

One&Only The Palm West Crescent ☎ 04 440 1010, ⊛ thepalm.oneandonlyresorts.com; map p.83. A haven of intimate, understated luxury amid the ever-increasing string of bling sprouting up around the Palm – small, peaceful and very civilized (apart from the fearsome price tag, although special online offers can sometimes make rates less punishing). The style is quasi-Moorish, with hints of the Alhambra in Granada, and neat gardens lining a gorgeous pool, and there's also a fine spa and almost half a kilometre of private beach. A boat shuttle runs guests over to the mainland from the hotel's own marina, where you'll also find the attractive waterside *101* bar-restaurant (see p.121). **4200dh**

Rixos East Crescent ☎ 04 457 5555, ⊛ rixos.com; map p.83. In a fine position at the very southern tip of the East Crescent, facing the skyscrapers of the mainland, this sprawling five-star resort offers plenty of beach, sweeping views, and a good range of activities plus kids' club to keep families entertained, although at this price you might prefer to head for *Atlantis*. **2250dh**

DUBAI MARINA

Amwaj Rotana The Walk at Jumeirah Beach Residence ☎ 04 428 2000, ⊛ rotana.com/amwajrotana; map p.83. This slick, modern hotel is a real bargain compared to other nearby establishments – although it's set slightly away from the seafront, so you'll have to mix with the hoi polloi on the marina public beach over the road if you want to get onto the sand. In-house facilities include a good-sized pool and a couple of decent restaurants, while the stylish rooms come with impressive sea and Palm Jumeirah views from higher floors. **800dh**

Arjaan by Rotana Dubai Media City Al Sufouh Rd, Dubai Media City ☎ 04 436 0000, ⊛ rotana.com/arjaanhotelapartments; map p.83. Modern high-rise apartment-hotel opposite the *One&Only Royal Mirage* and towering above Al Sufouh Rd, offering competitively priced one- to three-bed apartments with small kitchenettes – and superb views from higher floors. **1000dh**

★ **Grosvenor House** Al Sufouh Rd ☎ 04 399 8888, ⊛ grosvenorhouse-dubai.com; Dubai Marina metro; map p.83. One of Dubai's smoothest hotels, set slightly away from the seafront in a pair of elegantly tapering skyscrapers (the new Tower 2 being a recent addition to the original hotel, located in Tower 1). The entire hotel is a model of contemporary cool, from the suave public areas right through to the elegantly furnished rooms, decorated in muted whites, creams and cottons, and with big picture windows afford sweeping views over the marina and coast. There's also a pool, two excellent spas (see box, pp.96–97), and one of the city's best selection of restaurants and bars (see p.115 & p.122), while guests also have free use of the beach and facilities at the nearby *Royal Méridien*. **1440dh**

Hilton Dubai Jumeirah Resort The Walk at Jumeirah Beach Residence ☎ 04 399 1111, ⊛ hilton.com/dubai; Jumeirah Lake Towers metro; map p.83. This glitzy Hilton boasts lots of shiny metal and an air of cosmopolitan chic – it's more of a city-slicker's beach bolthole than family seaside resort, and the place tends to attract a glam young local crowd. Rooms are bright and cheerfully decorated, but facilities are relatively limited compared to nearby places, although you do get a spa, health club, watersports centre, kids' club and the excellent *BiCE* Italian restaurant (see p.115). Outside there's a medium-sized pool and lovely terraced gardens running down to the sea, though the hotel beach is on the small side, and the sunloungers are rather packed in. **1240dh**

Le Méridien Mina Seyahi Al Sufouh Rd ☎ 04 399 3333, ⊛ lemeridien-minaseyahi.com; Nakheel metro; map p.83. This venerable old five-star has just emerged

8

from lengthy and long-overdue renovations, and is now looking better than it probably ever did, with nicely updated rooms and public areas – although the main draw remains the hotel's superb grounds and big swathe of beach, one of the largest of any of the marina hotels. The kicking *Barasti* beachside bar (see p.122) is also worth a visit. 1800dh

Le Royal Méridien Beach Resort and Spa The Walk at Jumeirah Beach Residence ☎04 399 5555, ⓦleroyalmeridien-dubai.com; Dubai Marina metro; map p.83. This large and slightly overblown five-star is comfortable enough, lacking the style of some other places along the beach although compensating with its extensive grounds and beach, complete with three larger-than-average pools – excellent for families. Facilities include the ostentatious, Roman-themed Caracalla Spa (see box, p.96), a smart gym, tennis and squash courts, a kids' club and a good number of restaurants, including the excellent *Rhodes Twenty10* (see p.115). 1800dh

Oasis Beach Tower The Walk at Jumeirah Beach Residence ☎04 399 4444, ⓦoasisbeachtower.com; Dubai Marina metro; map p.83. Shiny high-rise apartment hotel right in the thick of the Marina action with assorted two- to four-bed apartments, all with spacious living and dining areas and fully equipped kitchens. There's also a decent second-floor pool, and the Marina public beach is just over the road. 1800dh

★ **One&Only Royal Mirage** Al Sufouh Rd ☎04 399 9999, ⓦroyalmirage.oneandonlyresorts.com; Nakheel metro; map p.83. The most romantic hotel in town, this dreamy resort is the perfect *One Thousand and One Nights* fantasy made flesh, with a superb sequence of quasi-Moroccan-style buildings scattered amid extensive, palm-filled grounds. It's particularly stunning at night, when the labyrinthine sequence of beautifully sculpted and tiled courtyards, hallways and corridors – and the thousands of palms – are illuminated. The whole complex is actually three hotels in one: *The Palace*, the *Arabian Court*, and the *Residence & Spa*, each a little bit more sumptuous (and expensive) than the last. Rooms are attractively appointed, with Arabian decor, reproduction antique wooden furniture and colourful rugs, while facilities include a 1km stretch of

private beach, four pools, the delectable Oriental hammam-style spa (see box, p.97) and some of the best restaurants and bars in town (see pp.115–116 & p.122) – all at sometimes surprisingly good rates. 2200dh

Ritz-Carlton The Walk at Jumeirah Beach Residence ☎04 399 4000, ⓦritzcarlton.com; Dubai Marina metro; map p.83. Set in a low-rise, Tuscan-style ochre building this very stylish establishment is one of the classiest and most eye-wateringly expensive in the city, and makes for a refreshing change from the in-your-face high-rises surrounding it. Rooms are spacious, with slightly chintzy European-style decor, while public areas have the air of a luxurious old country house, especially in the sumptuous lobby lounge. There's also a big and very quiet stretch of private beach and gardens, while children are surprisingly well catered for, with a big kids' club, covered outdoor play area and their own pool. Other facilities include tennis and squash courts, an attractive spa (see box, p.97) and one of the smartest gyms in town. 3000dh

Sheraton Jumeirah Beach The Walk at Jumeirah Beach Residence ☎04 399 5533, ⓦsheraton.com /jumeirahbeach; Jumeirah Lake Towers metro; map p.83. The area's most low-key five-star, beginning to look like a bit of an ancient relic now compared to the thrusting high-rises engulfing it on all sides, but still with a certain old-fashioned charm. It's particularly good for families, with extensive palm-studded gardens and beach, while kids get their own pool area, shaded playground and the Pirates day-care club. There's also a range of watersports available, plus squash courts, gym, sauna and steam room. Usually a bit cheaper than the nearby competition, but still no bargain. 1440dh

The Westin Dubai Al Sufouh Rd ☎04 399 3333, ⓦwestinminaseyahi.com; Nakheel metro; map p.83. It's difficult to love this pompous Neoclassical eyesore (with wind towers) – a strong contender for the fiercely contested prize of Dubai's ugliest hotel – although the huge and attractive grounds, enormous pool and attractive spa partly compensate, while the rooms themselves are surprisingly tasteful compared to the exterior. Significantly overpriced compared to the competition at current rates, however. 2250dh

8

AROUND DUBAI

If you want to get away from the city proper, a couple of resorts offer visitors the chance to enjoy the emirate's unspoilt desert hinterlands. As well as those listed below we also cover hotels in **Abu Dhabi** (see p.175), **Al Ain** (see p.158), on the **east coast** (see p.162) and in **Hatta** (see p.164).

Bab Al Shams Desert Resort and Spa ☎04 381 3231, ⓦmeydanhotels.com/babalshams; map p.145. Hidden out in the desert a 45min drive from the airport, this gorgeous resort occupies a wonderfully atmospheric replica Arabian fort and offers a complete change of pace and style from the city five-stars, with desert camel- and

horse riding or falconry displays the order of the day, rather than lounging on the beach. Rooms are decorated in traditional Gulf style, with rustic ochre walls and Bedouin-style fabrics, while facilities include a magnificent infinity pool and a good selection of restaurants, including *Al Hadheerah* – Dubai's first traditional Arabian open-air desert restaurant, complete with belly dancers and live band. 1300dh

Desert Palm ☎04 323 8888, ⓦdesertpalm .peraquum.com; map p.145. On the edge of Dubai, around a 20min drive from the city centre, the *Desert Palm* is a pleasantly laidback suburban bolthole, surrounded by polo fields, with distant views of the skyscrapers along Sheikh Zayed Rd. The suites and villas (there are no rooms) are beautifully designed and equipped with fancy mod cons like pre-loaded iPods and espresso machines; villas come with private pool and indoor and outdoor rain showers. Facilities include the excellent *Rare* steakhouse and the superb in-house Lime Spa (see box, p.96). 1050dh

Kempinski Hotel Ajman ☎06 714 5555, ⓦkempinski .com/en/ajman/hotel-ajman/welcome; map p.145. Very chilled-out beachside resort hotel in the sleepy emirate of Ajman, a 1hr drive north of Dubai, but feeling a million miles away from the big city. The hotel's main attraction is its blissful strip of beach and attractive gardens, backed up by the usual five-star amenities including a spa and fitness centre – very nice, although a bit overpriced at current rates. 1300dh

Al Maha Desert Resort and Spa Dubai Desert Conservation Reserve, Al Ain Rd ☎04 832 9900, ⓦal-maha.com; map p.145. Some 60km from Dubai, this very exclusive, very expensive resort occupies a picture-perfect setting amid the pristine Dubai Desert Conservation Reserve (see p.159) – gazelles and rare Arabian oryx can often been seen wandering through the grounds. The resort is styled like a Bedouin encampment, with stunning views of the surrounding dunes and accommodation in tented suites with handcrafted furnishings and artefacts, plus small private pools. Activities include falconry, camel treks, horseriding, archery, 4WD desert drives and guided nature walks; or you can just relax in the resort's serene spa. Full board including two desert activities per day around 6500dh

8

PIERCHIC

Eating

It's almost impossible not to eat well in Dubai, whatever your budget. If you've got cash to burn, the city offers a superb spread of top-quality restaurants (including a growing number of places run under the auspices of various international celebrity chefs), with gourmet food served up in some of its most magical locations. There are also plenty of good cheap eats to be had too, from cheap and cheerful curry houses to the plentiful shwarma stands and kebab cafés. Dubai is a particularly fine place to sample the many different types of Middle Eastern (aka "Lebanese") cuisine, with restaurants across the city offering varying takes on the classic dishes of the region, usually featuring a big range of classic mezze and succulent grilled meats, sometimes with a good selection of shisha (waterpipes) on the side.

9

As you'd expect given Dubai's cosmopolitan make-up, a huge variety of other international cuisines are also represented. Italian, Iranian, Thai, Japanese and Chinese are all popular, and **Indian** food is particularly good, with inexpensive but often surprisingly excellent curry houses scattered all over the city centre catering to Dubai's large subcontinental population.

We've specifically advised making **reservations** at places that tend to get booked solid some time (possibly weeks) in advance, though it's worth booking at any upscale restaurant just to be on the safe side. Note that only hotel restaurants and a very small number of mall-based establishments have **alcohol** licences (see box, p.118). You won't find booze at independent restaurants and cafés.

CITYWIDE

A few international franchises have established a presence in Dubai, but a refreshing number of the city's major chains are local businesses which have made good, and are now spreading citywide.

Automatic Branches in the Al Khaleej Centre, Al Mankhool Rd, Bur Dubai (map p.38); on Sheikh Zayed Rd, just north of the Rose Rayhaan hotel (map pp.64–65); Jumeirah Rd, just north of the zoo (map pp.72–73); and on the upper level of The Walk at Jumeirah Beach Residence in Dubai Marina, roughly opposite the Ritz-Carlton hotel (map p.83). Hearty Lebanese food in a string of comfortable and fuss-free outlets around the city, well prepared and very reasonably priced, with a decent range of mezze (from 12dh) plus grills and kebabs (from 28dh) and some more expensive seafood options. Daily 10am–midnight.

Dôme Branches at BurJuman, Bur Dubai (map p.38); DIFC (map pp.64–65); Dubai Mall (map pp.64–65); Jumaira Plaza, Jumeirah Rd, opposite the Village Mall (map pp.72–73); Souk Madinat Jumeirah (map p.78); and Ibn Battuta Mall (map p.83); ⓦ domecafes.ae. Citywide café chain (originally from Australia) – nothing fancy, but a reliable source of good coffee and cheap grub including pasta, pizzas, soups, salads, burgers and a few more substantial international mains. Also very competitively priced daily specials, with mains for around 27–42dh. Daily 8am–10pm.

Japengo Branches at the Palm Strip Mall, Jumeirah Rd (map pp.72–73); plus at BurJuman (map p.38); Wafi (map p.57); Festival City (map p.57); Dubai Mall (map pp.64–65); Souk Madinat Jumeirah (map p.78); Mall of the Emirates (map p.78); and Ibn Battuta Mall (map p.83); ⓦ binhendi.com/v2/japengo.htm. One of the most shamelessly eclectic menus in town, based around a longish list of Japanese standards (sushi, sashimi, maki) spliced together with Middle Eastern mezze, Southeast Asian stir-fries, Italian pizzas and pastas, plus sandwiches, salads and a range of Japengo "classics" (meaning anything from taquitos to fish and chips). The end result of this culinary free-for-all is much tastier and more consistent than you might expect, and prices are reasonable too (most mains 50–80dh). Now has branches across the city, although the original branch on Jumeirah Rd is still the funkiest and most appealing. Daily 8.30am–1am.

Le Pain Quotidien Branches at Dubai Mall (map pp.64–65); Mall of the Emirates (map p.78); and The Walk at Jumeirah Beach Residence (map p.83); ⓦ lepainquotidien.ae. Major Belgian chain, with attractively rustic wooden decor and authentic Flemish fare, including good tartines (open-faced sandwiches; 30–45dh) and mains (45–60dh) like *waterzooi*, Flemish beef stew and lamb cassoulet – or try the novel lentil soup in a bowl made out of bread. Just a shame there's no beer – although the tangy home-made lemonade almost compensates. Daily 7.30am–11pm.

More Branches at the Festival Centre (map p.57); DIFC (map pp.64–65); Dubai Mall (map pp.64–65); Mall of Emirates (map p.78); and the Gold and Diamond Park

---

FRIDAY BRUNCH

The **Dubai Friday brunch** is a highlight of the weekly social calendar among the city's Western expat community – a bit like the British Sunday lunch, only with a lot more booze. Restaurants across the city open for brunch from around noon, often with all-you-can-eat (and sometimes drink) offers which attract crowds of partying expats letting off steam at the end of the long working week. Check *Time Out Dubai* (ⓦ timeoutdubai.com) for the latest offers.

Good **places for brunch** include *Spectrum on One* (see p.111), *Left Bank* at Souk al Bahar (see p.120), *Thai Kitchen* (see p.108) and *Zuma* (see p.112), although arguably the city's most spectacular brunch is held at *Al Qasr* hotel (see p.99) – so big that guests are given a map of the various food stations to help them navigate the incredible culinary spread provided.

9

> **DHOW DINNER CRUISES**
>
> The city's popular dhow dinner cruises are covered in Basics (see p.25)

(map p.78); ⓦmorecafe.biz. This citywide chain of attractive European-style cafés is a good place either for breakfast, lunch, a light dinner or just a cup of superior coffee, with moreish sandwiches and home-made pasta (45–60dh) plus an eclectic selection of international mains (55–80dh). The branch at the Dubai Mall, with a big terrace overlooking the Dubai Fountain and Burj Khalifa, is particularly nice. Free wi-fi. Daily 8am–11pm.

Shakespeare & Co Branches on the south side of Al Attar Business Tower, 37th St, off Sheikh Zayed Rd, roughly opposite the Ritz-Carlton hotel (map pp.64–65); Souk al Bahar (map pp.64–65); Dubai Mall (map pp.64–65); Village Mall, Jumeirah Rd (map pp.72–73); Marina Mall (map p.83); ⓦshakespeareandco.ae. Ever-expanding café-cum-coffee-shop chain, characterized by its distinctively chintzy decor – a kind of high-camp Victoriana, usually with cherubs. Food includes a wide selection of soups, salads,

saj, sandwiches and crêpes (from 35dh), plus more substantial mains. The original branch at Al Attar Business Tower has relatively restrained decor, and a nice shisha tent; the newest outlet, at the Marina Mall, is contrastingly pink and flouncy. Daily 7am–1am.

Wafi Gourmet Branches at Wafi (two outlets; map p.57); Festival Centre (map p.57); and Dubai Mall (map pp.64–65); ⓦwafigourmet.com. Dubai-wide offshoot of the original and much-loved deli-cum-café at Wafi (see p.56), serving up a big range of hot and cold mezze (from 27dh), grills (from 55dh) plus a good selection of more expensive seafood mains. Daily 10am–10pm.

Zaatar w Zeit Branches on Sheikh Zayed Rd, just north of the Shangri-La hotel (map pp.64–65); Dubai Mall (map pp.64–65); The Walk at Jumeirah Beach Residence (map p.83); Marina Walk in the Marina (map p.83); Ibn Battuta Mall (map p.83); ⓦzaatarwzeit .net. Cheap fast food with a Lebanese twist is the focus here, with various kinds of *manakish* (a kind of Middle Eastern-style pizza served with thyme, yoghurt and cheese) and other Lebanese-style snacks, plus wraps, salads and pizzas. Mains 15–35dh. Daily 24hr.

BUR DUBAI

Bur Dubai is one of the best places in the city for cheap curry (rivalled only by Karama), while there are also a number of attractive Arabian-style cafés and Lebanese restaurants, although not much in the way of other cuisines apart from a couple of lame pizzerias and a few fast-food outlets. If you want a wider spread of international cuisine, your best bet is to either head over the Creek to Deira or make for the food court at the BurJuman mall (see p.134).

Aangan Dhow Palace Hotel, Kuwait Rd ☎04 359 9992, ⓦfacebook.com/AanganAtDhowPalaceHotel; Al Karama metro; map p.38. If you want really good mainstream Indian food but aren't too fussed about atmosphere or ambience, this is the place to come. The decor is boring and the atmosphere is often borderline chaos – with half a dozen extended Indian families trying to make themselves heard over the (admittedly, rather good) in-house Indian band. The food, however, is top-notch, with richly flavoured renditions of classic North Indian meat and veg tandooris and curries, served up in big portions and with a fair helping of spice. Mains around 45–55dh (veg) and 60–90dh (meat). Daily 12.30–3.30pm & 7pm–2am.

★ **Antique Bazaar** Four Points Sheraton, Khalid bin al Waleed Rd ☎04 397 7333, ⓦantiquebazaar-dubai .com; Al Fahidi metro; map p.38. This pretty little Indian restaurant looks like a forgotten corner of some Rajput palace, littered with assorted subcontinental artefacts and dishing up a fair selection of North Indian favourites with reasonable aplomb. There's also the added incentive of a very passable resident band (nightly from 9pm) churning out Bollywood tunes, plus a couple of female dancers twirling around in gauzy costumes. Not the place for a quiet romantic dinner, but good fun otherwise. Mains from

around 40dh (veg), 50–55dh (meat). Daily 12.30–3pm & 7.30pm–2.30am, closed Fri lunch.

Arabian Tea House Café Al Fahidi St, next to the main entrance to Bastakiya ☎04 353 5071, ⓦfacebook .com/ArabianTeaHouseCafe; Al Fahidi metro; map p.38. Formerly the *Basta Arts Café*, this lovely little courtyard café is set in the idyllic garden of a traditional old Bastakiya house. The menu features a good range of light meals (pasta, quiches, jacket potatoes), plus sandwiches and salads (from 30dh), assorted breakfasts (from 22dh) and decent juices and smoothies. Daily 8am–8pm.

Bastakiah Nights Bastakiya ☎04 353 7772, ⓦfacebook.com (search for "Bastakiah N Rest"); Al Fahidi metro; map p.38. One of the most beautiful places to eat in central Dubai, occupying a superbly restored old house in Bastakiya – the perfect place to indulge in a few Orientalist fantasies. The food (mains 45–70dh) doesn't

---

> **TOP 5 CAFÉS**
>
> **Arabian Tea House Café** See above
> **Belgian Beer Café** See p.110
> **Lime Tree Café** See p.113
> **Al Mallah** See p.110
> **XVA Café** See p.106

9

quite match up with a short and rather dull menu featuring the usual Middle Eastern (plus a couple of Iranian) standards, but when the setting's this good, you might not care. Daily 11am–11pm.

Bayt al Wakeel Mackenzie House, near the main entrance of the Textile Souk ☎ 04 353 0530; Al Ghubaiba metro; map p.38. The small menu of rather pedestrian Arabian food won't win any awards, but the convenient location near the entrance to the Textile Souk and the setting – either on an attractive terrace jutting out into the Creek or inside the historic old Mackenzie House (see p.42) itself – more than compensate. Mezze 15dh, mains 30–40dh (plus some more expensive seafood dishes 60–75dh). Daily noon–midnight.

★ **Kan Zaman** Next to the Diving Village, Shindagha ☎ 04 393 9913, ⓦ alkoufa.com; Al Ghubaiba metro; map p.38. Occupying a beautiful creekside location, this large Middle Eastern restaurant is one of the best places in the city for a blast of authentic Arabian atmosphere – usually full of local Emiratis and expat Arabs puffing on shisha after dark. There's a big selection of mezze (most under 20dh) plus meat and seafood grills (40dh), as well as an excellent shisha selection. Daily 11am–3.30am.

Saravanaa Bhavan Khalifa bin Saeed Building, 3a St ☎ 04 353 9988, ⓦ saravanabhavan.com; Al Ghubaiba metro; map p.38. The most conveniently located of several Dubai branches of this much-loved South Indian vegetarian restaurant chain from Chennai, about 100m west of the Bur Dubai Abra Station, between the HSBC and Bank of Baroda buildings. The menu features an encyclopedic array of favourites, ranging from South Indian dosas, *iddlis* and *uppuma* through to classic North Indian veg curries, plus a few Chinese dishes. Given the rock-bottom prices (mains 12–15dh), quality is remarkably high. Daily 7.30am–11pm.

Vasanta Bhavan Vasantam Hotel, Al Nahda St ☎ 04 393 8006, ⓦ thevasantabhavan.com/Dubai.html; Al Ghubaiba metro; map p.38. Of the hundreds of little curry houses dotted around Bur Dubai, this cosy little vegetarian establishment is one of the best. Food is served upstairs in a comfortable and peaceful dining room, with an excellent range of North and South Indian standards, richly flavoured and at giveaway prices. Mains 7–12dh. Daily 7am–11.30pm.

XVA Café Bastakiya ☎ 04 353 5383, ⓦ xvahotel.com; Al Fahidi metro; map p.38. Tucked away in an alley at the back of Bastakiya, this shady courtyard café serves up good vegetarian food including flavoursome salads and sandwiches (22–33dh) and assorted light meals (33–38dh) with a Middle Eastern twist, plus good breakfasts. Daily except Fri 9am–7pm.

Yakitori-Tei Ascot Hotel, Khalid bin al Waleed Rd ☎ 04 352 0900, ⓦ facebook.com/YakitoriTeiAscotHotel; Al Fahidi metro; map p.38. If you want something that's not curry in Bur Dubai this is your best bet. The mainly Japanese menu (mains mostly 55–85dh) ticks all the usual boxes, with competently prepared stir-fries, sushi, sashimi, maki, yakitori and curries, and there's also a cursory list of Thai classics (around 50dh) and jugs of draught sake to wash it all down with. Daily 12.30–3pm (last orders) & 6.30–11.30pm.

DEIRA

Deira provides an interesting mix of up- and downmarket eating options, with assorted fancy restaurants in the area's five-star hotels and cheap eats at a smattering of good street cafés – the area around *Al Aroos Damascus* on Al Muraqqabat Road is particularly good for Middle Eastern food.

Al Aroos Damascus Al Muraqqabat Rd ☎ 04 221 9825, ⓦ aroosdamascus.com; Al Rigga metro; map p.49. One of a number of lively local Middle Eastern restaurants along Al Muraqqabat Rd – Dubai's "Little Iraq" – and parallel Al Rigga Rd, underwhelming by day but fun by night when the restos get going and crowds fill out the broad swathes of pavement seats – it all feels distinctly Mediterranean Middle East rather than Arabian Gulf. The menu runs through all the usual Lebanese mezze and grills, well cooked, reasonably priced (mains from just 20dh) and served in such huge portions it's difficult to see how they actually make you any money. If *Al Aroos* is full or doesn't appeal, try the slightly more upmarket *Samad al Iraqi* just down the road, or *Al Safadi* next to the metro station on Al Rigga Rd. Daily 7am–3pm.

Ashiana Sheraton Dubai Creek, Baniyas Rd ☎ 04 207 1733, ⓦ sheratondubaicreek.com; Union metro; map p.49. This pleasantly sedate and old-fashioned restaurant has been going seemingly forever, but remains consistently popular, offering an interesting selection of modern Indo-European fusion dishes (think tandoori lamb saddle or pan-fried duck in tamarind sauce) backed up by a few old-school subcontinental classics like chicken tikka and *palak paneer*. Live music at all meals. Mains 75–125dh. Daily 7.30–11.30pm, plus Sun–Thurs noon–3pm.

Ashwaq Perfume Souk, Sikkat al Khail Rd ☎ 04 226 1164; Al Ras metro; map p.49. Just 100m or so from the entrance to the bustling Gold Souk, this is one of the busiest and best of Deira's various shwarma stands, with melt-in-the-mouth shwarma sandwiches (5dh) and plates (20dh) and big fruit juices (from 10dh). The perfect place for a cheap lunch, especially if you can snag a seat at one of the pavement tables – brilliant for people-watching. Sat–Thurs 10am–midnight, Fri 3pm–midnight.

The China Club Radisson Blu Dubai Deira Creek Hotel, Baniyas Rd ☎ 04 222 7171, ⓦ radissonblu.com/hotel -dubaideiracreek; Union metro; map p.49. The best Chinese restaurant in central Dubai, offering a daily "Yum

TOP 5 CHEAP EATS

Al Aroos Damascus See opposite
Ashwaq See opposite
Betawi See p.108
Delhi Darbar See below
Hatam al Tai See below

Cha" dim sum buffet (99dh per person) at lunchtimes, and à la carte in the evening, with well-prepared standards – live seafood, stir-fries and noodles – along with the restaurant's signature dim sum (32–46dh) and Peking duck. Most mains 60–90dh. Daily noon–3pm & 7–11pm.

Al Dawaar Hyatt Regency, Corniche Rd ☎ 04 317 2222, ⓦ dubai.regency.hyatt.com; Palm Deira metro; map p.49. Dubai's only revolving restaurant, balanced atop the gargantuan *Hyatt Regency* and offering superlative city views – each revolution takes 1hr 30min, so you should get to see the whole 360-degree panorama if you don't eat too fast. Food is buffet only (175dh at lunch; 235dh at dinner, excluding drinks), featuring a mix of Mediterranean, Arabian, Asian and Japanese dishes plus the restaurant's signature US prime ribs– not the city's greatest culinary experience, but a decent accompaniment to the head turning vistas outside. Daily 12.30–3.30pm & 6.30pm–midnight.

Delhi Darbar Al Sabkha Rd ☎ 04 235 6161, ⓦ delhi -darbar.com; Palm Deira metro; map p.49. Unpretentious but excellent little no-frills restaurant serving up heartwarming meat kebabs, tandooris and Mughlai-style dishes (from 22dh) along with a good selection of veg curries (from 15dh) and superb tandoori rotis at just 1.50dh a pop. Daily 9am –midnight.

Focaccia Hyatt Regency, Corniche Rd ☎ 04 210 1234, ⓦ dubai.regency.hyatt.com; Palm Deira metro; map p.49. This rambling Italian restaurant feels more like a rather smart country club than a city-centre restaurant, with

a casual ambience and soothing Gulf views. Food features a mix of traditional and modern Italian cuisine, with a seasonally changing menu and a mix of pasta and risottos (60–75dh), plus meat and fish mains (85–120dh). Daily except Sat 7pm–midnight, plus Fri brunch 12.30–4pm.

Hatam al Tai Just south of Baniyas Square, behind Gift Village ☎ 04 224 7776; Baniyas Square metro; map p.49. Bustling, no-frills café serving meaty and filling Iranian food – kebabs, stews, shwarma plates and biriyanis – at bargain prices (30–40dh). If there's no space, *Shiraz Nights* next door makes a very acceptable alternative. The shwarma stands outside both these places are also good for a snack on the go. Daily 6am–12.30pm.

Shabestan Radisson Blu Dubai Deira Creek Hotel, Baniyas Rd ☎ 04 222 7171, ⓦ radissonblu.com/hotel -dubaideiracreek; Union metro; map p.49. This posh but rather plain Iranian restaurant retains a loyal following among Emiratis and expat Iranians thanks to its huge (if rather pricey) *chelo* kebabs, fish stews and other Persian specialities like *baghalah polo* (slow-cooked lamb) and *zereshk polo* (baked chicken with wild berries). There's also a resident two-piece band (nightly except Sat) plus lovely creekside views if you can get a seat near the window. Mains 95–135dh. Daily 12.30– 3.15pm & 7.30–11.15pm (last orders).

★ **Table 9 by Nick and Scott** Hilton Dubai Creek, Baniyas Rd ☎ 04 212 7551, ⓦ table9dubai.com; Al Rigga metro; map p.49. Occupying the Hilton dining room which formerly hosted Gordon Ramsay's much-loved *Verre* restaurant, now relaunched as *Table 9* by Ramsay's protégés Nick Alvis and Scott Price. Top-notch modern European fine dining is still the order of the day, but with a more relaxed ambience and a flexible approach to dining: you can mix and match "larger" and "smaller" plates including classics like pork belly and sea bass with cockles through to more quirky concoctions like duck with ceps and liquorice. Smaller/larger plates 80dh/100dh; tasting menus 300dh (vegetarian)/450dh (non-vegetarian). Daily 7pm–midnight.

THE INNER SUBURBS

Dubai's inner suburbs offer a range of eating options, with an excellent selection of inexpensive curry houses and Middle Eastern cafés in **Karama** and **Satwa**, and more upmarket options in **Oud Metha** (including an excellent cluster of places in Wafi), **Festival City**, and ranged along the side of the Creek in **Garhoud**.

GARHOUD

Boardwalk/Aquarium Dubai Creek Yacht Club ☎ 04 295 6000, ⓦ dubaigolf.com/dubai-creek-golf-yacht -club; Deira City Centre metro; map p.57. Seemingly always packed, unpretentious *Boardwalk* occupies a spectacular perch on the creekside, with stunning city views. The menu meanders through an eclectic range of international dishes – anything from chicken makhani or an Arabic mixed grill to fish and chips (mains 60–90dh) – and there's a decent wine list. Alternatively, head for the more upmarket *Aquarium* seafood restaurant upstairs (☎ 04 295 6000; mains from around 90dh;

daily 7.30–11pm), which has similar creekside views plus a spectacular fish tank. Sun–Thurs noon–12.30am, Fri & Sat 8am–12.30am.

QD's Dubai Creek Yacht Club ☎ 04 295 6000, ⓦ dubaigolf .com/dubai-creek-golf-yacht-club; Deira City Centre metro; map p.57. Fun and good-value restaurant-cum-bar- cum-shisha café in a superb location athwart a large open-air terrace overlooking the Creek. The cheap and cheerful pub- grub-style menu features lots of pizzas and Lebanese kebabs (mains from around 50dh), and there's also a big selection of shisha and a well-stocked bar. Daily 5pm–2am.

9

TOP 5 MIDDLE EASTERN FOOD

Kan Zaman See p.106
Khan Murjan Restaurant See below
Al Nafoorah See p.111
Shabestan See p.107
Tagine See p.116

★ **Thai Kitchen** Park Hyatt ☎ 04 602 1818, ⓦ dubai .park.hyatt.com; Deira City Centre metro; map p.57. Occupying part of the *Park Hyatt*'s lovely creekside terrace, this superb restaurant offers all the usual Thai classics alongside a few more unusual regional specialities. Food is served in small, tapas-sized portions (35–55dh), meaning that you can work your way through a much wider range of dishes and flavours than you'd normally be able to – although three dishes per person will probably suffice, whatever the waiters may tell you. Daily 7pm–midnight, plus Fri brunch 12.30–4pm.

OUD METHA

Asha's Wafi ☎ 04 324 4100, ⓦ ashasrestaurants.com; Dubai Healthcare City metro; map p.57. Owned by legendary Bollywood chanteuse Asha Bhosle, this sleek, modern restaurant serves up an interesting menu featuring traditional North Indian classics alongside offerings from Bhosle's own family cookbook, including unusual specialities like Goan brown cashew chicken curry or green fish curry. Mains 70–95dh. Daily 12.30–3pm & 7pm–midnight.

★ **Khan Murjan Restaurant** Souk Khan Murjan, Wafi ☎ 04 327 9795, ⓦ bit.ly/KhanMurjan; Dubai Healthcare City metro; map p.57. The centrepiece of the spectacular Khan Murjan Souk (see p.56), this beautiful courtyard restaurant has proved a big hit with the city's Emiratis and expat Arabs, thanks to the traditional atmosphere and unusually wide-ranging Middle Eastern menu. All the usual Lebanese favourites are present and correct, alongside various Egyptian, Moroccan and Turkish classics and local Gulf dishes like *fouga* (a kind of Emirati-style chicken biriyani) and *goboli* (rice cooked with lamb, spices, onions and raisins). Mains from around 70dh. Daily 10am–1am.

Lan Kwai Fong 10th St, diagonally opposite the Mövenpick Hotel ☎ 04 335 3680, ⓦ facebook.com (search for "Lan Kwai Fong Dubai"); Oud Metha metro; map p.57. One of the best budget Chinese restaurants in the city, boasting a loyal following among the city's expat Chinese community, who come for the Hong Kong-style food and moreish Peking duck. The big menu also features plenty of meat and veg options along with seafood, dim sum and claypot sizzlers. Mains from 30dh. Daily noon–3pm & 6.30–11.30pm.

Lemongrass Opposite Lamcy Plaza ☎ 04 334 2325, ⓦ lemongrassrestaurants.com; Oud Metha metro;

map p.57. Long-running Oud Metha stalwart, occupying a good-looking modern restaurant and delivering what is still probably the best cheap Thai food in the city, with authentically spicy curries, stir-fries, soups, salads and a decent selection of seafood, all backed up with smooth and attentive service. Most mains 40–60dh. Daily noon–midnight.

Medzo Wafi ☎ 04 324 4100, ⓦ pyramidsrestaurants atwafi.com; Dubai Healthcare City metro; map p.57. Suave little restaurant with a cosy old-school European-style dining room and a good selection of Italian-cum-Mediterranean cuisine – pastas, pizzas and risottos (65–75dh) along with more substantial meat and seafood mains (from 100dh) – all bursting with sunny southern flavours. Daily 12.30–3pm & 7–11.30pm.

Sevilles Wafi ☎ 04 324 4100, ⓦ pyramidsrestaurants atwafi.com; Dubai Healthcare City metro; map p.57. Spanish cuisine makes a rare Dubai appearance at this attractive Wafi restaurant, with a rustic wood-and-brick interior plus outdoor terrace. There's a decent spread of traditional tapas, assorted meat and fish mains (including six kinds of paella), plus Iberian wines to wash it all down with. Mains from 70dh. Daily noon–1am (Tues–Fri until 2am).

KARAMA

Betawi 4b St, off Sheikh Khalifa bin Zayed St; Khalid bin al Waleed metro; map p.57. Tucked away in a Karama backstreet, this utterly ordinary-looking, shoebox-sized café is the unlikely source of probably the best Indonesian cooking in the city – and at bargain prices. There's no atmosphere and scarcely room to move your elbows, let alone swing a cat, but the food is excellent, including well-prepared versions of classic dishes like *sate ayam*, *nasi goreng*, *mee goreng*, *gado gado* and *nasi padang* – best accompanied with a glass of delicious, authentically fluorescent *es campur*. Mains around 25dh. To reach it go down the small side road roughly opposite Spinneys and past the south side of the *Park Regis Kris Inn* and *Bombay Chowpatty* café and straight on to *Bikanervala* restaurant; turn left at *Bikanervala* and you'll see *Betawi* on the opposite side of the street about 50m further down. Daily noon–10pm, Fri from 2pm.

Sukh Sagar Sheikh Khalifa bin Zayed St ☎ 04 396 7222, ⓦ sukhsagar.com; Al Karama metro; map p.57. An offshoot of the well-known Mumbai chain, and the best of the many places to eat strung out along this section of Sheikh Khalifa bin Zayed St. The interior is so cosy it's hard not to fall asleep at your table, while food comprises an excellent selection of vegetarian cuisine from north and south India including delicious Mumbai-style street-food classics like *pav bhaji*, *bhel puri* and *sev puri*. Excellent value, with huge portions and virtually everything under 25dh. Daily 9am–midnight.

9

SATWA

Al Mallah 2nd December St ☎ 04 398 4962; World Trade Centre or Al Jafiliya metros; map p.58. A classic slice of Satwa nightlife, this no-frills Lebanese café churns out good shwarmas, grills and other Middle Eastern food at bargain prices (mezze around 10dh, mains around 30dh) to a lively local crowd; the pavement terrace is a great place to people-watch. If there's no space here, *Beirut*, just down the road, is very similar and almost as good. Daily 7am–3am.

Pars Satwa Roundabout, just behind Chelsea Plaza Hotel ☎ 04 398 9222, ⓦ parsuae.com; World Trade Centre or Al Jafiliya metros; map p.58. Attractive garden restaurant offering big portions of well-prepared Iranian food, including the usual meat kebabs and stews, plus a smattering of seafood. Mains 45–65dh. Daily 6–11.30pm (Fri until 12.30am).

Ravi's Al Satwa Rd, just south of Satwa Roundabout; World Trade Centre or Al Jafiliya metros; map p.58. This famous little Pakistani café, between the copycat *Ravi Palace* and *Rawi Palace* restaurants, attracts a loyal local and expat clientele thanks to its tasty array of subcontinental standards – veg, chicken and mutton curries, biriyanis and breads – although it's no longer quite as absurdly cheap as it once was, with mains for around 15–20dh. The interior is usually packed, and it's more fun (despite the traffic) to sit out on the pavement and watch the street life of Satwa drift by. Daily 5am–3am.

FESTIVAL CITY

Belgian Beer Café Crowne Plaza Hotel, off Crescent Drive ☎ 04 701 1127, ⓦ facebook.com/belgianbeer cafedubai; map p.57. This convivial Belgian-style pub-cum-restaurant serves mainly as a drinking venue (see p.119), but is also a good place for a nourishing helping of traditional Belgian cuisine, usually featuring Flemish classics like *waterzooi*, carbonade, and the inevitable mussels. Mains 70–80dh. Daily noon–2am (Fri & Sat until 3am).

Reflets par Pierre Gagnaire InterContinental Hotel, off Crescent Drive ☎ 04 701 1111, ⓦ facebook.com /refletsparpierregagnaire; map p.57. Opened in 2008 by multiple Michelin-starred French chef Pierre Gagnaire, *Reflets* has established itself as one of the city's top European fine-dining experiences, showcasing Gagnaire's innovative and superbly crafted modern French cuisine. The short menu features a mix of regularly changing meat and seafood creations – anything from blue Atlantic lobster to wild pigeon – backed up by heaps of luscious little *amuses-bouches*. The service is super-smooth, there's a spectacularly expensive wine list and the over-the-top purple decor with pink chandeliers adds a further flourish – although the floor-to-ceiling mirrored toilets aren't to everyone's taste. It's seriously expensive though – expect to pay around 2000dh per person total once you've factored in drinks. Daily 7–11.30pm.

SHEIKH ZAYED ROAD AND DOWNTOWN DUBAI

Most of **Sheikh Zayed Road**'s top restaurants are tucked unobtrusively away in the strip's various five-star hotels, although there's a lively café scene down at street level, including the original branch of the ever expanding *Shakespeare & Co* chain (see p.105), while a number of places also do an enjoyable sideline in shisha, pulling in a loyal crowd of locals and expat Arabs. There's another good clutch of inexpensive cafés at the **DIFC** (see p.63) including attractive branches of *More* and *Dôme* (see p.104), as well as a couple of alluring top-end options. Further south, the stunning waterfront at **Downtown Dubai** is ringed with further cafés and restaurants, with cheaper establishments on the Dubai Mall side of the water, and more upmarket options over on the opposite side in Souk al Bahar and *The Palace* hotel.

SHEIKH ZAYED ROAD

Ayoush off Sheikh Zayed Rd; Emirates Towers metro; map pp.64–65. Pleasant little restaurant tucked just off Sheikh Zayed Rd opposite the Emirates Towers in a miniature courtyard-cum-faux-garden, with palm trees wrapped in twinkly lights and a cheery soundtrack of classic Arabic tunes (which *almost* mask the roar of nearby traffic). A popular hangout among Emiratis and expat Arabs thanks to its extensive shisha selection (no fewer than 24 varieties; 25–50dh), and there's also above-average Lebanese food (mains 40–60dh) and excellent, if pricey, juices (25dh). Daily 24hr.

Benjarong Dusit Thani Hotel, Sheikh Zayed Rd ☎ 04 317 4515, ⓦ facebook.com/BenjarongDTDU; Financial Centre metro; map pp.64–65. No surprises that the signature restaurant at this excellent Thai-owned hotel offers some of the best Royal Thai cooking in Dubai. Set in a

delicately painted wooden pavilion on the 24th floor, it covers pretty much every aspect of the country's cuisine. There's a particularly good selection of fish and seafood, plus the usual meat stir-fries and red and yellow curries, and they also do a lively Friday brunch. Most mains 55–75dh. Daily noon–3pm & 7–10.30pm (last orders).

The Exchange Grill Fairmont Hotel, Sheikh Zayed Rd ☎ 04 311 8559, ⓦ fairmont.com; World Trade Centre metro; map pp.64–65. This small and rather exclusive steakhouse feels more like a room in a private gentlemen's club than a public restaurant, with just fourteen tables surrounded by huge leather armchairs. The menu of Premium Gold Angus and Wagyu cuts (215–295dh) is supplemented with a few upmarket seafood dishes, and there's an extensive wine list. Daily 7pm–midnight.

Hoi An Shangri-La Hotel, Sheikh Zayed Rd ☎ 04 405 2703, ⓦ shangri-la.com; Financial Centre metro; map

TOP 5 PLACES TO POSE

Armani Ristorante See p.112
Buddha Bar See p.115
Okku See below
Sho Cho See p.113
Zuma See p.112

pp.64–65. Hybrid Vietnamese–French cuisine is the speciality here, served in an elegant wood-panelled restaurant. Traditional Asian dishes and ingredients are combined with modern Continental cooking techniques to produce unusual creations like five-spice grilled Australian lamb chops with green beans, nectarine and plum sauce. Mains 110–140dh. Daily 7–11pm.

★ **La Petite Maison** Building 8, Gate Village, DIFC ☎04 439 0505, ⓦlpmdubai.ae; Emirates Towers metro; map pp.64–65. An offshoot of the famous Nice restaurant, this is as authentic as French restaurants come in the UAE, offering traditional *cuisine niçoise* in a bright white dining room which feels intimate and pleasantly formal but not excessively starchy. Cooking blends Gallic haute cuisine with a dash of Mediterranean zing, the seasonally changing menu featuring, for example, carpaccio of scallops or octopus in lemon oil and slow-cooked duck legs in an orange glaze or mushroom rigatoni. Most mains 120–200dh. Reservations usually essential. Daily noon–3.30pm & 7–11.30pm.

Marrakech Shangri-La Hotel, Sheikh Zayed Rd ☎04 405 2703, ⓦshangri-la.com; Financial Centre metro; map pp.64–65. Vies with *Tagine* (see p.116) for the title of Dubai's best Moroccan restaurant. The decor – a subtle melange of pale green tiles and Moorish cusped arches – is lovely, while the menu includes a good spread of authentic Moroccan cooking, ranging from the usual couscous and tagine dishes through to traditional favourites like *harira*, *pastilla* (pigeon pie) and *tangia*. Most mains 70–80dh. Daily except Sun 7–11pm.

★ **Al Nafoorah** Emirates Towers Boulevard ☎04 330 0000; Emirates Towers metro; map pp.64–65. One of the city's best places for Middle Eastern food, *Al Nafoorah* looks more like a slightly starchy Parisian establishment than a traditional Lebanese restaurant., with floor-length white tablecloths, flouncy chandeliers and tasteful old black-and-white photos on the walls. What's on offer is the real deal, however, from the superb array of mezze through to the perfectly cooked selection of fish, meat grills and kebabs. Mezze from 30dh, mains from 60dh. Daily 12.30–3pm (Fri & Sat from 1pm) & 7–11pm.

★ **The Noodle House** Emirates Towers Boulevard ☎04 319 8757, ⓦthenoodlehouse.com; Emirates Towers metro; map pp.64–65. A Dubai institution, this cheapish and very cheerful noodle bar caters to an endless stream of diners who huddle up on long communal tables

to refuel on excellent Southeast and East Asian food, with a mix of Thai, Chinese, Malay, Singaporean and Indonesian dishes. Reservations aren't accepted, so you might have to queue at busy times. There are other branches at Madinat Jumeirah and the BurJuman centre, though neither has yet quite managed to recreate the atmosphere of the original. Most mains around 60dh. Daily noon–11.30pm.

Okku H Hotel, Sheikh Zayed Rd ☎04 501 8777, ⓦokkudubai.com; World Trade Centre metro; map pp.64–65. Swanky Japanese bar-club-restaurant in the former *Monarch Hotel*, which vies with nearby *Zuma* (see p.112) for the title of the coolest *izakaya*-style sushi-and-saki joint in town, with a moody interior full of beautiful people and an authentic menu of Japanese cuisine including some of the best sushi and sashimi in town (45–100dh), "small plates" (anything from soft-shell crab to chicken yakitori; 50–125dh) through to more substantial "large plates" (including the inevitable *Nobu*-style black cod in miso; mostly 100–180dh). DJ nights on Thurs, Fri and Sun attract a party crowd, and the Friday brunch is top-notch. Daily noon–3pm & 7pm–3am.

Shang Palace Shangri-La Hotel, Sheikh Zayed Rd ☎04 405 2703, ⓦshangri-la.com; Financial Centre metro; map pp.64–65. This intimate circular restaurant specializes in top-notch traditional Cantonese and Szechuan cooking – with a particularly good selection of seafood ranging from *hammour* (grouper) to lobster and mud crab, plus meat and veg claypots. Mains 90–120dh. Daily noon–3pm & 7–11pm.

Spectrum on One Fairmont Hotel, Sheikh Zayed Rd ☎04 311 8101, ⓦfairmont.com; World Trade Centre metro; map pp.64–65. This good-looking modern restaurant would be a nice place to eat whatever was on the menu, but it also boasts a unique selling point – it has no fewer than seven separate kitchens, each specializing in a different cuisine, so you can mix and match from Arabian, Indian, Chinese, Japanese, Thai, European and seafood menus as you fancy. The whole concept is typical of Dubai's more-is-more approach to life, and the food is actually pretty good – and where else could you experience a meal of sashimi, chicken tikka masala and crème brûlée, followed by a pot of English breakfast tea? Most mains 100–150dh. Also hosts one of the city's most opulent Friday brunches (295dh brunch only, 550dh with unlimited champagne; bookings strongly recommended). Daily 6.30pm–12.30am (last orders), plus Fri noon–3pm.

Teatro Towers Rotana Hotel, Sheikh Zayed Rd ☎04 343 8000, ⓦrotana.com; Financial Centre metro; map pp.64–65. This long-running Sheikh Zayed Rd favourite is one of the strip's livelier and less exclusive offerings, with theatrically themed decor and a mix-and-match menu featuring a range of Thai, Chinese, Italian and Indian, plus sushi and sashimi, competently prepared and affordably priced. Mains 60–110dh. Daily 6–11.30pm (last orders).

9

TOP 5 RESTAURANTS WITH VIEWS

At.mosphere See below
La Parilla See opposite
Al Muntaha See p.114
Thiptara See opposite
Vu's Restaurant See below

Vu's Restaurant Jumeirah Emirates Towers Hotel, Sheikh Zayed Rd ☎04 319 8088, ⓦjumeirah.com; Emirates Towers metro; map pp.64–65. Perched up on the 50th floor of the *Jumeirah Emirates Towers* hotel, this smart and rather formal restaurant is the second highest in the city. The view, of course, is a major draw, but the restaurant itself is one of the city's top fine-dining venues, with a short but very sophisticated menu of modern European cuisine – arctic char with tarragon gnocchi, for example, or braised Wagyu beef brisket with bone-marrow and bourguignon sauce. Visit either for the brisk three-course business lunch (150dh) or for a more relaxed evening à la carte experience. Mains from 200dh. Sun–Thurs 12.30–3pm & 7.30pm–midnight, plus Fri 7.30pm–midnight.

Zuma Building 6, Gate Village, DIFC ☎04 425 5660, ⓦzumarestaurant.com; Emirates Towers metro; map pp.64–65. Very hip new Japanese bar-restaurant, discreetly tucked away in a corner of the Gate Village, with a dining area (including sushi counter and *robata* grill) downstairs, and a bar-lounge above – the whole place smoother than George Clooney on ice. Informal *izakaya*-style dining – with shared dishes brought to your table in no particular sequence – is the order of the day, although the food itself, including melt-in-the-mouth sushi and sushimi plus more substantial mains, is absolutely top-notch (with prices to match) and would look quite at home in a Michelin-starred restaurant. Portions are on the small side and the bill can quickly stack up, however, particularly if you indulge in the extensive list of fine wines and superior sake. Mains 80–165dh; express lunch menu 80dh. DJ nightly from around 9pm playing house and other sounds. Reservations almost always essential. Daily: restaurant 12.30–2.45pm (last orders) & 7pm–1am (Thurs & Fri until 2am); bar 12.30pm–1 or 2am.

DOWNTOWN DUBAI

Armani Ristorante/Armani Amal Burj Khalifa ☎04 888 3888, ⓦdubai.armanihotels.com; Burj Khalifa/Dubai Mall metro; map pp.64–65. The smooth new *Armani* hotel (see p.98) offers a wide range of dining options at its various in-house restaurants – although if you're not staying at the hotel you'll need to reserve in advance to gain admittance. All are kitted out in generic minimalist Armani decor with a profusion of muted oatmeal whites and charcoal greys which you'll find either achingly cool or pretentiously dull depending on the cut of your jib, and which makes it rather difficult to tell any of the different venues apart, although it does concentrate attention on the food, which is sometimes very good (as it should be given the prices). Top of the tree is the signature *Armani Ristorante* (mains 140–290dh), serving fine-dining interpretations of regional Italian cuisine, particularly Tuscan dishes, with a regularly changing menu brimful of market-fresh ingredients and artfully crafted dishes – foie gras and date terrine with pears and an espresso reduction, for example, or veal cheek, morels and truffle – backed up by a huge wine list. The hotel's *Armani Amal* restaurant also gets good reviews for its inventive regional Indian cuisine (mains 130–180dh) with a European twist. Daily 7–11.30pm.

At.mosphere Burj Khalifa ☎04 888 3444, ⓦatmosphereburjkhalifa.com; Burj Khalifa/Dubai Mall metro; map pp.64–65. *At.mosphere*'s selling point couldn't be simpler: this is the world's highest bar and restaurant, located almost half a kilometre above ground level on the 122nd floor of the world's tallest building. There are two options here. The cheaper is to visit *The Lounge* (minimum spend 200dh – meaning that a mixed couple can visit for 100dh per head) for a drink or a pricey afternoon tea (290dh) – a good way of seeing the tower if you want to avoid the crowds of the "At the Top" tour (see p.68). If you want to go the whole hog, *The Restaurant* (mains 260–360dh) offers upmarket international meat and seafood dishes in its svelte dining room, although at these prices you're probably better off heading to one of the Armani restaurants downstairs. The Restaurant daily 12.30–3pm & 7–11.30pm; The Lounge noon–2am.

BiCE Mare Souk al Bahar ☎04 423 0982, ⓦbicemare.com; Burj Khalifa/Dubai Mall metro; map pp.64–65. Sister establishment to the Dubai Marina *BiCE* (see p.115), with a chic minimalist modern dining room and great terrace overlooking the Dubai Fountain. Italian-style seafood dominates the menu, with assorted seafood pastas (from 140dh) and other maritime *secondi piatti* (from 180dh) – the seared scallops with asparagus and black truffle wins rave reviews. No alcohol served 4–6pm. Daily noon–11.30pm (last orders).

Organic Foods Lower Ground Floor, Dubai Mall ☎04 434 0577, ⓦorganicfoodsandcafe.com; Burj Khalifa/Dubai Mall metro; map pp.64–65. Despite its size and profusion of food outlets, the Dubai Mall isn't overly blessed with good places to eat, and this is one of its better offerings. The café itself (which doubles as an organic food store) is spacious and usually blessedly peaceful compared to most other cafés in the mall, while the menu features a good selection of additive-free offerings. These include an eclectic selection of mains (mostly around 50dh) stretching from burgers, fish and chips and pasta through to salmon risotto and tofu stir-fry, plus cheaper (25–40dh) salads, sandwiches and pizzas. Sun–Wed 8.30am–10pm, Thurs–Sat until midnight.

Thiptara The Palace Hotel, Old Town ☎04 428 7961, ⓦtheaddress.com/en/dining/thiptara; Burj Khalifa /Dubai Mall metro; map pp.64–65. This beautiful Thai restaurant, set in a traditional wooden pavilion jutting out into the waters of the lake behind the Dubai Mall, offers probably the best night-time view of the Burj Khalifa and Dubai Fountain. The menu is strongest on seafood, but also offers a fair spread of meat dishes (though few veg options). Most mains 90–150dh. Reservations recommended. Daily 7–11.30pm.

JUMEIRAH

Eating options in beachside Jumeirah are relatively thin on the ground, although there's a cluster of places in the *Dubai Marine Beach Resort* including the enduringly popular *Sho Cho*, as well as a few other places along Jumeirah Road including branches of *Automatic* and *More* (see p.104) and the much-loved *Lime Tree Café*.

Lime Tree Café Jumeirah Rd ☎04 349 8498, ⓦthelimetreecafe.com; map pp.72–73. Eternally popular with Jumeirah's large community of expat wives and ladies-who-lunch, this cheery little establishment feels more like a neighbourhood café in some upwardly mobile suburb of London or Melbourne than anything remotely Arabian. It's a great place to people-watch, while the food's pretty good too, with moreish wraps, focaccias, paninis, quiches and salads, fat cakes and a good selection of tasty fruit juices. Daily 7.30am–6pm.

Sho Cho Dubai Marine Beach Resort, Jumeirah Rd ☎04 346 1111, ⓦdxbmarine.com/Sho-Cho; map pp.72–73. This chic little bar-restaurant is best known for its cool little outside terrace bar (see p.121), but also dishes up a reasonable selection of sushi, sashimi and other Japanese fare (mains from 90dh). Daily 7pm–2am or later (kitchen closes at midnight).

THE BURJ AL ARAB AND AROUND

The Burj al Arab and surrounding hotels are home to some of the city's swankiest restaurants. For less financially punishing dining, the place to head for is Souk Madinat Jumeirah, which is home to numerous cafés and restaurants including branches of *Dôme* (see p.104), *The Noodle House* (see p.111), and *Japengo* (see p.104), among lots of other places, many of them spread out along the Madinat's picturesque waterfront.

Après Mall of the Emirates ☎04 341 2575, ⓦmalloftheemirates.com; Mall of the Emirates metro; map p.78. Cool bar-restaurant with surreal views over the snowy slopes of Ski Dubai through big picture windows and a good range of international food (mains 85–160dh) – anything from bouillabaisse to fish and chips, plus excellent thin-crust pizzas (around 70dh). It's also a fun spot for a drink, with an extensive drinks selection and kick-ass cocktails. Daily 11.30am–1am (Thurs & Fri until 2am).

La Parrilla 25th floor, Jumeirah Beach Hotel, Jumeirah Rd ☎04 406 8999, ⓦbit.ly/JBHhotel; map p.78. Perched atop the *Jumeirah Beach Hotel*, this Argentinian-themed steakhouse boasts superb views of the Burj al Arab, excellent Argentinian, Australian and Wagyu steaks (165–475dh) and an appealing splash of Latin atmosphere, with live music and tango dancers nightly (except Sun) – ask nicely and the manageress might even sing you a song. Daily 6.30pm–midnight.

Left Bank Souk Madinat Jumeirah ☎04 368 6171; map p.78. Jostling for elbow room among the string of incredibly popular eating and drinking spots along the Souk Madinat Jumeirah waterfront, this sleek modern bar-restaurant offers a good spot to watch the passing scene if you can bag a table on the outside terrace (although the convivial dining room inside is nice too).

The regularly changing menu (mains 90–165dh) features an eclectic selection of good (if pricey) international food – wild sea bass or confit duck leg through to curry of the day, Lancashire hotpot or fish and chips. Or just come for a drink. Daily 10.30am–2am (Wed–Fri until 3am).

Al Mahara Burj al Arab ☎04 301 7600, ⓦburj-al -arab.com; map p.78. Perhaps the more appealing of the Burj al Arab's two signature restaurants, *Al Mahara* looks like some kind of fantastic underwater grotto, entered through a huge golden arch and with seats arranged around a giant fish tank. There's a range of gourmet international seafood to choose from – Atlantic sea bass, lobster thermidor and so on – plus a couple of meat options, although the prices are enough to make you weep into your obsiblue shrimps tartare with octopus carpaccio. Mains around 370dh. Daily 12.30–3pm & 7pm–midnight.

TOP 5 FOR FINE DINING

Indego by Vineet See p.115
La Petite Maison See p.111
Reflets par Pierre Gagnaire See p.110
Rhodes Mezzanine See p.115
Table 9 by Nick and Scott See p.107

9

Al Muntaha Burj al Arab ☎04 301 7600, ⓦburj-al -arab.com; map p.78. For the ultimate splurge in the Burj, head to *Al Muntaha* ("The Highest"), referring to the restaurant's stunning location at the summit of the famed hotel, although it does equally well to describe the prices. The menu features fine international dining – anything from Wagyu fillet Rossini to wild sea bass – and the views are spectacular, although you may find the psychedelic decor a little *de trop*. If you just want have a quick look it's much cheaper to come for a drink at the attached *Skyview Bar* (see p.121). Mains 325–525dh; set lunch 480dh; Friday brunch 560dh. Daily 12.30–3pm (Fri 10am–3.30pm) & 7pm–midnight.

Pai Thai Al Qasr Hotel, Madinat Jumeirah ☎04 366 8888, ⓦmadinatjumeirah.com; map p.78. This beautiful Thai restaurant is one of the city's most romantic places to eat, with stunning Burj al Arab views from the candlelit terrace and live music murmuring gently in the background. Food includes all the usual Thai classics, such as spicy salads, meat and seafood curries – not the most original menu in town, although given the setting you probably won't care. Mains 80–200dh. Daily 6–11.30pm.

★ **Pierchic** Al Qasr Hotel, Madinat Jumeirah ☎04 366 8888, ⓦmadinatjumeirah.com; map p.78. One of the city's most spectacularly situated restaurants, perched at the end of a breezy pier jutting out in front of the grandiose *al Qasr* hotel, and with unbeatable views of the nearby Burj al Arab, *Jumeirah Beach Hotel* and Madinat Jumeirah. The short, mainly seafood menu has prices to match the location, with a selection of international-style fine-dining fish and seafood offerings, ranging from Dover sole to Canadian lobster, plus a couple of meat choices. Mains around 200dh. Daily 1–3pm & 7–11.30pm.

Zheng He Mina A'Salam Hotel, Madinat Jumeirah ☎04 366 6730, ⓦmadinatjumeirah.com; map p.78. This classy Chinese restaurant – generally reckoned one of the best in the city – offers a range of Chinese (mainly Cantonese) fine dining (mains 90–180dh). There's nothing particularly innovative about the menu, although quality is high and the setting memorable, with seating either inside the svelte restaurant itself or outside on the beautiful Burj-facing terrace. Daily noon–3pm & 7–11.30pm.

THE PALM JUMEIRAH AND DUBAI MARINA

There's a dense cluster of places to eat around **Dubai Marina**. Upmarket options are, as ever, concentrated in the area's various five-star hotels, though there are plenty of more down-to-earth places along the lively The Walk at Jumeirah Beach Residence (see p.86) and Marina Walk (see p.87) – the latter is particularly appealing after dark, with a long string of buzzing marina-side cafés and restaurants. Heading out to **The Palm Jumeirah**, eating options are mainly confined to the resort hotels, notably *Atlantis* and the various sumptuous restaurants at the stunning *Jumeirah Zabeel Saray*.

THE PALM JUMEIRAH

Amala Jumeirah Zabeel Saray Hotel, West Crescent ☎04 453 0444, ⓦjumeirah.com; map p.83. The most popular of the *Zabeel Saray's* stunning collection of restaurants, and not to be confused with the *Amal* restaurant at the *Armani* hotel (see p.112) – not that you're likely too, once you've seen them both. Where the *Amal* is all designer discretion, *Amala* (like all the *Zabeel Saray* venues) is a great big roaring statement of visual intent, opulently decorated and unmistakably Indian – or at least a kind of Bollywood version of India. Food matches the decor, with a selection of traditional and well-prepared (if not particularly original) North Indian dishes – Mughlai-style curries and tandooris – with the fixed price of 285dh per head allowing you to order as much as you like from the à la carte menu – good value, assuming you arrive sufficiently hungry. Daily 6pm–1am.

Ronda Locatelli Atlantis ☎04 426 2626, ⓦatlantisthepalm.com/restaurants; map p.83. The most affordable and accessible (not to mention family-friendly) of Atlantis's various celebrity-chef restaurants, *Ronda Locatelli* feels more like a casual modern Italian diner than a Michelin palace, with a straightforward menu of pizzas (65–90dh) cooked in the kitchen's wood-fired brick oven, pasta (90–120dh) plus more elaborate mains (115–200dh), highlighting Giorgio Locatelli's rustic and fuss-free culinary style, using fine ingredients to maximum effect. Daily noon–2.45pm (last orders) & 6–10.30pm (last orders; Thurs & Fri until 11.30pm); pizzas only 3–5pm.

Vôi Jumeirah Zabeel Saray Hotel, West Crescent ☎04 453 0444, ⓦjumeirah.com; map p.83. Occupying a grand old-world-style dining room – all high ceilings, white linen and chandeliers, like something out of a Balzac novel – *Vôi* specializes in colonial-style French-Vietnamese cuisine (mains 185–290dh), with some dishes leaning towards Paris, and others towards Southeast Asia – seared lobster tail with black beans, bean sprouts and mango-artichoke salad, for instance, or sautéed veal medallion, cep mushrooms and edamame beans. A resident mixologist prepares a good range of unusual cocktails and mocktails. Daily 7pm–midnight.

TOP 5 MOST ROMANTIC PLACES TO EAT

Bastakiah Nights See p.105
Eauzone See opposite
Al Mahara See p.113
Pai Thai See above
Pierchic See above

DUBAI MARINA

BiCE Hilton Dubai Jumeirah Resort, The Walk at Jumeirah Beach Residence ☎04 318 2520, ⊕hilton .com/dubai; Jumeirah Lake Towers metro; map p.83. This smooth modern Italian restaurant is generally reckoned the best in the southern part of the city (it's pronounced "Bee-Chay" – the nickname of Beatrice Ruggeri, who founded the original *BiCE* restaurant in Milan in 1926). Food includes tasty pizzas and pastas (70–90dh) bursting with fresh ingredients and flavours, plus a mix of meat and seafood mains (from 170dh) including regional classics like Sicilian rigatoni and more contemporary creations like lobster carpaccio. Daily 12.30–3pm & 7–11.30pm.

★ **Buddha Bar** Grosvenor House Hotel, Al Sufouh Rd ☎04 317 6833, ⊕buddhabar.com; Dubai Marina metro; map p.83. Modelled after the famous Parisian joint, this superb bar-restaurant is a sight in its own right: a huge, sepulchral space hung with dozens of red-lantern chandeliers and presided over by an enormous golden Buddha (looking like a rather supercilious *maitre d'*). The menu features a fine array of Japanese and pan-Asian cooking, with sushi, maki and sashimi plates alongside Thai- and Chinese-inspired meat, seafood and vegetarian mains. It's decidedly pricey for what you get, with most mains around 200dh, but the setting is superb. Alternatively, just pop in for a drink to sample the atmosphere and try one of the bar's long, minty cocktails. Advance reservations recommended. Daily 8pm–2am (Thurs & Fri until 3am).

Eauzone Arabian Courtyard, One&Only Royal Mirage, Al Sufouh Rd ☎04 315 2412, ⊕royalmirage.oneand onlyresorts.com; Nakheel metro; map p.83. Regularly voted the most romantic restaurant in Dubai, with seating within little Arabian tents set up amid the beautifully floodlit waters of one of the hotel's swimming pools – which seems to transform by night into a luminous, palm-studded lagoon. Food is an obligatory three- to five-course set menu (from 260dh) featuring European meat and seafood dishes, some with an Asian twist. The only problem is getting a reservation; if you can't, console yourself with a drink at the beautiful attached bar – just make sure you don't fall into the water on your way out. It's also open for lunch, when there's a much cheaper menu of salads, sandwiches and light meals (60–100dh), although it doesn't look nearly as beautiful as by night. Daily noon–11.30pm.

Frankie's The Walk at Jumeirah Beach Residence ☎04 399 4311, ⊕facebook.com/FrankiesDubai; Dubai Marina metro; map p.83. The foodie lovechild of champion jockey Frankie Dettori in association with Marco Pierre White, this cosy restaurant has a casual bistro feel, with hints of American family diner, and is much less posey than you might expect given its celebrity chef connection. Food is Italian with a mixed menu of reasonably priced

pizzas and pastas (from 70dh), plus more elaborate meat and seafood mains (from 150dh), all well prepared and backed up by one of the Marina's best drinks lists. Daily 6.30pm–12.30am.

★ **Indego by Vineet** Grosvenor House Hotel, Al Sufouh Rd ☎04 317 6000, ⊕luxurycollection.com /grosvenorhouse; Dubai Marina metro; map p.83. Overseen by Vineet Bhatia, India's first Michelin-starred chef, this stylish restaurant showcases his distinctive style of contemporary Indian cooking, blending international ingredients and classical cooking techniques with Indian spices and flavours to unusual effect – think lamb chop biriyani or tandoori lobster. Mains 140–220dh. Daily 12.30–3pm (Fri & Sat until 4pm) & 7pm–midnight.

Nina Arabian Courtyard, One&Only Royal Mirage, Al Sufouh Rd ☎04 315 2412; Nakheel metro; map p.83. Along with *Indego by Vineet* (see above), this is Dubai's most innovative Indian restaurant, offering a similar fusion of subcontinental and international ingredients and methods – anything from traditional butter chicken through to frogs' legs and rambutan in pickling five spices. The sumptuous orange decor, complete with oddly mismatched chandeliers, red Chinese lanterns and quasi-Moroccan arches, adds its own curious touch of hybrid magic. Mains from 90–130dh. Daily 7–11.30pm (last orders).

Al Qaherah 1940 Dubai Marina Walk ☎04 447 0047; Dubai Marina metro; map p.83. One of the prettiest of the long string of cafés and restaurants now lining Marina Walk, "Cairo 1940" occupies a neat little slice of terrace dotted with potted plants and colonial-era Cairene street signs (shame about the TVs). The menu continues the Egyptian-cum-North African theme, with classics like *kushari*, *sharkaseya* and *mulukhiyah* (mains 40–60dh) and other regional favourites, although offbeat spellings may confuse – "flafel" is easy enough to decipher, while "fool" is *foul* and a "toajin" is a tagine – although what "frick with meat", "psara" and "meat paper" are is anyone's guess. Daily 9am–3am.

Rhodes Mezzanine Grosvenor House Hotel, Al Sufouh Rd ☎04 317 6000, ⊕luxurycollection.com /grosvenorhouse; Dubai Marina metro; map p.83. Dubai flagship restaurant of UK chef Gary Rhodes, with a short but inventive menu showcasing his distinctive brand of modern European cuisine, with British classics given a French makeover, including signature Rhodes' desserts like jam roly-poly and bread-and-butter pudding. Starters 90–160dh, mains 195–250dh – or try the tasting menu, with smaller portions at just 60–165dh per dish. Daily except Sun 7–11.30pm.

★ **Rhodes Twenty10** Le Royal Méridien Beach Resort and Spa, The Walk at Jumeirah Beach Residence ☎04 316 5505, ⊕leroyalmeridien-dubai.com; Dubai Marina metro; map p.83. Gary Rhodes' second Dubai restaurant is

9

a much more casual, and affordable, affair than his flagship *Mezzanine* (see p.115). Food features an excellent range of "European-inspired cuisine infused with a touch of the Middle East" – crispy duck *pastilla* with harissa hollandaise, for instance, or spicy chicken with saffron curry risotto – alongside burgers, steaks, British classics like steak-and-kidney pie and fish and chips and Rhodes' signature confit pork belly. Most mains 120–190dh. Daily except Mon 7pm–midnight.

Tagine The Palace, One&Only Royal Mirage, Al Sufouh Rd ☎ 04 315 2412, ⓦ royalmirage.oneandonlyresorts .com; Nakheel metro; map p.83. Sumptuous little Moroccan restaurant, the beautiful Moorish decor complemented by authentic North African cooking including classics like *pastilla*, *tangia* and a selection of delicious tagines. Resident musicians provide good live music most nights. Mains around 100dh. Daily except Mon 7–11.30pm (last orders).

360°

Drinking

You won't go thirsty in Dubai, and the huge number of drinking holes tucked away all over the city attests to the extraordinary degree to which this Muslim city has gone in accommodating Western tastes. The best bars encapsulate Dubai at its most beguiling and opulent, whether your taste is for lounging on cushions in alfresco Arabian-themed venues or sipping champagne in cool, contemporary cocktail bars. Superlative views are often thrown in for good measure, whether from a perch atop one of the city's tallest skyscrapers or at one of its many waterfront venues, some of which offer sweeping coastal or creekside panoramas. Most larger hotels also have English-style pubs, with obligatory faux-wooden decor and banks of TVs showing the latest sporting events – a lot less stylish than the city's bars, but usually a bit cheaper.

10

Not surprisingly, boozing in Dubai comes at a **price**, thanks to high government taxes. A pint of beer will usually set you back around 30–35dh in a pub (more in a bar, assuming draught beer's available, which it often isn't), a glass of wine around 40dh and a basic cocktail around 50dh. Costs in the city's pubs can be cut (slightly) by looking out for happy hours and special promotions, usually chalked up on a blackboard behind the bar.

Most bars **open** at 6 or 7pm and stay open till around 1–3am; pubs generally open from around noon until 2am; some places stop serving alcohol between 2 and 4pm (although they may stay open for food and soft drinks). Most of the city's more upmarket drinking holes accept **reservations** (phone numbers for relevant places are listed), although the more club-style DJ bars often require a certain minimum spend in return for booking you a table. Smarter bars usually have some kind of **dress code** – don't be surprised if you get turned away if you rock up in shorts and T-shirt.

Although Dubai is extremely liberal (at least compared to the rest of the region) in its provision of alcohol, be aware that any form of **public drunkenness** is strongly frowned upon, and may even get you arrested, particularly if accompanied by any form of lewd behaviour, which can be taken to include even fairly innocuous acts like kissing in public (see p.29). The city also has a zero-tolerance policy towards **drink-driving** – worth remembering if you get behind the wheel on the morning after a heavy night, since even the faintest trace of alcohol in your system is likely to land you in jail.

BUR DUBAI

George & Dragon Ambassador Hotel, Al Falah St ☏04 393 9444, ⓦastamb.com; Al Ghubaiba metro; map p.38. This simple little pub won't win any style awards but has the important distinction of serving up the cheapest beer in the city; at the time of writing it was the only place in Dubai where you could reliably pick up a pint for around 20dh – so long as you don't mind the sometimes borderline scuzzy atmosphere. Daily noon–1am.

Sherlock Holmes Arabian Courtyard Hotel, Al Fahidi St ☏04 351 9111, ⓦarabiancourtyard.com; Al Fahidi metro; map p.38. One of the nicer English pubs in Bur Dubai, with a relaxed atmosphere, flock wallpaper, leatherette chairs and glass cases full of vaguely Sherlock

Holmes-related memorabilia. Also does decent pub food. Daily noon–2am (no alcohol served 4–6pm).

★ **Viceroy Bar** Four Points Sheraton Hotel, Khalid bin al Waleed Rd ☏04 397 7444, ⓦfourpoints.com /burdubai; Al Fahidi metro; map p.38. This traditional English-style pub is the nicest in Bur Dubai, complete with fake oak-beamed ceiling, authentic wooden bar and oodles of comfy leather armchairs. There's a decent range of draught beers and other drinks, plus assorted sports on the overhead TVs, and it's also a conveniently short stagger to the excellent *Antique Bazaar* Indian restaurant (see p.38). Daily 12.30pm–midnight.

DEIRA

Issimo Cocktail Lounge Hilton Dubai Creek Hotel, Baniyas Rd ☏04 227 1111, ⓦhilton.com/dubai; Al Rigga metro; map p.49. Occupying a corner of the *Hilton*'s ultramodern, chrome-obsessed ground floor, this chic little cocktail bar has a cute boat-shaped bar and a refreshingly unposey atmosphere – and is also one of the city's few non-smoking drinking holes. A good spot for an aperitif or

digestif before or after a meal at *Table 9* (see p.107) upstairs. Daily noon–4pm & 6pm–1.30am.

The Pub Radisson Blu Dubai Deira Creek Hotel, Baniyas Rd ☏04 222 7171, ⓦradissonblu.com/hotel-dubai deiracreek; Union metro; map p.49. Spacious and usually fairly peaceful English-style pub, complete with the usual fake wooden bar and lots of TVs screening global sports.

LADIES' NIGHTS

Ladies' nights are something of a Dubai institution. These are basically an attempt to drum up custom during the quieter midweek evenings – they're usually held on Wednesday, Thursday or, most commonly, Tuesday nights – with various places around the city offering all sorts of deals to women, ranging from a couple of free cocktails up to complimentary champagne all night. Just be aware that where ladies lead, would-be amorous blokes inevitably follow. Pick up a copy of *Time Out Dubai* for latest listings.

10

Happy hour (20 percent discounts) daily 6–9pm. Daily noon–4pm & 6pm–midnight.

Up on the Tenth 10th floor, Radisson Blu Dubai Deira Creek Hotel, Baniyas Rd ☎ 04 205 7033, ⊛ radissonblu .com/hotel-dubaideiracreek; Union metro; map p.49. Not the most stylish venue in Dubai – the 80s-style mirrored Manhattan skyline effect behind the bar is so dated it's almost an antique and the whole place is poky and often stinks of cigars. However, it also offers just about the best Creek views to be had in the city centre, with memorable vistas of the water framed by the twinkling towers of Deira. Arrive early, grab a window seat and watch the city light up. A jazz singer and pianist perform daily (except Fri) from 10pm till late. Daily 6.30pm–3am.

THE INNER SUBURBS

★ **Belgian Beer Café** Crowne Plaza Hotel, Festival City ☎ 04 701 2222, ⊛ facebook.com/belgianbeercafe dubai; map p.57. This convivial Belgian-style pub-cum-restaurant is one of the highlights of the Festival City development, with an eye-catching traditional wooden interior, an excellent range of speciality beers on tap or by the bottle (including draught Hoegaarden, Leffe and Belle-Vue Kriek) and good traditional Flemish cuisine (see p.110). Daily noon–2am (Fri & Sat until 3am).

Eclipse 26th floor, InterContinental Hotel, Festival City ☎ 04 701 1111; map p.57. Swanky modern bar at the top of the fancy Festival City *InterCon*, offering huge views over Sheikh Zayed Rd and the Creek, plus a good range of beers, wines and cocktails. Alternatively, check out the hotel's equally smooth waterside *Vista* bar terrace, with sweeping city skyline views and a decent shisha selection. Daily 6pm–2am.

★ **The Terrace** Park Hyatt Hotel, Garhoud ☎ 04 602 1234, ⊛ dubai.park.hyatt.com; Deira City Centre metro; map p.57. Seductive (if pricey) waterside bar, with seating either indoors or outside on the terrace overlooking the Creek and the numerous fancy yachts parked at the adjacent marina. It's all very romantic and mellow, the mood helped along by smooth chill-out music and a nice selection of cocktails and other tipples, backed up by an upmarket bistro menu and seafood bar (mains 70–85dh). Daily noon–2am.

Vintage Wafi, Oud Metha ☎ 04 701 2222, ⊛ pyramidsrestaurantsatwafi.com; Dubai Healthcare City metro; map p.57. This cosy little wine bar is perhaps the nicest in the city, with a good spread of international vintages, including a decent selection by the glass, and a convivial atmosphere. There's also champagnes, beers, spirits and soft drinks, plus a few superior bar snacks. Daily except Thurs 5pm–1am.

SHEIKH ZAYED ROAD AND DOWNTOWN DUBAI

SHEIKH ZAYED ROAD

The Agency Emirates Towers Boulevard shopping complex ☎ 04 319 8741; Emirates Towers metro; map pp.64–65. Sedate-looking wood-panelled wine bar serving up a decent selection of vintages from all the world's major wine-producing countries by the glass or bottle, plus assorted champagnes, cocktails and beers, and fancy bar snacks. Daily noon–1am (Fri & Sat until midnight only).

Blue Bar Novotel World Trade Centre, Sheikh Zayed Rd ☎ 04 332 0000, ⊛ facebook.com (search for "Blue Bar Dubai"); World Trade Centre metro; map pp.64–65. This stylish little bar is a pleasant spot for a mellow drink earlier in the evening, with a sedate crowd and a good selection of speciality Belgian beers, plus cocktails, wines, premium whiskies and superior bar meals. Things can get lively later on in the evening from Thurs to Sat when there's a live band playing a mix of blues, jazz, classic rock and pop (from around 9.30pm until 1am). Happy hour daily 6–8pm (buy one get one free). Daily 2pm–2am.

Cin Cin Fairmont Hotel, Sheikh Zayed Rd ☎ 04 311 8559, ⊛ fairmont.com/dubai/dining/cincin; World Trade Centre metro; map pp.64–65. Upmarket, dimly lit lounge bar attracting a mix of monied bon viveurs and flash young party animals, although the atmosphere's generally pretty sedate. Wine-buffs can choose from around 450 vintages; there's also a well-stocked selection

TOP 5 TRADITIONAL PUBS

Belgian Beer Café See above
Double Decker See p.120
Fibber Magee's See p.120
Long's Bar See p.120
Viceroy Bar See opposite

10

TOP 5 BARS WITH VIEWS

At.mosphere See below
Bar 44 See p.122
Neos See below
Up on the Tenth See p.119
Vu's Bar See below

of vodkas and rare whiskies to browse, as well as a special "cigar bar" with walk-in humidor. Daily 7pm–2am.

Double Decker Al Murooj Rotana Hotel, Financial Centre Rd ⓦrotana.com/almuroojrotana; Financial Centre metro; map pp.64–65. One of the liveliest pubs in town, with quirky decor themed after the old London Routemaster buses and usually busy with a more-than-averagely tanked-up crowd of expats and Western tourists. Live music every Fri, and a DJ from around 9pm the rest of the week. Daily noon–3am.

★ **Fibber Magee's** Off Sheikh Zayed Rd ☎04 332 2400, ⓦfibbersdubai.com; Emirates Towers metro; map pp.64–65. One of the city's best-kept secrets, and probably Dubai's most successful stab at a traditional European pub, with a spacious, very nicely done out wood-beamed interior (and mercifully few TVs, to boot), and a good selection of draught tipples including Kilkenny, Guinness, Magners, London Pride and Peroni (with pints from just 20dh during the daily 4–7pm happy hour). There's also regular live music and good, homely pub food. To reach it, go down the small side road between *Jashan* restaurant and *Zoom* (just south of the *Radisson* hotel) and it's on your left in the bottom of the *Stables* restaurant building. Daily noon–2.30am (last orders).

iKandy Shangri-La Hotel, Sheikh Zayed Rd ☎04 405 2703, ⓦshangri-la.com; Financial Centre metro; map pp.64–65. Ibiza-style chill-out venue set around the poolside terrace on the fourth floor of the *Shangri-La*, with big white sofas on which to recline and ambient music in the background. Very nice, although drink prices are sky high. Daily 6pm–2am; closed April–Sept.

Long's Bar Towers Rotana Hotel, Sheikh Zayed Rd ☎04 312 2202, ⓦrotana.com/towersrotana; Financial Centre metro; map pp.64–65. Proud home to the longest bar in the Middle East, this English-style pub offers one of the strip's more convivial and downmarket drinking holes. There are all the usual tipples, pop-rock soundtrack, TV sports and other Dubai pub essentials, plus a separate dining area serving up basic pub grub. The small dance area sees action during the irregular DJ and live music nights, and – in a slightly more spontaneous fashion – towards closing time during the bar's innumerable drinks promotions. Daily noon–3am.

Oscar's Vine Society Crowne Plaza Hotel, Sheikh Zayed Rd ☎04 331 1111; Emirates Towers metro; map pp.64–65. If you like your wine bars rustic and with a

lingering smell of cheese, you'll love *Oscar's*, which manages a fair impression of a provençale wine cellar in the unlikely setting of the fourth floor of the *Crowne Plaza*. Tipples include a decent spread of international wines, with assorted French-style light meals and snacks to accompany, and very jolly service. Happy hour 6–7pm (buy one get one free). Daily 6pm–midnight (Thurs until 1am).

Vu's Bar 51st floor, Jumeirah Emirates Towers Hotel, Sheikh Zayed Rd ☎04 319 8088, ⓦjumeirah.com; Emirates Towers metro; map pp.64–65. On the 51st floor of Dubai's top business hotel, this is one of the highest licensed perches in Dubai. The small, capsule-like bar itself, with floor-to-ceiling windows on one side, feels like the business end of a space rocket, and the muted music, dark decor, dim lighting and rather subdued ambience means there's not much to distract one from contemplation of the endless city lights below. Prices are above average, as you'd expect (beer bottles 40dh, cocktails from 55dh, wines from 62dh) although there's a vast selection of tipples to choose from, plus a good cigar selection. Daily 6pm–3am.

DOWNTOWN DUBAI

At.mosphere 122nd floor, Burj Khalifa ☎04 888 3444, ⓦatmosphereburjkhalifa.com; map pp.64–65. The alcoholic equivalent of the mile-high club, *At.mosphere* is the world's highest bar and restaurant, located almost half a kilometre above ground level on the 122nd floor of the Burj Khalifa. Decor is svelte and modern, although you're eyes will inevitably be drawn to the huge views outside. There's a minimum spend of 200dh (per couple) if you want to visit the bar – where they also do light meals and pricey afternoon teas (290dh) – or you can choose to eat at the even pricier restaurant (see p.112). Daily noon–2am.

Left Bank Souk al Bahar, Old Town ☎04 368 4501, ⓦemiratesleisureretail.com/Brands/LeftBank.aspx; Burj Khalifa/Dubai Mall metro; map pp.64–65. Svelte little bar-restaurant tucked away in Souk al Bahar, sleepy by day but often kicking after dark, particularly on ladies' nights (currently Wed) when members of the fairer sex can sup virtually for free. Decent drinks selection, including reasonable cocktails and draught beer, and a passable menu of bistro-style international mains (75–195dh). Daily noon–2am.

Neos 63rd floor, The Address Downtown Dubai Hotel, Sheikh Mohammed bin Rashid Boulevard (Emaar Boulevard) ☎04 436 8888, ⓦtheaddress.com; Burj Khalifa/Dubai Mall metro; map pp.64–65. The second highest bar in Dubai (eclipsed only by *At.mosphere*), with great views over Downtown Dubai and the Burj Khalifa – although the overblown decor, smoky atmosphere, ostentatious crowd and steep wine, beer and cocktail prices may leave you shaken rather than stirred. Daily 6pm–3am.

JUMEIRAH

Sho Cho Dubai Marine Beach Resort, Jumeirah Rd ☎ 04 346 1111, ⓦ dxbmarine.com/Sho-Cho; map pp.72–73. This chic little bar-cum-Japanese restaurant – all arctic white and underwater blue – seems to have been around forever, but remains modestly popular among the city's

Lebanese and Bollywood party set, despite (or perhaps because of) the trumped-up door staff. A nightly DJ plays mainly house – although the biggest night at present is the pose-free 1980s session every Sun. Daily 7pm–2am or later (kitchen closes at midnight).

THE BURJ AL ARAB AND AROUND

360° Jumeirah Beach Hotel, Jumeirah Rd ☎ 04 406 8769, ⓦ 360dubai.com; map p.78. The ultimate Dubaian chill-out bar (if you don't mind the high prices and sometimes erratic service), spectacularly located at the end of a long breakwater which arcs out into the Gulf opposite the *Jumeirah Beach Hotel* and Burj al Arab, and offering sublime after-dark views of both. An entrance fee is occasionally charged when visiting DJs are in residence; you may also need to reserve in advance if planning to arrive before 10pm – check the website for details. Daily 5pm–2am.

★ **Bahri Bar** Mina A'Salam Hotel, Madinat Jumeirah ☎ 04 366 6730, ⓦ madinatjumeirah.com; map p.78. Superb little Arabian-style outdoor terrace, liberally scattered with canopied sofas, Moorish artefacts and Persian carpets, and offering drop-dead gorgeous views of the Burj and Madinat Jumeirah – particularly lovely towards sunset. Daily 4pm–2am (Thurs & Fri until 3am).

BarZar Souk Madinat Jumeirah ☎ 04 366 6730, ⓦ madinatjumeirah.com; map p.78. The bar here is pretty nondescript, but the big terrace outside is one of the Madinat's best chill out spaces, with views of the fake Arabian wind towers and waterways and lots of bean-bags to crash out on over drinks, plus a good range of shisha. Daily 5pm–2am (Tues, Thurs & Fri until 3am).

Koubba Al Qasr Hotel, Madinat Jumeirah ☎ 04 366 6730, ⓦ madinatjumeirah.com; map p.78. A kind of twin sister to the nearby *Bahri Bar* (see above), with similarly delectable Arabian-themed decor and jaw-dropping views over *Al Qasr* and the Burj al Arab from its spacious terrace. Daily 6pm–2am (Fri from 4pm).

Skyview Bar 27th floor, Burj al Arab ☎ 04 301 7600, ⓔ BAArestaurants@jumeirah.com; map p.78. Landmark bar perched near the summit of the Burj al Arab, with colourful psychedelic decor and vast sea and city views – coming for a drink here is currently the cheapest way to see the inside of this fabulous hotel (see p.77). The huge drinks list majors in cocktails (from 100dh), but also sports a decent spread of wines, spirits, mocktails and even a few beers; alternatively, go for the lavish, seven-course afternoon teas (450dh). There's a minimum spend of 250dh per person, and you'll need to reserve in advance via email. Daily: afternoon tea 1–6pm; drinks 7pm–2am.

Uptown Bar Jumeirah Beach Hotel, Jumeirah Rd ☎ 04 406 8769, ⓦ bit.ly/JBHhotel; map p.78. Superb views of the Burj al Arab and southern Dubai are the main draw at this place, located on the 24th floor of the *Jumeirah Beach Hotel*. There's indoor and outdoor seating, plus a reasonable drinks list, although the decor is disappointingly humdrum for such a fine perch. Daily 6pm–1.30am.

THE PALM JUMEIRAH AND DUBAI MARINA

THE PALM JUMEIRAH

101 Dining Lounge and Bar One&Only The Palm, West Crescent ☎ 04 440 1030, ⓦ thepalm.oneandonlyresorts .com; map p.83. Overlooking the private marina of the swish new *One&Only The Palm* hotel, *101* doesn't quite know whether it wants to be a restaurant or a bar, with a dining room inside serving up a vaguely Spanish-style menu of tapas and assorted light Mediterranean meals, and a terrace over the water outside with live DJ most evenings and stunning views across to the massed skyscrapers of the marina opposite. Pricey, but worth it for the views. Daily 11am–1am.

C Club Jumeirah Zabeel Saray Hotel, West Crescent ☎ 04 453 0444, ⓦ jumeirah.com; map p.83. Fancy cigar lounge with OTT Neoclassical styling that wouldn't look out of place in your average English stately home. The "C" stands for cigars, cognac and chocolate (each represented in the decor by a different shade of dark wood), and there's a big selection of all three, including special chocolate-and-cognac pairings, as well as fine malts, spirits and other

tipples. Live jazz on Thurs & Fri from 8pm. Daily 6pm–1am.

Voda Bar Jumeirah Zabeel Saray Hotel ☎ 04 453 0444, ⓦ jumeirah.com; map p.83. Wacky cocktail bar in the über-stylish *Jumeirah Zabeel Saray* hotel – the white decor and pod-chairs look vaguely sci-fi futuristic, while the faux-Renaissance painted ceiling looks, well, just odd. There's an impressive drinks list, with excellent cocktails, plus good sushi to accompany and a live DJ from 9pm. Expensive, although offering regular promotions, including ladies' nights every Tues and daily happy hours (7–9pm). Daily 6pm–3am, (Fri from 4.30pm).

> ## TOP 5 BARS FOR MUSIC
>
> **360°** See above
> **Blue Bar** See p.119
> **Rooftop Bar** See p.122
> **Sho Cho** See above
> **Siddharta Lounge** See p.122

10

> ## TOP 5 BARS BY THE WATER
> **101 Dining Lounge and Bar** See p.121
> **360°** See p.121
> **Barasti Bar** See below
> **The Terrace** See p.119
> **Up on the Tenth** See p.119

DUBAI MARINA

★ **Bar 44** 44th floor, Grosvenor House Hotel, Al Sufouh Rd ☎ 04 399 8888, ⓦ luxurycollection.com /grosvenorhouse; Dubai Marina metro; map p.83. On the hotel's 44th floor, this svelte contemporary bar offers peerless 360-degree views of the entire marina development, with twinkling high-rises stretching away in every direction – as memorable a view of the southern city as you're likely to get short of climbing into a helicopter. The drinks list is as upmarket as the setting, with a big selection of wallet-emptying champagnes alongside fine malt whiskies, cool cocktails and other designer beverages (wine from 58dh, cocktails from 60dh, champagne from 148dh – or a cool 50,000dh for a bottle of 1981 Krug). Daily 6pm–2am (Thurs until 3am).

★ **Barasti Bar** Le Méridien Mina Sehayi, Al Sufouh Rd ☎ 04 318 1313, ⓦ barastibeach.com; Nakheel metro; map p.83. One of southern Dubai's most consistently popular nightspots, this fun, two-level beachside bar is more or less always packed with an eclectic crowd of tourists and expats. Downstairs is usually more Ibiza chill-out, with cool ambient music, shisha and loungers on the sand, while the pubbier upstairs is generally noisier, with

live DJs and a party atmosphere. Daily noon–2am.

★ **Rooftop Bar** Arabian Courtyard, One&Only Royal Mirage, Al Sufouh Rd ☎ 04 315 2412, ⓦ royalmirage .oneandonlyresorts.com; Nakheel metro; map p.83. On the roof of the *Royal Mirage*, this is one of Dubai's ultimate Orientalist fantasies, with seductive Moorish decor, cushion-strewn pavilions, silver-tray tables and other assorted Arabian artefacts – while the vaguely psychedelic lighting and smooth sounds from the live DJ add to the *One Thousand and One Nights* ambience. The downstairs bar-cum-pub area has a fine outdoor terrace, but otherwise isn't so nice. Daily 5pm–1am.

Siddharta Lounge Tower Two, Grosvenor House Hotel, Al Sufouh Rd ☎ 04 317 6000, ⓦ luxurycollection.com /grosvenorhouse; Dubai Marina metro; map p.83. Swanky new addition to the *Grosvenor House*'s ever-increasing array of top-end places to eat and drink. Outdoors is a cool poolside terrace and bar, inside a "palm area" with shisha lounge – all snowy-white decor with the occasional gold armchair. A nightly DJ provides a chill-out soundtrack, warming up as the evening wears on. Food and drinks are ordered off the menu of the adjacent *Buddha Bar* (see p.115), except there's no sushi. Daily 5pm–1am (Thurs & Fri until 2am).

West Beach Bistro & Sports Lounge Mövenpick Hotel, The Walk at Jumeirah Beach Residence ☎ 04 449 8888, ⓦ moevenpick-hotels.com; Jumeirah Lake Towers metro; map p.83. Cool sports bar right in the thick of the marina action with good bistro food and a huge main screen for big events, plus pool table and excellent happy hour deals. Daily noon–1am.

THE THIRD LINE GALLERY

Nightlife, entertainment and the arts

Like pretty much everywhere else in the Gulf, Dubai only really gets going in the cooler evening and night-time hours. As dusk falls, the streets light up in a blaze of neon and the pavements begin to fill up with a cosmopolitan crowd of Emiratis, Arabs, Westerners, Indians and Filipinos. The city's vibrant nightlife takes many forms. Western expats and tourists tend to make for the city's restaurants, bars and clubs, while locals and expat Arabs can be found relaxing in the city's myriad shisha cafés. Souks and shopping malls across the city fill up with crowds of consumers from all walks of Dubai society – most remain remarkably busy right up to when they close around midnight; bars and clubs meanwhile kick on until the small hours.

Dubai has a reasonably busy **clubbing** scene, driven by a mix of Western expats and tourists along with the city's large expat Arab (particularly Lebanese) community. Music tends to be a fairly mainstream selection of house, hip-hop and r'n'b (perhaps with a splash of Arabic pop), although a healthy number of visiting international DJs help keep things fresh. The emphasis at more upmarket places still tends to be on posing and pouting – expect to see lots of beautiful young things from Beirut or Bombay quaffing champagne and inspecting their make-up – although there's more fashion-free and egalitarian clubbing to be had at places like *Zinc* and *N'dulge*, the latter being Dubai's nearest equivalent to an Ibiza-style superclub.

In terms of more **cultural** diversions, there's significantly less on offer. Dubai is widely derided as the city that culture forgot – and in many ways the stereotype is richly deserved. The city has five-star hotels, luxury spas, celebrity chefs and shopping malls aplenty, but until a few years back lacked even a single functioning theatre. Even now, the city's musical life is largely limited to Filipino cover bands and the occasional big-name visiting rock act.

Yet things are changing – albeit slowly. Dubai now hosts a decent range of cultural festivals, including good film and jazz events (see p.29 & p.27), although outside festival time the city's cultural calendar can feel decidedly undernourished. Where Dubai has scored a major success, however, is in establishing itself as the Gulf's **art capital**, boasting a remarkable number of independent galleries; many of these are set up in unlikely places around the city by expats from around the Arab world and showcase a healthy spread of cutting-edge work by a range of international artists.

CLUBS

Club venues come and go on an annual basis, so it's worth checking the latest **listings** in *Time Out Dubai* (⊛ timeoutdubai .com) or visit ⊛ platinumlist.ae to find out what's new and happening; ⊛ yadig.com is (along with the *Time Out* website) the best source of local user reviews. Entrance **charges** generally vary depending on who's playing; occasionally it's free, but more usually expect to pay 50–100dh. Unfortunately, quite a few places (including several high-profile venues) suffer from truly lousy **service** – with neanderthal bouncers, officious waiters and pushy bartenders as standard. We haven't bothered listing the worse offenders, but even the places listed below aren't always as good as they should be. Note too that most places also have a **couples-only policy** (which may or may not be enforced depending on how busy they are) – in general it's also worth dressing to impress, or prepare to be turned away. As well as the following places, quite a few **bars** – places like *Sho Cho* and *360°* – have regular live DJs and a club-like ambience later on at night (see box, p.121), particularly if there's a special event on.

Armani Privé Armani Hotel, Burj Khalifa ☎ 04 888 3308, ⊛ dubai.armanihotels.com; Burj Khalifa/Dubai Mall metro; map pp.64–65. This self-styled "VIP lounge" hosts the usual mix of local and international DJs, with fancy decor and an above-average soundtrack, although if the staff don't like your face it's about as much fun as spending an evening poking yourself in the eye with a large fork. Daily except Sun 10pm–3am.

Boudoir Dubai Marine Beach Resort, Jumeirah Rd ☎ 04 345 5995 or ☎ 346 1111, ⊛ myboudoir.com; map pp.72–73. This sultry bar-cum-nightclub looks like the apartment of an upper-class nineteenth-century Parisian courtesan, with plush red drapes, chintzy chandeliers and an indecent number of mirrors (think Émile Zola with tequila slammers). There's a regular DJ on Tues, Thurs & Fri (ladies also get free champers all night on these evenings), plus occasional visiting international DJs at other times; on other nights it's more of a bar. Blokes will probably need to be in a (mixed-sex) couple to get in. Daily 9pm–3am.

Cirque du Soir Fairmont Hotel, Sheikh Zayed Rd ☎ 056 115 4507, ⊛ cirquedusoirdubai.com; World Trade Centre metro; map pp.64–65. An offshoot of the original London club (Lady Gaga is a big fan), this top-end venue at the *Fairmont* is half club, half music hall, with big-top-inspired decor and assorted performers including burlesque podium dancers, kooky clowns and juggling waiters – with a proper stage show later at night. Mon, Tues, Thurs & Fri 10.30pm–3am.

Domeland by Chi Al Nasr Leisureland, Oud Metha ☎ 04 337 9471; Oud Metha metro; map p.57. Formerly *Chi@ TheLodge*, this was Dubai's first mega-club when it opened a few years back, with space for 3500. It's now been somewhat overtaken by newer and fancier places, although still hosts the occasional big-name DJ and other themed events. Entrance charges vary, depending on what's on. Check *Time Out Dubai* for details of forthcoming events.

Kasbar The Palace, One&Only Royal Mirage, Al Sufouh Rd ☎ 04 315 2412, ⊛ royalmirage.oneandonlyresorts .com; Nakheel metro; map p.83. This superior-looking club shares the opulent Moroccan styling of the rest of the *Royal Mirage* complex, with the resident DJ serving up a mixed menu of Arabian and international tunes. It's sometimes lively, but at other times there's more of a crowd and a better atmosphere at the hotel's *Rooftop Bar* (see p.122). Hotel guests free; non-guests 65dh. Daily 9pm–2/3am.

Nasimi Beach Atlantis, The Palm ☎04 426 2626, ⓦnasimibeach.com; map p.83. Blissed-out beach club which functions as a bar-restaurant during the day and then turns more club-like later on as the resident DJ fires up the tunes. Events include regular, riotously popular beach and full-moon parties. Daily except Sun: restaurant noon–11.30pm; bar, lounge and beach 9am–1am (Fri until 2am); closed during summer (usually April–Sept).

N'dulge Atlantis, The Palm ☎055 200 4322 or ☎04 426 0561, ⓦatlantisthepalm.com/thingstodo/ndulgenightclub.aspx; map p.83. Formerly *The Sanctuary*, *N'dulge* has taken over *Chi@The Lodge's* mantle of Dubai's leading superclub, with space for around 3000 punters on its two big dancefloors inside and a lovely chill-out and shisha terrace outside. The eclectic music policy, with different tunes in each of the three areas, means you should find something you like. Daily 9pm–3am.

Trilogy Souk Madinat Jumeirah ☎04 366 6917,

ⓦtrilogy.ae; map p.78. Dubai's best-looking club, with moody Arabian styling and a medium-sized dancefloor. *The Rooftop* bar offers lovely views over the Madinat, while the main club area hosts big-name visiting DJs, as well as local acts. The Rooftop Mon–Sat 10pm–3am (closed in summer – roughly April to Sept); club Tues, Thurs & Fri only.

Velvet Underground Royal Ascot Hotel, Khalid bin al Waleed Rd ☎050 962 4222, ⓦvelvetundergrounddubai .com; Al Fahidi metro; map p.38. Bringing an unexpected dash of club culture to deepest Bur Dubai, *Velvet Underground* (formerly *Eleganté*) serves up an eclectic mix of music (with local and occasional international DJs) ranging from hip-hop and r'n'b through to Bollywood, Arabic and African. Free before midnight, after which men pay 100dh. Tues–Sun 10.30pm–3am.

Zinc Crowne Plaza Hotel, Sheikh Zayed Rd ☎050 151 5609, ⓦfacebook.com/zincnightclub; Emirates Towers metro; map pp.64–65. One of the longest running and most enduringly popular clubs in Dubai, thanks to an eclectic soundtrack, unposey atmosphere and the off-duty air crews that frequent it. Music is a mix of retro, r'n'b, hip-hop and house depending on the night. Entrance 100dh Thurs–Sun, 50dh Mon–Wed. Daily 10pm–3am.

11

SHISHA CAFÉS

For an authentic Arabian alternative to the pub, club or bar, nothing beats a visit to one of Dubai's **shisha cafés**. These are the places where local Emiratis and expat Arabs tend to head when they want to kick back, lounging around over endless cups of coffee while puffing away on a shisha (also known as waterpipe), filling the air with aromatic clouds of perfumed smoke – far more fragrant than your average smoke-filled pub. Many of Dubai's Arabian restaurants also do a good line in shisha, and the best places will have twenty or more varieties to choose from, with all sorts of fruit-scented flavours, plus a house special or two. Along with the places listed below, **other good places for shisha** include bars such as *BarZar* at Souk Madinat Jumeirah (see p.121) and *360°* at the *Jumeirah Beach Hotel* (see p.121), along with cafés such as *Kan Zaman* in Bur Dubai (see p.106), *QD's* in Garhoud (see p.107), and the Al Attar Business Tower branch of *Shakespeare & Co* on Sheikh Zayed Road (see p.105).

A'Rukn The Courtyard Souk Madinat Jumeirah ☎04 366 6730, ⓦmadinatjumeirah.com; map p.78. The picturesque central courtyard of the Madinat Jumeirah is a captivating place to kick back over a pricey shisha (65–85dh) and watch the engaging night-time life of the souk – from sunburnt tourists to robed Emiratis and their *abbeya*-clad wives – roll past. There are also mezze and Lebanese grills to snack on, plus a decent drinks list, making this one of the few places in the city where you can enjoy a shisha and a tipple at the same time. Daily 6pm–midnight.

Arabian Courtyard Arabian Courtyard, One&Only Royal Mirage ☎04 315 2412, ⓦroyalmirage.oneand onlyresorts.com; Nakheel metro; map p.83. This beautiful Moroccan-style courtyard, with fairy-lit palms and seating in pretty little open-sided tented pavilions, provides the magical setting for one of Dubai's most romantic shisha venues. Choose from twelve varieties of shisha (45–50dh), plus assorted mezze, Lebanese grills and a big list of beers, wines and cocktails. Daily 7pm–1/2am.

Creek View Restaurant Baniyas Rd ☎04 223 3223; Baniyas Square metro; map p.49. This convivial little open-air café scores highly for its breezy creekside location and lively late-night atmosphere, when it's usually busy with a mix of shisha-puffing locals and tourists. It's a good place for an after-dinner smoke and coffee (with ten types of shisha at 24–26dh), although the food (mainly mezze and kebabs) is mediocre and the music cheesier than an Edam factory. Daily 10am–2am.

Al Hakawati Marina Walk, Dubai Marina ☎04 368 2346, ⓦalhakawaticafe.com; Dubai Marina metro; map p.83. One of the liveliest and most appealing of the many cafés dotted along Marina Walk. The sign's easy to miss, but the café itself is pretty obvious, with an eye-catching scatter of red, kilim-covered sofas shaded by a little grove of potted trees – all in all, a very fair impression of a traditional Levantine garden café amid the thrusting skyscrapers. There are ten types of shisha on offer (21dh), and the food – a mishmash of Arabian and Western – isn't bad either. Daily 9am–2am.

LIVE MUSIC

Dubai's regular live music scene is pretty limited, although the city is increasingly featuring on the tours of big-name international acts, and things look up considerably during the Dubai International Jazz Festival (see p.27), not to mention the Womad festival down the road at Abu Dhabi (see p.28).

Atelier ⊛ theatelierworld.com. Launched in 2012, this major new music promoter has already brought a host of international acts to the city – from Nelly and 50 Cent through to Duffy and Craig David – playing to big crowds at the Meydan complex (see p.61). Events are currently staged monthly except during summer. Check the website for forthcoming shows.

Dubai Media City Amphitheatre Dubai Media City; Nakheel metro; map p.83. In the heart of Dubai Media City and with a capacity of 15,000, this spacious outdoor arena is the city's main venue for big shows by visiting international music acts, and also hosts the annual Dubai International Jazz Festival (see p.27). Check ⊛ timeoutdubai.com for details of forthcoming events.

The Fridge 5 Alserkal Ave, off Sheikh Zayed Rd interchange 3, Al Quoz ☎ 04 347 7793, ⊛ thefridge dubai.com; Noor Islamic Bank metro; map p.78. Based in a two-storey warehouse in the industrial (and increasingly arty) district of Al Quoz, *The Fridge* stages what are often the most original and interesting music events in town, with a mission to support local musicians in every genre – jazz, rock, hip-hop, classical or whatever else.

Jambase Souk Madinat Jumeirah ☎ 04 366 6730, ⊛ jumeirah.com; map p.78. Popular live music bar hosting a variety of enthusiastic local cover bands: not the most original music you'll ever hear, but the cracking party atmosphere generally compensates. Daily except Sun 7pm–2am (Thurs & Fri until 3am).

The Music Hall Jumeirah Zabeel Saray Hotel, West Crescent, The Palm ⊛ themusichall.com; map p.83. Opened at the beginning of 2013, this upmarket supper club-cum-music hall promises to bring something a bit different to the city's entertainment scene, with shows featuring an eclectic variety of ten-minute acts – anything from Arabian or Indian through to salsa or gipsy fusion – interspersed with DJ sets and accompanied by lavish food. Minimum spend applies. Thurs, Fri & hols.

The Music Room Majestic Hotel, Mankhool Rd ⊛ themusicroomdubai.com; Al Fahidi metro; map p.38. This dimly lit hotel pub serves up a classic slice of offbeat Bur Dubai nightlife, with the resident cover band performing most nights to a loyal crowd of tanked-up tourists and expats singing along to Bon Jovi classics, plus lots of Thai working girls touting for custom from their barside stools. Daily 6pm–3am.

Peppermint Experience World Trade Centre, Sheikh Zayed Rd ☎ 050 357 1113, ⊛ peppermint -experience.com; World Trade Centre metro. Leading local music promoter bringing regular big-name DJs and other acts to the city. Check the website for forthcoming events.

CINEMA

Dubai is well equipped with a string of modern multiplexes serving up all the latest Hollywood blockbusters, plus a few Bollywood flicks and the occasional Arabic film – although screenings of alternative and arthouse cinema are rare outside the excellent Dubai International Film Festival (see p.27). It's worth bearing in mind that the authorities **censor** any scenes featuring nudity, sex, drugs and homosexuality, as well as anything of a sensitive religious or political nature. In addition, audiences are generally less well behaved than in Western cinemas, with noisy teenagers and out-of-control kids the norm, usually accompanied by assorted mobile phone conversations and much noisy crunching of popcorn. **Tickets** cost around 35–50dh, while some cinemas have also introduced so-called "Gold" and "Grand" class screenings in their smaller auditoriums (tickets around 100dh) complete with luxurious reclining seats and personal table service.

Golden Cinema Bur Dubai, opposite Al Ghubaiba metro ⊛ goldencinemadubai.com. For something a bit different from the usual Hollywood fare, head to the Golden Cinema, which caters to the local Indian community with regular screenings of Bollywood, Tamil and Malayalam films – particularly lively on Fri.

Grand Cinemas Branches include the Grand Cineplex at Wafi, Oud Metha; the Grand Festival at Festival City; the Grand, Mercato mall, Jumeirah; and the Megaplex, Ibn Battuta Mall ⊛ grandcinemas.com. The city's largest cinema chain, with a range of multiplexes.

Lamcy Plaza Cinema Lamcy Plaza, Oud Metha ☎ 04 336 8808, ⊛ lamcyplaza.com/movie.htm; Oud Metha metro. This no-frills old stalwart is a fun place to take in an Indian film among a lively local crowd.

Movies Under the Stars Rooftop Gardens, Wafi, Oud Metha ☎ 04 324 4100, ⊛ wafi.com; Dubai Healthcare City metro. Free open-air films screened every Sun (8.30pm) from Oct to May, with seating on beanbags and an enjoyably informal and chilled-out atmosphere.

Vox Deira City Centre, Garhoud; Mall of the Emirates ⊛ voxcinemas.com. Two large modern multiplexes.

THEATRE

Dubai's theatrical scene remains decidedly moribund. The good news is that the city now possesses a couple of decent theatres, although the bad news is that neither of them is yet staging anything particularly worth seeing, unless you're lucky enough to time your visit to coincide with the arrival of one of the international productions which occasionally stop by. In the meantime it's left largely to the groundbreaking DUCTAC to keep the cultural fires burning.

Dubai Community and Arts Centre (DUCTAC) Mall of the Emirates ☎ 04 341 4777, ⓦ ductac.org; Mall of the Emirates metro. A rare and refreshing burst of alternative creative spirit, DUCTAC is home to the excellent little Centrepoint Theatre, Kilachand Studio Theatre and Manu Chhabria Arts Centre which collectively host an engaging and eclectic array of productions, including film, music and theatre, with the emphasis on local and community-based projects.

Madinat Theatre Madinat Jumeirah ☎ 04 366 6546, ⓦ madinattheatre.com. Squirrelled away in the depths of the Madinat Jumeirah, this was Dubai's first proper theatre when it opened a few years back, although the pedestrian programme of events – featuring an uninspiring mix of mainstream musicals, theatrical performances and other assorted lowbrow crowd-pleasers – hasn't yet done much to invigorate Dubai's flagging cultural credentials.

ART GALLERIES

11

Art galleries have positively mushroomed over Dubai during the past few years – the places below are just some of the better known venues. For comprehensive listings, check out ⓦ artinthecity.com, which also covers galleries in Sharjah and Abu Dhabi. The (unlikely) hub of the city's art scene was formerly the rundown industrial area of **Al Quoz**, off Sheikh Zayed Road (between interchanges 3 and 4; First Gulf Bank metro), whose low rents attracted a string of gallery owners from across the Arab world, although Al Quoz is now increasingly rivalled by the dense cluster of more upmarket galleries that have sprung up in the **Gate Village** at the DIFC (see p.64; Emirates Tower metro). The city also hosts two big annual arts **festivals** in mid-March, when Art Dubai and the Bastakiya Art Fair hit town (see p.28).

BUR DUBAI

Majlis Gallery Al Fahidi Roundabout, next to the main entrance into Bastakiya, Bur Dubai ☎ 04 353 6233, ⓦ themajlisgallery.com; Al Fahidi metro. Set in a pretty old Bastakiya house, this is the oldest gallery in the city, founded in 1989 by English interior designer Alison Collins (who still co-owns it), and hosting monthly exhibitions showcasing the work of Emirati and international artists. Sat–Thurs 10am–6pm.

GATE VILLAGE, DIFC

artsawa Building 8 ☎ 04 340 8660, ⓦ artsawa.com. Exhibitions of work by both emerging and established Middle Eastern artists. Sat–Thurs 10am–7pm.

Artspace Building 3 ☎ 04 323 0820, ⓦ artspace-dubai .com. Upmarket gallery specializing in work by leading painters and sculptors from across the Middle East. Sun–Thurs 10am–8pm.

ayyam gallery Building 3 ☎ 04 439 2395, ⓦ ayyamgallery.com. Leading Syrian-owned gallery (they also have branches in Beirut, Damascus, Jeddah and London, plus a second Dubai branch in Al Quoz) promoting work by Arabian and Iranian artists. Sat–Thurs 10am–8pm.

Cuadro Building 10 ☎ 04 425 0400, ⓦ cuadroart.com. Exhibitions of works by leading international artists in a variety of media – painting, photography, sculpture and printmaking. Also runs an interesting education programme including lectures, workshops and panel discussions, plus artist residencies. Sun–Thurs 10am–8pm, Sat noon–6pm.

The Empty Quarter Building 2 ☎ 04 323 1210, ⓦ theemptyquarter.com. The only Dubai gallery devoted exclusively to photography, with fine art, documentary and photojournalism exhibitions of work by top Middle Eastern and international talent. Sun–Thurs 10am 10pm, Sat 2–8pm.

Opera Gallery Building 3 ☎ 04 304 5518, ⓦ operagallery.com. Part of an international gallery chain, representing mainstream paintings and drawings by major international twentieth- and twenty-first-century artists. Also have a second branch in the Dubai Mall. Sun–Thurs 10am–8pm, Sat noon–8pm.

XVA Gallery Building 7 ⓦ xvagallery.com. One of the city's oldest galleries, recently relocated to the Gate Village from its old home at the XVA hotel and café in Bastakiya, and focusing mainly on big-name artists from Arabia and Iran. Sun–Thurs 10am–6pm.

AL QUOZ

Courtyard Gallery Sheikh Zayed Rd, off interchange 3 (exit 43) ⓦ courtyardgallerydubai.com. One of the city's largest galleries, hosting local Arab and Iranian artists alongside big European names. Part of a quaint and colourful little complex which also includes its own café and a couple of handicraft shops. Sun–Thurs 10am–6pm.

Gallery Isabelle van den Eynde Sheikh Zayed Rd, off interchange 3 (exit 43) ☎ 04 323 5052, ⓦ ivde.net. Formerly the B21 Gallery, this is one of the city's more cutting-edge venues, priding itself on nurturing and showcasing the talents of the young Arab artists. Sat–Thurs 10am–7pm.

Green Art Gallery Sheikh Zayed Rd, off interchange 3 (exit 43) ☎04 346 9305, ✆gagallery.com. One of the longest established galleries in the city, particularly known for its role in promoting the work of Arab artists. Sat–Thurs 10am–7pm.

thejamjar Sheikh Zayed Rd, off interchange 4 (exit 39), Al Quoz ☎04 341 7303, ✆thejamjardubai.com. Part gallery, part community project, thejamjar exhibits work by local and international artists and also provides a range of other facilities and events including art classes for children and adults and a "DIY Painting Studio" where you can have a crack at painting; all materials are provided free. Mon–Thurs & Sat 10am–8pm, Fri 2–8pm.

The Third Line Sheikh Zayed Rd, off interchange 3 (exit 43) ☎04 341 1367, ✆thethirdline.com. Focusing on the work of Arab artists, this is one of Dubai's most experimental venues, with engaging displays of painting, photography and assorted installations. Sat–Thurs 10am–7pm.

11

SOUK MADINAT JUMEIRAH

Shopping

Dubai is shopaholic heaven. This is the city that boasts the world's largest shopping mall and whose major annual event is the Dubai Shopping Festival (see p.27) – even its name sounds suspiciously like "do buy". The seriousness with which Dubai takes its retail therapy is evident in the lavishness of many of the spectacular modern malls that dot the city, some of them virtual tourist attractions In their own right, attracting an eclectic crowd of local Emiratis, Western tourists and bargain-hunting Indian and Filipino expats. Alternatively, there's still plenty of old-fashioned Arabian shopping to be found in the souks of Deira and Bur Dubai, piled high with traditional items like gold, perfume and spices at cut-throat prices – which can often be lowered still further if you fancy a spot of good-natured haggling.

Opening hours for mall shops are usually 10am to 10pm; some stay open until midnight between Thursday and Saturday, while a few remain closed on Fridays until 2pm. Opening hours in souks are more variable: in general most places open from 10am to 10pm, though many close in the afternoon from around 1 to 4/5pm depending on the whim of the owner. **Bargaining** is the norm in the souks; prices in mall shops are fixed.

BOOKS AND MUSIC

Borders Mall of the Emirates ☎ 04 341 5758; Mall of the Emirates metro; map p.78. One of the city's few reliable sources of decent reading matter. Other branches at Marina Mall (map p.83) and Ibn Battuta Mall (map p.83). Daily 10am–10pm (Thurs–Sat until midnight).

★ **Kinokuniya (Book World)** Second floor, Dubai Mall ☎ 04 434 0111, ⓦ kinokuniya.com/ae; Burj Khalifa/Dubai Mall metro; map pp.64–65. This local outpost of the famous Japanese chain is far and away Dubai's best bookshop – a vast emporium stuffed with a simply massive array of titles, ranging from mainstream novels, travel guides and magazines through to graphic novels, works in French and German and a brilliant manga selection. Daily 10am–10pm (Thurs–Sat until midnight).

Magrudy's Jumeirah Rd, Jumeirah ☎ 04 344 4193; ⓦ magrudy.com; map pp.72–73. The city's oldest

bookshop, and still one of the best, although note that all the good stuff is kept on the easily missed upstairs floor. Sat–Thurs 9am–10pm, Fri 2–10pm.

Virgin Megastore Dubai Mall ☎ 04 325 3330, ⓦ virginmegastore.me; Burj Khalifa/Dubai Mall metro; map pp.64–65. Dubai offshoot of the now defunct UK chain, mainly of interest (high-street nostalgia apart) for its selection of Arabic pop and other music from Morocco to Iraq – anything from traditional oud recitals or the legendary Um Kalthoum through to contemporary superstars like Amr Diab and Nancy Ajram, as well as recordings by many Gulf and Emirati musicians. Other branches at BurJuman (map p.38), Deira City Centre (map p.57), Mercato (map pp.72–73) and Mall of the Emirates (map p.78). Daily 10am–10pm (Thurs–Sat until midnight).

CLOTHES AND SHOES

Aizone Mall of the Emirates ☎ 04 347 9333; Mall of the Emirates metro; map p.78. Originally from Beirut, Aizone majors in chic and very pricey partywear (mainly for ladies; the token menswear offerings are very dull). The emphasis is on skimpy frocks, figure-hugging dresses and

outrageously tiny tops, although there's usually also a decent selection of more practical indie-label designs which won't immediately blow off in a high wind. There's a second branch at the Dubai Mall (map pp.64–65). Daily 10am–10pm (Thurs–Sat until midnight).

WHAT TO BUY

Almost everything, is the answer. **Gold**, **diamonds** and other precious stones are cheaper here than just about anywhere else in the world. Dubai is also good for cheap **spices** and Middle Eastern **food**, purchased either in the Deira souks or a local supermarket; dates are a particularly good buy. Other bargains are local **perfumes**, **clothes** and **shoes**, including pretty little Arabian-style embroidered slippers – or you could go the whole hog and kit yourself out in a traditional *dishdasha* or *abbeya*. The city also has a thriving **carpet** trade (though you might want to check the Blue Souk in Sharjah too) ranging from inexpensive kilims to heirloom-quality Persian rugs. Arabian **souvenirs** are another obvious choice and there are heaps of collectable antiques such as old coffee pots, khanjars, wooden boxes and antique Bedouin jewellery, along with shisha pipes and frankincense, not to mention plenty of memorably awful toy camels, mosque alarm clocks and Burj al Arab paperweights. Recordings of Arabian **music** are another interesting buy, although for a quintessentially Dubaian memento, check out some of the vast array of **fake designer** stuff on offer in Karama (see p.135) and Bur Dubai.

For (genuine) contemporary **fashion**, all the world's top brands are represented in Dubai's malls. In fact, label fatigue sets in pretty rapidly during any shopping tour of the city and you might prefer to forego looking at yet more Armani in favour of searching out some of the city's small number of more interesting independent boutiques like S*uce (see opposite) or Ginger & Lace (see opposite) – or just take your revenge on the dominant brands by buying a pile of fakes from Karama. Most major labels have their own stores; alternatively, check out what's available at one of the city's increasing number of flagship international **department stores**, which now include Harvey Nichols, Galeries Lafayette, Bloomingdale's and Saks Fifth Avenue.

12

TAILORING IN DUBAI

Although not as well known for its tailoring industry as places like Hong Kong, Bangkok or India, Dubai is a decent place to get tailor-made clothes run up at fairly modest prices. A good tailor will be able to copy any existing garment you bring in or, alternatively, make up clothes from a photograph or even a hand-drawn design. The best place to head to is the Meena Bazaar area of Bur Dubai, particularly **Al Hisn Street** (off Al Fahidi Street near the Dubai Museum), where you'll find a line of tailors along the west side of the road – Dream Girl Tailors (see below) is a good bet.

Dream Girl Tailors Al Hisn St ☎ 04 388 0070; Al Fahidi metro; map p.38. One of the best and most reliable of the Al Hisn St tailors (see box above), who will charge you around 60dh for a shirt or trousers, or from 150dh for a dress (not including material). Sat–Thurs 10am–1pm & 4–10pm, Fri 6–9pm only.

Fabindia Nashwan Building, Al Mankhool Rd (nr Eppco Petrol Station, south of the junction with Kuwait Rd), Bur Dubai ☎ 04 398 9633, ⓦ fabindia.com; Al Karama metro; map p.38. Well-known Indian chain selling a wide range of clothing and homeware combining the best of traditional subcontinental craftsmanship with chic contemporary designs in vibrant colours – all at very affordable prices. Inconveniently located, but worth the hike. Sat–Thurs 10am–9pm, Fri 2–10pm.

Ginger & Lace Wafi ☎ 04 324 5699; Dubai Healthcare City metro; map p.57. One of the best of the (admittedly few) independent boutiques in Dubai, selling a range of funky ladieswear sourced from international designers. There's a second branch at the Ibn Battuta Mall (map p.83). Daily 10am–10pm (Thurs & Fri until midnight).

Harvey Nichols Mall of the Emirates ☎ 04 409 8888, ⓦ harveynichols.com; Mall of the Emirates metro; map p.78. The flagship shop of one of Dubai's flagship malls, this suave, minimalist three-storey department store offers a vast array of international labels, including British classics like Vivienne Westwood and Alexander McQueen. Daily 10am–10pm (Thurs–Sat until midnight).

Mumbai Se Dubai Mall ☎ 04 434 0626, ⓦ facebook .com/mumbaiseuae; Burj Khalifa/Dubai Mall metro; map pp.64–65. Top-end designer Indian fashions (ladieswear only) at prices to match – the place to go if you want to feel like Bollywood royalty. Other branches at Festival Centre (map p.57) and Marina Mall (map p.83). Daily 10am–10pm (Thurs–Sat until midnight).

Não do Brasil Second Floor, Dubai Mall ☎ 04 431 3772, ⓦ naodobrasil.com; Burj Khalifa/Dubai Mall metro; map pp.64–65. One of the most eye-catching shops in the Dubai Mall and a virtual work of art in its own right, stuffed full of funky trainers in colourful patterns handcrafted under ethical conditions in Brazil. Surprisingly affordable, too. Daily 10am–10pm (Thurs–Sat until midnight).

Priceless Al Maktoum Rd, near Deira Clock Tower ☎ 04 221 5444; Al Rigga metro; map p.57. Worth the schlep down Al Maktoum Rd for the excellent spread of top designer menswear and ladieswear – Armani, Yves Saint-Laurent, Gucci and the like – all sold at big discounts; two-thirds off label prices is standard. Sat–Thurs 10am–10pm, Fri 2–10pm.

S*uce The Village Mall, Jumeirah ☎ 04 344 7270, ⓦ shopatsauce.com; map pp.72–73. The city's leading independent boutique, stocking a wide range of designs you won't find anywhere else, usually with the emphasis on colourful hippychick chic, plus a good range of funky accessories. Sat–Thurs 10am–10pm, Fri 4–10pm.

ELECTRONICS

Carrefour The various Dubai branches of the French hypermarket (see p.132) offer a vast selection of bargain-basement electronics and accessories – laptops, tablets, phones and plenty more – although mainly featuring less fashionable (or, indeed, downright obscure) brands.

Khalid bin al Waleed Road Bur Dubai; Al Fahidi metro. The massed computer and electronics shops lining Khalid bin al Waleed Rd around the junction with Al Mankhool Rd are heaven for technophiles in search of a deal, with everything from cut-price PCs to mobile phone accessories at discount prices; be prepared to shop around. It's also worth checking out the nearby Al Ain Centre on Al Mankhool Rd, which is also stuffed with mountains of digital gadgets.

FOOD

★ **Bateel Dates** BurJuman ☎ 04 359 7932, ⓦ bateel .com; Khalid bin al Waleed metro (exit 3); map p.38. The best dates in the city, grown in Bateel's own plantations in Saudi Arabia and sold either plain, covered in chocolate or stuffed with ingredients such as almonds and slices of lemon or orange. Other offerings include date biscuits, juice and jam, along with concoctions like date pesto and date mustard, plus a small selection of fine (date-free) chocolates. They also do nice gift boxes if you're looking for a present. Other branches at Deira City Centre (map p.57), Festival Centre (map p.57), Souk al Bahar (map pp.64–65) and Dubai Mall (map pp.64–65). Daily 10am–10pm (Thurs & Fri until 11pm).

12

Carrefour Mall of the Emirates ☎04 409 4888, ⓦcarrefouruae.com; Mall of the Emirates metro; map p.78. This vast French hypermarket chain might not be the most atmospheric place to shop in the city, but is one of the best places to pick up just about any kind of Middle Eastern foodstuff you fancy, including dates, sweets like halva and baklava, teas, tropical fruits, nuts, spices, Arabian honey, Turkish coffee, saffron, caviar, *labneh* and olives. Also a good source of electronics (see p.131), kitchenware, rugs, perfumes and all sorts of other stuff, often at bargain-basement prices. Other branches near Al Ghubaiba Bus Station in Bur Dubai (daily 8am–midnight; map p.38), Deira City Centre (map p.57), and Marina Mall (map p.83). Daily 9am–midnight.

Spice Souk Deira; Al Ras metro. All sort of spices and other local specialities (see p.51).

Wafi Gourmet Wafi, Oud Metha ☎04 327 9940, ⓦwafigourmet.com; Dubai Healthcare City metro; map p.57. The ultimate Dubai deli, this little slice of foodie heaven is piled high with tempting Middle Eastern items, including big buckets of olives, nuts, spices and dried fruits, and trays of date rolls, baklava and fine chocolates. The shop also has its own restaurant, in case you can't wait to get stuck in, offering instant gratification with a range of tasty kebabs, mezze and seafood. Daily 10am–10pm (Thurs & Fri until midnight).

HANDICRAFTS, CARPETS AND SOUVENIRS

★ **The Camel Company** Mall of the Emirates ☎04 340 2670, ⓦcamelcompany.ae; Mall of the Emirates metro; map p.78. This dromedary-obsessed shop stocks Dubai's cutest selection of stuffed toy camels – vastly superior to the usual hump-backed horrors on offer elsewhere in the city – plus camel mugs, camel cards, camel T-shirts and so on. Other branches at Dubai Mall (map pp.64–65), Souk al Bahar (map pp.64–65), Souk Madinat Jumeirah (map p.78) and Ibn Battuta Mall (map p.83). Daily 10am–10pm (Thurs–Sat until midnight).

Deira Tower Baniyas Square, Deira; Baniyas Square metro; map p.49. Home to the biggest collection of rug shops in the city, the so-called Deira Tower "Carpet Souk" comprises thirty-odd stores spread over the ground and first floors of this large office block. There's a massive amount of stuff on sale, ranging from huge, museum-quality Persian heirlooms to ghastly framed carpet pictures and other tat, but it's mostly good quality, and likely to work out cheaper than in one of the city's mall-based rug shops. Most shops open 10am–9pm (although many close from around 2pm to 4/5pm).

★ **Gallery One** Mall of the Emirates ☎04 341 4488, ⓦg-1.com; Mall of the Emirates metro; map p.78. Citywide gallery chain selling a good range of superb, limited-edition photographs of Dubai – expensive, but not outrageous – as well as other fine-art photography and superior postcards. Other branches at Dubai Mall (map pp.64–65), Souk al Bahar (map pp.64–65) and Souk Madinat Jumeirah (map p.78). Daily 10am–10pm (Thurs–Sat until midnight).

Gift Village Baniyas Square (next door to Hatam al Tai café), Deira ☎04 294 6858, ⓦgift-village.com; Baniyas Square metro; map p.49. A veritable Aladdin's cave of discounted everything, from pure tat through to designer desirables, including perfumes, electronics, clothing, bags, sports equipment, household appliances and cuddly toys. Daily 9am–1am (closed Fri noon–3pm).

International Aladdin Shoes Textile Souk, Bur Dubai (next to Bur Dubai Old Souk Abra Station) ☎055 515 4351; Al Ghubaiba metro; map p.38. In a prime position, this eye-catching little stall (no sign) in the midst of the Textile Souk stocks a gorgeous selection of colourful embroidered ladies slippers (65–200dh) along with lovely embroidered belts. Daily 8am–11pm.

Al Jaber Gallery Dubai Mall ☎04 339 8556, ⓦaljabergallery.ae; Burj Khalifa/Dubai Mall metro; map pp.64–65. Dubai's leading purveyor of low-grade Arabian "handicrafts". Look hard enough and you might find some half-decent stuff, including attractive old traditional wooden boxes and coffee pots, though the shop is perhaps best regarded as a source of hilarious kitsch – dodgy daggers, constipated camels, fluorescent shisha pipes and the like. Kids will love it. Other branches at Deira City Centre (map p.57), Mall of the Emirates (map p.78), Souk Madinat Jumeirah (map p.78) and Marina Mall (map p.83). Daily 10am–10pm (Thurs–Sat until midnight).

Pride of Kashmir Mall of the Emirates ☎04 341 4477, ⓦprideofkashmir.com; Mall of the Emirates metro; map p.78. One of the leading citywide handicrafts chains, more upmarket than Al Jaber Gallery (see above) but perfectly affordable. Stock usually includes carpets and kilims alongside antiques (and cleverly aged fake antiques), pashminas and traditional-style wooden furniture. Other branches at Souk al Bahar (map pp.64–65) and Souk Madinat Jumeirah (map p.78). Daily 10am–10pm (Thurs–Sat until midnight).

JEWELLERY AND PERFUME

Ajmal BurJuman ☎04 351 5505, ⓦajmalperfume.com; Khalid bin al Waleed metro (exit 3); map p.38. Dubai's leading perfumiers, offering a wide range of fragrances including traditional *attar*-based Arabian scents. If you don't like any of the ready-made perfumes on offer you can make up your own from the big glass bottles on display behind the

counter. Other branches at Sikkat al Khail Rd, Deira (daily 10am–10pm; map p.49), Khan Murjan Souk (map p.57), Deira City Centre (map p.57) and Mall of the Emirates (map p.78). Daily 10am–10pm (Thurs & Fri until 11pm).

Damas Dubai Mall ☏ 04 339 8846, ⓦ damasjewel.com; Burj Khalifa/Dubai Mall metro; map pp.64–65. Ubiquitous chain of jewellery shops, with branches in virtually every mall in the city. Gold and diamond jewellery predominate, and designs range from classic Italian to chintzy Arabian. Other branches across the city. Daily 10am–10pm (Thurs–Sat until midnight).

Gold and Diamond Park Sheikh Zayed Rd between interchanges 3 and 4 ⓦ goldanddiamondpark.com; First Gulf Bank metro; map p.78. This low-key little mall is the place to come if you want diamonds, which retail here for barely half the price you'd expect to pay back home. The ninety-odd shops are stuffed full of diamond-encrusted jewellery; most is made according to European rather than Arabian designs, with a good range of pieces in classic Italian styles. You'll also find a few other precious stones and platinum jewellery for sale, plus a small amount of gold. Some places can also knock up custom-made designs. Daily 10am–10pm.

Gold Souk Deira; Al Ras metro. Huge selection of gold in Dubai's most famous souk (see p.48).

Perfume Souk Deira; Al Ras metro. Local and international brands from a string of shops – or mix your own (see p.53). Most shops open around 10am–10pm, although some may close roughly 1–4/5pm, and also on Fri mornings.

MALLS

BurJuman Corner of Khalid bin al Waleed and Sheikh Zayed roads, Bur Dubai ⓦ burjuman.com; Khalid bin Al Waleed metro (exit 3); map p.38. The best city-centre mall, BurJuman remains enduringly popular with tourists and locals alike thanks to its 300-plus shops and convenient location. The older and relatively run-of-the-mill section has branches of Virgin (see p.130), Ajmal (see p.132) and Bateel Dates (see p.131), while a posh extension at the mall's south end combines stylish architecture with a chain of upmarket shops, including the flagship Saks Fifth Avenue department store. Daily 10am–10pm (Thurs & Fri until 11pm).

Deira City Centre Garhoud ⓦ deiracitycentre.com; Deira City Centre metro; map p.57. Long overtaken in the glamour and glitz stakes by newer shopping centres, this big old mall nevertheless remains one of the most popular in the city among less label-conscious consumers. It also offers a quintessential slice of Dubaian life, attracting everyone from veiled Emirati women to bargain-crazed Russian carpet-baggers – though the crowds can make the whole place rather chaotic and exhausting. The 340-plus outlets here have a largely (though not exclusively) downmarket, bargain-basement emphasis, although it's also worth checking out the "Jewellery Court" on Level 1, featuring an extraordinary collection of jewellery and watch shops selling everything from svelte Italian designs to the most outrageous, gem-encrusted Arabian bling imaginable, at equally fabulous prices. Think diamonds – lots of them. Daily 10am–10pm (Thurs–Sat until midnight).

Dubai Mall Downtown Dubai ⓦ thedubaimall.com; Burj Khalifa/Dubai Mall metro; map pp.64–65. With a stupendous 1200-odd shops, this mother of all malls (see p.68) has pretty much everything you'll ever need to buy, and branches of just about every chain that does business in the city; some of the few that aren't here can be found in the adjacent Souk al Bahar (see p.136). Highlights include the flagship Bloomingdale's and Galeries Lafayette department stores; "Fashion Avenue", home to the biggest array of designer labels in Dubai; and the attractively chintzy "Souk" area, with a further 120 shops selling gold, jewellery and Arabian perfumes. Upstairs you'll find a Dubai branch of Hamleys, the famous London toyshop, plus Kinokuniya (see p.130), while the basement holds a massive Waitrose supermarket. Daily 10am–10pm (Thurs–Sat until midnight).

Festival Centre Festival City ⓦ festivalcentre.com; map p.57. The centrepiece of the new Festival City development, this big new mall (see p.60) is nicely designed, with attractive waterfront walks and a big (albeit fairly predictable) range of shops – although the frustrating lack of maps makes it remarkably difficult to actually find anything. Daily 10am–10pm (Thurs–Sat until midnight).

★ **Ibn Battuta Mall** Between interchanges 5 and 6, Sheikh Zayed Rd ⓦ ibnbattutamall.com; Ibn Battuta metro; map p.83. This Ibn Battuta-inspired mall is worth a visit for its stunning decor alone (see p.88) – although as a shopping experience it's a bit underpowered. Shops include branches of Borders (see p.130), The Toy Store (see p.143) and Ginger & Lace (see p.131) – and it's worth a look at the entertaining Daiso in the Andalucia court, a kind of Japanese pound shop with everything for 7dh. Daily 10am–10pm (Thurs–Sat until midnight).

★ **Mall of the Emirates** Interchange 4, Sheikh Zayed Rd ⓦ malloftheemirates.com; Mall of the Emirates metro; map p.78. Perhaps the best one-stop shopping destination in the city (see p.80), with around 500 stores to browse, good places to eat and drink and the surreal snow-covered slopes of Ski Dubai to ogle. Highlights include the flagship Harvey Nichols department store (see p.131), the impressive new Fashion Dome and the "Arabian Souk", housing various handicrafts and carpet outlets. There's also a big Borders – one of the few really good bookshops in the

12

city (see p.130) – and a well-stocked Toy Store, scattered with giant stuffed animals and selling everything from Teletubbies to T-Rexes. Daily 10am–10pm (Thurs–Sat until midnight).

Marina Mall Sheikh Zayed Rd, Dubai Marina ⓦ marinamall.ae; Jumeirah Lake Towers metro; map p.83. Aimed more at local Marina residents than visiting tourists, this bright modern mall is worth a visit if you're in the area and fancy a bit of clothes shopping (the central atrium looks like a kind of postmodern temple of designer brands), but not worth a special visit otherwise. Daily 10am–10pm (Thurs & Fri until midnight).

★ **Mercato** Jumeirah Rd, Jumeirah ⓦ mercato shoppingmall.com; map pp.72–73. This kitsch Italian-themed mall (see p.74) is relatively small compared to many others in the city, but packs in a good selection of rather upmarket outlets aimed at affluent local villa dwellers, including a decent range of mainstream designer labels. Daily 10am–10pm (Fri until midnight).

The Village Mall Jumeirah Beach Rd, Jumeirah ⓦ thevillagedubai.com; map pp.72–73. The best of the various small malls scattered along the northern end of Jumeirah Beach Rd, attractively designed and home to the excellent S*uce boutique (see p.131) and a boutique selling the work of top Indian designer Ayesha Depala, plus a homely little branch of *Shakespeare & Co* (see p.105). Sat–Thurs 10am–10pm, Fri 4–10pm.

★ **Wafi** Oud Metha ⓦ waficity.com; Dubai Healthcare City metro; map p.57. This zany Egyptian-themed mall makes for a pleasantly superior shopping experience, with quirky decor and a refreshingly peaceful atmosphere, while the attached Khan Murjan Souk (see below) is one of the best places in the city to shop for traditional arts and crafts. Wafi is particularly good for independent ladies' fashion, with outlets including Ginger & Lace (see p.131), the over-the-top Valleydez and the more understated By Malene Berger (showcasing work by the leading Danish designer) and Desert Rose – not to mention Noura Ashley, full of quietly opulent black *abbeyas*. Daily 10am–10pm (Thurs & Fri until midnight).

SOUKS

The Gold, Perfume and Spice souks are covered in the Deira chapter (see p.48, p.53 & p.51).

Karama Souk Karama; Al Karama metro; map p.57. This open-air concrete complex in Karama is the best place to explore Dubai's roaring trade in fake designer gear and offers the perfect opportunity to stock up on anything from dodgy D&G to the latest Manchester United football strip, although sadly the uniquely amateurish forgeries – think "Adibas" and "Hugo Bros" – which used to be one of the souk's specialities are no longer seen, following crackdowns by the city authorities. The little shops here have racks full of reasonable-quality imitation designer clothing and sportswear, while there are also plenty of fake designer bags and "genuine fake watches" to be had. A few low-grade souvenir shops can also be found dotted around the souk selling kitsch classics like mosque-shaped alarm clocks, pictures made from sand and miniature Burj al Arabs moulded in glass. The poky little Karama Centre nearby has some nice Indian ladieswear, including pretty *shalwar kameez*, plus jewellery. Most shops open daily 10am–10pm.

★ **Khan Murjan Souk** Wafi, Oud Metha ⓦ wafi.com /souk-in-dubai; Dubai Healthcare City metro; map p.57.

SHOPPING FOR FAKES

Despite ongoing government clampdowns, Dubai's vibrant trade in **counterfeit goods** (bags, watches, sunglasses, pens, counterfeit DVDs and so on) is still going strong, and for many visitors the acquisition of a top-notch fake Chanel bag or Gucci watch at a fraction of the price of the real thing may be the shopping highlight of a visit to the city – although the brands and city authorities won't thank you for saying so. Spend any amount of time in **Karama Souk**, the **Gold Souk** or around **Al Fahidi Street** in Bur Dubai and you'll be repeatedly importuned with offers of "cheap copy watches" or "copy bags".

Fakes are often on public display in shops, although they may be kept in backrooms away from prying official eyes. Many fakes are still relatively expensive – you're unlikely to find bigger-ticket items like bags and watches for much under US$50, and plenty of items cost double that, although they'll still be a lot cheaper than the real thing. Many fakes look pretty convincing at a casual glance (it's been suggested some counterfeits are actually manufactured in the same factories that produce the genuine items and aren't really fakes at all, but just seconds or "overmakes"), although longevity varies considerably; some fakes can fall to pieces within a fortnight, while others might last just as long as the real thing. It's essential to check quality carefully – particularly stitching and zips – and you should also be prepared to shop around and bargain like crazy. Don't be afraid to walk away if you can't get the price you want – you'll have plenty of other offers.

12

This eye-catching new development (see p.56) is one of Dubai's most seductive attempts at taking a humble collection of shops and turning them into a full-blown Orientalist fantasy – retail therapy masquerading as culture, although in Dubai it's often difficult to separate the two. The hundred-plus stores here comprise the city's best and most upmarket array of traditional crafts shops, selling just about every kind of Arabian geegaw, artefact and antique you can think of (and lots you probably can't). Daily 10am–10pm (Thurs & Fri until midnight).

Souk al Bahar Old Town Island ⓦ soukalbahar.ae; Burj Khalifa/Dubai Mall metro; map pp.64–65. Seemingly an afterthought to the massive Dubai Mall next door, the Arabian-themed Souk al Bahar specializes in local arts and crafts shops. Branches of Pride of Kashmir, Al Jaber Gallery and Gallery One (see p.132), among others, are all here, plus a few independent fashion boutiques. The underpowered decor, gloomy lighting and bizarrely confusing layout don't encourage you to stay long, however, while many shops remain untenanted and the whole place feels bizarrely underused compared to its always-packed neighbour. Sat–Thurs 10am–10pm, Fri 2–10pm.

★ **Souk Madinat Jumeirah** Madinat Jumeirah ⓦ madinatjumeirah.com; map p.78. At the heart of the Madinat Jumeirah, this superb recreation of a "traditional" souk serves up a beguiling mix of shopping, eating and drinking opportunities either within its narrow, wood-framed passageways or on the lagoon-facing terraces outside. Like all good bazaars, the layout is mazy and disorienting, although not so big that you'll ever be far from where you want to be. The superb array of shops (including branches of Al Jaber Gallery, Pride of Kashmir, Camel Company and Gallery One; see p.132) are mainly concerned with traditional arts and crafts – anything from ouds and embroidered slippers to Moroccan hanging lamps and tagine pots. Daily 10am–10pm.

12

ABU DHABI F1 GRAND PRIX

Sport and outdoor activities

Despite the sometimes punishing climate, Dubai (and neighbouring Abu Dhabi) boast a top-notch calendar of annual sporting events, including leading tennis and rugby tournaments, the Abu Dhabi Formula 1 Grand Prix and the Dubai World Cup, the world's richest horse race. The city also hosts occasional international cricket test and one-day matches as well as a pair of prestigious golf tournaments, including the DP World Tour Championship, the season-ending finale to the European Tour. For those who want to get active, there's a fair range of outdoor pursuits on offer, including world-class diving, plenty of watersports, assorted desert activities, plus a spectacular selection of golf courses. If you need a break from the heat head indoors, where you can hit the slopes at Ski Dubai or glide about on the Dubai Ice Rink.

ANNUAL SPORTING EVENTS

13

Dubai Marathon ⊛ dubaimarathon.org. Mid-Jan. A leading international marathon that attracts top distance runners like three-time champion Haile Gebrselassie. The route leads from the city centre all the way down the coast to Dubai Media City, and back again.

Dubai Desert Classic Emirates Golf Club ⊛ dubaidesertclassic.com. Four days in late Jan/early Feb. First staged in 1989, the Dubai Desert Classic has established itself as an important – and very lucrative – event in the PGA European Tour. Past winners feature a virtual who's who of the game's leading players, including Ernie Els, Tiger Woods, Colin Montgomerie, Seve Ballesteros and Rory McIlroy (who is sponsored by the local Jumeirah hotel chain). Tickets around 175dh, or you can watch the early practice rounds for free.

Wild Wadi's Swim Burj al Arab Feb. Popular charity swim attracting hundreds of amateur competitors who tackle an 800m route around the Burj al Arab, offering a rare chance to see the Burj (literally) from the waves.

Dubai Tennis Championships Dubai Tennis Stadium, Garhoud ⊛ dubaitennischampionships.com. Two weeks in late Feb/early March. Well-established fixture on the international ATP and WTA calendar, attracting many of the world's leading players. Past winners have included Rafael Nadal, Venus Williams, Andy Roddick, Novak Djokovic and five-time champion Roger Federer. Tickets start at a remarkably modest 50dh.

Dubai World Cup Meydan Racecourse ⊛ dubaiworldcup.com. March. The world's richest horse race, and the climax of the city's annual racing calendar, with a massive US$10 million in prize money. Tickets from 350dh.

Abu Dhabi Desert Challenge ⊛ abudhabidesert challenge.com. One week in March/April. Formerly known as the UAE Desert Challenge: rally drivers, bikers and quad-bikers race each other across the desert regions of Abu Dhabi emirate in one of the Middle East's leading motorsports events (and the second round of the FIA Cross Country Rally World Cup).

Traditional dhow racing Dubai International Marine Club ⊛ dimc.ae. April/May. A rare opportunity to see the Gulf's traditional wooden dhows under sail.

Abu Dhabi F1 Grand Prix Yas Marina Circuit ⊛ yasmarinacircuit.com. Three days in Nov. The crown jewel in the Middle Eastern sporting calendar, held annually at the spectacular Yas Marina Circuit (see opposite) since 2009. Tickets from around 1500dh.

DP World Tour Championship Earth course, Jumeirah Golf Estates ⊛ dpworldtourchampionship.com. Four days in Nov. The showpiece finale of the European Tour's season-long "Race to Dubai", during which the top sixty players battle it out at the spectacular Greg Norman-designed "Earth" course. Not only that, but entrance is free.

Al Habtoor Tennis Challenge ⊛ habtoortennis.com. One week in Nov/Dec. Ladies' tennis event, attracting a mix of top-100 players alongside up-and-coming younger talents, and a great place to get up close to some of the future stars of the sport. The event has previously been held at the *Habtoor Grand Resort* in Dubai Marina, but may move to a new venue in Business Bay in the future.

Dubai Rugby Sevens The Sevens stadium, Al Ain Rd ⊛ dubairugby7s.com. Three days in late Nov/early Dec. This annual IRB Sevens World Series tournament is one of the highlights of the international rugby sevens calendar, featuring top national teams from around the globe, with recent winners including England, South Africa and New Zealand. Also provides the excuse for some of the city's most raucous partying. Tickets free on opening day, then from 240dh.

Dubai Ladies Masters Emirates Golf Club ⊛ dubailadiesmasters.com. Four days in Dec. First staged in 2006 and now an established fixture in the Ladies European Tour, attracting some of the world's top female golfers. Tickets 195dh.

Mubadala World Championship Zayed Sports City, Abu Dhabi ⊛ mubadalawtc.com. Three days in late Dec. Self-styled "world championship" featuring six of the world's top male tennis players battling for big bucks.

FOOTBALL IN DUBAI AND THE UAE

Football attracts a fervent following in Dubai – as throughout the Gulf – with local TV stations serving up an endless stream of both local and European games, including plenty of Premier League action. The UAE runs its own professional football league, with twelve participating teams, including five from Dubai, which compete in various tournaments including the Etisalat Pro-League and Etisalat Cup. The two biggest Dubai clubs are **Al Wasl** (⊛ alwaslsc.ae), who play at Zabeel Club (and were briefly managed by Diego Maradona in 2012), and **Al Ahli**, who play at Rashid Stadium, and who are perhaps best known in the West for their unsuccessful attempts to headhunt the then Spurs manager Harry Redknapp in 2011. The UAE has also enjoyed considerable success at international level, winning the 2007 and 2013 Gulf Cups (the local equivalent of the European Championships) – although they've qualified for the World Cup just once, in 1990, losing all three games.

13

OTHER SPECTATOR SPORTS VENUES

Dubai Autodrome Dubailand ⓦdubaiautodrome
.com. FIA-approved circuit which hosts various events
including the Dubai 24 Hour, a kind of Middle Eastern Le
Mans. You can also have a drive yourself in a variety of cars
either on the main circuit or on the Kartdrome karting
track; check the website for details.

Dubai Sports City Dubailand ⓦdubaisportscity.ae.
This vast new sporting complex (still under construction at
the time of writing) hosts a variety of events but is best
known as a cricket venue, regularly hosting matches
between the major national sides and serving as the de
facto home ground of the Pakistan cricket team, who due
to security concerns haven't played a match on Pakistani
soil since 2009.

Al Marmoum Race Track Around 40km from Dubai off
exit 37 of the Al Ain Rd ☎055 676 0006, ⓦdcrc.ae
(Arabic only). Home to Dubai traditional camel races – one
of Dubai's most evocative sights as dozens of camels gallop

across the sands to the enthusiastic cheers of local
dromedary fanciers. Races are held from Oct to March at
7am or 2pm, although there's no fixed schedule. For details
of forthcoming meets call the race track on the number
above. Entrance free.

Meydan Racecourse Meydan ⓦmeydan.ae. The
spectacular Meydan Stadium (see p.61) is the major venue
for Dubai's extensive programme of horse-racing (there are
also races at Jebel Ali racetrack, in the far south of the city).
The racing season runs from Nov to March; details can be
found on ⓦemiratesracing.com. Just don't expect to make
any money at the bookies – betting is illegal in the UAE.

Yas Marina Circuit Yas Island, Abu Dhabi
ⓦyasmarinacircuit.com. A chance to put down some
rubber on Abu Dhabi's state-of-the-art F1 track as driver or
passenger in a selection of wheels ranging from classic
Aston to single-seater F3000. Karting and drag-racing
experiences also available.

DIVING AND WATERSPORTS

Dubai itself has only limited **diving** opportunities – the offshore marine environment has been significantly damaged by
development and there are no natural reefs – although a number of wreck dives lie reasonably close to shore. It does,
however, lie within easy striking distance of outstanding dive sites off the UAE's east coast in Fujairah, and off the
Musandam peninsula in Oman (see box, p.163), both of which are only a couple of hours' drive away. For more detailed
information about the region's dive sites, pick up a copy of the *UAE Underwater Explorer* guidebook, available at bookshops
throughout the city. **Watersports** facilities are available at all the beachside hotels (see box, p.87). Typical offerings
include sailing, windsurfing, kayaking, banana-boating, wakeboarding and deep-sea fishing. The city also boasts several
water parks, including Wild Wadi (see p.79) and Aquaventure (see p.85) as well as the recently opened Yas Waterworld
on Yas Island in Abu Dhabi (see p.143).

DIVING AND WATERSPORTS OPERATORS

Al Boom Diving Branches at Atlantis and Le Méridien
Al Aqah Beach, Fujairah ☎04 342 2993,
ⓦalboomdiving.com. The city's leading dive operator,
offering a range of PADI courses and dives, plus Musandam
excursions.

Kitefly Dubai Kite Beach, Umm Suqeim ☎050 254
7440, ⓦkitesurf.ae. One of several kitesurfing operators
working off Kite Beach (between the Dubai Offshore Sailing
Club and Jumeirah Beach Park). Others include Kite Surfing
UAE (ⓦkitesurfinguae.com) and Dukite (ⓦdukite.com).

The Pavilion Dive Centre Jumeirah Beach Hotel ☎04
406 8828, ⓦbit.ly/Paviliondive. Offers a range of on-site

PADI courses and introductory dives, plus dives to nearby
wrecks and excursions to Musandam.

Sky and Sea Adventures ☎04 399 9005,
ⓦwatersportsdubai.com. Leading local watersports
operator, operating out of the Sheraton and Hilton hotels in
Dubai Marina and offering activities including
wakeboarding, windsurfing, bodyboarding, snorkelling,
kayaking, parasailing and sailing. Also arrange PADI dive
courses and wreck and reef dives.

Surf Dubai Umm Suqeim ☎050 504 3020,
ⓦsurfingdubai.com. Individual and group surf lessons off
Umm Suqeim open beach by the Burj al Arab, plus board
rental and repair.

SKYDIVING, BALLOONING AND FLYING

As well as the following, you can also take to the skies on a variety of helicopter and seaplane trips around the city (see p.25).

Balloon Adventures Emirates ☎04 285 4949,
ⓦballooning.ae. Memorable sunrise flights over the
desert around Al Ain. 995dh per person.

iFly Dubai Mirdif City Centre mall, Mirdif
ⓦtheplaymania.com/ifly; Rashidiya metro. Don a flying
suit and take to the air (sort of) at this fun attraction. For

215dh you're put in a wind tunnel and then blown a few
metres into the air by powerful jet of air which holds you
hovering aloft, while you try to look cool. Full instruction
provided. Daily 10am–11pm (Thurs–Sat until midnight).

Skydive Dubai Near the Grosvenor House hotel, Dubai
Marina ☎050 153 3222, ⓦskydivedubai.ae; Dubai

13

Marina metro. Dubai's ultimate adrenaline rush, with various packages catering to both first-time tandem jumpers and experienced skydivers. Jumps take place in the spectacular skies above southern Dubai and the Palm Jumeirah, currently costing 1750dh for a tandem jump. They also run a training school in the desert.

GOLF

Golf is big business in Dubai, and the city has an outstanding selection of international-standard courses. Prices are sky-high though, and you'll be lucky to get a round anywhere for less than 500dh. There are further world-class courses down the road in Abu Dhabi (see ⓦ golfinabudhabi.com/en for details).

Arabian Ranches Golf Club Dubailand ⓦ arabian ranchesgolfdubai.com. Striking modern course (created by Ian Baker-Finch and Nicklaus Design) consisting of a grass links-style course set in the middle of natural desert.

Al Badia Golf Course Festival City ⓦ albadiagolfclub .ae. Attractive Creekside course in the southern city centre designed by Robert Trent Jones II with an oasis-style theme. It holds lots of water features and a variety of teeing angles and hole lengths to suit both serious and recreational players.

Dubai Creek Golf Club Garhoud ⓦ dubaigolf.com. Famous for its spiky-roofed clubhouse (see p.56), this Thomas Bjørn-designed course enjoys a superb creekside setting, and there's also a floodlit nine-hole par-3 course for after-dark swingers. It's also one of the most affordable clubs for visitors.

The Els Club Dubai Sports City, Dubailand ⓦ elsclubdubai.com. Spectacular "desert links" course, with greens and fairways surrounded by rolling dunes and untouched desert scenery, and with a range of tees and hole lengths to suit ability.

Emirates Golf Club Emirates Hills ⓦ dubaigolf.com. The oldest all-grass championship course in the Gulf, and probably still the most prestigious, centred around a striking Bedouin tent-style clubhouse. Current home of the Dubai Desert Classic (see p.138).

Jumeirah Golf Estates Dubai Sports City, Dubailand ⓦ jumeirahgolfestates.com. Huge, dedicated golfing "community" boasting two separate state-of-the-art courses – "Fire" and "Earth" – designed by Greg Norman, Vijay Singh respectively, and set amid dramatic desert scenery.

The Montgomerie Dubai Emirates Hills ⓦ themontgomerie.com. Links-style course designed by the eponymous Scotsman, featuring top-notch facilities and many unusual features, such as the world's largest green (playable from a 360-degree teeing ground).

INDOOR ACTIVITIES AND WINTER SPORTS

Dubai Ice Rink Dubai Mall ⓦ dubaiicerink.com; Burj Khalifa/Dubai Mall metro. Olympic-sized ice rink offering a range of open-to-all public sessions (55dh including skate rental), plus "disco sessions" and learn-to-skate classes. Check the website for the latest schedule.

Ski Dubai Mall of the Emirates ⓦ skidxb.com; Mall of the Emirates metro. Go skiing in the middle of the desert (see p.80).

The Wall Dubai World Trade Centre ⓦ climbingdubai .com/wall.html; World Trade Centre metro. Open-air climbing wall, the highest in the UAE, with a range of routes for different abilities, including some challenging overhangs for more advanced climbers. There's also a special "speedwall" on which two climbers can race one another over identical routes, and climbing lessons are available. From 60dh. Sun–Wed 3–11pm, Fri & Sat 2–10pm.

DESERT ACTIVITIES AND TREKKING

A range of desert excursions and "safaris" are offered by the city's various tour operators – for full details of trips and operators are covered in Basics (see p.25) – although by and large the selection of activities is disappointingly stereotypical, and most trips involve being sat in the back of a vehicle while someone drives you across the desert or through the mountains. Slightly more active alternatives (offered by most local tour operators) include **camel safaris**, often featuring a bit of sand-boarding en route, while adrenaline junkies will enjoy the chance to try their hand at riding a **dune-buggy** or **quad-bike** across the dunes. A couple of places (see p.25) offer specialist **off-road desert driving** courses; experienced drivers with a 4WD should pick up a copy of the *UAE Off-Road Explorer* by Shelley Frost, available at bookshops around the city, which lists twenty off-road routes with maps and GPS coordinates. Trips featuring the traditional Arabian pursuit of **falconry** are also sometimes offered by tour operators; alternatively, contact specialist operator Shaheen Xtreme (see p.25). There are also myriad **trekking** possibilities in the craggy Hajar mountains in the east and north of the UAE, although at present their tourist potential remains largely unexploited.

DUBAI AQUARIUM, DUBAI MALL

Kids' Dubai

Dubai has a vast array of diversions for children. Dedicated kids' attractions range from sedate edutainment-themed places such as Children's City and the quirky KidZania through to the white-knuckle thrills of Sega Republic and Abu Dhabi's Ferrari World, while Dubai's huge array of family-friendly attractions includes superb water parks, dolphinariums, and the Middle East's only snowdome. And when you're done with those, there are plenty of more low-key pleasures to hand, including simply messing around on the beach. Older children will also enjoy the city's traditional Arabian atmosphere and the opportunity of getting out into the desert on a sunset safari, complete with dune-bashing, camel rides and belly dancing. On the downside, many attractions come with fairly hefty price tags attached, and family entrance fees can quickly put a significant hole in even deep wallets.

If you're planning a family holiday to Dubai it's worth noting that most of the city's beach hotels have their own in-house **kids' clubs**, providing free childcare while you get on with some serious sunbathing or shopping. These clubs usually cater for ages 4 to 12 (under-4s are sometimes admitted, though a parent or guardian will need to stay in attendance), but be sure to check exactly what's included before booking. Most hotels can also arrange **babysitting** services for a fee.

Most of the city's larger **shopping malls** have dedicated kids' play areas featuring various attractions ranging from soft-play equipment and gentle coin-operated rides for toddlers up to arcade games and other attractions for older kids. Entrance to all these areas is free, although individual attractions within them are chargeable. The main places are Fun City (ⓦfuncity.ae; BurJuman, Mercato and Ibn Battuta malls), Magic Planet (ⓦtheplaymania .com/magicplanet; Mall of the Emirates and Deira City Centre) and the Wafi Encounter Zone at Wafi. The city's malls also host a wide range of **children's events and entertainers** during the Dubai Shopping Festival (see p.27) and Dubai Summer Surprises (see p.28).

DEDICATED KIDS' ATTRACTIONS

Children's City Creek Park, Oud Metha ☎04 334 0808, ⓦchildrencity.ae; Dubai Healthcare City metro. Occupying a series of brightly coloured red and blue buildings – modelled after children's play bricks – towards the southern end of Creek Park, Children's City is aimed at kids aged 2–15, with a subtle educational slant. A series of galleries with fun interactive exhibits and lots of touchscreens cover subjects including physical science, nature, international culture and space exploration. There's also a play space, while kids aged 2–5 can muck around with sand and water in the toddlers' area. 15dh; children aged 3–15 10dh; under-2s free; family ticket for 2 adults and 2 children 40dh; 5dh park entry fee. Sat–Thurs 9am–8pm, Fri 3–9pm.

Dubai Dolphinarium Creek Park (just inside the park near Gate #1), Oud Metha, ☎04 336 9773, ⓦdubaidolphinarium.ae; Dubai Healthcare City metro. Twice-daily shows (Mon–Sat at 11am & 6pm; also Fri & Sat at 3pm; adults 100dh, children 50dh) starring the dolphinarium's three resident bottlenose dolphins and four seals. Alternatively, you can go swimming with the dolphins (Mon–Thurs hourly 1–4pm; advance reservations required; 2100dh for up to 3 people, 550dh each additional person).

Ferrari World Yas Island, Abu Dhabi ☎02 496 8001, ⓦferrariworldabudhabi.com. The blockbuster attraction at Abu Dhabi's Yas Island (see p.174), the "world's biggest indoor theme park" (as it's billed) offers a wide range of Ferrari-themed rides and displays which will appeal both to kids and grown-ups, including the chance to drive an F1 simulator or to ride the Formula Rosso roller coaster (the world's fastest) or to experience race-day acceleration in the G Force "tower of speed" – as well as numerous gentler family-oriented rides. Dedicated motorsports enthusiasts will also enjoy the big display of classic and contemporary Ferraris, and the virtual tour of the firm's famous Maranello factory. Adults and children over 1.3m 225dh; under 1.3m 185dh; under-3s free. Daily except Mon 11am–10pm.

KidZania Second floor, Dubai Mall ⓦkidzania.ae; Burj Khalifa/Dubai Mall metro. Innovative edutainment attraction based on an imaginary, miniaturized city where the kids are in charge. Children get the chance to dress up and roleplay from 75 different grown-up professions (anything from airline pilot to archeologist), getting involved in the commercial life of the "city" and even earning their own money en route. Ages 17 and over 95dh; ages 4–16 140dh; ages 2–3 95dh; under-2s free. Daily 10am–9pm.

SEGA Republic Second floor, Dubai Mall ⓦsegarepublic.com; Burj Khalifa/Dubai Mall metro. Huge indoor theme park featuring a range of adrenaline-pumping rides and other amusements for kids of all ages, although more likely to appeal to older children. Five

TOP 5 FAMILY-FRIENDLY HOTELS

Atlantis Huge beach and a superb range of children's facilities and in-house attractions including Aquaventure, Dolphin Bay and the Lost Chambers. See pp.84–85.

Bab al Shams Desert Resort and Spa An enjoyable and stress-free alternative to staying in Dubai proper, with a wide range of fun desert activities. See p.101.

Jumeirah Beach Hotel Brilliant kids' facilities, including huge grounds, pools and one of the city's best kids' clubs. See p.99.

Le Royal Méridien Beach Resort and Spa Vast swathe of beach, gardens and pools, plus good kids' club and watersports centre. See p.101.

Sheraton Jumeirah Beach Low-key and very family-friendly resort, with good kids' facilities and rates which are often significantly lower than those at other beachside hotels. See p.101.

FREE (OR ALMOST FREE) BEACHES

If you want some sand but don't fancy stumping up the punishing prices levied by the various five-star hotels (see box, p.87) there are other options. Easily the nicest is the lovely **Jumeirah Beach Park**, although there are a number of other places scattered around the city – albeit with minimal facilities.

Jumeirah Beach Park Jumeirah Rd, Jumeirah. Gorgeous stretch of lifeguard-protected white-sand beach with plenty of facilities (see p.74). 5dh. Daily 8am–10.30pm, Thurs–Sat until 11pm; Mon ladies and boys aged up to 4 only.

Al Mamzar Park At the far eastern edge of Deira, close to the border with Sharjah. One of Dubai's biggest parks, with well over a mile of fine sand and facilities including a children's playground and amusement arcades, swimming pool, spacious palm-shaded lawns and impressive views of Sharjah. 5dh.

Daily 8am–11pm (Thurs–Sat until 11.30pm); Wed ladies and boys aged up to 4 only.

Russian Beach Immediately south of the Dubai Marine Beach Resort (see p.98). Large but decidedly bare and windswept stretch of sand at the north end of Jumeirah, almost in the shadow of the enormous cranes and gantries of Port Rashid. Free. Open 24hr.

Umm Suqeim beach Immediately north of the Burj al Arab. Nice stretch of sand (but no facilities) with dramatic views of the Burj. Free. Open 24hr.

14

themed "zones" cover a range of wildlife, sporting and high-speed rides and activities, including the "Wild Jungle" ride, the Spin Gear indoor horizontal spinning-coaster and the Sonic Hopper drop tower; there's also a big selection of Sega arcade games with prizes. 160dh for one-day pass (including 10 video games); 220dh for one-day pass (including 200dh credit for games); general admission ticket 10dh, with pay as you go for individual rides (15–30dh). Daily 10am–11pm (Thurs–Sat until 1am).

Wonderland Next to Garhoud Bridge, Oud Metha ☏ 04 324 1222, ⓦ wonderlanduae.com; Dubai Healthcare City metro. Old-fashioned theme park with a

variety of rides (mostly 5–10dh) and other attractions including a rollercoaster, powercarts, pirate ship and bumper cars, plus the modest Splashland water park (daily 10am–6pm). Adults 15dh, children aged 4–12 10dh. Daily 10am–10pm.

Yas Waterworld Yas Island, Abu Dhabi ☏ 02 414 2000, ⓦ yaswaterworld.com. Over forty rides, slides and other attractions for all ages and swimming abilities, from the gentle Tot's Playground through to the stomach-churning Jebel Drop waterslide. 225dh; children below 1.1m tall 185dh; under-3s free. Daily: March–May, Sept & Oct 10am–7pm; June–Aug 10am–8pm; Nov–Feb 10am–6pm.

OTHER KIDS' ACTIVITIES

Activities Top of the list for kids are the city's various water parks and other marine attractions, including Wild Wadi (see p.79), Aquaventure and Dolphin Bay (see p.85), not to mention the various watersports offered at the marina hotels (see p.87). Active older kids will also enjoy Dubai Ice Rink (see p.140) and the surreal Ski Dubai (see p.80), while there are various other activities ranging from ballooning to wall-climbing (see p.140).

Sights In terms of general attractions there are plenty of sights in the city likely to amuse the offspring. These include nature-related activities like a visit to the Dubai

Aquarium (see p.69), The Lost Chambers at the *Atlantis* resort (see p.85) and Dubai Zoo (see p.73). A ride on the cable car above Creek Park (see p.58) is another possibility, as is the spectacular Dubai Fountain (see p.69).

Tours There are a number of child-friendly tours available in and around the city. Most kids will enjoy a desert safari (see p.26), while within the city itself there are enjoyable rides aboard the engaging Wonder Bus (see p.25), not to mention abra rides and cruises across or along the Creek (see p.22 & p.25).

TOP 5 CHILDREN'S SHOPS

The Camel Company Cute camels galore – a guaranteed child-pleaser. Locations across the city. See p.132.

Hamleys Branch of the famous London toy store, located in the Dubai Mall (see p.134).

Al Jaber Gallery The place for kitsch Arabian handicrafts, with locations citywide. See p.132.

The Toy Store Dubai's leading toy shop, with branches in the Mall of the Emirates (see p.134), Marina Mall (see p.135) and Ibn Battuta Mall (see p.134), offering everything from Teletubbies to Roboraptors.

Toys R Us Head to the Festival Centre (see p.134) for a reliable source of all the latest kiddie crazes.

Day-trips

Not until you leave it do you realize how unrepresentative Dubai is of the UAE as a whole, and a visit to any of the neighbouring emirates offers an interesting alternative perspective on life in the Gulf. The easiest day-trip is to the nearby city of Sharjah, now virtually a suburb of Dubai, which boasts a fine array of museums devoted to various aspects of the UAE's traditional religion and culture. A two-hour drive south of Dubai, the "garden city" of Al Ain offers a pleasantly laidback contrast to life on the coast, with a string of traditional mud-brick forts, souks and a wonderful oasis. Heading across country from Dubai, the tranquil east coast of the UAE offers dramatic mountain scenery and a string of beautiful – and still largely deserted – beaches.

Sharjah

Just 10km north up the coast, the city of **SHARJAH** seems at first sight like simply an extension of Dubai, with whose northern suburbs it now merges seamlessly in an ugly concrete sprawl. Physically, the two cities may have virtually fused into one, but culturally they remain light years apart. Sharjah has a distinctively different flavour, having clung much more firmly to its traditional Islamic roots, with none of Dubai's freewheeling glitz and tourist fleshpots – and precious few tourists either.

Sharjah's appeal is far from obvious. Physically it's the most unattractive place in the UAE, a desperately ugly sprawl of concrete high-rises and traffic, while at ground level the entire city, despite its size, seems oddly lacking in any kind of street life or definite personality. There *are* compensations, however, mainly in the shape of the city's fine array of museums devoted to various aspects of Islamic culture and local Emirati life, all of which offer some recompense for Sharjah's architectural squalor and puritanical regime (see box, p.147). These include the world-class **Museum of Islamic Civilization**, the excellent **Sharjah Art Gallery**, the impressive new **Sharjah Heritage Museum**, and the engaging **Al Mahatta** aviation museum. Further attractions include the massive **Blue Souk**, one of the largest in the UAE, and **Souq al Arsa**, one of the prettiest.

15

All the central attractions are clustered close together and easily covered on foot, although to reach the Blue Souk and Al Mahatta Museum you might prefer to hop into one of Sharjah's plentiful **taxis**.

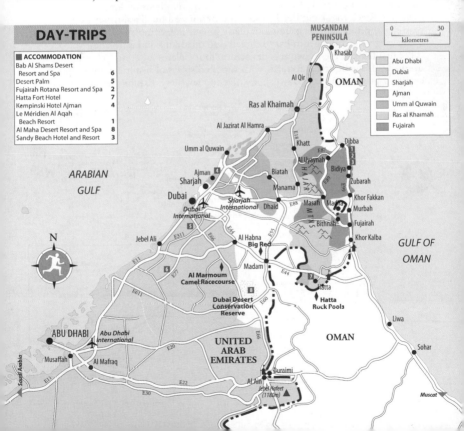

15

Sharjah Museum of Islamic Civilization

Corniche St • Sat–Thurs 8am–8pm, Fri 4–8pm • 5dh • ☎ 06 565 5455, ⓦ islamicmuseum.ae

The main reason for trekking out to Sharjah is to visit the superb **Sharjah Museum of Islamic Civilization**, which occupies the beautifully restored former Souk al Majara building along the waterfront, topped with a distinctive golden dome. The museum offers an absorbing overview of the massive – and often unheralded – contributions to global culture made by Muslim scientists, artists and architects over the past five hundred years or so, although some of the displays are irritatingly self-congratulatory, and occasionally veer into pure ahistorical propaganda (like the attempt to claim the purely Hindu Jantar Mantar observatory in Jaipur, India, as a work of Islamic provenance).

The museum is spread over two levels. Downstairs, the **Abu Bakr Gallery of Islamic Faith** has extensive displays on the elaborate rituals associated with the traditional Haj pilgrimage to Mecca. These are accompanied by a range of absorbing exhibits, including fascinating photos of Mecca, and a large piece of *kiswah*, the sheet of black cloth with Koranic texts richly embroidered in gold thread that was formerly used to drape the *kaaba* in the city's Masjid al Haram.

On the opposite side of the ground floor, the **Ibn al Haitham Gallery of Science and Technology** showcases the extensive contributions made by Arab scholars to scientific innovation over the centuries. Absorbing displays cover Islamic contributions to fields such as chemistry, medicine and astronomy, emphasizing the degree to which Arab scientists led the medieval world (standard scientific terms like zenith, azimuth, algorithm and algebra all derive from Arabic, as do hundreds of names of stars, including Rigel, Algol and Betelgeuse). The sections on medieval navigation, map-making and stargazing are particularly interesting, complete with lots of quaint medieval gear including armillary spheres, wall quadrants and astrolabes.

The first floor of the museum is devoted to four galleries offering a chronological overview of **Islamic arts and crafts**, with superb displays of historic manuscripts, ceramics, glass, armour, woodwork, textiles and jewellery. Exhibits include the first-ever

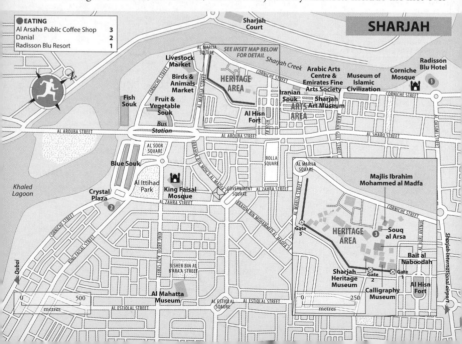

SHARJAH'S ISLAMIC LAWS

Among the relatively liberal Islamic emirates of the UAE, Sharjah is infamous for its hardline stance on matters of dress, alcohol and the relationship between the sexes. These derive from the close financial ties linking Sharjah with **Saudi Arabia**. In 1989, a Saudi consortium provided a financial rescue package after the emirate's banking system collapsed with debts of over US$500 million. Saudi advisers subsequently succeeded in persuading Sharjah's ruler to introduce a version of **sharia**-style law, and Saudi influence remains strong to this day. Many locals bemoan the stultifying effect these laws have had on the emirate's development – particularly painful given that, up until the 1950s, Sharjah was one of the most developed and cosmopolitan cities in the lower Gulf. Alcohol is banned, making it the only dry emirate in the UAE; the wearing of tight or revealing clothing in public areas is likely to get you into trouble with locals or the police; couples "not in a legally acceptable relationship" are, according to the emirate's "decency laws", not even meant to be alone in public together (in 2010 police even started going door to door in an attempt to round up cohabiting unmarried couples). Punishments for more serious offences include imprisonment and flogging. In practice, unmarried Western couples behaving in a respectable manner are extremely unlikely to experience any hassle. There have, however, been repeated reports of Asian and Arab expat workers being arrested by the city's hardline police and being carted off into detention.

15

map of the then known world (ie Eurasia), created by Moroccan cartographer Al Shereef al Idrisi in 1099 – a surprisingly accurate document, although slightly baffling at first sight since it's oriented upside down, with south at the top.

Sharjah Creek

Stretching away outside the Islamic Museum is Sharjah's broad **Creek**, which describes a leisurely parabola around the northern edge of the city centre before terminating in the expansive Khaled Lagoon. The Creek was formerly central to Sharjah's commercial fortunes – at least until the city's rulers carelessly allowed it to silt up during the 1950s and become impassable to larger shipping. This allowed Dubai to leapfrog Sharjah in commercial importance, sending the latter into a long economic decline from which it has yet to recover.

Despite being long since eclipsed by Dubai's various ports, Sharjah's Creek still sees a considerable amount of commercial shipping both modern and traditional, usually with a few old-fashioned wooden dhows moored up on the far side of the water beneath a long line of spiky gantries – like bits of random Meccano poking up at the sky. The waterfront **Corniche** is also one of the very few places in the city that might tempt you to an extended stroll, with sweeping views downriver (right) to the twin minarets of the impressive **Corniche Mosque** and upriver (across the water, left) to the grandiose **Sharjah Court** building.

Sharjah Art Museum and around

Just off Corniche St; from the waterfront follow the sign to the Corniche Post Office and then to the Sharjah Art Foundation, or access from Al Burj Ave, behind Al Hisn fort • Sat–Thurs 8am–8pm, Fri 4–8pm • Free • ☎ 06 568 8222, ⊛ sharjahmuseums.ae

Occupying a large modern wind towered building just off Corniche Street, the **Sharjah Art Museum** is the major showpiece in Sharjah's attempts to position itself as a serious player in the international art scene, and the principal venue of the famous Sharjah Biennial (see box, p.148). The ground floor is devoted to temporary exhibitions, usually featuring local and/or Arab artists of varying originality and ability. Much more interesting is the permanent **Orientalist collection** upstairs, which focuses on paintings by nineteenth-century European artists depicting life in Islamic lands. The collection is centred on a wonderful selection of lithographs by Scottish artist David Roberts drawn from his celebrated *Sketches in the Holy Land and Syria*,

---

THE SHARJAH BIENNIAL

The Sharjah Art Museum provides the main venue for the **Sharjah Biennial**
(Ⓦ sharjahbiennial.org), held from March to May every odd-numbered year. First staged in
1993, the Biennial is now a major fixture on the international art calendar and has gained a
reputation for innovation notably at odds with Sharjah's ultra-conservative cultural regime.
Things came to a head during the 2011 Biennial when director Jack Persekian was sacked by
the ruler of Sharjah, Sheikh Sultan bin Mohammad al Qassimi, after allegations that one of the
festival's exhibits – *Maportaliche/Ecritures Sauvages* by Algerian artist Mustapha Benfodil,
featuring 23 headless mannequins dressed as two football teams and a referee – contained
"offensive" texts printed on the dummies' shirts, while a number of demonstrators peacefully
protesting the killings of pro-democracy activists in Bahrain were simultaneously hauled off by
police for questioning.

15

based on a journey through the Middle East in 1838–39. Roberts' work remains one
of the quintessential visual expressions of Orientalism, with canvases showing
picturesquely robed natives reclining in carefully staged postures amid even more
picturesque mosques, forts and assorted ruins.

Art galleries

Emirates Fine Arts Society ☏ 06 568 4488, Ⓦ sharjahtourism.ae/en/heritage/arts **Arabic Arts Centre** Ⓦ www.sdci.gov.ae/english
/arabicartcenter.html

While you're here, it's also worth having a look at the attractive cluster of restored
traditional buildings opposite the museum, backing onto the adjacent Iranian souk
and home to a few further art galleries including the low-key **Emirates Fine Arts Society**
and **Arabic Arts Centre**, which stage occasional exhibitions.

Al Hisn Fort

Al Burj Ave

At the very heart of the city is the modest **Al Hisn Fort** of 1820, the most enduring symbol
of old Sharjah, originally home to the ruling Al Qassimi family and the rallying point in
days gone by for all important city gatherings, although it's now ignominiously hemmed
in by ugly apartment blocks. The fort (and interesting museum within) was formerly open
to the public but has been closed for extensive renovations for several years now, with no
reopening date currently in sight. Most of the building you see now is actually a modern
reconstruction, the original having been largely demolished in 1969. Sharjah's current
ruler, Sheikh Sultan bin Mohammad al Qassimi (then crown prince) flew back from
university in Cairo in an attempt to halt the fort's destruction but arrived too late to save
anything of the original apart from a single tower – although he subsequently had his
revenge on the wreckers by having the entire edifice rebuilt painstakingly from scratch.

Rolla Square

At the southern end of Al Burj Avenue, the landmark **Rolla Square** is currently fenced
off as part of a major redevelopment project. The "square" (actually more of a park) has
traditionally served as the city's major meeting place, famous for the vast banyan tree
(*rolla* in Arabic) which stood here until 1978. A striking modern sculpture – half-tree,
half-tent – now stands in its place.

Heritage Area

The area west of Al Hisn Fort was formerly the heart of old Sharjah, a quarter of
traditional Emirati houses arranged around a sequence of spacious, lopsided squares and
labyrinthine alleyways, and enclosed in a long section of reconstructed city wall. The
entire area has now been meticulously renovated and relaunched as the city's so-called
Heritage Area, home to several interesting museums and the engaging Souq al Arsa.

Bait al Naboodah

Heritage Area • Sat–Thurs 8am–8pm, Fri 4–8pm • 5dh • ☎ 06 568 1738, ⓦ sharjahmuseums.ae

Situated in an atmospheric old house opposite the Souq al Arsa (see below), the **Bait al Naboodah** offers an interesting re-creation of traditional family life in Sharjah. The main draw is the rambling two-storey building itself, one of the most attractive in the UAE, arranged around a spacious central courtyard with exposed coral-brick walls and wooden verandas supported by incongruous Greek-style wooden columns. Only the rooms on the ground floor are open. These include a string of bedrooms furnished in traditional Gulf style, with canopied wooden beds and floor cushions, the walls hung with old rifles, clocks and radios. There are also a couple of rustic kitchens, a small *majlis* (with a few pictures of the Al Naboodah family who once lived here) and a traditional games room with quaint local toys including a cute toy car made out of two old oil cans, with food tins for wheels. A couple of further rooms are devoted to the restoration of the house and another has insightful exhibits on traditional Emirati architecture. For an eyeful of contemporary Emirati architecture, climb the stairs up to the rooftop for a view of Sharjah's uninspiring concrete skyline.

15

Calligraphy Museum

Heritage Area (reachable via the small alleyway by the entrance to the Sharjah Heritage Museum) • Sat–Thurs 8am–8pm, Fri 4–8pm • Free • ☎ 06 568 0006, ⓦ sharjahmuseums.ae

Sharjah's small but worthwhile **Calligraphy Museum** provides a rare showcase for the under-appreciated skills of Arabian calligraphers, featuring artworks from across the Islamic world dating from the 1970s to the present day. Exhibits in the main room focus on eye-poppingly intricate examples of traditional calligraphy using ink on paper; exhibits in the smaller second room feature more outlandish examples of calligraphic art executed in wood and ceramics, alongside quasi-abstract paintings incorporating assorted calligraphic elements.

Sharjah Heritage Museum

Heritage Area • Sat–Thurs 8am–8pm, Fri 4–8pm • Free • ☎ 06 568 0006, ⓦ sharjahmuseums.ae

Housed in the venerable Bait Saeed al Taweel ("House of Said the Tall"), the excellent new **Sharjah Heritage Museum** is one of the best collections of its kind anywhere in the UAE. Wide-ranging and well-explained exhibits cover all the usual bases – traditional dress, architecture, social customs, the pearling trade and so on – with many insights into lesser-known local customs en route. These include the entertaining revelation that a person who refused to join their family for dinner would be given a cooking pot with a large rock inside; the fact that widows were formerly discouraged from looking either at the moon or at their own reflections (mirrors were covered in cloth to prevent accidental eye contact); and the observation that boys were commonly circumcised – by the local barber.

Souq al Arsa and around

Heritage Area • Most shops open roughly 10am–1/2pm & 4/5–10pm (closed Fri morning)

Bounding the northern side of the Heritage Area, the **Souq al Arsa** is far and away the prettiest in Sharjah, if not the whole of the UAE. The souk is centred around an atmospheric central pillared courtyard, flanked by carpet shops and the quaint little *Al Arsaha Public Coffee Shop* (see p.151), beyond which radiates an intriguing tangle of alleyways. The coral-stone shops are stuffed with all sorts of colourful local handicrafts as well as an eclectic selection of random curios and collectibles which might include anything from wind-up gramophones and antique cameras through to Saddam Hussein-era Iraqi banknotes or a stuffed crocodile head.

Tucked into one side of the Souq al Arsa is the small and eminently missable Eslah School Museum – a couple of old classrooms with wooden desks and photographs of former pupils. More interesting is the **Majlis Ibrahim Mohammed al Madfa**, hidden away around the back (north) side of the Souq al Arsa and one of the prettiest buildings in the Heritage Area, topped by a diminutive round wind tower, said to be the only one in the UAE.

The Blue Souk

King Faisal St • Most shops open roughly 10am–10pm, although many close between around 1pm and 4pm

A kilometre west of the city centre, the huge **Blue Souk** (officially known as the Central Souk) is Sharjah's most visited and photographed attraction, occupying an enormous, eye-catching and ungainly pair of buildings which – despite the myriad wind towers, blue tiling and other Arabian decorative touches – bear an uncanny resemblance to a large railway station. The souk is best known for its numerous carpet shops, which stock a vast range of Persian and other rugs at prices that are generally significantly cheaper than in Dubai. If you're not after rugs, there are plenty of electronics, clothes, jewellery and handicrafts shops to browse, although Souq al Arsa has a better selection of Arabian souvenirs and the range of goods on offer is fairly underwhelming compared to Dubai.

15

Around the Blue Souk

The area around the Blue Souk is unusually green and pleasant compared to the rest of Sharjah's concrete jungle, centred on the cheery **Ittihad Park** and the neatly manicured lawns of Al Soor Square. It's also where you're most strongly reminded of Sharjah's pronounced Saudi leanings (see box, p.147), with a pair of major thoroughfares – King Abdul Aziz and King Faisal streets – named in honour of two of the kingdom's most notable former leaders, and the impressive **King Faisal Mosque** rising close by.

The streets north of the Blue Souk are home to the city's major wholesale markets, including areas devoted to fruit and veg, a waterside fish market and a rustic livestock souk. Most interesting is the **Birds and Animals Market**, comprising a couple of arcades of shops selling a miscellany of tropical birds, cats, fish, geese and pigeons plus a few places specializing in magnificent hunting falcons, which stand hooded on their pillars with patrician aloofness – the finest birds can change hands for thousands of dollars.

Al Mahatta Museum

Bisher bin al Bara'a St (Street 23), off King Abdul Aziz St • Sat–Thurs 8am–8pm, Fri 4–8pm • 5dh • ☎ 06 573 3079, ⓦ bit.ly/AlMahatta

Around a kilometre south of the Blue Souk lies the unexpectedly absorbing **Al Mahatta Museum**, devoted to the history of aviation in Sharjah. It occupies the buildings of what was until 1977 the city's airport, complete with aircraft hangar, air traffic control tower and passenger guest house (the runway was incorporated into what is now King Abdul Aziz Street). The cavernous **hangar** contains five planes (plus the nose of a 1952 De Havilland Comet, the world's first commercial jet aircraft) dating from the 1930s to the 1950s. Most were formerly used by Gulf Aviation (the forerunner of Gulf Air) and range in size from an impressive Douglas DC3 (1945) to a diminutive De Havilland Dove (1947) dangling from the ceiling. All look marvellously antique and only marginally air-worthy, although one (a 1954 Heron) was flown commercially in Australia until as recently as 1995.

The remainder of the museum occupies the old **rest house**, built for passengers overnighting at the airport and containing fascinating displays about the first commercial flights to Sharjah. These were launched in 1932 by Imperial Airways using a creaky old Hanno biplane (looking like something straight out of *Wacky Races*) to cover the 7000km from London to Karachi – a three-day flight, with overnight stops in Cairo and Sharjah. Further rooms are stuffed full of assorted aircraft components – engines, propellors, instruments, tailfins – plus a final hall exploring flight in the natural world. At the end of your visit you may be shown *Air Outpost*, a marvellous fifteen-minute documentary on the original Imperial Airways London–Karachi flights made by Strand Films in 1937 – well worth a look on YouTube even if you don't manage to get to the museum.

ARRIVAL AND DEPARTURE

SHARJAH

The city's significantly lower rents mean that many people commute daily from Sharjah to Dubai, resulting in the main highway's now-notorious **traffic jams**, at their worst between 7am and 10am when heading into Dubai, and from 5pm to 8pm travelling back towards Sharjah. Visiting Sharjah from Dubai, you'll be travelling in the opposite direction to most of the traffic, but the roads can still get congested so it's worth avoiding the peak hours, if possible. Depending on traffic the journey takes anything from 40min to well over an hour.

By air Sharjah's international airport (ⓦshj-airport.gov .ae), around 15km inland from the city centre along the E88 Dhaid road, serves a wide range of destinations across Arabia and Asia. A cab to the Sharjah city centre will cost around 50dh; alternatively, airport buses (routes #14, #15, #88 and #99; ⓦmowasalat.ae) run regularly into town (departures roughly every 15–20min; 5dh).

By bus 24hr buses (every 20–25min; 7dh) run from Bur Dubai's Al Ghubaiba bus station (see p.23) to the main bus

terminal in Sharjah a short distance east of the Blue Souk.

By taxi Taxis in Dubai levy a 20dh surcharge to travel to Sharjah; count on around 60–70dh from central Dubai to Sharjah in total.

Tours A convenient alternative to travelling under your own steam is to take a tour of Sharjah with a Dubai-based operator (see p.25). These cost around 150dh, sometimes including a brief visit to the neighbouring emirate of Ajman as well.

15

GETTING AROUND

By taxi There are plenty of taxis in Sharjah for short hops around the city. All are metered, with similar prices to

Dubai and a basic flag fare of 3dh (minimum charge 5dh; 1dh/750m).

EATING

Eating in Sharjah is a fairly utilitarian business. There are a fair number of places for a quick spot of lunch or dinner, but nowhere that really deserves a special visit on account of its food or atmosphere alone, with the exception of the engaging *Al Arsaha Public Coffee Shop*. There's also a peaceful little café in the Sharjah Art Museum, and you can get a decent cup of coffee at the *New York Café* on the ground floor of the Crystal Plaza, just south of the Blue Souk. Don't go looking for a beer, however: alcohol in Sharjah is completely forbidden.

★ **Al Arsaha Public Coffee Shop** Souq al Arsa. At the heart of the pretty Souq al Arsa, this quaint and personable little café offers a beguiling window on local life, with old photos of the UAE on the rattan-covered walls, colourful tables covered in big Lipton's tea logos and an entertaining local clientele. It's a good place to grab a glass of mint tea or a cup of coffee, and they also serve up mountainous, spicy biryanis (chicken, mutton or fish; 20dh). Daily 8am–9pm.
Danial Crystal Plaza, Al Zahra Rd ☎06 574 4668, ⓦdanialrestaurant.com. This no-frills restaurant on the second floor of the Crystal Plaza, immediately south of the

Blue Souk, serves up above-average lunch and dinner buffets (55dh) featuring a mix of Middle Eastern and international fare. Daily 12.30pm–12.30am.
Radisson Blu Resort Corniche St ☎06 565 7777, ⓦradissonblu.com/resort-sharjah. A ten-minute taxi ride east of the city centre, the *Radisson* has Sharjah's best selection of eating outlets, including *Canton China* (daily 8am–midnight), the beachside *Calypso!* (daily 10am–11pm) and *Café at the Falls* (daily 12.30–3.30pm & 7–11pm) located in the hotel's striking, tropical-rainforest-themed atrium.

Al Ain and around

For a complete change of pace and scenery, a day-trip out to the sedate desert city of **AL AIN**, some 130km inland from Dubai on the border with Oman, offers the perfect antidote to the rip-roaring pace of life on the coast. The UAE's fourth largest city and only major inland settlement, Al Ain – and the twin city of **BURAIMI**, on the Omani side of the border – grew up around the string of six oases whose densely packed swathes of palms still provide the modern city with one of its most attractive features. The city served as an important staging post on trading routes between Oman and the Gulf, a fact attested to by the numerous forts that dot the area and by the rich archeological remains found in the vicinity, evidence of continuous settlement dating back to Neolithic times. In 2011 Al Ain was designated a UNESCO World Heritage Site – the first in the UAE – on account of the historical and cultural significance of its oases, ancient *falaj* irrigation systems and archeological remnants.

Al Ain is actually part of **Abu Dhabi emirate** and is also celebrated as the birthplace of Sheikh Zayed bin Sultan al Nahyan (see box, p.172), Abu Dhabi's revered former ruler and first president of the UAE, who served as the city's governor before taking over the reins of power in Abu Dhabi in 1966. Al Ain's verdant, tree-lined streets are evidence of Sheikh Zayed's obsession with "greening" the desert, while the string of shady oases which dot the area have led to its popular moniker as the Gulf's Garden City. Al Ain's slightly elevated position also makes it a popular summer retreat for wealthy Emiratis on account of the less humid air, although in truth you're unlikely to notice much difference.

There are plenty of low-key attractions here to fill up a day or overnight trip including the old-fashioned **Al Ain National Museum**, the idyllic **Al Ain Oasis** and a string of mud-brick forts including the beautifully restored **Al Jahili Fort**. The largely unspoilt desert scenery surrounding Al Ain is home to a further smattering of sights, including the **Hili Archeological Park**, the state-of-the-art **Al Ain Zoo** and the craggy summit of **Jebel Hafeet**. It's also reasonably straightforward to hop across the border to visit the Omani city of Buraimi, home to a pair of fine forts and a bustling string of souks.

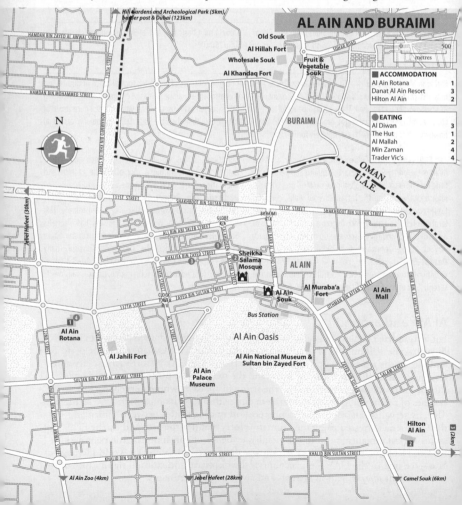

> ## AL AIN ORIENTATION
>
> Historically, Al Ain has always been an oasis rather than a city – and the place you see today has formed as a result of scattered villages slowly growing together, rather than a single settlement growing outwards from a central core. All of which explains Al Ain's otherwise bafflingly spread-out city plan, with endless grids of identikit streets and roundabouts sprawling across the desert for well over 20km in every direction. The fact that every main road looks exactly like every other main road can lead to intense confusion if you get lost, although the many helpful brown tourist signs are a life-saver if you're driving yourself.

Al Ain National Museum

Off Zayed bin Sultan St • Sat, Sun & Tues–Thurs 8.30am–7.30pm, Fri 3–7.30pm, closed Mon • 3dh; includes Sultan bin Zayed Fort • ☎ 03 764 1595, ⓦ bit.ly/AlAinMuseum

The old-fashioned but entertaining **Al Ain National Museum** is well worth a look before diving into the rest of the city. The first section sports the usual dusty displays on local life and culture (featuring some marvellous photos of Abu Dhabi emirate in the 1960s) alongside quirkier exhibits such as a core sample (1950) from Ras Sadr 1, the oldest oil well in Abu Dhabi emirate, and a fragment of lunar rock collected by Apollo XVII in 1972. Look out too for the entertaining mishmash of gifts presented by various luminaries to Sheikh Zayed over the years, including Egyptian president Gamal Nasser (a pair of large embossed plates) and the celebrated female Palestinian freedom fighter Lyla Khaled (a bullet). The second section offers a comprehensive overview of the archeology of the UAE, including extensive artefacts from sites such as Umm an Nar, near Abu Dhabi, and Jebel Hafeet and Hili (see p.156), just outside Al Ain. Most of the exhibits are fairly unexciting, but they're well displayed and explained, offering an interesting picture of local cultural and commercial links right back to the Sumerian era.

Sultan bin Zayed Fort

Off Zayed bin Sultan St • Sat, Sun & Tues–Thurs 8.30am–7.30pm, Fri 3–7.30pm, closed Mon • 3dh; includes Al Ain National Museum

Right next to the Al Ain National Museum, the **Sultan bin Zayed Fort** (or Eastern Fort) is one of the eighteen or so scattered around Al Ain and the surrounding desert. Best known as the birthplace of Sheikh Zayed, the picturesque three-towered structure houses a superb collection of 1960s and 1970s black-and-white photos from around the Gulf, while the picturesque little courtyard at its centre is dotted with a trio of trees and a couple of little traditional palm-thatched *barasti* huts – humble beginnings for the sheikh who would subsequently become one of the world's richest men.

Al Muraba'a Fort

No set hours, but usually open in daylight hours, assuming the caretaker's around • Free

One of the many old forts dotted about the city and surrounding countryside, **Al Muraba'a Fort** was built during the 1940s by Sheikh Zayed during his spell as governor of Al Ain and has now been meticulously restored – providing an incongruous mud-brick memento of times past amid the humdrum architecture of downtown Al Ain. The layout follows the usual pattern, with a large courtyard surrounded by a low crenellated wall and an impressive three-storey **keep** within, built from the traditional admixture of mud brick, clay and gypsum. Inside, stairs lead up past a few small bare rooms, their walls peppered with tiny loopholes, just large enough to accommodate the tip of a rifle, to the top-floor *majlis*, with pretty carved windows and a rustic wooden ceiling insulated with straw.

Al Ain Oasis

Between Al Ain St and Zayed bin Sultan St • Daily sunrise–sunset • Free

South of the centre, spreading west from the National Museum, a dusty green wall of palms announces the presence of the beautiful **Al Ain Oasis**, the largest of the various oases scattered across the city (the name Al Ain, means, literally, "The

15

A NASTY AFFAIR AT THE BURAIMI OASIS

A sleepy backwater for much of its history, Al Ain and Buraimi briefly captured the world's attention in the early 1950s as a result of the so-called **Buraimi Dispute** – one of the defining events in the twentieth-century history of Abu Dhabi and Oman, and one which neatly encapsulates the Wild West atmosphere of the early days of oil prospecting in the Gulf. The origin of the dispute lay in Saudi Arabia's claim in 1949 to sovereignty over large parts of what was traditionally considered territory belonging to Abu Dhabi and Oman, including the Buraimi Oasis. The Saudis (supported by the US Aramco oil company) backed up their claim by referring to previous periods of Saudi occupation dating back to the early nineteenth century, although their real interest in Buraimi stemmed from the belief that large amounts of oil lay buried in the region.

In 1952 a small group of Saudi Arabian soldiers occupied **Hamasa**, one of three Omani villages in the oasis, claiming it for Saudi Arabia and embarking on a campaign of bribery in an attempt to obtain professions of loyalty from local villagers. They also attempted to bribe **Sheikh Zayed**, then governor of Al Ain, tempting him with the huge sum of US$42 million – an offer which Sheikh Zayed pointedly refused. The affair was debated in both the UK Parliament and at the United Nations, although attempts at international arbitration finally broke down in 1955. Shortly afterwards the Saudis were driven out of Hamasa by the Trucial Oman Levies, a British-backed force based in Sharjah (for an eyewitness account of this action, read Edward Henderson's *Arabian Destiny*; see p.194). The dispute wasn't fully resolved until 1974, when an agreement was reached between King Faisal of Saudi Arabia and Sheikh Zayed (who had subsequently become ruler of Abu Dhabi and first president of the newly independent UAE). Ironically, after all the fuss, the area proved singularly lacking in oil.

The dispute gave Buraimi its proverbial fifteen minutes of fame, even inspiring an episode of *The Goon Show* entitled "The Nasty Affair at the Buraimi Oasis". More importantly, it put a final end to centuries of Saudi incursions into Abu Dhabi and Oman, as well as establishing the legendary reputation of Sheikh Zayed, who succeeded in repulsing the oil-rich Saudis and their American cronies long before Abu Dhabi had found its own huge oil reserves. As one foreign observer put it, "He [Zayed] was very proud that, when he had nothing, he told them to get stuffed."

Spring"). This is easily the most idyllic spot in the city, with a mazy network of little walled lanes running between densely planted thickets of trees. There are an estimated 150,000-odd date palms here, along with mango, fig, banana and orange trees, their roots watered in the summer months using traditional *falaj* irrigation channels, which bring water down from the mountains over a distance of some 30km. It's a wonderfully peaceful spot, the silence only broken by the calls to prayer from the two mosques nestled among the palms, and pleasantly cool as well. There are eight entrances dotted around the perimeter of the oasis, although given the disorienting tangle of roads within you're unlikely to end up coming out where you entered.

Al Ain Souk

Immediately in front of the bus station, **Al Ain Souk** is home to the city's main meat, fruit and vegetable market. Housed in a long, functional warehouse-style building, the souk is stocked with the usual picturesque piles of produce (along with the dangling carcasses of animals in the meat section), prettiest at the structure's west end, where Indian traders sit enthroned amid huge mounds of fruit and vegetables. The souk attracts a colourful cast of characters, including patrician-looking Omani men with splendid beards and big white turbans, along with heavily veiled local Bedouin women in their distinctive metal face masks.

Sheikha Salama Mosque

Corner of Salahudeen al Ayubi and Zayed bin Sultan streets

Right in the centre of the city stands Al Ain's newest landmark, the sleek **Sheikha Salama Mosque**, which replaced the previous Sheikha Salama Mosque built by Sheikh Zayed in honour of his mother but unceremoniously demolished in 2007. The new mosque is the largest and easily the best-looking place of worship in the city, with space for almost five thousand worshippers and a striking design mixing traditional and modern, including a pair of tall, square, faintly Moroccan-looking minarets at one end – but, unusually, no dome. It's also worth trying to have a look through the doors (if open) for a look at the striking courtyard and ablutions fountain within.

Al Ain Palace Museum

Al Ain St • Sat, Sun & Tues–Thurs 8.30am–7.30pm, Fri 3–7.30pm, closed Mon • Free • ☎ 03 751 7755, ⓦ bit.ly/AlAinPalace

On the western side of Al Ain Oasis stands the **Al Ain Palace Museum**, occupying one of the various forts around Al Ain owned by the ruling Nahyan family of Abu Dhabi and hallowed thanks to its associations with Sheikh Zayed. The sprawling complex is pleasant enough, with rambling, orangey-pink buildings arranged around a sequence of five courtyards and small gardens, although the palace's thirty-odd rooms, including assorted bedrooms, *majlis* and a small school, aren't particularly interesting.

Al Jahili Fort

120th St, off Sultan bin Zayed al Awwal St • Sat, Sun & Tues–Thurs 8.30am–7.30pm, Fri 3–7.30pm, closed Mon • Free

Of Al Ain's various mud-brick forts, **Al Jahili Fort**, built in 1898, is easily the most impressive, with an fine battlemented main tower and a spacious central courtyard. The much-photographed circular tower on the northern side – with four levels of diminishing size, each topped with a line of triangular battlements – probably pre-dates the rest of the fort.

The fort is also home to the excellent little **Mubarak bin London** exhibition, devoted to the life of legendary explorer **Wilfred Thesiger** (1910–2003). Thesiger – or Mubarak bin London (the "Blessed Son of London") as he was known to his Arab friends – stayed at the fort in the late 1940s at the end of one of the two pioneering journeys across the deserts of the Empty Quarter which later formed the centrepiece of *Arabian Sands*, his classic narrative of Middle Eastern exploration. The exhibition showcases some of Thesiger's superb photography, along with an interesting short film and assorted personal effects, plus a few photographs of the explorer and his close friend Sheikh Zayed (to whom Thesiger bore an uncanny resemblance).

Hili Gardens and Archeological Park

Daily 9am–10pm • Free

About 8km north of the centre, the **Hili Gardens and Archeological Park** is the site of one of the most important archeological sites in the UAE – many finds from here are displayed in the Al Ain Museum, which also provides a good explanation of their significance. The main surviving structure is the so-called "**Hili Grand Tomb**", a circular mausoleum dating from the third century BC, made from large, finely cut and fitted slabs of stones. A quaint carving of two people framed by a pair of long-horned oryx decorates the rear entrance, while a second, less well-preserved circular tomb can be seen nearby in the enclosure signed **Tombs E and N**. Most of this tomb's walls have disappeared, revealing the six tiny chambers within which around six hundred people were buried over a hundred-year period.

Other remains scattered around the park include the outline of a further building ("Hili 10"), with well-preserved foundations right next to the entrance, and the more extensive remains of the "**Hili 1**" settlement, although unless you're a trained archeologist it's difficult to make much sense of what looks like a big heap of dried mud.

15

Camel Souk

Off the Oman road, near Bawadi mall, about 9km from the city centre

Al Ain's old-fashioned **Camel Souk** (actually just a series of pens in the open desert) is worth a visit, despite being a bit tricky to find, attracting a lively crowd of local camel-fanciers haggling over dozens of dromedaries lined up for sale. The souk is busiest in the mornings before around 10am, although low-key trading may continue throughout the day. Be aware that there are some very pushy traders here who may demand massively inflated tips for showing you around or allowing you to take photographs of their animals. Always agree a sum in advance: around 20dh should suffice, although they may demand ten times that figure.

To reach the souk, find the roundabout in front of the *Hilton* hotel and follow the road towards the Oman border at Mazyad. After about 6km you'll see the huge new Bawadi mall on your left. Do a U-turn at the next roundabout, 1km or so beyond the mall, and start driving back towards Al Ain. The souk is off the road on your right, about 500m before you get back to the Bawadi mall.

Al Ain Zoo

Off Nahyan al Awwal St • Daily 9am–8pm • 15dh; children aged 3–12 5dh; under-3s free • ⓣ 03 782 8188, ⓦ awpr.ae

On the southwestern edge of town, around 7km from the centre, the excellent **Al Ain Zoo** is a guaranteed crowd-pleaser for both kids and adults. There are over four thousand animals here, humanely housed in large open pens spread around the very spacious grounds. Inmates include plenty of African fauna – big cats, giraffes, zebras and rhinos (including rare South African white lions and Nubian giraffes) – along with numerous Arabian animals and birds. The zoo has played an important role in conserving endangered local species including the Arabian oryx, leopard, and Houbara bustard – no fewer than 72 antelopes and gazelles of various species were born here in 2010 alone.

Jebel Hafeet

Taxis cost around 100dh

The soaring 1180-metre **Jebel Hafeet** (or Hafit), 30km south of Al Ain on the Omani border, is a popular retreat for locals wanting to escape the heat of the desert plains, and is worth a visit if you have your own vehicle or are prepared to stump up the taxi fare. The second-highest mountain in the UAE, Jebel Hafeet's distinctively craggy outline (resembling – according to some – the tail of a dragon) provides an impressive backdrop to the city and is especially pretty after dark, when the lights lining the road up it seem to hang suspended in midair. You can drive to the top in half an hour or less along the excellent road, from where there are peerless views over the surrounding Hajar mountains. The outdoor terrace at the *Mercure Grand* hotel, perched just below the summit, makes a memorable – if often surprisingly chilly – spot for a drink.

Into Oman: Buraimi

Citizens of most Western countries can buy a visa on the spot at the Hili border post for 5 Omani rials (approximately 10dh)

About 1km north of central Al Ain lies the contiguous Omani city of **Buraimi**, now increasingly overshadowed by its more progressive neighbour. The city-centre border post between the two was closed in 2006 to all except Gulf Cooperation Council (GCC) citizens, meaning that if you want to visit you'll have to enter Oman via the border post north of Al Ain at Hili, where full border formalities are in force.

Modern Buraimi offers an interesting introduction to Oman – not that massively different to Al Ain, admittedly, although with a slightly more colourful crowd of locals (including the occasional women sporting traditional Bedu face masks, and men wearing jauntily embroidered Omani caps rather than the *ghutra* headdress favoured in the UAE). The main road through town (the Sohar road) just east of Al Hillah fort is particularly colourful, with an incredible quantity of ladies' tailoring shops stuffed full of extravagantly embroidered clothes and adorned with brilliant neon signs.

Al Hillah Fort

Sun–Thurs 8am–2pm • Free

Right in the middle of town is the historic **Al Hillah Fort**, a low-slung sandstone edifice, rather plain and box-like from the outside. It's actually a walled residential complex rather than a proper fort – the walls come with the usual battlements and rifle slits, but there are no proper defensive towers or outer walls. The entrance gateway leads into a large gravel courtyard, empty save for a small mosque. Go right from here to reach the complex's second courtyard, where you'll find one of Oman's finest clusters of traditional residential buildings, with three impressive two-storey buildings, embellished with superb wooden doors and carved details including unusual windows formed of interlocking triangles. Climb to the roofs of any of the three for fine views over the complex.

The souks

Surrounding Al Hillah Fort is Buraimi's interesting huddle of souks. Immediately north of the fort is the engaging **old souk**, in a small white building with a fake watchtower at its centre, full of little shops selling spices, shoes, food, walking sticks and traditional toy rifles, while the area at the rear hosts stalls run by local Bedu women selling locally produced honey and rosewater.

South of the fort, the large **fruit and vegetable souk** occupies a rather grand edifice resembling a kind of postmodern fort, with Indian and Pakistani traders presiding over vast piles of colourful comestibles. The **wholesale souk** next door (in a similar building) is usually quieter, with merchandise including big piles of dried fish, sacks of dates and large bundles of wood stacked up in every direction.

Al Khandaq Fort

Sun–Thurs 8am–2pm • Free

A short walk south of the souks is the immaculately restored **Al Khandaq Fort**, set in a slightly elevated position above a dried-up wadi and surrounded by a deep moat. The fort is modest in size but prettily decorated, with diminutive, slope-sided round towers adorned with zigzagging triangles and chevrons, slightly reminiscent of Al Jahili Fort in Al Ain. Most of the interior is occupied by a large gravel courtyard from where ramps and steps lead up to a walkway around the battlements, offering sweeping views over the dusty palms below.

ARRIVAL AND DEPARTURE   AL AIN

By minibus Minibuses (hourly 6.30am–11.30pm; 1hr 30min–2hr; 20dh) run between Al Ghubaiba bus station in Bur Dubai and Al Ain's bus station.

Tours Tours are offered by virtually all the Dubai operators listed in Basics (see p.25) and cost around 220dh for a day-long tour of Al Ain's major attractions.

GETTING AROUND

By taxi There are plenty of taxis on the streets – and passing drivers of empty cabs often hoot at likely looking fares. Most taxis in Al Ain are now modern silver vehicles, although you might see a few of the city's older gold and white cars. All are metered, with a flag fare of 3.5dh.

ACCOMMODATION

Al Ain isn't exactly overflowing with accommodation options. Apart from the three low-key five-stars listed below there are a few drab and overpriced places dotted around the centre, but no budget options.

Al Ain Rotana 120th St ☎ 03 754 5111, ⓦ rotana.com /alainrotana. The fanciest of the city's three five-star hotels, and conveniently close to the city centre, with pleasantly chintzy Arabian decor, spacious gardens and a nice pool. Rooms are very spacious and well appointed, and there are also a couple of good in-house restaurants (see opposite). **800dh**

Danat Al Ain Resort Al Salam St ☎ 03 704 6000, ⓦ danathotels.com. Formerly the *Al Ain InterContinental*, this very peaceful hotel on the edge of town is set amid extensive gardens and with attractively refurbished rooms. **800dh**

Hilton Al Ain Khalid bin Sultan St ☎03 678 6666, ⓦhilton.com. Run-of-the-mill and rather dated hotel, though the grounds and pools are spacious and attractive and rates are sometimes slightly lower than at the city's other two five-stars. <u>750dh</u>

EATING

There's a smattering of simple restaurants and cafés in the city centre – the best selection is along **Khalifa bin Zayed Street** – while there are also several coffee shops in the smart, modern **Al Ain Mall**, including a typically chintzy branch of *Shakespeare & Co* (see p.105). For more upmarket restaurants you'll need to head out to one of the city's trio of five-star hotels listed above; these are also where you'll find the city's only **licensed** venues.

Al Diwan Khalifa bin Zayed St ☎03 764 4445. Rustic-looking restaurant with very cheery staff and a menu of mainly Lebanese and Iranian classics – grilled pigeon, *chelo* kebabs, chicken and meat *arayes*, assorted mezze and a wide selection of (pricier) seafood. Most mains 35–50dh. Daily 8am–midnight.

★ **The Hut** Khalifa bin Zayed St ☎03 751 6526. An unexpected find, this cosy little café looks more like an English country teashop than anything you'd expect to discover in the depths of the UAE. There's a good selection of teas, coffees, juices, cakes and pastries, plus a short menu of sandwiches (served with mountainous piles of chips) from as little as 18dh. Excellent value. Daily 8am–1pm.

Al Mallah Khalifa bin Zayed St. Simple but consistently popular little café serving up big and tasty Lebanese grills and juices, plus takeaway shwarmas. Mains around 25dh. Daily 8am–midnight.

Min Zaman Al Ain Rotana hotel ☎03 754 5111, ⓦrotana.com/alainrotana. The swankiest Lebanese restaurant in town, with a classy range of the usual Middle Eastern classics. Sit either in the attractive dining room or outside on the terrace overlooking the hotel gardens. There also an Arabian band and belly dancer most nights. Most mains around 60dh. Daily 7pm–2am.

Trader Vic's Al Ain Rotana hotel ☎03 703 1086, ⓦtradervics.com. Al Ain branch of the Gulf-wide chain with a lively party atmosphere, potent cocktails and a wide-ranging, if expensive, international menu featuring stir-fries, curries, pizzas, steaks and seafood – anything from Omani lobster to New York-style sirloin. Licensed. Mains from around 85dh. Daily 12.30–3.30pm & 7–11.30pm.

Dubai Desert Conservation Reserve

E66 highway, around 50km from Dubai, 75km from Al Ain • ⓦddcr.org

Unfortunately, much of the desert around Dubai is a total mess, disfigured by endless building works, pylons, petrol stations and other unforgivable clutter. For a taste of real, unadulterated desert, the best place to head is the superb **Dubai Desert Conservation Reserve**. Interestingly, this is not an untouched piece of original desert, but one which has been systematically rehabilitated over the past decade and restored to something approaching its original condition – perhaps offering a model of what could be done elsewhere to rejuvenate Dubai's beautiful but severely damaged natural environment.

The reserve encloses 250 square kilometres of shifting dunes, dotted with stunted acacia, firebush and indigenous *ghaf* trees, and serves as a refuge for 33 local mammal and reptile species, including rare and endangered creatures such as the oryx, Arabian mountain gazelle, sand gazelle, Arabian red fox and sand fox.

Access to the reserve is carefully controlled; the cheapest option is to come on a visit with one of the small and select group of Dubai operators who are allowed to run **tours** here – at present, Arabian Adventures, Lama, Travco and Alpha (see p.25). Alternatively, you can stay in the reserve at the idyllic but wickedly expensive *Al Maha* resort (see p.102).

The east coast

The **east coast** of the UAE is almost the exact opposite of the west. Compared to the country's heavily developed Arabian Gulf seaboard, the Indian Ocean-facing east is only thinly settled and still relatively untouched. Somnolent and scenic, the east is a popular weekend destination, just two hours' drive away, for visitors from Dubai, who come to loll around on the largely deserted beaches dotting the coast.

15

THE EMIRATES OF THE EAST

The division of the tip of the Arabian peninsula between the seven emirates of the UAE and Oman is a complicated little jigsaw puzzle. The borders were formalized by British colonial officials who simply wandered around the peninsula for months asking the inhabitants of every village which sheikh they owed allegiance to, and drew up the boundaries accordingly. Most of the area covered here falls within the Emirate of Fujairah, though Masafi belongs to Ras Al Khaimah and Khor Fakkan to Sharjah, while Dibba is divided into three districts: Dibba Muhallab, ruled by Fujairah; Dibba al Hisn, ruled by Sharjah; and Dibba Bayah, which belongs to Oman.

Much of the east is dominated by the magnificent **Hajar Mountains**, which bisect the region and run on into Oman. The UAE section of the Hajar rise to a highest point of 1527m at Jebel Yibir, inland from Dibba in the far north of the country, and provide a scenic backdrop to the length of the eastern coast, metamorphosing from slate grey to deep red as the light changes through the course of the day.

There are a number of low-key sights scattered around the east coast, including the old fort at **Fujairah** and the UAE's oldest mosque at **Bidiya**, although for many visitors the main attraction is the trio of attractive beachside resorts which dot the beautiful **Al Aqah Beach**.

Masafi

Most tours to the east coast stop en route at the small town of **MASAFI**, the western gateway to the Hajar Mountains and around 80km from Dubai. Masafi is famous for two things: the first is water – this is where the eponymous mineral water, sold all over the Emirates, is bottled; the second is the town's so-called **Friday Market** (open daily, despite its name, around 8am–10pm). Strung along either side of the busy main road, this heavily visited and decidedly characterless highway bazaar survives largely on the passing coach-party trade. The market is best for carpets, and you can occasionally unearth a few decent items here (and at cheaper prices than Dubai), although most of the stock is kitsch factory-made tat – if you ever wanted a rug embellished with an enormous portrait of Sheikh Zayed, for example, now's your chance.

Dibba

Pushed right up against the border with Oman is the sleepy coastal town of **DIBBA**. This quiet little spot was the site of one of the major battles of early Islamic history in 633 AD (a year after the Prophet Mohammed's death) when the forces of the caliph Abu Bakr defeated those of a local ruler who had renounced Islam. A large cemetery outside town is traditionally believed to house the remains of the apostates killed in the battle.

Modern Dibba has something of a split personality, being divided into three parts: Dibba Bayah on the Omani side, Dibba Muhallab, part of the UAE's Emirate of Fujairah, and Dibba al Hisn, part of the UAE's Emirate of Sharjah. Fujairah's **Dibba Muhallab** is easily the largest most developed of the three areas, and one of the UAE's more pleasant towns, built on a pleasingly human scale, with neat apartment blocks, tree-lined streets and a sweeping seafront corniche giving the whole place a pleasantly Mediterranean air. A couple of huge mosques, each sporting a quartet of minarets, rise proudly above the corniche, while the town also demonstrates the typical Emirati penchant for decorating roundabouts with oversized statues – in this case ranging from a coffeepot and a watchtower through to an oil lamp and a pile of earthenware pottery. Sharjah's **Dibba al Hisn** is smaller, with a rather toy-town main street lined with identikit faux-Arabian villas and office blocks.

Into Oman: Dibba Bayah

Passports need to be shown, but there are no border formalities and a visa isn't required

It's possible to hop over the Omani border into the even quieter and significantly less developed **Dibba Bayah**. The pleasant seafront here is fringed with a fine arc of golden sand, plus the occasional fishing boat, while just inland stands a large, rather plain fort (not open to the public; follow the brown signs inland to "Daba Castle", left of the main road through town about 750m north of the border checkpoint).

It's possible to travel north from here along the rough, graded track into the mountains as far as the official border post at Wadi Bih some 35km further on, though the border is closed to all but Omani and UAE nationals.

Al Aqah Beach

Dibba is the jumping-off point for the lovely **Al Aqah Beach**, a fine stretch of golden sand with a trio of upmarket hotels (see p.162), all of which make a good spot for a meal or an overnight stay. The long swathe of unspoilt coastline hereabouts ranks among the UAE's most attractive destinations if you want to get out of Dubai for a few days, and gets busy at weekends with city-dwellers escaping the urban rush. The waters around the curiously shaped rock – popularly known as **Snoopy Island** on account of its supposed resemblance to the famous cartoon dog – directly offshore, opposite the *Sandy Beach Motel*, are a popular spot for diving and snorkelling.

Bidiya

The small fishing village of **BIDIYA**, around 7km south of Snoopy Island and 25km south of Dibba, is famous as the site of the UAE's oldest mosque (and, for once, "old" doesn't mean 1975), dating back to the fifteenth century. It's a rustic little structure made of mud brick and gypsum, topped by four very flat, small domes; visitors are sometimes allowed into the small and dimly lit interior, which is supported by a single column. Behind the mosque, steps lead up to the top of the hill behind, studded with a couple of watchtowers and offering superb views over the Hajar mountains.

Khor Fakkan

Roughly halfway down the east coast, the sizeable town of **KHOR FAKKAN** (or Khawr Fakkan) sprawls round a superb bay, one of the loveliest in the UAE. The town is part of the booze-free and ultra-conservative Sharjah emirate, and hasn't enjoyed the tourist boom its location would otherwise suggest. It's a pleasant spot for a brief visit though, with a fine seafront corniche complete with fish market, a tempting stretch of beach (although, this being Sharjah, modest beachwear is advised) and views of another popular diving spot, Sharq Island, sometimes mistranslated as the rather alarming "Shark Island", although *sharq* is in fact simply the Arabic for "east".

MADHA

About halfway between Khor Fakkan and Fujairah lies the curious Omani exclave of **Madha** – a tiny dot of Omani territory (comprising just 75 square kilometres) completely surrounded by the UAE. The area is reached via a single surfaced road off the main coastal highway between Khor Fakkan and Fujairah city near the district of Qurayya.

There's nothing particular to see here, beyond the unremarkable modern town of Madha itself, surrounded by mountains. The enclave is notable mainly for one geopolitical oddity: the village of **Nahwa** (a few kilometres further along the road past Madha town, at the end of the tarmac). Bizarrely, this village actually belongs to the UAE emirate of Sharjah, creating a Russian-doll effect whereby the UAE territory of Nahwa is enclosed within the Omani district of Madha, which is enclosed by the UAE emirates of Fujairah and Sharjah – which are themselves bookended by Omani territory on either side.

15

Fujairah

The largest settlement on the east coast, **FUJAIRAH** (or "Fujairah city" as it's often described to distinguish it from the eponymous emirate) is fairly unexciting, although its urban sprawl and modest cluster of high-rises come as something of a surprise after the unspoilt surrounding countryside. Fujairah has recently enjoyed something of a minor boom, mainly on the back of economic developments in neighbouring emirates, especially Dubai. The focus of much of this is the city's massive oil-refuelling port – the world's third largest after Singapore and Rotterdam – at the southern end of town, which is where most of the UAE's oil is exported from, as its east coast location saves shipping from making a two-day dog-leg around the tip of the Arabian peninsula. There's usually a line of tankers several kilometres long offshore waiting for their turn at the pumps.

The main sight in town is the photogenic **Fujairah Fort** (not currently open to the public), off Madhab Road on the northern edge of the city centre. Dating back to the sixteenth century, this is the most picture-perfect of the UAE's many forts, set atop a large plinth and with high, bare walls rising to a pretty cluster of towers and battlements, dramatically framed by an outcrop of the Hajar Mountains. Immediately south of the fort, the rather pedestrian **Fujairah Museum** (Sun–Thurs 8am–1pm & 4–6pm, Fri 2–6pm; 2dh) houses a run-of-the-mill collection of local weaponry, jewellery and archeological displays.

15

ARRIVAL AND DEPARTURE

THE EAST COAST

By car Public transport around the east is sketchy, and won't get you very far in a day. However, vehicle rental is a possibility, and once you've managed to get out of Dubai, the roads in the east are some of the emptiest and most driver-friendly in the country.

Tours Most of the Dubai tour operators listed in Basics (see p.25) offer day-tours of the east, usually costing around 200–250dh.

ACCOMMODATION AND EATING

If you want to spend a night or two on the east coast, the three best places to stay are the trio of upmarket hotels on Al Aqah Beach. For eating, both the *Fujairah Rotana* and *Le Méridien* have a wide range of all-day cafés and restaurants. Coach parties normally head for the *Sandy Beach Resort* – although the buffet lunches are pretty awful.

Fujairah Rotana Resort and Spa E99 coastal highway, 1km south of the Le Méridien Al Aqah ☏ 09 244 9888, ⓦ rotana.com; map p.145. Close to the landmark *Le Méridien Al Aqah*, the equally large though rather less overpowering *Fujairah Rotana Resort & Spa* offers similar five-star luxury and an equivalent spread of facilities and in-house activities. 700dh

Le Méridien Al Aqah Beach Resort E99 coastal highway ☏ 09 244 9000, ⓦ lemeridien-alaqah.com; map p.145. Towering over the northern end of Al Aqah Beach the

---

BULLFIGHTING FUJAIRAH-STYLE

If you happen to be around Fujairah on a Friday afternoon don't miss the chance to watch one of the town's traditional **bull-butting** contests (*mnattah* in Arabic). The sport is said to have been introduced to the Gulf by the Portuguese sometime during the seventeenth or eighteenth centuries; unlike Spanish bullfighting, the bulls fight one another, rather than a matador. And although there's plenty of bovine testosterone floating around, no blood is spilled – although spectators occasionally have to dash for cover if one of the bulls decides to make a run for it.

The highly prized Brahma bulls which take part in the contests are brought in from across the UAE; animals are fed up on a diet of milk, honey and butter and weigh around a ton. The bulls are led into the ring by their handlers, after which the "arena master" – a challenging and potentially lethal occupation – takes charge. All being well, the bulls will lock horns and begin to test their strength against the other, although some simply can't be bothered, and just stand around eyeing up the crowd. Bouts last two or three minutes. The winning bull is the one that succeeds in pushing the other one out of the ring, although many contests end in a draw.

The bull-butting ground (an open area with tethering posts) is at the southern end of town between the seafont Corniche Street and the main coastal highway. Meetings start around 4.30–5pm on Fridays year-round and last a couple of hours.

INTO OMAN: THE MUSANDAM PENINSULA

Around two and a half hours' drive north of Dubai lies Oman's **Musandam peninsula**, perhaps the most scenically spectacular area in the entire Gulf, as the towering red-rock Hajar mountains fall precipitously into the blue waters of the Arabian Gulf, creating a labyrinthine system of steep-sided fjords (**khors**), channels and islands. This is one of the region's most pristine natural wildernesses, thinly populated and boasting a magically unspoilt marine environment, including pods of frolicking humpback dolphins and the occasional basking shark. The contrast with Dubai could hardly be greater.

Until the last few decades this was one of the least accessible places in Arabia, and even now there are few roads into or around the peninsula. The easiest way to explore is **by boat**, offering superlative views of the surrounding *khors*. Various boat trips, usually aboard a traditional wooden dhow, start from **Khasab**, the peninsula's main town, most of them heading up into **Khor Ash Sham**, the largest of Musandam's many *khors*, ringed with remote fishing villages. Alternatively, local operators also offer dramatic trips into Musandam's **mountainous interior**, following the rough road (4WD only) which climbs dramatically up the towering Jebel Harim ("Mountain of Women"), the peninsula's highest peak.

VISITING MUSANDAM FROM DUBAI

The peninsula is separated from the rest of Oman by a large stretch of UAE territory, and is actually a lot easier to visit from Dubai than from Muscat. Musandam is just about possible as a **day-trip** from Dubai, if you make a very early start. Leaving at around 6am, you'll have time for a five-hour boat ride or mountain safari before heading back, although you probably won't be back in Dubai anytime much before 10pm. It usually takes about half an hour each way to clear the UAE–Oman border post and you should be able to get an Omani visa on the spot. The peninsula also makes a good destination for a longer **two- or three-night** stay. An increasing number of local tour operators (see p.25) now offer one-day excursions, as well as longer diving and other trips. Alternatively contact the excellent **Khasab Travel and Tours** (in Dubai ☏04 266 9950, ⊛khasabtours.com).

15

landmark *Le Méridien Al Aqah Beach Resort* is an impressive high-rise colossus which looks like it's been airlifted directly from Dubai Marina and plonked down on this sleepy stretch of coast. The hotel serves up plenty of five-star style, with facilities including a spa, dive centre and kids' club, plus extensive gardens and private beach. **1000dh**

Sandy Beach Hotel and Resort E99 coastal highway, 1km south of the Fujairah Rotana ☏09 244 5555, ⊛sandybm.com; map p.145. A low-key alternative to Al Aqah's two five-star resorts, with accommodation in a range of beach chalets and hotel rooms, plus diving and watersports centres. **700dh**

Hatta

An easy day-trip from Dubai is to the village of **HATTA**, a small enclave of Dubai territory around 115km from the city centre and close to the east coast. Built in the shadow of the magnificently craggy Hajar mountains, the village was founded in the sixteenth century and once served as an important staging post on the overland route from Oman to Dubai, as the watchtowers which dot the surrounding hillsides testify. Many people come to visit the **Hatta Heritage Village**, one of the UAE's most appealing museums of traditional life, while the town and surrounding countryside is a popular weekend getaway from Dubai, partly on account of its fractionally cooler temperatures and lower humidity, although things are pretty somnolent during the week.

Hatta Heritage Village

Approaching from Dubai, turn right at the roundabout in front of the *Hatta Fort Hotel*, from where it's about a 3km drive uphill • Sat–Thurs 8am–8pm, Fri 2–8pm • Free • ☏04 852 1374, ⊛bit.ly/HattaHeritage

The main attraction hereabouts is the extensive **Hatta Heritage Village**. Scattered across a rugged hillside ringed by craggy mountains, the village comprises a number of low and unusually solid-looking traditional structures with tiny windows and stout teak

15

BIG RED

Driving from Dubai to Hatta (just before you reach the Oman border) you'll notice a huge sand dune off on your left. Known as **Big Red**, this is one of the most popular off-road destinations in the UAE and often crawling with 4WDs and quad-bikers attempting to make their way to the top; many Dubai tour operators use the stretch of less elevated dunes on the other side of the road for dune-bashing excursions during their afternoon desert safaris (see p.26). You can hire your own quad bike from the outlet next to the main road if you fancy a crack at the sands, or just a spin around the flat quad-bike course next to the highway.

---

doors. Restoration here has been relatively light compared to similar heritage sites in the UAE, which adds to the village's rather rustic appeal.

Inside the complex the first building you reach is also the largest, **Al Husen** fort, its rooms filled with displays of dusty weaponry and a *majlis* with unusually tiny windows. There's also a "traditional house" and other smaller buildings with exhibits on traditional folklore, palm tree products and a "poets' *majlis*". The path up through the village eventually climbs up to one of Hatta's two **watchtowers**, from where there are fine panoramic views. A second watchtower, roughly opposite the entrance to the Heritage Village, is reached by a short footpath and worth the climb for the further superb views from the top.

Hatta Rock Pools

The pools are best accessed by 4WD and quite tricky to find, so if you're interested ask for directions locally; there are no border checks but it's worth carrying your passport just in case, and remember UAE rental cars won't be insured while you're in Oman, unless you've made special arrangements

The only other attraction nearby are the **Hatta Rock Pools**, around 20km from Hatta over the border in Oman. The pools sit inside a kind of miniature canyon which has been carved by water erosion out of the rocky floor of the surrounding *wadi*. It's an attractive spot for a dip, although it gets overrun at weekends and has been rather spoilt by the rubbish, graffiti and other junk left by day-trippers.

ARRIVAL AND DEPARTURE   HATTA

By car Hatta is just over an hour's drive along a fast modern highway. The highway passes through a small section of Oman en route – there are cursory checkpoints entering and leaving Oman territory, but visitors aren't required to produce any paperwork, although note that unless you've made special arrangements, UAE rental cars aren't insured while you're in Oman. The Oman stretch is also notably less developed than the UAE territory on either side, with unspoilt stretches of rocky desert stretching away to the Hajar mountains in the distance.

By shared taxi/bus Shared taxis (25dh per person) carrying seven passengers leave when full from ranks at the Gold Souk Bus Station and Al Sabkha Bus Station, both in Deira. You might also check at Al Ghubaiba and the Gold Souk bus stations to see if there are any bus services running when you visit.

ACCOMMODATION AND EATING

Hatta Fort Hotel E44 highway ☎04 809 9333, ⓦjaresortshotels.com; map p.145. Appealing, rather old-fashioned country resort, with fine mountain views, attractive gardens and a spacious pool with its own little rocky waterfall. It's a popular retreat at weekends, when it can get absolutely overrun, but is very peaceful at other times. There's a 50dh per person entrance charge on Fri and Sat, redeemable against food and drink at one of the hotel's trio of restaurants. <u>600dh</u>

SHEIKH ZAYED MOSQUE

Abu Dhabi

The capital of the UAE, Abu Dhabi is the very model of a modern Gulf petro-city: thoroughly contemporary, shamelessly wealthy and decidedly staid. Abu Dhabi's lightning change from obscure fishing village into modern city-state within the past thirty years is perhaps the most dramatic of all the stories of oil-driven transformation that dot the region, and although the city's endless glass-fronted high-rises and multi-lane highways can seem fairly uninspiring on first acquaintance, locals take understandable pride in the city's remarkable recent metamorphosis. For the casual visitor, modern Abu Dhabi is mainly interesting for how it contrasts with its more famous neighbour – an Arabian Washington to Dubai's Las Vegas. Specific sights are relatively thin on the ground, and much of the pleasure of a visit lies in wandering through the city centre and along the handsome waterfront Corniche Road.

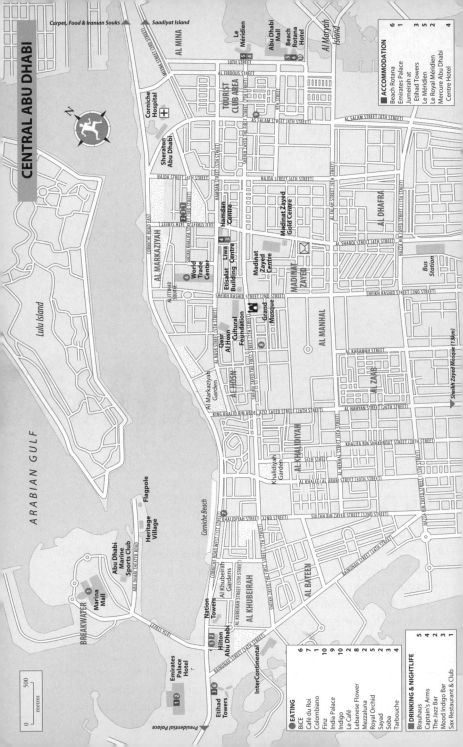

CENTRAL ABU DHABI

Carpet, Food & Iranian Souks

Saadiyat Island

AL MINA

Le Méridien

Abu Dhabi Mall

Beach Rotana Hotel

Al Maryah Island

10TH STREET

AL FIRDOUS STREET

TOURIST CLUB AREA

Corniche Hospital

AS SALAM STREET (8TH STREET)

AL SALAM STREET (8TH STREET)

MINA STREET (11TH STREET)

Sheraton Abu Dhabi

NAJDA STREET (6TH STREET)

NAJDA STREET (6TH STREET)

AL DHAFRA

HAMDAN STREET (5TH STREET)

Hamdan Centre

Madinat Zayed Gold Centre

AL MARKAZIYAH

CORNICHE ROAD EAST

World Trade Center

Etisalat Building

Liwa Centre

Madinat Zayed Centre

Bus Station

SHEIKH KHALIFA STREET (3RD STREET)

AL NASR STREET (5TH STREET)

KUTTHAB SQUARE

SHEIKH RASHID STREET (2ND STREET)

MADINAT ZAYED

AL SHARQI STREET (4TH STREET)

SHEIKH RASHID STREET (2ND STREET)

Qasr Al Hosn

Cultural Foundation

Grand Mosque

AL MANHAL

HAZZA BIN ZAYED STREET (11TH STREET)

Al Markaziyah Garden

AL HOSN

AL ZAAB

AL KARAMAH STREET

ARABIAN GULF

Lulu Island

KING KHALID BIN ABDEL AZIZ SAEED STREET (26TH STREET)

AL NAHYAN STREET (26TH STREET)

Sheikh Zayed Mosque (13km)

KHALIFA BIN SHAKHBOUT STREET (28TH STREET)

AL KHALIDIYAH

16TH STREET

Khalidiyah Garden

AL KHALEEJ AL ARABI STREET (30TH STREET)

Corniche Beach

CORNICHE ROAD WEST (1ST STREET)

KHALIDIYAH STREET (32ND STREET)

SULTAN BIN ZAYED STREET (32ND STREET)

Flagpole

Heritage Village

Abu Dhabi Marine Sports Club

ABU DHABI THEATRE ROAD

Al Khubeirah Gardens

AL KHUBEIRAH STREET (5TH STREET)

AL KHUBEIRAH

AL BATEEN

BAINUNAH STREET (34TH STREET)

BREAKWATER

Marina Mall

Nation Towers

Hilton Abu Dhabi

InterContinental

14TH STREET

ZAYED THE FIRST STREET (7TH STREET)

Emirates Palace Hotel

Etihad Towers

Presidential Palace

N

0 500 metres

■ ACCOMMODATION

Beach Rotana	6
Emirates Palace	1
Jumeirah at Etihad Towers	3
Le Méridien	5
Le Royal Méridien	2
Mercure Abu Dhabi	4
Centre Hotel	

● EATING

BiCE	6
Café du Roi	7
Colombiano	1
Finz	10
India Palace	9
Indigo	10
Le Café	2
Lebanese Flower	8
Mezzaluna	5
Royal Orchid	3
Sayad	3
Soba	3
Tarbouche	4

■ DRINKING & NIGHTLIFE

Brauhaus	5
Captain's Arms	4
The Jazz Bar	2
Mood Indigo Bar	3
Sax Restaurant & Club	1

ABU DHABI ORIENTATION

Abu Dhabi isn't as vastly spread out as Dubai, but still stretches over a considerable area – even the city centre's main sights are too widely scattered to be comfortably walkable (it's 8km from the *Emirates Palace* on the southwest side of the centre to the Abu Dhabi Mall on the opposite flank). Fortunately there are plenty of inexpensive city taxis (see p.175) available to ferry you around the city, as well as for longer trips out to the Sheikh Zayed Mosque (15km from the centre) and beyond.

The city is actually built on an island, connected to the mainland by three bridges: (from north to south) **Sheikh Zayed Bridge**, **Al Maqtaa Bridge** and **Mussafah Bridge**. These bridges connect in turn to the three main roads across the island: **Al Salam Street**, **Al Maktoum Street** and **Al Khaleej al Arabi Street**. Memorize this basic layout, and you'll hopefully not go too far wrong.

Route-finding and orientation are generally straightforward thanks to the city's fairly regular grid plan, although potential confusion is provided by the city's **street names**. All major roads have both a **number** and a **name** (or sometimes two). Odd-numbered roads run up and down the island, starting with the Corniche Road (1st Street); even-numbered roads run across the island. Names are more complicated. Most major roads have a modern Arabic name, although different parts of the same street may have different names (the city-centre 5th Street, for example, is known as Al Nasr Street at one end and Hamdan bin Mohammed Street – or just Hamdan Street – at the other). A few old pre-independence names also remain in occasional use (7th Street, for example: officially Sheikh Zayed the First Street but also known as Electra Street; or 9th Street, officially Al Falah Road but also occasionally referred to as Old Passport Road). Road signs generally show a mix of numbers and modern names.

16

The city's two standout attractions are the stunning **Sheikh Zayed Mosque**, one of the world's largest and most extravagant places of Islamic worship, and the ultra-opulent **Emirates Palace Hotel**. Other attractions include the memorable new souk at the **World Trade Center**, and the contrastingly traditional **Heritage Village**, offering superb views of the Corniche Road.

Emirates Palace Hotel

Corniche Rd West • ☎ 02 690 9000, ⓦ emiratespalace.com

Standing in solitary splendour at the western end of the city is the vast **Emirates Palace Hotel**. Opened in 2005, it was intended to rival Dubai's Burj al Arab and provide Abu Dhabi with a similarly iconic "seven-star" landmark – although in fact the two buildings could hardly be more different. Driveways climb up through the grounds to the main entrance to the hotel, which sits in an elevated position above the sea and surrounding gardens. It's impressively stage-managed, although the only really unusual thing about the building is its sheer size: 1km in length, 114 domes, 140 elevators, 2000 staff and so on. The quasi-Arabian design, meanwhile, is disappointingly pedestrian and much of the exterior looks strangely drab and even a little bit cheap – ironic, really, given that the hotel is believed to have been the most expensive ever built (at a rumoured cost of US$3 billion). All of which means the *Emirates Palace* is as cautiously conservative as the Burj al Arab is daringly futuristic and innovative – which says a lot about the contrasting outlooks of the two very different cities which they represent.

The **interior** is far more memorable, centred on a dazzling central dome-cum-atrium, with vast quantities of marble and huge chandeliers. Cavernous corridors stretch out for what seem like miles towards the rooms in the two huge flanking wings – you can work up a healthy appetite just walking between your room and the lobby, and even staff have been known to get lost. The six "ruler's suites", with gold-plated fittings throughout, are more conveniently situated, but are reserved for visiting heads of state. Visitors with cash to drop can shop to impress at the world's first gold vending machine (in the lobby), which dispenses over three hundred pure-gold products, including miniature gold ingots. Non-guests can visit for a meal at one of the numerous restaurants, or drop in for one of the sumptuous afternoon teas (see p.176) – but dress well to avoid being turned away at the gate.

The vast new building you can see directly behind the *Emirates Palace* (and designed in a similar style) is Abu Dhabi's new **Presidential Palace**, under construction at the time of writing but planned on an unprecedentedly monumental scale which may eventually make even the *Emirates Palace* look relatively understated by comparison.

Heritage Village

Breakwater • Sat–Thurs 9am–5pm, Fri 3.30–9pm • Free • ☎ 02 681 4455, ⓦ bit.ly/UAE_Heritage_Village

Dramatically situated on the Corniche Road-facing side of the Breakwater – a small protuberance of reclaimed land jutting out from its southern end – the **Heritage Village** offers a slice of traditional Abu Dhabi done up for the visiting coach parties who flock here for whistle-stop visits. The "village" consists of picturesque *barasti* huts, plus a small **museum** (though it hardly ever seems to be open), and has spectacular views over the water to the Corniche Road. Opposite the museum is a string of **workshops** where local artisans – carpenters, potters and brass-makers and so on – can sometimes be seen at work. The so-called "traditional market", however, is basically just a few ladies flogging cheap handicrafts out of a line of *barasti* huts.

Immediately beyond the Heritage Village you can't fail to notice the enormous **flagpole**, visible for miles around. At 123m, this was formerly claimed to be the tallest in the world, until topped by one in Jordan in 2003 (which, ironically, was made in Dubai).

Marina Mall

Marina Village, Breakwater • Sat–Thurs 10am–10pm, Fri 2–10pm • ⓦ marinamall.ae

Dominating the centre of the Breakwater, the large **Marina Mall**, an attractive modern complex built around a series of tented courtyards and fountains, is one of the city's two top shopping destinations, along with the glitzy Abu Dhabi Mall on the opposite side of town. The mall's main attraction for non-shoppers is its views of the long string of glass-faced high-rises lining the Corniche Road. These are best appreciated from the soaring **Burj al Marina** tower, located at the back of the mall, which can be visited for the price of an expensive drink at the 41st-floor *Colombiano* coffee shop (see p.176) immediately below.

Corniche Road

ⓦ bit.ly/AD_Corniche

Driving through modern Abu Dhabi's suburban sprawl, it's easy not to notice that the city is built on an island rather than on the mainland itself; it wasn't until the construction of the Maqtaa Bridge in 1966 that the two were connected. The city's waterfront location is best appreciated from the sweeping, waterfront **Corniche Road**, which runs for the best part of 5km along Abu Dhabi's western edge. The road is lined by spacious gardens on either side and flanked by a long line of glass-clad high-rises which both encapsulate the modern city's internationalist credentials and provide Abu Dhabi with its most memorable views (although the waterfront as a whole is perhaps best appreciated from the Heritage Village across the water). Two of the city's most striking recent developments can be found at the southern end of the Corniche Road: the huge new **Etihad Towers** complex (ⓦ etihadtowers.com), a cluster of five futuristic skyscrapers, and the nearby **NationsTowers** development (not quite finished at the time of writing), comprising two further similarly neck-cricking towers of slightly unequal height, joined at the top by a vertiginous sky-bridge.

16

The Corniche Road is also a popular spot with local residents catching (or shooting) the breeze, particularly towards dusk, when it fills up with a diverse crowd of promenading Emiratis, jogging Europeans and picnicking Indians. There's also an attractive blue-flag **beach** with safe swimming stretching from near the *Hilton* to Al Khaleej al Arabi Street (which is where you'll find the main entrance).

Qasr al Hosn and around

Al Nasr St (5th St) • ⓦ bit.ly/Qasr-al-Hosn

More or less at the very centre of Abu Dhabi sits **Qasr al Hosn** ("The Palace Fort"), the oldest building in Abu Dhabi. The fort started life around 1761 as a single round watchtower built to defend the only freshwater well in Abu Dhabi, and was subsequently expanded in 1793, becoming the residence of Abu Dhabi's ruling Al Nahyan family. In 1939, Sheikh Shakhbut bin Sultan al Nahyan, the elder brother of Sheikh Zayed, began to significantly enlarge the complex using income raised from the first oil-prospecting concessions granted to foreign companies.

The fort continued to serve as the ruler's palace and seat of government until Sheikh Zayed came to power in 1966, at which point the ruling family decamped and the fort was given over to purely administrative uses. It was eventually renovated, acquiring a bright new covering of white-painted concrete – hence its popular name of the "White Fort". The large and rather plain whitewashed structure you see today is of no particular architectural distinction, although the rambling battlemented walls, dotted with a few watchtowers, are modestly pretty. The fort was being renovated again at the time of writing and is due to reopen as a major new museum of Abu Dhabi's historical and cultural heritage – although no one seems to have any idea of when this might happen.

Cultural Foundation

Al Nasr St (5th St) • ⓦ adach.ae/en

The city's sleek, modern **Cultural Foundation** is currently closed as part of the Qasr al Hosn redevelopment, with no confirmed reopening date in sight. The foundation formerly hosted various collections, including the National Library and Archives, along with regular temporary exhibitions, film screenings and concerts.

World Trade Center and around

ⓦ wtcad.ae **Souk** Sun–Thurs 10am–10pm, Fri 3–11pm, Sat 10am–11pm

Standing on the site of the city's former main souk, the huge new **World Trade Center** (previously known as the Central Market) is one of central Abu Dhabi's most interesting recent developments. Much of the complex is concentrated in a pair of shiny cylindrical skyscrapers – Trust Tower and The Domain – although the main attraction is the marvellous new **souk** (or "World Trade Center Central Market", as it now seems officially to be known), designed by Foster & Partners and offering a memorable postmodern take on the traditional Arabian bazaar. Classical Islamic motifs blend seamlessly with modern materials, the souk's design featuring sleek wooden latticework screens (like a contemporary reworking of the traditional *mashrabiya*), geometrical stained-glass windows and marvellous (if incongruous) cast-iron lifts, while the muted lighting and gusts of wafting spices add to the romance – part chaste Zen minimalism, part Arabian Nights harem.

Many of the **shops** on the upper levels are yet to open, although most on the ground floor are now open for business including several handicrafts and souvenir shops, and dedicated honey and spice shops. There are also a couple of places to eat in the central atrium (see p.177) and a very chintzy branch of *Shakespeare & Co* (see p.105).

16

On the southwestern side of the World Trade Center, **Al Ittihad** ("Union") **Square** is home to an arresting sequence of oversized sculptures, including a vast cannon, enormous perfume bottle and gargantuan coffeepot – an endearingly quirky contrast to the drab surrounding architecture.

Downtown Abu Dhabi

The area immediately east of Sheikh Rashid Street (2nd Street) is the heart of downtown Abu Dhabi, and where you'll find the city's liveliest street life and densest concentration of cafés and shops. The parallel **Hamdan Street** and **Sheikh Zayed the First Street** are the two major thoroughfares, each lined with identikit office blocks stacked tightly together like Lego bricks.

Just south of the latter lies the **Madinat Zayed Gold Centre** (Sat–Thurs 9am–2pm & 4–11pm, Fri 4–11pm), Abu Dhabi's low-key equivalent to Dubai's Gold Souk, with two floors of shops selling traditional and contemporary jewellery.

Tourist Club Area

Hugging Abu Dhabi's eastern waterfront (although the actual water is hidden away behind the buildings lining 10th Street), the **Tourist Club Area** is one of downtown's liveliest districts, home to the flash **Abu Dhabi Mall** as well as a dense cluster of upscale hotels, including the *Beach Rotana* and *Le Méridien*. Looking east from the upper floors of the mall or the grounds of the *Beach Rotana*, there are fine views over to the impressive cluster of buildings on **Al Maryah Island** (formerly Sowwah Island) now rising just over the water and including the new Abu Dhabi Financial Centre and huge new Cleveland Clinic.

Al Mina

You'll find Abu Dhabi's closest equivalent to a traditional souk in the workaday **Al Mina** port district, which stretches north of the Tourist Club Area. First up is the so-called **Carpet Souk**, a modest square surrounded by small shops. Most of the stock on offer consists of low-grade factory carpet, though some places have more valuable traditional rugs and kilims if you hunt around. A five-minute walk beyond here, the **Food Souk** is aimed largely at the wholesale trade, although there's a colourful line of date merchants at the southern end. A further ten minutes' walk northwest, the **Iranian Souk** sounds promising, but is mainly devoted to kitchenware and potted plants.

Sheikh Zayed Mosque

Between Al Ain and Al Khaleej al Arabi roads (around 30dh by taxi) • Sat–Thurs 9am–10pm, Fri 4.30–10pm (interior closed for about 30min during prayers – see ⓦ szgmc.ae/en/mosque-opening-hours for timings) • Free guided tours: Sun–Thurs at 10am, 11am & 4.30pm, Fri at 4.30pm & 8pm, Sat at 10am, 11am, 2pm, 4.30pm & 8pm • ☏ 02 441 6444, ⓦ szgmc.ae/en

Some 15km from central Abu Dhabi, the mighty **Sheikh Zayed Mosque** dominates all landward approaches to the city, its snowy-white mass of domes and minarets visible for miles around and providing a spectacular symbol of Islamic pride at the entrance to the capital of the UAE.

Completed in 2007, the mosque was commissioned by and named after Sheikh Zayed bin Sultan al Nahyan (see box, p.172), who lies buried in a modest white marble mausoleum close to the entrance. The mosque is one of the world's biggest – roughly the eighth largest, depending on how you measure it – and certainly the most expensive, having taken twelve years to build at a cost of around US$500 million. It's also unusual in being one of only two mosques in the UAE (along with the Jumeirah Mosque in Dubai; see p.72) **open to non-Muslims**. If visiting, you'll be expected to dress conservatively; female visitors not suitably attired will be offered a black *abbeya* robe to wear.

SHEIKH ZAYED AND THE RISE OF MODERN ABU DHABI

In matters of historical precedence, Abu Dhabi has had the clear advantage over Dubai. The town was established much earlier as an independent settlement and commercial centre, and also struck oil many years before (and in much greater quantities than) Dubai. The city has, however, always lagged behind its neighbour in terms of development. Much of the blame for this can be laid at the door of the insular, old-fashioned and often downright eccentric **Sheikh Shakhbut bin Sultan al Nahyan** (ruled 1926–1966). Despite the sudden wealth of oil revenues, Sheikh Shakhbut signally declined to make any notable improvements to his city, preferring to keep oil revenues locked up in a wooden chest under his bed.

Increasing frustration at the glacial pace of change (particularly when compared to events in burgeoning Dubai) led to Sheikh Shakhbut's overthrow in a peaceful coup in 1966, and his replacement by his younger brother, **Sheikh Zayed bin Sultan al Nahyan** (ruled 1966–2004), who had previously served as governor of Al Ain, proving a resourceful and charismatic leader. On becoming ruler he immediately set about transforming Abu Dhabi. Electricity and telephones were rapidly installed, followed by a new port and airport, schools and a university. Sheikh Zayed also initiated a vast public handout of accumulated oil money to cash-strapped locals and other impoverished families across the neighbouring emirates – an act of fabulous generosity which did much to establish his reputation, and paved the way for his role as leader of the UAE following independence in 1971, when he became the new country's first president.

16

The huge **exterior** is classically plain, framed by four 107m-high minarets and topped with some eighty domes. Entrance to the mosque is through a vast **courtyard** – capable of accommodating some 40,000 worshippers – surrounded by long lines of rather Moorish-looking arches, the columns picked out with *pietra dura* floral designs and topped with unusual gold capitals resembling bits of palm tree. Flanking one side of the courtyard, the vast **prayer hall** is a spectacular piece of contemporary Islamic design. The hall is home to the world's largest carpet (made in Iran by around twelve hundred artisans, measuring over 5000 square metres, containing some 2.2 million

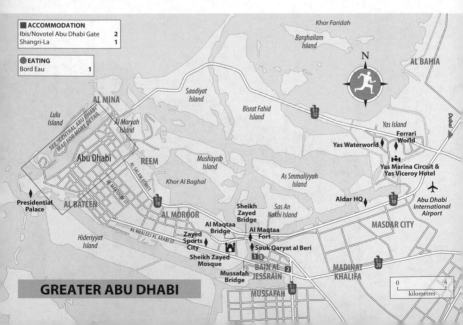

GREATER ABU DHABI

ACCOMMODATION
Ibis/Novotel Abu Dhabi Gate — 2
Shangri-La — 1

EATING
Bord Eau — 1

knots and weighing 47 tonnes) and the world's largest chandelier (made in Germany, measuring 10m in diameter, 15m tall and containing a million Swarowski crystals). It's not the world records which impress, however, so much as the extraordinary muted opulence of the design, with every surface richly carved and decorated, and the prayer hall's three massive chandeliers dangling overhead like enormous pieces of very expensive jewellery. Look out, too, for the hand-crafted panels made from Turkish Iznik tiles which decorate the corridors outside, and for the *qibla* wall itself, inscribed with the 99 names (qualities) of Allah in traditional Kufic calligraphy, subtly illuminated using fibre-optic lighting.

Between the Bridges

Three bridges connect Abu Dhabi with the mainland, crossing the narrow sea inlet which separates the city from the mainland close to one another about 15km from the centre. Crossing Al Maqtaa Bridge, the middle of the three, you'll probably notice an old **watchtower** sitting in the middle of the water, while just over the bridge you'll pass the quaint little **Al Maqtaa Fort** (not open to the public), which once guarded approaches to the city.

The area south of here, on the mainland between Al Maqtaa and Mussafah bridges – now popularly (if unimaginatively) known as **Between the Bridges** (Bain al Jessrain) – has become a major tourist destination with the recent opening of a string of hotels, including the opulent *Shangri-La* (see p.176).

Souk Qaryat al Beri

Between the Bridges waterfront · Sat–Thurs 10am–10pm, Fri 4–10pm · ⓦ soukqaryatalberi.com

Adjacent to the *Shangri-La* hotel, the **Souk Qaryat al Beri** has been done up in the usual faux-Arabian style. It's pretty modest compared to similar souks in Dubai, although the attractive waterfront promenade is good for a stroll, particularly after dark, or for a meal at one of its various cafés, including Abu Dhabi offshots of old Dubai favourites *Left Bank* (see p.113), *The Noodle House* (see p.111) and *Sho Cho* (see p.113).

Aldar HQ building

Take the signposted turn-off to Al Raha Beach (central) from the Dubai–Abu Dhabi highway

Driving into Abu Dhabi along the main Dubai highway you can't fail to notice the extraordinary new **Aldar HQ building**, headquarters of the Aldar property group and intended to form the centrepiece of the still-evolving Al Raha Beach development. Dubbed "the world's first circular skyscraper", it looks rather like an enormous magnifying glass, crisscrossed with a diagonal grid of steel supports which largely remove the need for internal columns. It's well worth a closer look, and you're free to go inside the lobby for a glimpse of the building's airy interior, while a café should have opened by the time you read this.

Yas Island

Access either from the Dubai highway or along the road via Saadiyat Island

About 30–35km from the centre on the outermost edges of the city, not far from the airport, **Yas Island** is now home to several of the city's key tourist attractions. Fast cars are the principal order of the day here thanks to the presence of the **Yas Marina Circuit**, which hosts the annual Abu Dhabi F1 Grand Prix along with various other races and activities (see p.139). Overlooking the circuit on one side and the island's swanky marina on the other you'll notice the dramatic **Yas Viceroy Hotel**, topped by a 217m-long undulating glass-and-steel canopy studded with over five thousand LEDs which ripple memorably with changing light displays after dark.

16

SAADIYAT ISLAND

Though it may currently be playing second fiddle to Dubai in the global tourism stakes, Abu Dhabi is increasingly looking for ways to challenge its upstart neighbour's pre-eminence in the region, backed by the emirate's apparently bottomless well of petrodollars – unlike credit-crunched Dubai, many of whose most ambitious projects have now been mothballed.

At the centre of Abu Dhabi's strategic vision is the new US$27 billion cultural district to be developed on the formerly uninhabited island of **Saadiyat** ("Island of Happiness"; ⓦ saadiyat .ae), a few kilometres from the city centre. Centrepiece of the development is a planned trio of world-class new **museums**, each in its own landmark building designed by one of the world's top architects, including the **Louvre Abu Dhabi**, housed in a huge flying-saucer-shaped edifice designed by French architect Jean Nouvel, a new Frank Gehry-designed **Guggenheim Museum** and a **Sheikh Zayed National Museum** by Foster & Partners. A further string of residential developments and tourist attractions has also been proposed, including a Gary Player golf course and a 9km beach lined with luxury hotels and marinas.

That at least was the plan, as first announced in 2006, although the three museums have so far notably failed to get built, while schedules have been repeatedly pushed back (latest estimates for opening dates are sometime in 2014–2015, although even these are beginning to seem optimistic). In addition, further promised landmark attractions – a new **Maritime Museum** by Japanese architect Tadao Ando and a **Performing Arts Centre** by Iraqi architect Zaha Hadid – now appear to be unlikely to open anytime in the foreseeable future, if at all. The development has also been rocked by repeated accusations that expat labourers working on the project have been subject to gross **human-rights violations**, leading to a boycott of the development by numerous international artists. Which isn't to say that Saadiyat's groundbreaking museums won't finally open one day, but that until then, it's best not to hold one's breath.

16

Ferrari World

Yas Island • Daily except Mon 11am–10pm • Adults and children over 1.3m 225dh; under 1.3m 185dh; under-3s free • ☏ 02 496 8001, ⓦ ferrariworldabudhabi.com

If you fancy a bit of Formula 1 action yourself, head to the jaw-droppingly huge **Ferrari World** theme park just down the road. Allegedly the world's largest indoor theme park (and occupying what looks like a vast red spaceship recently crash-landed) this offers a range of rides for hard-core adrenaline junkies and dedicated *tifosi* (see p.142). Other attractions on the island include a state-of-the-art water park and the Kyle Phillips-designed **Yas Links** golf course (ⓦ yaslinks.com) and **Yas Waterworld** (see p.143).

Masdar City

Masdar is clearly signposted from all major roads nearby; a free shuttle bus runs continuously between the small car park to the "city" itself (3min) • ⓦ masdarcity.ae

If somewhere like Yas Island is exactly what you'd expect in a place built on petroleum and in which the motor car is king, **Masdar City** is a complete surprise: the kernel of a brand-new zero-carbon, zero-waste green city, car-free and entirely self-sufficient in energy (using solar power and other renewable sources). Constructed at a cost of US$20 billion, the "city" (although it's actually more of a suburb), around 30km from the centre of Abu Dhabi and close to the airport, is eventually intended to cover around six square kilometres, providing a home to around 50,000 residents and 1500 businesses. The whole project was rather knocked back by the credit crunch and isn't now expected to get finished until 2025, but the small section so far completed is well worth a visit, and offers a tantalizing glimpse of what the 22nd-century city might just conceivably look like.

Exploring Masdar

Leave your vehicle in the car park, from where free shuttle buses make the three-minute drive to the "city" itself, depositing you at the main entrance to the development. Visitors are welcome to wander freely around the complex, although there's not much in the way of information beyond a smattering of signs. The scale of what's so far been built is fairly modest (barely a five-minute walk from one side to the other), although the originality of the overall concept is immediately apparent, with designs by Foster & Partners vaguely reminiscent in places of their superb souk at the new World Trade Center (see p.169).

The overall layout takes its cue from that of traditional Arabian cities, with narrow pedestrianized streets and shaded windows and walkways designed to protect against the searing desert heat and to funnel any available breezes into the complex. The architecture itself is fascinatingly eclectic – like some weird sci-fi future city, complete with automated electric "podcars" (although they'd been taken out of service at the time of writing). Parts of the complex, constructed out of curved facades of reddish sandstone with *mashrabiya*-type lattice work, look very faintly Arabian (or perhaps Indian), although other sections are entirely modernist, with dramatically sculpted steel and plate-glass buildings, a couple of strange pod-like structures (one covered in what looks like the shell of an enormous metal armadillo) and a remarkable postmodern wind tower at the centre of the complex.

Although very much a work in progress, Masdar is already a working community, with its own bank, mobile phone shop, café, travel agent and organic grocer's in place, while a number of leading international companies including Siemens, Mitsubishi and General Electric are expected to move in during 2013.

ARRIVAL AND GETTING AROUND   ABU DHABI

By air Abu Dhabi International Airport (airport code: AUH; Ⓦ abudhabiairport.ae) is on the eastern side of town, about 30km from the centre (a 30–45min drive, depending on traffic). All Etihad flights arrive at Terminal 3; other airlines touch down at Terminals 1 and 2. The easiest way to get into town is to catch a cab (around 60–70dh); alternatively, airport bus #901 runs regularly into the centre (every 40min; 3dh). If you're heading to Dubai you'll have to either go into central Abu Dhabi and pick up a bus there, or take a cab.

By bus Regular express buses (5.30am–11.30pm; every 30min; 2hr–2hr 30min; 15dh) run from Al Ghubaiba bus station in Bur Dubai to Abu Dhabi's main bus station, about 3km inland from the city centre.

Tours A convenient alternative to the bus is to take a tour from Dubai. Many Dubai tour operators (see p.25) offer Abu Dhabi day-trips, generally costing around 220dh.

Taxis Abu Dhabi's various attractions are very spread out, but there are plenty of metered taxis around town (flag fare 3.50dh).

16

ACCOMMODATION

Abu Dhabi has a good spread of **upmarket** and **mid-range** hotels, but absolutely nothing for **budget** travellers. As throughout the UAE, rates fluctuate considerably according to season and demand – the prices quoted below are intended only as a rough guide. For exact prices, consult the various hotel websites.

Beach Rotana 10th St, Tourist Club Area ☎ 02 697 9000, Ⓦ www.rotana.com/beachrotana; map p.166. Smart, modern resort-style hotel right in the thick of the downtown action. Rooms are spacious and attractively styled, and there's a nice stretch of waterfront beach and gardens, plus an excellent spread of places to eat and drink. <u>1000dh</u>

Emirates Palace Corniche Rd West ☎ 02 690 9000, Ⓦ emiratespalace.com; map p.166. Abu Dhabi's landmark hotel (see p.167) is the favoured residence of visiting heads of state and assorted celebrities, with every luxury you could think of, including lots of swanky restaurants and a vast swathe of beach. Rates aren't always as crushingly expensive as you might expect – check the website for offers. <u>1500dh</u>

Ibis/Novotel Abu Dhabi Gate Road 34, Gate City, Bain al Jessrain ☎ 02 508 9999, Ⓦ accorhotels.com;

map p.172. Twin hotels set in a single monumental high-rise in Bain al Jessrain district, 1km or so inland from the Between the Bridges area, only recently opened and still shiny brand new. The main attraction is price, with simple, modern and very competitively priced rooms in the *Ibis* section, and fancier (but still very affordable) lodgings in the four-star *Novotel*. There are a few adequate in-house dining options, and a very pleasant poolside bar, but nothing else in the neighbourhood. Convenient for the airport, although rather a long way from everywhere else – and not to be confused with the old *Novotel* (now the *Mercure Abu Dhabi*) in the city centre (see p.176). *Ibis* <u>240dh</u>, *Novotel* <u>440dh</u>

Jumeirah at Etihad Towers Etihad Towers, Corniche Rd West ☎ 02 811 5555, Ⓦ bit.ly/Jumeirah_Etihad; map p.166. Swanky new hotel occupying one of the five futuristic skyscrapers of the landmark Etihad Towers development – a cutting-edge alternative to the staid *Emirates Palace* opposite. Rooms are large, luxurious and full of state-of-the-art mod cons, while facilities include three pools, private beach and a serene spa. **1200dh**

Le Méridien 10th St, Tourist Club Area ☏ 02 644 6666, ⓦ lemeridien.com/abudhabi; map p.166. Pleasantly old-fashioned hotel with a vaguely old-world European air and attractive rooms decorated in warm reds and oranges. Plus points include the central location, attractive oceanfront gardens with a smallish bit of beach and a decent collection of restaurants, all at very competitive rates. **550dh**

Le Royal Méridien Sheikh Khalifa St, Al Markaziyah ☏ 02 674 2020, ⓦ lemeridien.com/royalabudhabi; map p.166. Chic but affordable modern hotel catering to a mix of business and tourist visitors, with stylish, rather minimalist, modern rooms and a better-than-average selection of in-house eating and drinking venues (see below). It's not

actually on the beach, though there are attractive walled gardens with a pair of pools. **650dh**

Mercure Abu Dhabi Centre Hotel Hamdan St ☏ 02 633 3555, ⓦ novotel.com; map p.166. This no-frills business hotel bang in the city centre is nothing to get excited about but the rooms are well equipped and comfortable, and rates are often as cheap as anywhere in town. **400dh**

Shangri-La Qaryat al Beri ☏ 02 509 8888, ⓦ shangri-la .com/abudhabi; map p.172. One of the city's most alluring hotels, with gorgeous Arabian Nights decor, huge gardens, four pools, the lovely Chi spa, a gorgeous infinity pool which appears to be flowing straight into the sea and wonderful views of the Sheikh Zayed Mosque. The main drawback is the location, about 10km from the centre near Al Maqta Bridge but some distance from anywhere else. Restaurants include the signature *Shang Palace* and *Hoi An*, modelled after their twins in Dubai (see p.111 & p.110), and the chic modern French *Bord Eau* (see below). **1200dh**

EATING

Even more so than in Dubai, eating in Abu Dhabi revolves around the big hotels – although there are a few cheaper options also worth hunting out if you're on a budget. For instant gratification, there are various cheap fast-food joints scattered along and around Hamdan Street and in the Marina Mall and Abu Dhabi Mall food courts.

16

BiCE Jumeirah at Etihad Towers Hotel, Corniche Rd West ☏ 02 811 5666, ⓦ bit.ly/Jumeirah_Etihad; map p.166. Abu Dhabi branch of the popular Italian chain, with a similar menu of flavourful Italian meat, fish and pasta dishes to its cousin in Dubai (see p.115). Daily noon–3pm & 7–11pm.

Bord Eau Shangri-La Hotel, Qaryat al Beri ☏ 02 509 8888, ⓦ shangri-la.com/abudhabi; map p.172. One of the city's top restaurants, offering fine modern French dining from a short menu of meat and fish mains (210–260dh) in a fancy, high-ceilinged dining room. Daily 7–11.30pm.

Café du Roi Al Hana Plaza, Corniche Rd West ☏ 02 681 6151, ⓦ cafeduroi.com; map p.166. Popular and long-established French-style café with Filipino waitresses and a largely Emirati clientele. There's a choice of indoor and outdoor seating, a long menu of snacks and light meals (from 30dh) and the best coffee in this part of town. Daily 6.30am–12.30am.

Colombiano 41st Floor, Burj al Marina, Marina Mall ☏ 02 681 9009, ⓦ colombianocoffeehouse.com; map p.166. Bog-standard coffee-shop-cum-café in a spectacular setting at the top of the Burj al Marina tower (see p.168). Prices reflect the sky-high location, with coffee from 27dh and a range of sandwiches, wraps, salads, pasta and pizza from around 50dh – expensive, but worth it for the views. Daily 9am–12.30am.

Finz Beach Rotana Hotel, 10th St, Tourist Club Area ☏ 02 697 9350, ⓦ www.rotana.com/beachrotana; map p.166. One of the best seafood restaurants in town,

occupying an unusual A-frame wooden dining room and terrace looking over the water to the shiny new Al Maryah Island developments. The menu features a wide selection of fish and seafood prepared in a variety of international styles, ranging from old favourites like sole meunière and beer-battered fish and chips to more elaborate creations like ocean trout in light curry foam and red mullet with truffle quinoa. There are also a few meat and vegetarian options, plus a good wine list. Mains from 140dh. Daily 12.30–3.30pm & 7–11.30pm.

India Palace As Salam St, Tourist Club Area ☏ 02 644 8777, ⓦ indiapalace.ae; map p.166. Long-established and pleasantly old-fashioned Indian restaurant, serving up a big spread of tasty and very reasonably priced North Indian meat, seafood and veg offerings, including tandoori dishes, *kadais* and Lucknow-style *dum pukht* biriyanis. Veg mains from 25dh, non-veg from 35dh. Daily noon–midnight.

Indigo Beach Rotana Hotel, 10th St, Tourist Club Area ☏ 02 697 9334, ⓦ www.rotana.com/beachrotana; map p.166. Good-looking modern Indian restaurant serving well-prepared North Indian meat tandooris and biriyanis, plus a few seafood and veg options – try the signature Sikandari raan (195dh for 2): roasted lamb stuffed with prunes, onions and cheese. Mains from around 100dh (meat) and 70dh (veg). Daily except Sun 12.30–3.30pm & 6.30–11.30pm.

Le Café Emirates Palace Hotel, Corniche Rd West ☏ 02 690 7999, ⓦ emiratespalace.com; map p.166. The beautiful foyer café of this opulent hotel makes a memorable setting for one of the Middle East's most sumptuous afternoon teas; choose either traditional English or Arabian style (served 2–6pm; 275dh). Otherwise drinks (including the Emirates Palace Cappuccino, topped with flakes of 24-carat gold), snacks and light meals are served throughout the day. Minimum spend 100dh. Daily 6.30am–1am.

Lebanese Flower Off 26th St ☎02 665 8700; map p.166. One of a line of colourful Lebanese restaurants (which also includes the neighbouring *Beirut Roastery*, *Lebanon Flower Bakery* and *Maatouk* café), this enduringly popular restaurant is the best place in the city to fill up on inexpensive Middle Eastern food, with a well-prepared range of fish and meat grills, kebabs (35–50dh) and mezze. Daily 7.30am–3am.

Mezzaluna Emirates Palace Hotel, Corniche Rd West ☎02 690 7999, ⓦemiratespalace.com; map p.166. One of the more affordable of the *Emirates Palace*'s string of upmarket eating venues, serving traditional Italian and Mediterranean cuisine including a good range of antipasti and pasta dishes, plus lavish meat and seafood *secondi piatti*. Mains 100–225dh. Daily 12.30–3pm & 7–11pm.

Royal Orchid Hilton Abu Dhabi Hotel, Corniche Rd West ☎02 681 1900, ⓦroyalorchid.ae; map p.166. Tucked away in the *Hilton*, this is one of the oldest restaurants in the city and is still going strong, thanks to its good and reasonably priced range of Thai and Chinese food. Mains from around 75dh. Daily noon–midnight.

Sayad Emirates Palace Hotel, Corniche Rd West ☎02 690 7999, ⓦemiratespalace.com; map p.166. The hotel's exclusive signature restaurant specializes in top-notch international seafood (Sayad is Arabic for "fisherman"), served up in a strangely calming dining space which glows softly with muted underwater blues and greens. Mains 125–240dh. Daily 6.30–11.30pm.

Soba Le Royal Méridien Hotel, Sheikh Khalifa St, Al Markaziyah ☎02 674 2020, ⓦleroyalmeridien abudhabi.com; map p.166. Cool, contemporary Asian restaurant serving up a mix of Thai, Japanese, Indonesian and Korean meat and seafood dishes, including good sushi, maki and sashimi. Mains from around 80dh. Daily noon–3pm & 7–11.30pm.

Tarbouche Central Market, World Trade Center ☎02 628 2220; map p.166. Occupying half of the serene central atrium of the Central Market, this is a pleasant spot for lunch, with a decent selection of mainstream Middle Eastern offerings (mezze from 20dh, grills from 40dh), plus a few sandwiches and salads (from 25dh). If the setting appeals but you don't fancy Lebanese, make for *Chapters*, occupying the other half of the atrium, which serves up assorted pizzas and other international mains at similar prices. Daily 9am–midnight.

16

DRINKING AND NIGHTLIFE

Abu Dhabi lacks Dubai's alluring range of swanky cocktail bars and other upscale establishments, although there's still a good range of places to drink, with virtually every hotel in the city hosting some kind of licensed venue. These follow essentially the same formula as in Dubai, with a mix of cheery British-style **pubs** and more upmarket (and expensive) **bars**, sometimes with live music or DJ.

Brauhaus Beach Rotana Hotel, 10th St, Tourist Club Area ☎02 697 9000, ⓦwww.rotana.com/beachrotana; map p.166. This convivial pub-cum-restaurant makes a surprisingly convincing stab at an authentic Bavarian *bierkeller*, with speciality German beers on tap or by the bottle and a good range of food to soak it all up with, served to an accompaniment of Bavarian marching bands and other Teutonic sounds. Very popular, so arrive early if you want to bag a seat. Sun–Wed 4pm–1am, Thurs–Sat noon–1am.

Captain's Arms Le Méridien Hotel, 10th St, Tourist Club Area ☎02 644 0348, ⓦcaptainsarms-abudhabi.com; map p.166. Cheery British-style pub with attractive outdoor seating overlooking the hotel gardens and nourishing pub grub. Daily noon–1am.

The Jazz Bar Hilton Abu Dhabi Hotel, Corniche Rd West ☎02 692 4562; map p.166. Long-established after-hours venue, with a good live jazz band nightly and a rather gentrified atmosphere. Sun–Fri 7pm–12.30am, Thurs & Fri until 1.30am.

Mood Indigo Bar Mercure Abu Dhabi Centre Hotel, Hamdan St ☎02 633 3555; map p.166. This under-used hotel bar-cum-pub is one of the best places in the city for a quiet, inexpensive pint. The atmosphere is relaxed, and there's discreet live jazz some evenings. Daily noon–2am, Thurs & Fri until 3am.

Sax Restaurant & Club Le Royal Méridien Hotel, Sheikh Khalifa St, Al Markaziyah ☎02 674 2020, ⓦleroyalmeridienabudhabi.com; map p.166. Plenty of sax appeal at this upmarket bar, with lots of cocktails, a small dancefloor and eclectic music, and one of the city's more glamorous crowds. Daily 7pm–2.30am, Thurs & Fri until 3.30am.

SHEIKH ZAYED ROAD, 1990

Contexts

History

Dubai's history has been shaped by its location at the southern end of the Arabian Gulf, squeezed between sand and sea. There has been some sort of human presence here since the beginning of the Bronze Age or earlier, though the region's harsh desert environment proved an effective barrier to sustained settlement and development until relatively recent times, save for a small and hardy population of itinerant Bedouin, fishermen and pearl divers. Not until the advent of oil and air-conditioning in the 1960s did the city's population rise above 100,000.

Early Dubai

The history of the Dubai area before the colonial era remains frustratingly vague. There are relatively abundant Bronze Age (c.3000–2000 BC) finds and a few later Ummayad (see below) remains, but virtually no other archeological or written records until the arrival of the British in the eighteenth century – an accurate reflection of the region's isolation, lack of development and historically low population levels.

Bronze Age archeological finds in the Dubai area include the remains of extensive settlements at Al Sufouh and Al Qusais, and inland at Hatta. The region was an important source of copper and appears to have enjoyed extensive trading connections which extended as far as the great Mesopotamian city of Ur (in what is now Iraq). From the third through to the seventh centuries AD, the region was loosely incorporated into the **Sassanian** empire, ruled from Iran. The Sassanians were displaced in the seventh century by the arrival of the **Ummayads** of Damascus, the first great Islamic dynasty. The Ummayads introduced Islam to the region, as well as stimulating local and overseas trade. The extensive remains of an Ummayad-era settlement have been discovered in **Jumeirah** (see p.74), including a caravanserai, suggesting that the area was an important staging post on the caravan route between Oman and Iraq.

Very little is known about the history of the Dubai area for the next thousand years. There's a passing reference to Dubai in the *Book of Roads and Kingdoms*, a collection of travellers' anecdotes and legends compiled by Arab–Andalucían geographer Abu Abdullah al-Bakri in around 1095. The first eyewitness account can be found in the *Voyage to Pegu, and Observations There* by **Gaspero Balbi**, describing the Venetian traveller's visit to the area in 1580 en route from Italy to Burma, with a brief mention of the coastal settlement of "Dibei" and its vibrant local pearl industry.

Early Dubai and the Trucial States

Dubai reappears in the historical record in the eighteenth century. During this period the territory which now makes up the UAE was largely controlled by two main tribal groupings. The first, the **Bani Yas**, were ruled by the Al Nahyan family from Abu

c.5000 BC	500–600 AD	c.630
Earliest human settlement in the southern Gulf	The UAE region becomes part of an extensive trade network dominated by the Sassanian (Iranian) empire; settlement of Jumeirah area	Arrival of Islam. The Islamic Umayyad dynasty displaces the Sassanids as the principal power in the region

Dhabi, and controlled the coast from Dubai to Qatar, as well as much of the region's desert hinterland. The second, the seafaring **Qawasim** (or Al Qasimi), were based further north in Sharjah and Ras al Khaimah, and had also established a significant presence on the far side of the Gulf along the southern coast of Iran.

The first **permanent settlement** around the Dubai Creek appears to have been established sometime during the eighteenth century by the Al Bu Falasah branch of the Bani Yas. This settlement remained, albeit loosely, under the control of the Bani Yas sheikhs in Abu Dhabi, but was regularly threatened by Qawasim incursions from the north.

At around the same time, the Gulf began to enter the mainstream of colonial politics thanks to its strategic location on the increasingly important sea route between Britain and India. By the later eighteenth century, the **British East India Company** had achieved a monopoly on the lucrative maritime trade with the Subcontinent, although their commercial interests were increasingly threatened by astute Qawasim sailors, who repeatedly outmanoeuvred and undercut their European rivals. Faced with this competition, the British began to concoct tales (probably fictitious) of Qawasim "piracy" against British and Indian shipping. In 1820, the Royal Navy launched a punitive attack against the Qawasim, landing seven thousand troops at Ras al Khaimah, bombarding the town's fort and forcing its rulers into an ignominious surrender – a reverse from which Qawasim power and prestige never entirely recovered.

Following their suppression of the Qawasim, the British signed a series of "anti-piracy" treaties with the rulers of the various Gulf emirates which now make up the UAE. These henceforth became known as the **Trucial States**, on account of the "truces" agreed with the British. The arrival of the British and the subsequent treaties did much to stabilize the political situation in the region, although by confirming the position of the ruling sheikhs it also had the effect of destroying local traditions of tribal democracy, whereby unpopular or incompetent rulers could be removed from office – an arrangement which was, therefore, very much to the advantage of the ruling families, if not always to their subjects.

The arrival of the Maktoums

For Dubai, the arrival of the British had the welcome result of significantly reducing Qawasim threats. Visiting in the late 1820s, the British Political Resident (the colonial official responsible for overseeing British interests throughout the Persian Gulf) described a town of some 1200 people, living in simple palm-thatch huts on the south side of the Creek (in what is now **Bur Dubai**) around the governor's small fort (Al Fahidi Fort, now the Dubai Museum), with three watchtowers equipped with old Portuguese cannons guarding the main approaches to the town.

It was in-fighting among the Bani Yas leaders of Abu Dhabi, however, that led to the real emergence of Dubai as a major force in the region. In 1833, the popular leader of the Abu Dhabi Bani Yas, Sheikh Tahnun, was assassinated by his half-brother, **Sheikh Khalifa**. Khalifa's coup d'état was not well received, and soon afterwards he was forced to suppress two uprisings with further bloodshed. By the summer of 1833, popular disgust at Khalifa's repressive regime led to around a thousand Bani Yas tribesmen

751 and onwards	1580	1833
The southern Gulf experiences a major boom in maritime trade following the shifting of the Islamic caliphate from Damascus to Baghdad	First European reference to Dubai, by the Venetian pearl merchant Gaspero Balbi	Around a thousand Bani Yas tribesmen from Abu Dhabi take control of Dubai under the leadership of Maktoum bin Buti

(perhaps a fifth of the local population) abandoning Abu Dhabi and trekking up the coast to establish themselves in Dubai.

The absconders were led by a certain **Maktoum bin Buti** and his uncle Obaid bin Said al Falasi. Arriving in Dubai (where they instantly doubled the local population), Maktoum and Obaid immediately took over the running of the town. This arrangement lasted until 1836, when Obaid died and Maktoum became sole leader – thus establishing the Maktoum family dynasty which endures to this day.

The initial position of Maktoum and his followers was precarious, however. Not surprisingly, the fratricidal Sheikh Khalifa was less than impressed by the mass defection, although following a series of clever diplomatic manoeuvres Maktoum bin Buti succeeded in establishing Dubai's independence from Abu Dhabi with the support of his powerful Qawasim neighbours to the north, who were naturally delighted to see their rivals in Abu Dhabi lose a significant slice of territory. Dubai was thus established as a buffer zone between Abu Dhabi and Qawasim territories – a small and relatively powerless enclave wedged between powerful and potentially hostile neighbours.

The early Maktoum years

Despite their precarious situation, the new Maktoum rulers began quickly to establish Dubai as a political and economic force in the lower Gulf. In 1835 the British signed a further round of treaties with the various Gulf emirates, now including Dubai, thus granting the newly independent settlement a measure of official recognition and British protection. Dubai's commercial life also flourished, a foretaste of things to come. Within a few years of Maktoum's arrival the town's souk had grown exponentially, while in 1841 the new district of **Deira** was established; the first on the north side of the Creek, it quickly rivalled Bur Dubai in commercial importance. Dubai's standing was further enhanced in 1845, when it helped to remove the perennially unpopular Sheikh Khalifa from power, ushering in a new period of close and cordial relations between Abu Dhabi and its breakaway neighbour.

Maktoum bin Buti died in 1852, and was succeeded in turn by his youngest brother Sheikh Said (ruled 1852–59), by Maktoum's eldest son, Sheikh Hasher (1859–86), and by Sheikh Hasher's brother Sheikh Rashid (1886–94). This stable succession of Maktoum rulers followed a consistent policy of forging strategic alliances with their more powerful neighbours abroad while achieving a modest level of economic prosperity at home. This was based largely on the city's flourishing **pearling industry**, which yielded some of the world's finest pearls, exported to London, Bombay and elsewhere. Meanwhile, the town was also establishing itself as an increasingly important local entrepôt, challenging the supremacy of both Abu Dhabi and neighbouring Sharjah.

British influence, meanwhile, continued to rise, thanks to the region's stategic location on the sea route to India. One by-product was the arrival of increasing numbers of **Indian traders** from the 1860s onwards, most of them working as representatives of British companies in India. In 1892 a new sequence of treaties were signed granting Britain the right to directly control all aspects of the rulers' foreign affairs – effectively relinquishing external sovereignty in exchange for British protection.

1835	1841	1894
Britain formally recognizes Dubai and enters into treaty with it	Settlement of Deira begins. Over the next decade the town grows rapidly, attracting a cosmopolitan population of Arabs, Iranians, Indians and Pakistanis	Dubai declared a free port by Sheikh Maktoum bin Hasher. Iranian merchants begin arriving in the city

Iranian influence

The uncanny ability of Dubai's Maktoum rulers to seize advantage of changing local conditions and turn them to spectacular profit is a recurrent motif in the emirate's history. Dubai's first great economic leap forward occurred during the reign of **Sheikh Maktoum bin Hasher** (ruled 1894–1906) as the result of changing circumstances across the Gulf in the flourishing Iranian port of **Lingah** (modern-day Bandar Lengeh), home to a prosperous community of Qawasim-descended merchants. All was not well in Lingah, however. The central government in Tehran, suspicious of the Qawasims' foreign origins, had begun subjecting them to increasingly punitive taxes and other onerous regulations, to the point where the entire community had begun to think about quitting the country completely.

Seeing the chance of attracting an expert commercial workforce in search of a new home, Sheikh Maktoum took drastic measures, abolishing customs duty and licences for vessels in Dubai, and turning the entire city into a free port, while sending emissaries to Lingah to talk up Dubai's commercial opportunities and offer free plots of land alongside the Creek for refugee merchants to establish new homes. Though many Qawasim decided to return to their ancestral homelands in Ras al Khaimah and Sharjah, a significant number (along with many Indian traders also previously based in Lingah) opted to set up shop in Dubai.

The results of Sheikh Maktoum bin Hasher's initiative changed the cultural and commercial face of the city forever. By 1901, five hundred of Lingah's Qawasim-descended Iranian merchants had settled in Dubai and the town had overtaken both Abu Dhabi and Sharjah as the region's largest port, while the new Iranian quarter the settlers established in **Bastakiya**, with its elaborate wind-towered houses, provided a model of modern urban development in a city which still largely consisted of simple palm-thatch shacks. The arrival of the Iranians also established Dubai as the leading overseas conduit for Iranian trade, channelling vast sums of money and merchandise through the city, which would henceforth play a role relative to Iran not unlike that which British Hong Kong played in relation to mainland China. Persian-descended Emiratis (*ajamis*) still continue to make up a sizeable proportion of the local population to this day.

Famine …

The massive commercial filip provided by the arrival of the Iranian merchants lent the city a new economic and cultural vibrancy which lasted for the best part of three decades. Further waves of merchants arrived in Dubai during the 1920s and 1930s from Iran, Abu Dhabi and Sharjah, attracted by the city's low taxes and trade-friendly environment.

The new-found prosperity was not to last, however, and the city's continued over-reliance on the pearling industry (which had become increasingly hamstrung by protectionist British regulations prohibiting the use of modern technology and diving equipment) proved fatal. The onset of the **Great Depression** in 1929 signalled the beginning of the end. Overseas demand for expensive precious stones dried up overnight, and the industry's death-knell was sounded shortly afterwards when Japanese scientists discovered a reliable method for creating cultured pearls, instantly wiping out traditional pearling in Dubai and elsewhere. The effect on Dubai's economy was

1912	1929 onwards	1939
Sheikh Saeed bin Maktoum becomes ruler of Dubai	Gradual collapse of the pearl trade following the Great Depression and Japanese discovery of artificial pearl culturing	Crushing of the merchants' *majlis* rebellion by the future Sheikh Rashid

catastrophic. Many of the city's businesses went bankrupt, Indian traders returned post-haste to Bombay, and the fledgling educational system collapsed. Food shortages and occasional famine became a recurrent feature, with locals reduced to catching and frying the swarms of locusts which periodically infested the city.

... and democracy

The ongoing economic crisis had major social consequences. Anger was widespread, much of it directed at the city's kindly but ineffectual ruler **Sheikh Saeed** (ruled 1912–58). As living conditions plummeted organized opposition to Sheikh Saeed's leadership gained momentum, with widespread demonstrations and two attempted coups. Despite widespread local poverty, Sheikh Saeed himself was earning an increasingly extravagant income through lucrative arrangements with the British including the rights to prospect for oil and to land seaplanes on the Creek.

As economic conditions systematically worsened, opposition to autocratic Maktoum rule expressed itself in the remarkable **merchants' majlis**, established in 1938 and led by a cousin of Sheikh Saeed – the closest approach to a genuine democracy ever seen in Dubai. The *majlis* set up a fifteen-member council which sought to enact a series of progressive reforms ranging from education and healthcare through to rubbish collection – as well as demanding that Sheikh Saeed hand over 85 percent of his personal income for public use. As tensions rose, the city reached a point of de facto civil war, with Sheikh Saeed and his loyal troop of Bedouin soldiers retaining control of Bur Dubai, while the rebels seized Deira.

The crisis was finally resolved in extraordinary circumstances (which tend, not surprisingly, to be glossed over in official histories of the city). The occasion was the 1939 wedding of Sheikh Saeed's eldest son – and future Dubai ruler – **Sheikh Rashid** to a daughter of a former ruler of Abu Dhabi, Sheikha Latifa, who had fled to Dubai some years previously. The rebels agreed to a temporary truce in order to allow Sheikh Rashid's wedding to go ahead at Sheikha Latifa's home, which happened to be located in rebel-held Deira. Sheikh Rashid arrived with his traditional entourage of rifle-toting Bedouin retainers, who took advantage of the truce to gun down a large proportion of the rebel *majlis*'s leaders. Many of those who survived were blinded in one eye and forced to "buy" their remaining eye on payment of a large ransom.

Deira was thus returned to Maktoum control, and Dubai's most promising democratic movement was annihilated. The wedding went ahead following the carnage. This was a notable event in its own right, in that it cemented relationships between the region's two major Bani Yas communities. Latifa would subsequently bear nine children by Rashid, including two future rulers of Dubai, meaning that future leaders of the city would now be cousins of the ruling Al Nahyan family in Abu Dhabi.

Sheikh Rashid

The wedding massacre in Deira in 1939 marked the arrival on the Dubai political scene of the charismatic, visionary and occasionally ruthless **Sheikh Rashid**, the man often described as the father of modern Dubai, and the ruler who (with the possible exception of his own son, current ruler Sheikh Mohammed) did more than anyone else to put modern Dubai on the global map.

1958	1960	1960–61
Death of Sheikh Saeed, succeeded by his son Sheikh Rashid. Huge oil reserves are found in Abu Dhabi	Dubai International Airport is opened	The Creek is dredged, establishing Dubai as the southern Gulf's major port

During the 1940s, Sheikh Rashid gradually took over the management of the city from his increasingly enfeebled father, Sheikh Saeed. Despite quashing the merchants' *majlis*, however, Sheikh Rashid was confronted with growing resistance centred on the international **Arab nationalism** movement, inspired by Egyptian president Gamal Nasser and promulgated in Dubai by the city's many well-educated foreign schoolteachers from Egypt, Iraq, Syria, Lebanon and Yemen. Local pan-Arabists called for a new socialist democracy, with an end to Maktoum rule and the severing of all ties to Britain. Not surprisingly, Sheikh Rashid and his followers had no sympathy with these aims, despite a series of riots and increasing political unrest throughout the 1940s and 1950s.

Dubai develops

Sheikh Saeed died in 1958, with leadership of the city formally passing to Sheikh Rashid. One of Rashid's first acts was the characteristically bold decision to **dredge the Creek**. The commercial lifeblood of Dubai, the Creek was in a bad way, having silted up so dramatically (the water, in places, being just less than 1m deep) that larger boats could no longer enter it to take on or unload cargo, increasingly crippling the city's commercial prospects. Despite the challenging cost and complexity of the job (around US$3 million, then equivalent to several years' worth of Dubai's annual GDP), Rashid pressed ahead with the project, raising money from local merchants and overseas bonds. By 1961 the Creek had been cleared, widened and deepened, establishing the city as the pre-eminent port in the region (Sharjah, by contrast, continued to allow its own Creek to silt up, losing virtually all its shipping business to Dubai as a result).

Shortly afterwards, Sheikh Rashid's leadership received an additional boost when **oil** was finally discovered in Dubai. The first commercially important deposits were discovered at the Fateh (Fortune) oilfield 25km offshore in 1966, with the first exports beginning in 1969. Although only ever a modest amount of oil compared to the vast reserves found in Abu Dhabi, the new revenues allowed Rashid to undertake a visionary series of **infrastructure developments** which laid the basis for Dubai's current prosperity. Many of these were derided at the time as being hopelessly ambitious, and yet in virtually every case history has proved Rashid's judgement to be faultless.

One of Rashid's first acts was to provide the city with its own **airport**, opened in 1960 (characteristically, the first in the Gulf to have its own duty-free shop), while the two sides of the Creek were finally connected with the opening of the **Maktoum Bridge** in 1963. Rashid's most famous – and successful – gamble, however, was the creation of a new deep-water port, **Port Rashid**. Original plans, based on future trade projections, were drawn up in 1967 for a port with four berths. Ignoring the predictions, Rashid ordered the port's capacity to be doubled, and then doubled again. The port finally opened in 1971 with sixteen berths – and was immediately oversubscribed.

Dubai's rising prosperity during the 1960s had an important **social payoff**. As the city grew increasingly wealthy, the pan-Arabist reforming fervour of the 1940s and 1950s began to cool. People gave up socialism and turned to shopping instead. Oil revenues allowed Rashid to exempt his subjects from all forms of taxation and to provide basic levels of free healthcare and housing for less well-off citizens. Dubai's leading merchant families and other bigwigs (including many prominent members of the reform movement) were bought off by being granted lucrative and exclusive trading licences and other concessions – a clever arrangement which stopped short of outright bribery,

1963	1966	1968
The first bridge across the Creek – Maktoum Bridge – is opened	Oil is discovered in the offshore Fateh field	The British announce their intention of quitting the region; discussions are held between the seven Trucial States on forming a new country

OIL IN DUBAI

The idea that Dubai is some kind of mega-rich oil sheikhdom is often heard, but has little basis in fact. The UAE as a whole sits on top of the world's fifth-largest discovered oil reserves and is the world's third-largest oil exporter. Some 95 percent of these reserves, however, are in Abu Dhabi, which struck oil in 1958 and has been living off it very comfortably ever since.

Dubai, by contrast, had to wait until 1966 to find a commercially viable source of oil and even this amounted to very little when compared with its neighbour's oil wealth – just four percent of total UAE deposits (further small fields were also discovered in Sharjah and Ras al Khaimah – the rest of the emirates got nothing). Despite the relatively modest finds, oil played a brief but vital role in the city's development, allowing Sheikh Rashid to invest in a range of infrastructure projects (see opposite). The oil boom was brief, however. In 1975, it accounted for almost two-thirds of the national GDP; a decade later it had dropped to fifty percent. Today the figure is under five percent, and falling, while according to latest estimates the emirate's reserves are expected to have been exhausted within twenty years.

but which offered a virtual licence to print money, as well as ensuring that the people concerned would henceforth have a vested interest in maintaining the status quo.

By the mid-1960s, the population of Dubai had topped 100,000. Some four thousand dhows were registered in the city, carrying a wide range of goods including textiles, gold and electronics, some of which were exported legally, although much was smuggled.

Independence

Further political challenges, however, lay just around the corner. In 1968, the British government suddenly announced plans to withdraw from the Gulf within three years. The ruling sheikhs, who had lived safely under the umbrella of British protection since 1820, were understandably alarmed, fearing that their tiny emirates might fall prey to much larger and more powerful states (Saudi Arabia, for example, had long claimed parts of Abu Dhabi emirate, while Iran has made a similar claim for Bahrain and other places in the Gulf). In a reversal of the usual colonial scenario, both Sheikh Zayed of Abu Dhabi and Sheikh Rashid urgently requested Britain to keep its military forces in the area beyond the proposed withdrawal date, even offering to pay for the cost of the troops themselves; the appeal, not surprisingly, was rejected on the grounds that it would cast British armed forces in a somewhat mercenary light.

The British encouraged the sheikhs to seek safety in numbers and to enter into a loose **confederation**, consisting of the seven emirates which now form the UAE, plus Qatar and Bahrain. Tensions between Qatar and Bahrain (then the most populous of the Gulf states) threw up irreconcilable differences and both withdrew from the proposed union, choosing to go it alone. Abu Dhabi and Dubai, however, agreed to unite, 135 years after their original split, along with Sharjah, Ras al Khaimah, Ajman, Umm al Quwain and Fujairah. Sheikh Rashid (whom the British had expected to lead the union) requested that Sheikh Zayed become the **first president** of the new country, perhaps realizing that Abu Dhabi's much larger size and far greater oil reserves – as well as Zayed's own natural charisma and fabled largesse (see box, p.172) – made him the natural choice of leader.

1969	1971	1970s and 1980s
Oil production begins	The British withdraw from the Trucial States, which are reformed as the United Arab Emirates. Opening of Port Rashid	Oil revenues are used to diversify Dubai's industrial base and create massive new infrastructure projects, such as the huge new Jebel Ali Port and Free Zone (1983), and the World Trade Centre (1979)

Independence duly arrived in December 1, 1971, with the newly formed country taking the name of the **United Arab Emirates** (Ras al Khaimah withdrew from the union at the last minute, but rejoined soon afterwards). Locally and abroad, there was a general sense of pessimism over the survival prospects of the fledgling country. The USSR initially refused to recognize the country, as did Saudi Arabia. Even worse, a few hours before independence Iranian forces occupied the two small Tunbs islands belonging to Ras al Khaimah, and another, Abu Musa, belonging to Sharjah (all of which they continue to occupy to this day). British warships stationed nearby signally failed to intervene.

Sheikh Mohammed and the boom years

Despite the initial misgivings, the newly independent UAE prospered. Political leadership continued to rest with the Al Nahyan family in Abu Dhabi, but Dubai remained easily the largest and most commercially vibrant city in the new country. Sheikh Rashid continued to plough oil revenues into further infrastructure developments including the landmark World Trade Centre (see p.64), as well as Jebel Ali Port and the new Shindagha Tunnel linking Deira and Bur Dubai. One of Sheikh Rashid's last major acts as ruler was to commission the city's new **dry docks**, opened in 1983. As ever, his timing was faultless. Within a year of the docks' opening, fighting broke out between Iran and Iraq, creating a steady supply of war-damaged vessels limping into Dubai for repairs.

In 1982, Rashid suffered a severe stroke, although he remained official ruler until his death in 1990, the increasingly infirm leader began to hand power over to his four sons. The eldest, the capable but low-key Sheikh Maktoum (ruled 1990–2006), was officially anointed heir to the throne, but over the following years it became increasingly apparent that it was Rashid's third son, current ruler **Sheikh Mohammed**, who was the driving force behind the city's ongoing development.

Under Mohammed, the already brisk pace of change turned into a whirlwind. During the 1980s and 1990s, as Mohammed's influence grew, the city began increasingly to diversify from its original base as a regional trade and shipping entrepôt. One key growth area was the development of the city's **tourism** industry. In the mid-1980s the city had 42 hotels with 4600 rooms; by 2008 it had around 40,000. In 1985, following a dispute with Gulf Air, Mohammed also launched **Emirates airline** in a bid to free Dubai from its dependence on other air carriers. (Emirates has gone on to become one of the world's most successful airlines and, as with many of Mohammed's schemes, has also been widely imitated by neighbouring emirates, including Abu Dhabi, whose own Etihad airline was founded in emulation).

Many other businesses were lured to the city by the creation of assorted **free trade zones** in which much of the UAE's normal red tape was strategically relaxed, including the ban on foreign ownership of the majority of any UAE business. The first free trade zone was established at **Jebel Ali**, which was followed by a string of more specialized hi-tech enclaves. The first two, **Internet City** and **Media City**, succeeded in attracting dozens of top international organizations to the city, ranging from Microsoft to the BBC. At the same time, the opening of the **Burj al Arab** in 1999 provided the city with an iconic landmark whose distinctive sail-shaped outline has probably done more than anything else to stamp Dubai on the global consciousness.

1985	1989	1990
Sheikh Mohammed founds Emirates airline	By the end of the 1980s the city's population has risen to over half a million, a fifty-fold increase in less than forty years	Death of Sheikh Rashid; Sheikh Maktoum becomes ruler of Dubai, though Crown Prince Sheikh Mohammed also exerts increasing influence over the city's development

As the new millennium arrived, the city went into overdrive. Sheikh Mohammed's ongoing attempts to position Dubai as a major global **financial centre** began to take shape with the opening of the Dubai Stock Exchange and Dubai International Financial Centre (DIFC). More importantly, in 2002 restrictions on foreign ownership of property were lifted, meaning that expats could suddenly buy their own homes, and foreign investors could enter the local property market. A massive **real estate boom** ensued. Foreign money poured in and construction companies went berserk, turning large parts of the city into an enormous building site – during the mid-noughties it was estimated that a quarter of all the world's cranes could be found in Dubai. At the same time work began on **Palm Jumeirah**, the first of the four artificial islands planned to line the coast, and other landmark developments including the gargantuan new *Atlantis* resort and the **Burj Khalifa** (or the Burj Dubai, as it was then known), the world's tallest building.

The credit crunch

November 2008 saw the spectacular opening of the grandiose new **Atlantis** resort, Dubai's latest mega-attraction – the launch party alone cost over US$20 million, the most expensive in history, with a million fireworks, a gaggle of A-list celebrities ranging from Robert de Niro to Richard Branson, and Kylie Minogue on stage. It marked, by all accounts, the end of an era.

Even while the *Atlantis* extravaganza was in progress, serious questions were being asked about Dubai's financial future. As 2008 became 2009, the global recession began to hit the city with alarming force. Overseas investors pulled their funds out, tourists stopped arriving and the Dubai's burgeoning real-estate market, which had been one of the biggest drivers of local economic growth, suddenly collapsed, with up to half the value of some properties being wiped off in a few weeks. Major developers like Nakheel, Emar and Damac announced that various landmark projects were being put on indefinite hold or cancelled. The Dubai Stock Market lost fifty percent of its value, while a sixty percent fall in the price of oil didn't help either. Rumours circulated that the airport car parks were being left full of vehicles abandoned by their expat owners as they flew back home to avoid bankruptcy and possible imprisonment.

Then, in November 2009, **Dubai World**, the emirate's biggest government company, with debts of US$59 billion, sparked worldwide financial panic when it announced that it would be unable to make scheduled debt repayments. The possible collapse of the Dubai economy suddenly became one of the major talking points in the ongoing global financial meltdown, raising the possibility that were Dubai to default on its loans (owed to a wide range of institutions worldwide, including a significant number of UK banks), the global recession would enter a new and even more toxic phase.

Dubai's sky-high ambition had suddenly turned into a colossal mountain of debt – around US$80 billion in total. And given that most of this was chalked up against government-owned firms, there seemed a genuine possibility that the entire emirate would go bankrupt. Foreign journalists lined up to take spiteful swipes at the struggling city, while the financial world held its breath waiting to see whether the oil-rich government in Abu Dhabi would come to the aid of its beleaguered neighbour. This they eventually did, to an estimated tune of around US$20 billion, although not before making Dubai sweat for a while. Rumours abounded that

1996	**1999**	**2006**
Dubai Shopping Festival held for the first time	Opening of the Burj al Arab	Death of Sheikh Maktoum; Sheikh Mohammed becomes ruler of Dubai

Abu Dhabi had been holding out for a stake in Dubai's prized Emirates airline and other key assets in return for the bailout, although instead they got naming rights to the Burj Khalifa (see box, p.68). Another glitterati-packed launch party heralded the opening of this landmark structure in early 2010, although it appeared somewhat valedictory: a symbol of the magnificent ambition which the city no longer had the cash to underwrite, and named after the ruler of a rival state.

To the present

Bankruptcy was thus averted, and although the city's prestige and financial standing may have taken a significant hit, reports of Dubai's demise have been greatly exaggerated. The years since the credit crunch have been strangely quiet compared to the previous tornado of change, and a number of headline mega-projects (Business Bay, the Palm Jebel Ali and Palm Deira islands, for instance) remain on hold, trapped in a limbo of semi-completion. At the same time, quiet progress has been made with the opening of the Metro Green Line in 2011 and continuing development around Sheikh Zayed Road, Dubai Marina and the Palm Jumeirah – while the discovery in 2010 of a new offshore oilfield added a further note of (cautious) optimism. The property market has also shown striking signs of recovery – so much so that in late 2012 the government introduced new laws aimed at preventing a repeat of the disastrous property bubble of the mid-2000s.

Real evidence that Dubai is rediscovering some of its former confidence, however, came with the announcement in December 2012 of plans for **Mohammed bin Rashid City** – a Brobdingnagian mega-project, disconcertingly similar to the failed Dubailand development (see box, p.88), to be built in collaboration with Universal Studios and featuring the usual theme parks, hundred-plus hotels and (it goes almost without saying) the world's biggest shopping mall. Whether any part of the thing ever actually gets built – or whether the announcement simply marks the first step in another cycle of potentially disastrous overenthusiasm – remains to be seen, but at least it offers fresh proof that though the party in Dubai may have slowed down it is still far from over.

2008	2010	2012
Credit crunch hits Dubai; emirate teeters on edge of bankruptcy; many major projects cancelled or mothballed	Opening of Burj Khalifa, the world's tallest building	Plans for ambitious new Mohammed bin Rashid City announced

Contemporary Dubai

Dubai is the modern world's most extraordinary urban experiment: an attempt to create a global city, from scratch, within the space of a few decades. Not surprisingly, there have been growing pains along the way, as Dubai attempts to enact its own vision of history on fast-forward. The city's landmark achievements and record-busting mega-projects have received plenty of coverage, although in the past few years foreign media have focused increasingly on Dubai's darker side, including human rights issues, environmental concerns and the city's alleged role in international terrorist networks. The uniquely multicultural expat society – and its relationship with its Emirati hosts – is another ongoing source of tension and potential instability, as the city's rulers and citizens argue over Dubai's identity, culture and eventual destination.

Demographic diversity

Dubai is perhaps the most **cosmopolitan** city on the planet, with residents from over two hundred countries calling it home. The emirate's population is overwhelmingly foreign, and native Emiratis – or "nationals", as they're often described – find themselves in an increasingly small minority. Of the UAE's population of slightly over five million, only nineteen percent are nationals; the figure is even lower in Dubai itself – some estimates put it at below five percent. Dubai's Emiratis thus find themselves forming just one small strand in the city's diverse cultural fabric, a situation which has led to increasing social tensions (see p.190).

The remainder of the city's populace is a veritable kaleidoscope of cultures. Nearly two-thirds are from **South Asia**, mainly Indian (around 1.7 million, including particularly large numbers from the state of Kerala), plus 1.25 million Pakistanis. Most of these are employed as low-skilled construction workers, taxi drivers and in various other menial positions, although there are also a significant number of wealthy and well-established Indian trading families who have been in the city for generations. A further quarter of the population comes from **other Arab countries** (mainly Palestine, Lebanon, Syria and Egypt) and **Iran** – Iranian merchants have traditionally provided Dubai with much of its commercial dynamism, while expat Arabs can be found in a wide range of jobs in the city's business and leisure sectors. There are also a large number of **Filipinos** (who provide the city with many of its waitresses, housemaids and nannies) plus a smaller but economically significant number of **expat Europeans** who supply essential financial, tourism and engineering expertise. As such, Dubai is not really a single city, but an agglomeration of dozens of self-contained ethnic enclaves, geographically contiguous but culturally quite separate. All of which lends the city its fascinatingly varied, but also decidedly dysfunctional, flavour.

The UAE's other demographic oddity is its **gender imbalance**. This is one of the most male-dominated countries on the planet, with 2.2 men for every woman in the country. The situation in Dubai is particularly uneven, with men forming around two-thirds of the population, making it one of the world's most sexually lopsided cities.

The ruling bargain: Emiratis and expats

Dubai has never been a **democracy** and, apart from a brief period in the 1930s (see p.183) has never looked like becoming one. The old tribal system of government by the ruling sheikh and his family remains deeply entrenched, regardless of the city's other impeccably modernist credentials. Despite appearances, the original system was not as autocratic as it might appear. Sheikhs were allowed to rule on the assumption that they acted in the best interests of their subjects, and did their best to provide for them – the so-called **ruling bargain**. Unpopular or incompetent leaders could be replaced, and often were. This simple but effective system of tribal democracy was seriously undermined by the British, who tended to confirm the position and privileges of whichever family happened to be in power, irrespective of their abilities. Fortunately the UAE, and Dubai in particular, has been blessed with a number of unusually effective and often prescient leaders – sheikhs Zayed, Rashid and Mohammed in particular – and there's certainly no way in which Dubai could have pursued its spectacularly rapid road to modernization under a traditional democracy.

The ruling bargain is still very much in force, in terms of the financial benefits which the sheikhs are expected to hand down to their subjects. Emirati **citizenship** is jealously guarded, and Dubai's native population benefit from a range of perks estimated to be worth over US$50,000 per year, including free land, university education, building grants and so on – not to mention a complete lack of income tax, and the possibility of earning easy additional money through renting out property or sponsoring foreign companies. The downside of this sheikh-led nanny-state model is that it has increasingly tended to mollycoddle its citizens into a state of privileged insensibility. Given their various guaranteed state subsidies and welfare benefits, around twenty percent of Emiratis simply decline to work, while those that do gravitate towards well-paid, low-skilled government jobs. The result is a notable lack of educated and entrepreneurial locals – which tends to place even more of the reins of economic power in the hands of foreigners (more than 99 percent of employees in private companies are expats). The situation has particularly concerned Sheikh Mohammed and his ruling circles, who have launched an ongoing **Emiratisation** programme over the past decade in order to encourage Emiratis to acquire skills and thus take up senior positions at private companies, although so far with relatively little success.

The rulers' disappointment in the apathy of their local workforce is one side of the equation. The flipside is the increasing resentment among some local Emiratis with what they see as the **sell-out** of their country and its traditional culture, and the fact that they now find themselves virtual strangers in their own homes. Despite Dubai's cosmopolitan make-up, there has been a remarkable lack of racial tension, although this may change. Increasing popular disgust at the insensitive behaviour of certain local Western expats and visitors is increasingly hardening local attitudes against foreigners.

Dubai's **expats**, in turn, find themselves in an ambivalent position. Emirati citizenship (with all its associated financial perks) is only very rarely granted to outsiders. Even those who have lived in the country for decades, including many people who were born in Dubai, have no rights to citizenship or even residence, instead holding the nationality of their parents' country – which they might never have visited. As such, Dubai is largely a city of transients, with foreigners living in Dubai on a sequence of three-year working visas, and with residence dependent on keeping their jobs and not falling foul of the authorities. Those from Europe, North America, Australia and New Zealand often come to Dubai, see out their contracts, and then go home again, giving the city's "Western" community its peculiarly rootless and impermanent flavour.

Humans rights and wrongs

Dubai's expat community comprises a huge range of ethnic and economic groups. At the bottom of the heap lie the **Indian and Pakistani labourers**, the city's most unsung and exploited community, who have provided the manpower to build modern Dubai but are denied any of its rewards. Most of the abuses are related to the **construction industry**, and its workforce of largely subcontinental labourers. Many of these immigrants live in labour camps in the most basic conditions, often working in dangerous circumstances in the heat of the Gulf sun, with fatalities all too common (an estimated 800 in 2007 alone). Workers' passports are routinely confiscated to prevent them from absconding, while pay is often held for months in arrears for the same reason. In addition, workers have no freedom of movement, being obliged by the terms of their visas to work for the employer who sponsored their arrival in Dubai. Pretty much all labourers also owe large sums of money to the employment agents back home who arranged their jobs for them, and spend much of their first year or two just paying off these fees. Workers are also routinely promised one wage before arriving in Dubai, but subsequently discover that their actual salary is far lower. What money they do manage to earn is sent back home to support their families. In Dubai itself, attempts are made to ensure that the workers remain largely invisible, prevented by security guards from entering the shopping malls and skyscrapers they helped to build.

Such workers are effectively little better than modern-day slaves. Though the principal offenders are the Gulf's large construction companies (including, ironically, a number of Indian firms) and employment agents in the Subcontinent, the Dubai government has acted with uncharacteristic lethargy in addressing the problems, and seems to regard it as more of a PR headache than a fundamental issue of human rights. Improvements are being made, but slowly. The ultimate challenge that forces Dubai to improve labour conditions may come from outside, however. Increasingly upbeat economic conditions in the Subcontinent mean that in future many Indians (if not Pakistanis) will be able to find better pay and working conditions at home. Which will be Dubai's loss – and India's gain.

The plight of the city's **housemaids** is sometimes even worse than that of its construction workers, as they risk suffering serious abuse in the privacy of their employer's home. **Human-trafficking** and forced prostitution (see p.34) is another major concern.

Terrorism and dirty money

Dubai's role in the international terrorist network is another issue that is frequently discussed, if little understood. The city's position is strangely ambiguous. On one hand, it is often held up as a potential target for Islamic extremists on account of its extremely liberal and Western-leaning regime. On the other, it's also frequently cited as a hub for international terrorist activities, and as the conduit through which terrorist finances are laundered and sent overseas. Repeated **threats** have been made against the city, but nothing has yet materialized (there seems to be no basis in the popular rumour that Dubai hasn't yet been attacked because it's paying protection money to Al Qaeda). The main possible trigger for an attack isn't Dubai's liberal regime, bars or (relatively) scantily clad Western women, but the presence of over a thousand US troops, including at the Jebel Ali Port. The country is protected by a very well-developed (and largely invisible) security system, while potentially troublesome local Islamist publications and organizations are routinely suppressed.

As for Dubai's reputation as an international **terrorist hub**, certainly the city's loose regulation and freewheeling commercial atmosphere – not to mention its proximity to Afghanistan, East Africa and, particularly, Iran (see box, p.52) – have made it a valuable transit point for money, arms, gold and drugs. Al Qaeda and other terrorist organizations have apparently used Dubai as a conduit for money-laundering, while the city has also been used as a base for various arms deals and dealers, including the notorious Victor Bout, the so-called "Merchant of Death" who banked in Dubai and operated a fleet of fifty cargo planes from Sharjah, shipping guns and weaponry around the region to repressive regimes such as Charles Taylor's Liberia. The city was also an international centre for nuclear weapons technology, which was smuggled from here to secret nuclear programmes in Iran, Libya and North Korea. Increasing government vigilance has succeeded in stamping out at least some of this traffic, and Dubai is no more guilty of actively harbouring and encouraging terrorists than London, Hamburg or New York. As is often pointed out, although two of the 9/11 terrorists may have come from the UAE, most of the hijackers learnt to fly in the USA.

Environmental disaster in the making?

Lingering concerns have also been raised about the city's **ecological credentials**. The facts make unpleasant reading. The UAE has the largest per capita environmental footprint of any country in the world (slightly above the US, almost double that of the UK, and three times the global average). Part of the reason can be found in Dubai's challenging climate, and the need for almost year-round air-conditioning, and its lack of natural water supplies, which have to be created using extremely energy-intensive desalination plants. Other causes of environmental over-consumption include the city's car-centred culture and inefficient public transport networks. Energy-busting city landmarks also burn up a prodigious amount of fuel, with Dubai's innumerable skyscrapers particularly to blame. Running elevators or pumping water up to the top of a forty-storey high-rise burns huge quantities of energy, while the glass-walled style favoured by most of the city's architects means that each building acts as a kind of giant greenhouse, thereby massively increasing air-conditioning requirements; it's been estimated that the Burj Khalifa requires cooling energy equivalent to that provided by 10,000 tons of melting ice per day. Other forms of physical damage to the environment are also commonplace: the possible environmental problems associated with the construction of various artificial Palm islands (see box, p.84) have been widely publicized, while preliminary work on the Palm Jebel Ali involved burying an entire national marine park under the island's foundations.

The profligate attitude towards energy consumption is perhaps a result of Dubai's location in one of the world's most oil-rich regions, while low-cost (or free) energy and water is provided as a matter of course to nationals, further encouraging waste. As a result, Dubai now actually consumes more energy than it produces and could soon find itself a victim of its own ecological rapaciousness, with its landmark string of artificial islands particularly at risk from rising sea levels. Ironically, it is oil-rich Abu Dhabi that has for once out-thought its neighbour, with schemes such as the vast new Masdar project, a low-rise, carbon-neutral development which will eventually serve as home to some 50,000 people.

A modern Córdoba?

In many ways, Dubai is a victim of its own success, and many aspects of the modern city that concern outsiders – its role in arms smuggling, money-laundering and human trafficking, for example – are a direct consequence of the *laissez-faire* policies that made the city such a huge hit in the first place. Meanwhile its extremely sensitive geopolitical situation at the heart of one of the world's most volatile regions has frequently put it under the international microscope and made it the object of negative – and frequently vituperative – media coverage in the West.

What is less widely appreciated are Dubai's massive achievements, of which the landmark skyscrapers, artificial islands and supersized malls are merely the most obvious, and superficial, expression. More important than any of these widely trumpeted (and just as frequently derided) mega-projects is Dubai's intangible contribution to Arab pride and Middle Eastern stability, and its role in providing an example of a stable and successful city based on commercial acumen, cultural liberalism and religious tolerance at the heart of one of the world's most dysfunctional regions. Sheikh Mohammed himself has suggested tenth-century Córdoba as a possible example of what the city may eventually become, alluding to the illustrious history of what was then one of Europe's more culturally and socially advanced cities, hosting a vibrant community of Muslims, Christians and Jews, and boasting some of the era's most spectacular architectural achievements. It's far too early to judge Dubai yet, or to decide whether it will succeed in living up to such lofty aspirations. Even so, it's worth bearing in mind that the city that is widely derided for its lack of culture and character could well turn out to be the focal point for a twenty-first-century Middle Eastern cultural and political renaissance, and a new and invaluable bridge between East and West.

Books

There aren't many books about Dubai, although the past couple of years have seen the publication of several interesting studies of the modern city. With one or two exceptions, don't expect to find any of these for sale in Dubai itself however. Books marked with the ★ symbol are particularly recommended.

Syed Ali *Dubai: Gilded Cage*. Detailed study of contemporary Dubai's relations with its massive expat community, from exploited Indian labourers to wealthy European expats, plus a good chapter on the social position of the city's Emiratis. Ploddingly written, but makes some sound points about the political and social structures that shape life in the city.

Anne Coles and Peter Jackson *Windtower: Houses of the Bastaki*. This beautiful coffee-table book offers a marvellous visual memento of old Dubai, with superb photographs of the architecture and inhabitants of Bastakiya back in the 1970s, accompanied by absorbing text.

Christopher M. Davidson *Dubai: The Vulnerability of Success*. Detailed, scholarly study of the history of Dubai, plus chapters on the city's social, political and economic workings, current challenges and future prospects. Full of fascinating detail, although rather a heavy read for non-specialists. Davidson has also provided a similarly in-depth account of Dubai's great rival in *Abu Dhabi: Oil and Beyond*, while his more recent *After the Sheikhs: The Coming Collapse of the Gulf Monarchies* offers a superb analysis of the effects of the Arab Spring and other socio-economic factors on the fossilized politics of the Gulf region, suggesting that the power of the various ruling families from Kuwait to Oman may finally be coming to an end, and in the very near future too.

Maha Gargash *The Sand Fish: A Novel from Dubai*. A rare novel from a native Dubaian, *The Sand Fish* is set in Dubai and the northern UAE in the 1950s. Narrated through the eyes of rebellious seventeen-year-old Noora, the third wife of an older man, it offers a vivid portrait of the city and its culture at the moment of transition from the traditional to modern era.

Edward Henderson *Arabian Destiny*. Published in 1988, *Arabian Destiny* describes Henderson's sojourn in the Gulf during the late 1940s and 1950s while working for the Petroleum Development (Trucial Coast). Much of the book is devoted to various events in neighbouring Oman, but there's a fascinating chapter on life in old Dubai, as well as forays into Al Ain and Abu Dhabi. Widely available in Dubai itself, although difficult to get hold of abroad.

★ **Jim Krane** *Dubai: The Story of the World's Fastest City* (published in North America as *City of Gold: Dubai and the Dream of Capitalism*). Far and away the best book on modern Dubai, packed with fascinating insights and offering a sympathetic but balanced account of the city's huge successes – and occasional failures. Krane systematically tackles pretty much every important aspect of Dubai's past and present, with absorbing accounts of the city's history and the personalities and achievements of its charismatic rulers through to vexed contemporary issues such as human rights abuses and environmental concerns, condensing a vast mass of detail into a compellingly readable roller coaster of a narrative.

Robin Moore *Dubai*. Rollicking Middle Eastern blockbuster by *French Connection* author Robin Moore, describing the gold-smuggling, oil-politicking and ladykilling exploits of disgraced US soldier James Fitzroy Lodd in late-1960s Dubai. The gung-ho narrative is of minimal literary value, admittedly, but paints a nice picture of pre-oil Dubai, while much of the historical background is surprisingly accurate, complete with cameo appearances by sheikhs Rashid and Zayed. An excellent poolside read.

Mohammad al Murr *Tales of Dubai* and *The Wink of the the Mona Lisa*. Two enjoyable collections of short stories by Mohammad al Murr (b.1955), set in Dubai during the 1970s and 80s and offering an engaging snapshot of the evolving city and its various colourful characters.

★ **Jonathan Raban** *Arabia*. Published in 1979, and still one of the best books ever written about the Middle East. It covers Raban's travels through the recently independent Gulf emirates, including chapters on Dubai and Abu Dhabi, before heading west to Yemen, Jordan and Egypt, with perceptive and entertaining accounts of the people and places encountered en route, all described in Raban's inimitable prose. Inevitably dated, but offers a wonderful portrait of the region at a moment of huge historical change.

Wilfred Thesiger *Arabian Sands*. This classic of desert exploration covers Thesiger's two traverses of the Empty Quarter in the late 1940s, including accounts of Al Ain and Abu Dhabi, plus a brief visit to Dubai en route.

Language

Language in Dubai is as complicated as the ethnic patchwork of people who inhabit the city. The city's official language is Arabic, spoken by nearly a third of the population, including local Emiratis, other Gulf Arabs and various Arabic-speaking expats from countries like Lebanon, Syria, Jordan and further afield. Hindi and Urdu are the mother tongues of many of the city's enormous number of Indian and Pakistani expats, although other Indian languages, most notably Malayalam, the native tongue of Kerala, as well as Tamil and Sinhalese (the majority language of Sri Lanka) are also spoken. Other Asian languages are also common, most notably Tagalog, the first language of the city's large Filipino community.

In practice, the city's most widely understood language is actually **English** (even if most speak it only as a second or third language), which serves as a link between all the city's various ethnic groups, as well as the principal language of the European expat community and the business and tourism sectors. Pretty much everyone in Dubai speaks at least a little English (ironically, even local Emiratis are now forced to revert to this foreign language in many of their everyday dealings in their own city).

Knowing the ethnic origin of the person you're speaking to is obviously the most important thing if you do attempt to strike out into a foreign tongue – speaking Arabic to an Indian taxi driver or a Filipino waitress is obviously a complete waste of time. The bottom line is that few of the people you come into contact with as a tourist in Dubai will be Arabic speakers, except in the city's Middle Eastern restaurants. And unless you're pretty fluent, trying to speak Arabic (or indeed any other language) in Dubai is mainly an exercise in diplomacy rather than a meaningful attempt to communicate, since the person you're addressing will almost certainly speak much better English than you do Arabic (or Hindi, or whatever). Having said that, there's no harm in giving it a go, and the person you're speaking to may be pleasantly entertained by your attempts to address him or her in their own language.

USEFUL ARABIC WORDS AND PHRASES

Hello (formal)	a'salaam alaykum (response: wa alaykum a'salaam)	OK	n'zayn
		How much?	bikaim?
		Do you speak English?	teh ki ingelezi?
Hello (informal)	marhaba/ahlan wasahlan	I don't speak Arabic	ma ah'ki arabi
Good morning	sabah al kheer	I understand	ana fahim (fem: ana fahma)
Good evening	masaa al kheer	I don't understand	ana ma fahim (fem: ana ma fahma)
Good night (to a man)	tisbah al kher		
(to a woman)	tisbahi al kher	My name is ...	Ismi ...
Goodbye	ma'assalama	What is your name?	Sho ismak?
Yes	na'am/aiwa	God willing!	Inshallah
No	la	I'm British	ana Britani
Please (to a man)	minfadlack	Irish	Irlandee
(to a woman)	minfadlick	American	Amerikanee
Excuse me	afwan	Canadian	Canadee
Thank you	shukran	Australian	Ostralee
You're welcome	afwan	from New Zealand	Noozeelandee
Sorry	afwan	Where are you from?	min wayn inta?

Where is?	wayn?	big/small	kabeer/saghir
fi	in	old/new	kadeem/jadeed
near/far	gareeb/ba'eed	day/night	yoom/layl
here/there	hina/hunak	today/tomorrow	al yoom/bokra
open/closed	maftooh/mseeker	perhaps	mumkin

NUMBERS

1	wahid	9	tissa
2	ithnayn	10	ashra
3	theletha	20	aishreen
4	arba'a	30	thelatheen
5	khamsa	40	arba'aeen
6	sitta	50	khamseen
7	saba'a	100	maya
8	themanya	1000	elf

FOOD GLOSSARY

The traditional Middle Eastern meal consists of a wide selection of small dishes known as **mezze** (or *meze*) shared between a number of diners. Most or all of the following dishes, dips and other ingredients are found in the city's better Middle Eastern (or "Lebanese", as they are usually described) **restaurants** and cafés, although note that vagaries in the transliteration from Arabic script to English can result in considerable variations in spelling.

arayes slices of pitta bread stuffed with spiced meat and baked

baba ghanouj all-purpose dip made from grilled aubergine (eggplant) mixed with ingredients like tomato, onion, lemon juice and garlic

burghul cracked wheat, often used as an ingredient in Middle Eastern dishes such as tabbouleh

falafel deep-fried balls of crushed chickpeas mixed with spices; usually served with bread and salad

fatayer miniature triangular pastries, usually filled with either cheese or spinach

fatteh dishes containing pieces of fried or roasted bread

fattoush salad made of tomatoes, cucumber, lettuce and mint mixed up with crispy little squares of deep-fried flatbread

foul madamas smooth dip made from fava beans (*foul*) blended with lemon juice, chillis and olive oil

halloumi grilled cheese

hammour common Gulf fish which often crops up on local menus; a bit like cod

humous crushed chickpeas blended with tahini, garlic and lemon; served as a basic side dish and eaten with virtually everything, from bread and vegetables through to meat dishes

jebne white cheese

kibbeh small ovals of deep-fried minced lamb mixed with cracked wheat and spices

kushari classic Egyptian dish featuring a mix of rice, lentils, noodles, macaroni and fried onion, topped with tomato sauce

labneh thick, creamy Arabian yoghurt, often flavoured with garlic or mint

loubia salad of green beans with tomatoes and onion

moutabal a slightly creamier version of *baba ghanouj*, thickened using yoghurt or tahini

mulukhiyah soup-cum-stew with a characteristically slimy texture, made from boiled *mulukhiyah* leaves.

saj Lebanese-style thin, round flatbread

saj manakish (or *mana'eesh*) pieces of *saj* sprinkled with herbs and oil – a kind of Middle Eastern mini-pizza

sambousek miniature pastries, filled with meat or cheese and then fried

sharkaseya chicken served in a creamy walnut sauce

shisha waterpipe (also known as hubbly-bubbly). Tobacco is filtered through the glass water-container at the base of the pipe, and so is milder (and less harmful) than normal cigarettes. Tobacco is usually available either plain or in various flavoured varieties; the best shisha cafés may have as many as twenty varieties.

shish taouk basic chicken kebab, with small pieces of meat grilled on a skewer and often served with garlic sauce

shwarma chicken or lamb kebabs, cut in narrow strips off a big hunk of meat roasted on a vertical spit (like the Turkish doner kebab) and served wrapped in flatbread with salad

tabbouleh finely chopped mixture of tomato, mint and cracked wheat

tahini paste made from sesame seeds

waraq aynab vine leaves stuffed with a mixture of rice and meat

zaatar a widely used seasoning made from a mixture of dried thyme (or oregano), salt and sesame seeds

zatoon olives

GLOSSARY

abbeya black, full-length women's traditional robe

abra small boat used to ferry passengers across the Creek (see p.22)

attar traditional perfume

bahar sea

barasti palm thatch used to construct traditional houses

bayt/bait house

burj tower

dar house

dhow generic term loosely used to describe all types of traditional wooden Arabian boat (see box, p.59)

dishdasha see *kandoura*

Eid ul Fitr festival celebrating the end of Ramadan (see box, p.28)

falaj traditional irrigation technique used to water date plantations, with water drawn from deep underground and carried to its destination along tiny earthen canals

funduk hotel

ghutra men's headscarf, usually white or red-and-white check

haj pilgrimage to Mecca

hosn/hisn fort

iftar the breaking of the fast after dark during Ramadan

iqal the rope-like black cords used to keep the *ghutra* on the head (traditionally used to tie together the legs of camels to stop them running off)

jebel hill or mountain

kandoura the full-length traditional robe worn by Gulf Arabs (also known as *dishdashas*). A decorative tassel, known as the *farokha* (or *tarboush*) often hangs from the collar. A long robe, or *basht*, is sometimes worn over the *dishdasha* on formal occasions, denoting the authority of the wearer

Al Khaleej The Gulf (translated locally as the Arabian Gulf, never as the Persian Gulf)

khanjar traditional curved dagger, usually made of silver

Al Khor The Creek

majlis meeting/reception room in a traditional Arabian house; the place where local or family problems were discussed and decisions taken

mashrabiya projecting window protected by a carved wooden latticework screen – although the term is often loosely used to describe any kind of elaborately carved latticework screen, whether or not a window is also present

masjid mosque

mina port

nakheel palm tree

oud Arabian lute; also the name of a key ingredient in Arabian perfumes derived from agarwood

qasr palace or castle

qibla the direction of Mecca, usually indicated by a sign or sticker in most hotel rooms in the city (and in mosques by a recessed niche known as the mihrab)

Ramadan see box, p.28

shayla women's black headscarf, worn with an *abbeya*

wadi dry river bed or valley

Small print and index

A ROUGH GUIDE TO ROUGH GUIDES

Published in 1982, the first Rough Guide – to Greece – was a student scheme that became a publishing phenomenon. Mark Ellingham, a recent graduate in English from Bristol University, had been travelling in Greece the previous summer and couldn't find the right guidebook. With a small group of friends he wrote his own guide, combining a highly contemporary, journalistic style with a thoroughly practical approach to travellers' needs.

The immediate success of the book spawned a series that rapidly covered dozens of destinations. And, in addition to impecunious backpackers, Rough Guides soon acquired a much broader readership that relished the guides' wit and inquisitiveness as much as their enthusiastic, critical approach and value-for-money ethos.

These days, Rough Guides include recommendations from budget to luxury and cover more than 200 destinations around the globe, as well as producing an ever-growing range of eBooks and apps.

Visit **roughguides.com** to see our latest publications.

Rough Guide credits

Editor: Edward Aves
Layout: Jessica Subramanian, Ankur Guha
Cartography: Katie Bennett
Picture editors: Mark Thomas, Tim Draper
Proofreader: Karen Parker
Managing editor: Keith Drew
Assistant editor: Dipika Dasgupta
Photographer: Tim Draper
Production: Charlotte Cade

Cover design: Wilf Matos, Jessica Subramanian
Editorial assistant: Olivia Rawes
Senior pre-press designer: Dan May
Creative operations manager: Jason Mitchell
Publisher: Joanna Kirby
Operations coordinator: Helen Blount
Publishing director (Travel): Clare Currie
Commercial manager: Gino Magnotta
Managing director: John Duhigg

Publishing information

This second edition published November 2013 by
Rough Guides Ltd,
80 Strand, London WC2R 0RL
11, Community Centre, Panchsheel Park,
New Delhi 110017, India
Distributed by the Penguin Group
Penguin Books Ltd,
80 Strand, London WC2R 0RL
Penguin Group (USA)
345 Hudson Street, NY 10014, USA
Penguin Group (Australia)
250 Camberwell Road, Camberwell,
Victoria 3124, Australia
Penguin Group (NZ)
67 Apollo Drive, Mairangi Bay, Auckland 1310,
New Zealand
Penguin Group (South Africa)
Block D, Rosebank Office Park, 181 Jan Smuts Avenue,
Parktown North, Gauteng, South Africa 2193
Rough Guides is represented in Canada by Tourmaline
Editions Inc. 662 King Street West, Suite 304, Toronto,
Ontario M5V 1M7
Printed in Singapore by Toppan Security Printing Pte. Ltd.

© Gavin Thomas, 2013
Maps © Rough Guides
No part of this book may be reproduced in any form
without permission from the publisher except for the
quotation of brief passages in reviews.
224pp includes index
A catalogue record for this book is available from the
British Library
ISBN: 978-1-40932-083-8

MIX
Paper from
responsible sources
FSC www.fsc.org FSC™ C018179

Help us update

We've gone to a lot of effort to ensure that the second
edition of **The Rough Guide to Dubai** is accurate and
up-to-date. However, things change – places get
"discovered", opening hours are notoriously fickle,
restaurants and rooms raise prices or lower standards. If
you feel we've got it wrong or left something out, we'd like
to know, and if you can remember the address, the price,
the hours, the phone number, so much the better.

Please send your comments with the subject line
"Rough Guide Dubai Update" to ✉ mail@uk.roughguides
.com. We'll credit all contributions and send a copy of the
next edition (or any other Rough Guide if you prefer) for
the very best emails.
Find more travel information, connect with fellow
travellers and plan your trip on ⓦ roughguides.com.

ABOUT THE AUTHOR

Gavin Thomas has worked for Rough Guides as a writer and editor since 1998; he is also the author of the *Rough Guide to Oman* and the *Rough Guide to Sri Lanka*, and co-author of the *Rough Guide to Rajasthan, Delhi & Agra*. His first experience of Dubai was during an unscheduled six-hour stopover at the airport, which impressed him so much that he decided to come back for more – the only time he has formed a lasting relationship with a major city on the basis of its duty-free facilities. He hopes one day to be able to walk down Al Fahidi Street without being offered a fake watch, and to say something in Arabic that somebody actually understands.

Acknowledgements

Thanks to James Smart for setting the ball rolling; to my editor and old compadre Edward Aves for giving the text a thorough spring-clean and for saving me from at least one major cheese-related embarrassment; and to Allison, for letting me go in the first place, and then for coming out in person and teaching me how to shop properly.

Photo credits

All photos © Rough Guides except the following:
(Key: t-top; c-centre; b-bottom; l-left; r-right)

p.2 Getty Images/Alan Copson
p.4 Getty Images/Frank de Luyck
p.9 Getty Images/John Miles (t)
p.15 Courtesy of *The Address Hotels + Resorts*/Nicolas Dumont (b)
p.16 Getty Images/Jonathan Kitchen (t)
p.90 Courtesy of *Jumeirah Zabeel Saray*
p.103 Chris Cypert/Chris Cypert
p.109 Courtesy of *Table 9 by Nick and Scott* (bl)
p.137 Getty Images/Marwan Naamani

p.141 Getty Images/Visions Of Our Land
p.144 Getty Images/Mohamed El Hebeishy
p.178 Alamy/Christine Osborne Pictures

Front cover Madinat Jumeirah and Burj al Arab © Corbis/ Georgina Bowater
Back cover Jumeirah beach and skyline © Getty Images/ Siegfried Layda (t); Bangles, Gold Souk © Rough Guides/ Tim Draper (bl); Dune-bashing in the desert © Rough Guides/Tim Draper (br)

Index

Maps are marked in grey

U

V

W

Y

Z

Maps
Index

City plan

The **city plan** on the pages that follow is divided as shown:

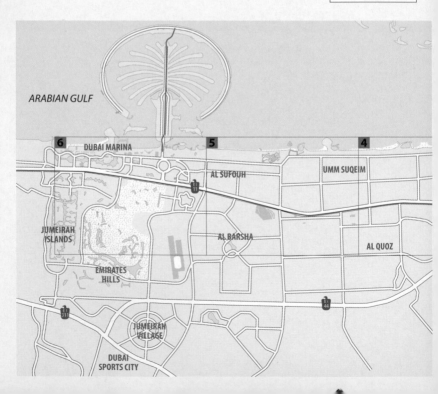

Map symbols

✈	Airport	🕌	Mosque	— —	Abra/ferry route	▥	Building
Ⓜ Ⓜ	Metro station	⛳	Golf course	- - - -	Footpath	▥	Souk/market
⚓	Abra station/ferry stop	⛲	Fountain	═══	Pedestrianized road	⬭	Stadium
✉	Post office	🚩	Border crossing	▢▢▢	Tunnel		Park
✚	Hospital	⌒⌒	Mountain range	▬▬	Metro		Beach
@	Internet access	▲	Mountain peak	▬▬	Monorail	⌄	Muslim cemetery
◆	Place of interest	⛼	Motor-racing circuit				

Listings key

- ■ Accommodation
- ● Eating
- ■ Drinking and nightlife
- ● Shopping

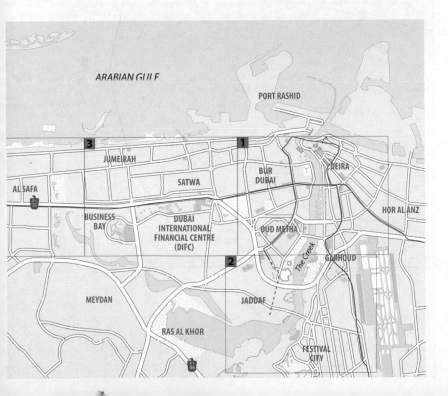

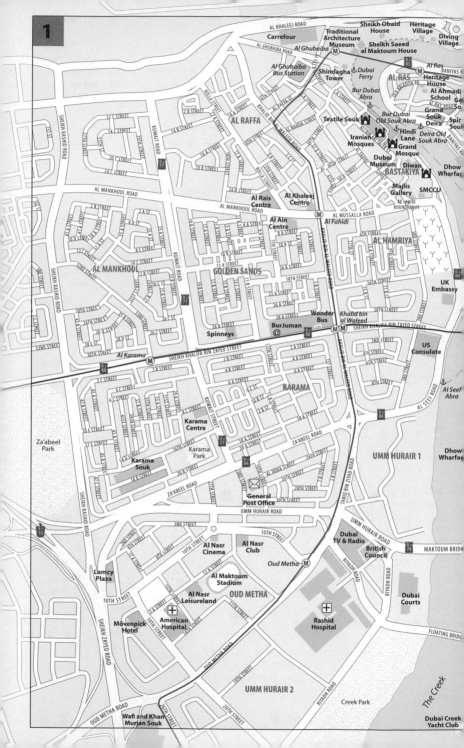

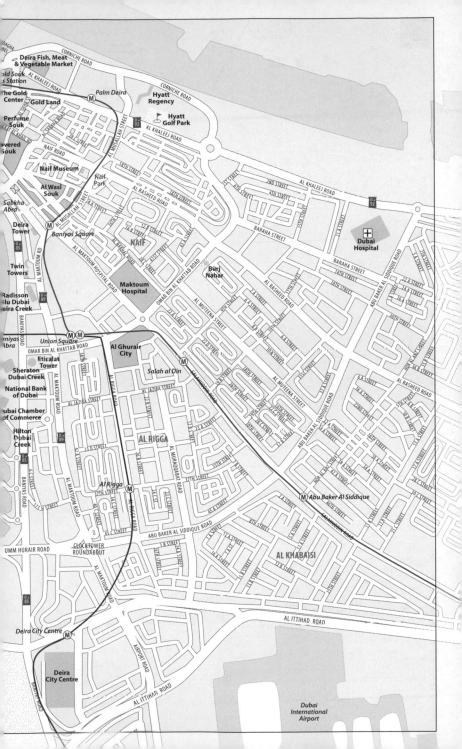

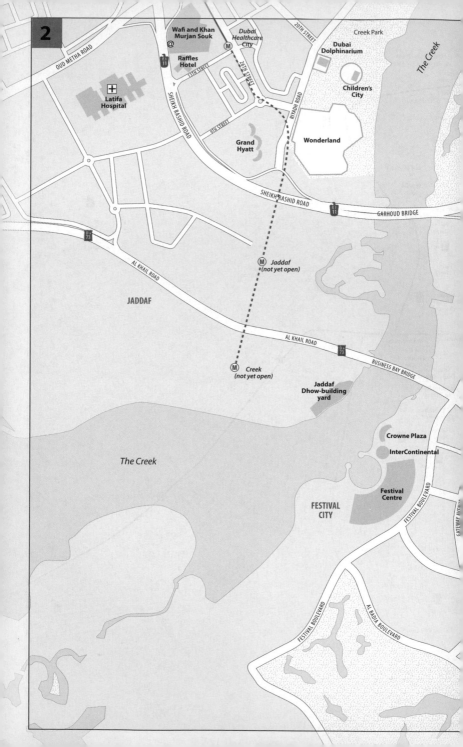

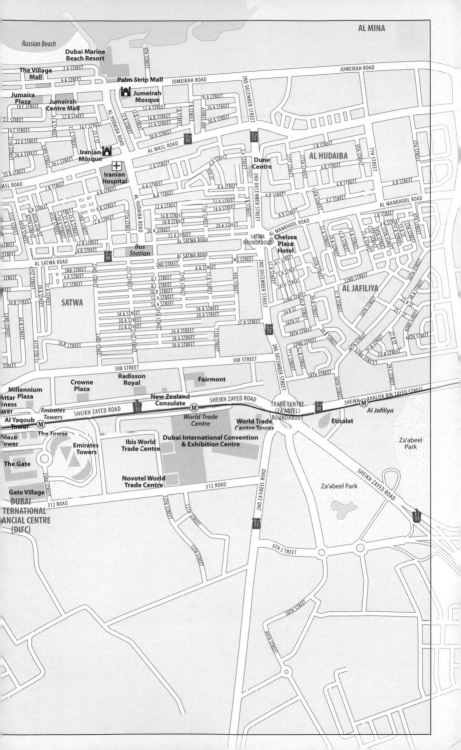

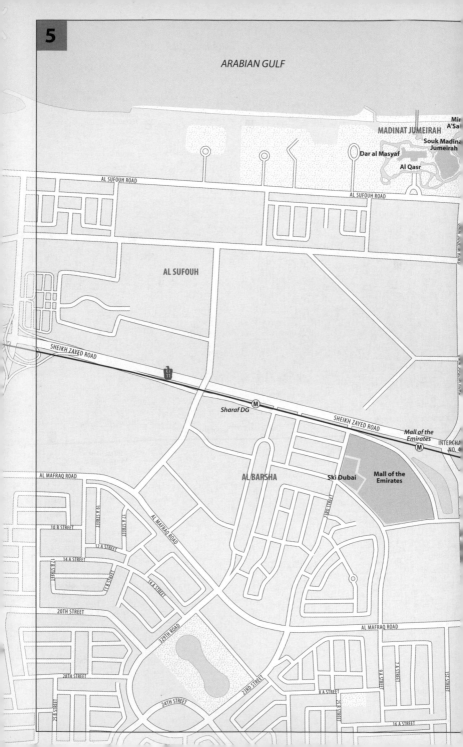

ARABIAN GULF

MADINAT JUMEIRAH

Mir
A'Sa

Souk Madina
Jumeirah

Dar al Masyaf

Al Qasr

AL SUFOUH ROAD

AL SUFOUH ROAD

AL SUFOUH

SHEIKH ZAYED ROAD

Sharaf DG

SHEIKH ZAYED ROAD

Mall of the
Emirates

INTERCHA
NO. 4

AL MAFRAQ ROAD

AL BARSHA

Ski Dubai

Mall of the
Emirates

19 A STREET

17 A STREET

10 B STREET

12 A STREET

AL MAFRAQ ROAD

14 A STREET

14 A STREET

20TH STREET

329 ROAD

AL MAFRAQ ROAD

28TH STREET

9 A STREET

7 A STREET

1 ST STREET

23RD STREET

8 A STREET

24TH STREET

16 A STREET

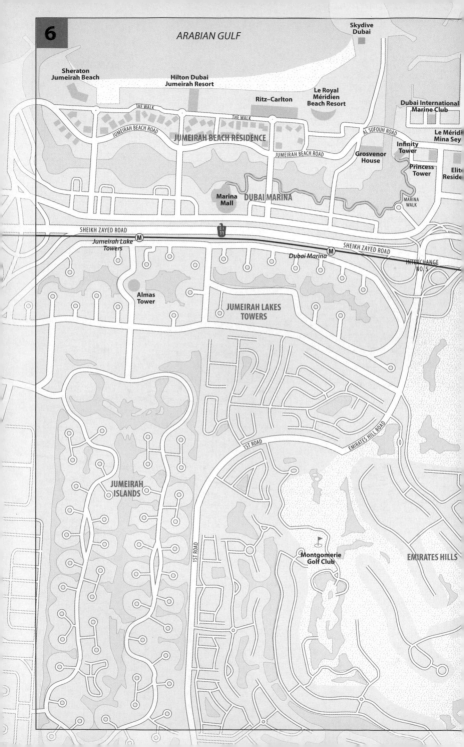

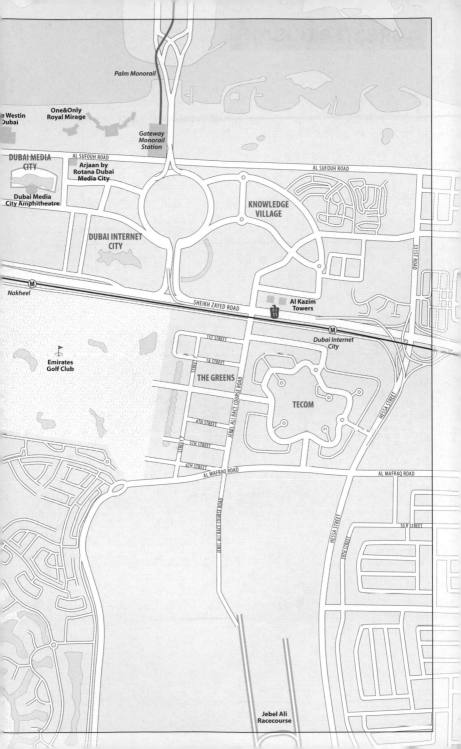

GREATER DUBAI

ARABIAN GULF

Palm Jebel Ali

Atlantis

Palm Jumeirah

DUBAI MARINA

Souk Madinat Jumeirah

Bu al A

Marina Mall

SHEIKH ZAYED ROAD

AL SUFOUH

Ibn Battuta Mall

SHEIKH ZAYED ROAD

JEBEL ALI FREEZONE

JEBEL ALI VILLAGE

THE GREENS

TECOM

JUMEIRAH ISLANDS

Mall of the Emirates

Jebel Ali Racecourse

AL BARSHA

EMIRATES HILLS

AL KHAIL ROAD

MOHAMMED BIN ZAYED ROAD (EMIRATES ROAD)

Fire & Earth

JUMEIRAH VILLAGE

JUMEIRAH GOLF ESTATES

Wind

The Els Club

Dubai Autodrome

DUBAI SPORTS CITY

MOHAMMED BIN ZAYED ROAD (EMIRATES ROAD)

Water

DUBAI MOTOR CITY

DUBAI INVESTMENT PARK

ARABIAN RANCHES

Arabian Ranches Golf Club

GLOBAL VILLAGE

Al Maktoum International Airport (under construction)

DUBAI BYPASS ROAD

DUBAILAND

DUBAI BYPASS ROAD

0		4

kilometres

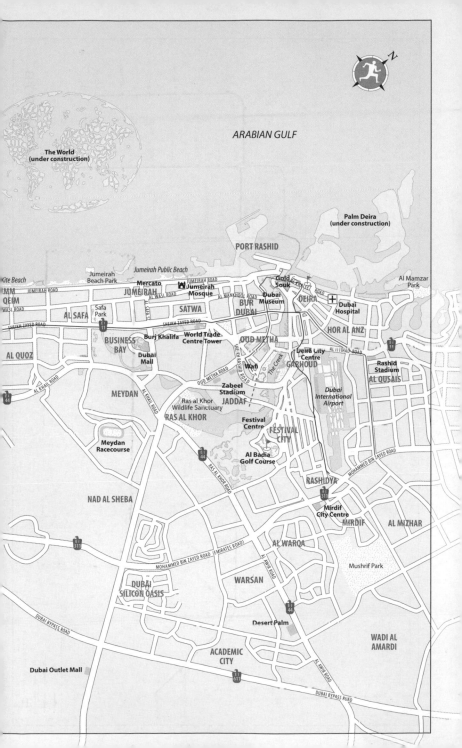

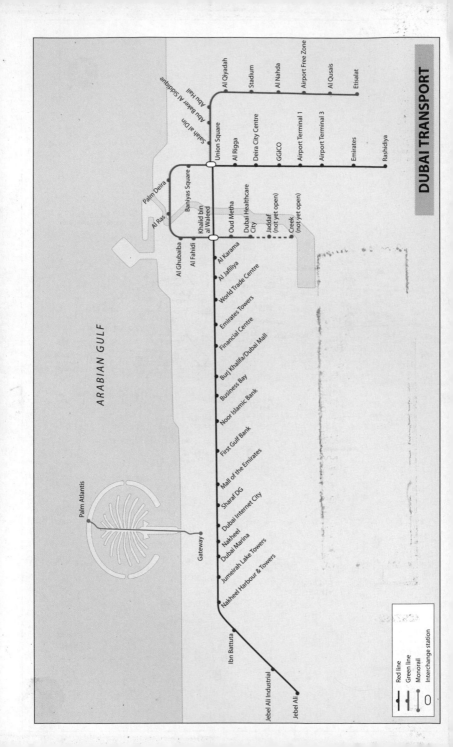

DUBAI TRANSPORT

ARABIAN GULF

Palm Atlantis

Gateway

Red line
Green line
Monorail
Interchange station

Abu Baker Al Siddique
Salah al Din
Abu Hail

Al Qiyadah
Stadium
Al Nahda
Airport Free Zone
Al Qusais
Etisalat

Union Square
Al Rigga
Deira City Centre
GGICO
Airport Terminal 1
Airport Terminal 3
Emirates
Rashidiya

Palm Deira
Al Ras
Baniyas Square

Khalid bin al Waleed
Oud Metha
Dubai Healthcare City
Jaddaf (not yet open)
Creek (not yet open)

Al Ghubaiba
Al Fahidi
Al Karama
Al Jafiliya
World Trade Centre
Emirates Towers
Financial Centre
Burj Khalifa/Dubai Mall
Business Bay
Noor Islamic Bank
First Gulf Bank
Mall of the Emirates
Sharaf DG
Dubai Internet City
Nakheel
Dubai Marina
Jumeirah Lake Towers
Nakheel Harbour & Towers

Ibn Battuta
Jebel Ali Industrial
Jebel Ali